Europe's Burden

The EU is many things: a civilizational ideal to emulate, an anchor of geopolitical stabilization, a generous donor, and a historical lesson on cooperation across nations. A fixer of national governance problems, however, it is not. In this book, Professor Alina Mungiu-Pippidi investigates the efficacy of the European Union's promotion of good governance through its funding and conditionalities both within EU proper and in the developing world. The evidence assembled shows that the EU's supposed power to transform the quality of governance is largely a myth. From Greece to Egypt and from Kosovo to Turkey, EU interventions in favor of good governance and anti-corruption policy have failed so far to trigger the domestic political dynamic needed to ensure sustainable change. Mungiu-Pippidi explores how we can better bridge the gap between the Europe of treaties and the reality of governance in Europe and beyond. This book will interest students and scholars of comparative politics, European politics, and development studies, particularly those examining governance and corruption.

Alina Mungiu-Pippidi has fought the cause of good governance as a journalist, strategic litigator, and scholar. She designed the Index for Public Integrity and several corruption control campaigns for civil society. Her theory on corruption has been outlined in *The Quest for Good Governance*, also from Cambridge University Press, and in several book chapters and journal articles, notably in *Nature* and *Journal of Democracy*.

Europe's Burden

Promoting Good Governance across Borders

Alina Mungiu-Pippidi

Hertie School of Governance, Berlin

CAMBRIDGE
UNIVERSITY PRESS

CAMBRIDGE
UNIVERSITY PRESS

University Printing House, Cambridge CB2 8BS, United Kingdom

One Liberty Plaza, 20th Floor, New York, NY 10006, USA

477 Williamstown Road, Port Melbourne, VIC 3207, Australia

314–321, 3rd Floor, Plot 3, Splendor Forum, Jasola District Centre,
New Delhi – 110025, India

79 Anson Road, #06–04/06, Singapore 079906

Cambridge University Press is part of the University of Cambridge.

It furthers the University's mission by disseminating knowledge in the pursuit of
education, learning, and research at the highest international levels of excellence.

www.cambridge.org
Information on this title: www.cambridge.org/9781108472425
DOI: 10.1017/9781108665537

© Alina Mungiu-Pippidi 2020

First published 2020

A catalogue record for this publication is available from the British Library.

Library of Congress Cataloging-in-Publication Data
Names: Mungiu-Pippidi, Alina, author.
Title: Europe's burden : promoting good governance across borders / Alina
Mungiu-Pippidi, Hertie School of Governance, Berlin.
Description: Cambridge, United Kingdom ; New York, NY : Cambridge
University Press, 2020. | Includes bibliographical references and index.
Identifiers: LCCN 2019028546 (print) | LCCN 2019028547 (ebook) | ISBN
9781108472425 (hardback) | ISBN 9781108665537 (epub)
Subjects: LCSH: Government accountability – European Union countries. |
Political corruption – European Union countries – Prevention. | Public
administration – Corrupt practices – European Union countries – Prevention. |
European Union countries – Politics and government.
Classification: LCC JN30 .M867 2020 (print) | LCC JN30 (ebook) | DDC
353.4/6094–dc23
LC record available at https://lccn.loc.gov/2019028546
LC ebook record available at https://lccn.loc.gov/2019028547

ISBN 978-1-108-47242-5 Hardback
ISBN 978-1-108-45966-2 Paperback

Contents

v

Figures

Tables

Acknowledgments

The research for this book was carried out within the ANTICORRP (anticorrp.eu) Seventh Framework Research Project (2012–2017) funded by DG Research, which included a work package on the role of EU aid in good governance. I worked as principal investigator with colleagues from the German Institute for Global Affairs (GIGA) and my own team at Hertie School of Governance in Berlin.

However, it is only fair to state that my many years of struggling alongside the development industry in the Balkans, the Caucasus and the former Soviet Union, as well as frustrating expert meetings in Brussels, are also responsible for my insight into the informal institutions discussed here and my longtime acquaintance with the actors and realities presented.

After the end of ANTICORRP, quite a few NGOs helped me organize focus groups and interviews in Ukraine, Moldova, Romania, Tunisia and Brussels. I visited and interviewed Brussels officials in Brussels, in Rome, and in the field offices of various countries – many of whom preferred to remain anonymous – as well as prosecutors, judges, civil society activists, and journalists. A number of the resulting case studies and a preliminary report of the main statistical findings appeared online on Anticorrp.eu in 2017, as well as in *Beyond the Panama Papers: The Performance of EU Good Governance Promotion* (Volume 4 of the *Anticorruption Report*, published by Verlag Barbara Budrich). The European Parliament's international trade committee, INTA, further commissioned me in 2018 to produce a state-of-the-art report on good governance conditionality and international trade, which informed findings in Chapter 3 of the present book. The Swedish government's development expert committee, EBA, commissioned me to provide a "lessons learned" paper for the donor community after ANTICORRP, which eventually became the article "Seven Steps to Control of Corruption: The Road Map," published by *Dædalus* in July 2018 (147[3]: 20–34). The ideas in that paper I presented at length at OECD Integrity Week meetings for two years in a row (2017, 2018) and in a series of IMF and World Bank meetings in 2018, and they shaped the present conclusions as well.

Special friends and mentors, such as Fraser Cameron and Richard Youngs, who had worked before on these topics, have helped substantially to get me started. Marc Plattner and Larry Diamond have provided input ever since my first article on this topic in *Journal of Democracy*, which was called "EU Accession is No End of History" – long before the democratic backslide of East Central Europe had become visible to the world. Tanja Börzel from Freie Universität Berlin gave our team her candid review and encouragement in a Brussels seminar generously organized by Carnegie Endowment and the Open Society Institute. Tens of academics volunteered to read the mini-chapters regarding their countries' institutional transformations – I thank the Greeks, Italians, Turks, and the rest who sent their critical insights, sometimes unsolicited and after hearing from friends what I was up to. I had a devoted editorial research team in Berlin: Ramin Dadašov worked on our models of globalization; Roberto Martinez Kukutschka worked on European crony capitalism; Aaron Burnett organized interviews; Jana Warkotsch worked on conditionality and MENA countries; Chris Norman, Natalia Alvarado Pachon, and Till Hartmann worked with the aid data; Elizabeth Miszta and Jacob Watson put the manuscript together, and our long-time editor Marcus Ferley provided the final touches. I owe thanks to Misi Fazekas at CEU and Barbara Budrich for allowing me to use figures from the *Anticorruption Report* in this book, and I need to thank our research officer, Cristina Marcuzzo at DG Research, for her trust in us during two intensive projects, ANTICORRP and DIGIWHIST. It was a privilege to work with the research teams of both projects. A seminar organized by Robert Rotberg at Harvard in 2017 and a talk on the Swiss model in Washington, DC, with Francesca Recanatini of the World Bank in 2018 fed me with great ideas and encouragement. Two anonymous reviewers from Cambridge University Press made precious comments that I was able (I hope) to address.

As I wrote this book entirely in 2018 after the end of ANTICORRP, none of the funders, colleagues, or interviewees are responsible for what I might have got wrong. My many thanks to everybody who shared their insights with me on what I eventually got right.

Abbreviations

ACA	anti-corruption agency
ACP	Africa, Caribbean and Pacific Group of States
ANAC	National Anti-Corruption Authority (Italy)
AKP	Justice and Development Party (Turkey)
BiH	Bosnia and Herzegovina
CCP	Coalition for a Clean Parliament (Romania)
CEEC	Central and Eastern European Countries
CEPEJ	European Commission for the Efficiency of Justice
CFSP	Common Foreign and Security Policy
CoC	Control of Corruption (a Worldwide Governance Indicator)
CoE	Council of Europe
CPI	Corruption Perception Index
CVM	cooperation and verification mechanism
DCFTA	Deep and Comprehensive Free Trade Area
DCI	Development Cooperation Instrument
DEVCO	Directorate for Development and Cooperation
DFID	Department for International Development (United Kingdom)
DG Home	Directorate-General for Migrant and Home Affairs
DG Just	Directorate-General for Justice and Consumers
DG NEAR	Directorate-General for Neighbourhood and Enlargement Negotiations
DPS	Democratic Party of Socialists (Montenegro)
EB	Eurobarometer
ECA	Europe and Central Asia (Chapter 4); European Court of Auditors
ECD	European Consensus on Development
ECHR	European Court of Human Rights
ECJ	European Court of Justice
EEAS	European External Action Service
EED	European Endowment for Democracy

EIDHR	European Instrument for Democracy and Human Rights
EITI	Extractive Industries Transparency Initiative
ELIAMEP	Hellenic Foundation for European and Foreign Policy (Greece)
EMU	Economic and Monetary Union
ENP	European Neighbourhood Policy
ENPI	European Neighborhood and Partnership Instrument
EPAP	European Partnership Action Plan
ERCAS	European Research Centre for Anti-Corruption and State-Building
EU	European Union
EULEX	European Union Rule of Law Mission in Kosovo
FCPA	Foreign Corrupt Practice(s) Act (USA)
FDI	foreign direct investment
FSU	former Soviet Union
GCR	Global Competitiveness Report
GDP	gross domestic product
GF	Governance Facility
Ghana-ARAP	Ghana Anti-Corruption, Rule of Law and Accountability Programme
GIFMIS	Government Integrated Financial and Management Information System (Ghana)
GIGA	German Institute for Global Affairs
GNI	gross national income
GRECO	Group of States Against Corruption (Council of Europe monitoring body)
GSP	Generalized System of Preferences
HDI	Human Development Index
IMF	International Monetary Fund
INLUCC	Instance nationale de lutte contre la corruption (Tunisia)
IPA	Instrument for Pre-accession Assistance
IPI	Index of Public Integrity
KAA	Kosovo Anti-corruption Agency
LAC	Latin America and the Caribbean
MCV	mechanism for cooperation and verification
MDG	Millennium Development Goals
MENA	Middle East and North Africa
MS	member state (of the European Union)
NABU	National Anti-corruption Bureau of Ukraine
NAD	National Anticorruption Directorate (Romania)

NIT	Nations in Transit (Freedom House Corruption Score)
ODA	official development assistance
ODC	other developing countries
OECD	Organisation for Economic Co-operation and Development
OHR	Office of the High Representative
OLAF	European Anti-Fraud Office
PAM	Public Accountability Mechanisms
PASOK	Panhellenic Socialist Movement (Greece)
RIS	Romanian Information Service
SAA	Stabilisation and Association Agreement
SPRING	Support for Partnership, Reforms and Inclusive Growth (EU project)
USAID	United States Agency for International Development
WB	World Bank
WGI	World Governance Indicators (from World Bank Institute)

1   The Blueprint

1.1   The Making of Switzerland: With a Little Help from Friends

There is one country in the world that is everybody's dream: Switzerland. The small Alpine republic is universally perceived as the world's highest achievement in democracy, human rights, the rule of law, and economic competitiveness. The end results of such achievements, of course, are prosperity and happiness, for which Switzerland also leads in global charts. Legend has it that some inner Swiss qualities have fashioned this miracle; perhaps some deeply ingrained virtue that the nation of clock makers possesses has spilled over into their splendid governance. Once achieved, the only other thing needed was protection from outside influence so that they could develop peacefully, which the Swiss then managed by means of their famous neutrality. The Swiss seem exceptional in having solved the main problem that nobody else, or only very few, have managed to solve and that is the kernel of the state-building challenge of our time. That solution is impartiality of the state to private interest, with the resulting capacity of balancing between various ethnic, religious, or economic groups so as to ensure ethical universalism as the norm – in other words everybody is treated equally and fairly. Building a Switzerland in Bosnia – or Iraq – has been many a reformer's dream but ultimately all have failed.

But that simple if powerful narrative is actually wrong. Even at first glance it is clear that happy Switzerland has not come about without difficulty, or overnight. By the mid-eighteenth century, Switzerland was a country dominated by privileges and restrictions on economic freedom (Tilly, 2009). Furthermore, it was plagued by religious, ethnic, and political conflict that would continue for more than a hundred years (Fischer, 1946). The public ethic was nonexistent: offices of governor were sold in return for the presumed benefit (in the form of bribes or appropriation received) of the office; crimes were punishable mostly by fines, because that seemed more convenient for an ever-deficient budget. If top officials were caught embezzling funds, they were simply replaced by way of punishment and suffered no other further inconvenience (ibid.). To cap it all, there were no usable public roads, schools, or hospitals, because the absence of any centralized power and the lack of solidarity across territories and social groups meant that most Swiss cantons were plagued by the same problems that prompt collective action in developing countries during our times, namely that nobody wanted to pay for public benefits. Still, at the beginning of the nineteenth century the variously contentious and self-centered interest groups somehow managed to form a nation, and it was a highly successful one, which took off economically from the beginning of the nineteenth century until it nearly surpassed England, Europe's first industrial nation, as the most competitive European economy (Biucchi, 1973).

This was no homegrown miracle, although certainly at the end of day it was the Swiss themselves who managed it. Even by 1802, though, their course had not yet been set. The first French occupation initiated in 1789 introduced the basics of a revolution in government – equal rights, separation of powers, centralization – according to the new rational and enlightened philosophy best described by Baron de Montesquieu, an intellectual and a magistrate, in his magnum opus *De l'Esprit des lois* (*The Spirit of Laws*). The French replaced the political system of the thirteen-canton confederation with the centralized unitary state of the Helvetic Republic, which soon collapsed because of underfunding and permanent conflict between federalist and centralist factions. There was a succession of coups and a civil war, plus a temporary retreat by the French state, although the French later intervened again as "mediator of the Swiss Confederation." In his words to the Swiss representatives in 1802, the First Consul Napoleon Bonaparte said:

Citizen representatives of the eighteen cantons of the Swiss Republic, the situation of your country is critical: moderation, prudence and the sacrifice of your passions are necessary for its salvation. [. . .]

Switzerland is not like any other state, neither in the succession of events over the centuries, nor in its geographical and topographical situation, and its extreme diversity of languages, religions and customs across its different parts.

Nature made your state a federation. Opposing it cannot be wise.

The circumstances and spirit of past centuries have made it that some nations are sovereign and others subject. A new environment and mood, changed from that of the past and closer to reason, have established the equality of rights between all parts of your territory.

The wish and interest of both you and the states surrounding you, therefore, favor:

1. The equality of rights between your eighteen cantons;
2. A voluntary and earnest renunciation of privileges on the part of patrician families;
3. A federal organization, so that each Canton organizes itself according to its religion, customs, interests and opinions;

The neutrality of your state, the prosperity of your commerce and a family-like administration are the only things that can make your people happy and sustain you.[1]

The federalists and the centralists each drafted a constitution, both of which were sent to Paris (Fischer, 1946). However, a third constitution was soon sent back from Paris, written by the first consul at the Malmaison Palace. That document, known as the Act of Mediation or Malmaison Constitution, was largely federalist but also introduced major changes that shaped the future of Switzerland. While restoring the federal system with largely independent cantons, the documents allowed for the creation of new cantons too, and the eventual addition of them led to the fading of the old line of conflict. The new political geography survived the conservative restoration of 1814–1815, as did the separation of powers and the abolition of privileges introduced earlier by the French. Some political equality between classes was lost, but it was gradually recovered in the following decades. In the end, present-day Switzerland resembles fairly closely the blueprint set by the Act of Mediation, certainly more so than all its other constitutional documents (Biucchi, 1973; Tilly, 2009). The Swiss industrial revolution followed closely and what is known in development theory as "take-off" unfolded gradually from the end of the eighteenth century until 1830, by which time the once primitive, highly constrained Alpine economy had reached global competitiveness (Biucchi, 1973, p. 628).

The French intervention in Switzerland did not come without major costs to the Alpine republic, both economic and in human lives. The Swiss paid dearly for each French occupation and subsequent economic exploitation, but they saw benefits too. First there were ten years of peace following the Act of Mediation, and then Napoleon's otherwise costly economic blockade of the British protected the Swiss cotton industry well enough to facilitate its take-off (ibid., p. 630). In a society dominated by inequality between town and country, between patricians and the people, and between people belonging to various linguistic, ethnic, and religious groups, ethical universalism could hardly have come easily, and in fact it

---

[1] Letter of Napoleon Bonaparte, First Consul and President, to the representatives of the Cantons of the Helvetic Republic, St Cloud, December 10, 1802 (Monnier, 2002, pp. 28–30).

took far longer for it to become the dominant norm than the brief French Revolution and Empire lasted. But the foreign intervention, based on political principles derived from the Enlightenment, managed to impose a blueprint that Swiss liberals fought to put into practice for decades afterwards. The French Revolution was emulated in quite a number of Swiss cities, and it provided likeminded Swiss liberals with the wind in their sails that they needed for reform. Many Swiss liberals had lived in Paris and been part of the intellectual ferment informing both the Revolution and the subsequent Empire. The same modernization and government rationalization efforts were attempted, although with less success, in other places occupied by the French, from the kingdoms of Prussia and Naples to aristocratic polities such as Venice and Malta. But only in Switzerland, and in combination with that country's particular circumstances and domestic agency, did the French modernization of government succeed to such an extent that the resulting democratization process made it into the textbooks. In short, foreign intervention, both intentionally and unintentionally, managed to stimulate three processes that helped to advance the norm of ethical universalism. First was the transformation of all particularistic trust networks into a political system based on equality, second was the insulation of public policy from categorical inequalities, and third the elimination or neutralization of power centers, which could otherwise have exercised their veto over public policy to the detriment of social welfare (Tilly, 2009). In conclusion, Enlightenment missionary zeal, promoted by Napoleon's staff in territories from Egypt to Switzerland, and the naked national interest of the French combined quite harmoniously to allow the French to engineer the transformation of Switzerland into what it became. No inner quality of Swiss society would by itself have led the Swiss to that position.

1.2   Topic of This Book

While few would dare to confess it openly, the same sort of "Making of Switzerland" type of intervention is what we in the present-day development industry are trying to replicate under the fancy names of "institutional change" or "good governance promotion" or "state-building." As there was limited success resulting from the macroeconomic reforms agreed by the Washington Consensus in the last decade of the twentieth century, it became necessary to amend them through a more context-sensitive approach. Since then, a considerable though by no means internally consistent body of research by the Bretton Woods institutions and academia has led to claims that "poor quality of institutions" present the major obstacle to development and prosperity; "poor-quality institutions" is the euphemism by which systematic corruption has mean-while come to be known. Critics of the Washington Consensus, such as Dani Rodrik or Joseph Stiglitz, have presented evidence that policies actually matter less than the institutional environment, and that classic growth recipes such as privatization might underperform in the wrong context (Rodrik, 2006; Stiglitz, 1999). In that view, centered on institu-tions, "what matters are the rules of the game in a society, as defined by prevailing explicit and implicit behavioral norms and the ability to create appropriate incentives for desirable economic behavior" (Rodrik and Subramanian, 2003). IMF economists Paulo Mauro, Vito Tanzi, and Hamid Davoodi established the first connections between corruption and growth on one hand, and corruption and government spending on the other (Mauro, 1995; Tanzi and Davoodi, 1998). Meanwhile, prosperity has been found to be associated with the rule of law, particularly in Anglo-Saxon systems (La Porta et al., 1998).

The argument was put most eloquently in an international best seller by James Robinson and Daron Acemoglu, who see the reason that some nations fail and others succeed in the persistence of "extractive institu-tions" of the sort that governing elites tend to promote over "inclusive" ones (Acemoglu and Robinson, 2012). An "augmented Washington Consensus" had already replaced the earlier one by the turn of the millen-nium, highlighting the importance of the rule of law for development. In the meantime, such arguments expanded in the academic policy commu-nity in various shapes and forms and have gradually become the mantra of development agencies over the past twenty years. In their most straightfor-ward form, a former World Bank president, James Wolfensohn, hit upon the idea of characterizing such suboptimal "institutions" (kleptocrats in government) in one word – "corruption" – and compared the spread of such governance contexts with cancer. However, while economists have some knowledge of how to create macro equilibria even if no universal keys to prosperity exist, building the rule of law and the control of corruption is virtually a virgin field for them.

Equally, repairing the institutional endowment of a developing country is a far more complex endeavor than removing the one-time kleptocrats in government, even if that is quite a challenge in itself with the exception of military occupation situations. Furthermore, replacing what historian Barrington Moore Jr. (1978) called "predatory elites," in other words changing the political regime, is even more difficult. After the unprece-dented spread of democracy with its third and fourth waves at the end of the twentieth century, it has become obvious that systematic corruption is more resistant to political competition than previously thought, and even new democratically elected elites find it easier to inherit the rents of the previous kleptocrats than to change the system (Mungiu-Pippidi, 2006a). Governance, defined in this book as the set of formal and informal institutions determining who gets what in a society, is more difficult to change than either one single government or one single corrupt political regime. Therefore, given that major social change is endogenous only in exceptional cases (Nisbet, 1992), one is tempted to say that there is room in the world for more Napoleon-style interventions.

The subject of this book is the systematic intervention by the European Union intended to improve governance in other countries, in particular to engineer change from systematic corruption to public integrity. I am interested in the topic as a particular case of the general research question that asks whether human agency from outside a country can influence the transition of a society from *corruption as governance norm* – where public resource distribution is systematically biased in favor of authority holders and those connected with them – to *corruption as an exception*, a state therefore that is largely autonomous from private interest and in which the allocation of public resources is based on ethical universalism (everyone treated equally and fairly). More specifically, I am interested in the motivations, mechanism, and performance of EU good governance promotion. To understand it, I will match theories of change and mechanisms of EU development aid to the models of institutional quality evolution advanced in corruption and political development studies.

The focus of this book is on the European Union for four main reasons.

First, the EU is the world's leading provider of official development assistance (ODA). OECD figures show that official development assistance provided by the EU and its member states reached EUR 75.5 billion in 2016, with EU collective ODA representing 0.51 percent of EU gross national income (EC, 2017c). While 25 percent of the recent growth of EU collective ODA between 2015 and 2016 was due to in-country refugee costs in the face of the EU's unprecedented migration crisis, between 2002 and 2014 the ODA dispersed only from EU institutions to developing countries tripled from just above USD 5 billion to over USD 16 billion. Moreover, around 12 percent of the total annual ODA from EU institutions was allocated to the government and civil society sector, which includes among other things development of public sector and administrative management, development of anti-corruption organizations and institutions, and legal and judicial development. Only humanitarian aid has received slightly more contributions in recent years than good governance aid. While USAID (United States Agency for International Development) sponsored projects worldwide between 2007 and 2013 that included anti-corruption activities amounting to about USD 6.7 billion (of which Iraq received one billion alone), in the same period the EU spent even more, with countries such as Turkey, Kosovo, and Palestine receiving billions of euros to strengthen the rule of law and control of corruption. Turkey alone received nearly EUR 1 billion to support the rule of law over the last decade.

Second, the EU has important conditionalities related to the rule of law and control of corruption in relation to its financial assistance. Indeed, "norms promotion" is a cornerstone of EU assistance, and the EU's foreign policy in general boasts of its "normative power," "soft power," or "smart power": in other words, the power to elevate others to EU values. Good governance conditions for EU financial assistance are clearly stipulated within political conditions: for instance, in the Cotonou Agreement with the so-called ACP countries (Africa, Caribbean, Pacific), in the European Neighborhood Policy (ENP) documents (for Eastern European and Mediterranean countries), and in the association and deep free trade agreements, aside from the general Copenhagen criteria for enlargement of the EU. The support from the EU to over 120 countries is generally conditional, albeit to very different extents, on good governance, or is even dedicated to it. EU aid activity represents therefore an excellent population of cases for evaluating the building of good governance and lessons learned.

Third, we find that beyond that group, EU Member States themselves present excellent cases to answer this research question, as quite a number of EU policies – for instance, the fiscal regulatory framework, the competition policies, and the absorption of EU funds – in fact demand good control of corruption and governance of high quality. Certain EU scholars have been arguing that the quality of the governance processes was deliberately developed to be an important criterion for the evaluation of the EU's overall democratic legitimacy, as a means by which EU-level institutional players have sought to counter claims about weak input from below leading to democratic deficit (Schmidt, 2013). The union has the unprecedented ambition to bring even its member states to comparably high quality of governance, due to the need to manage the common currency, the euro. An instrument to monitor governance, the European Semester, was thus developed by the European Commission to advise EU member states on matters that go far beyond fiscal governance, such as the business environment and public administration.[2]

Finally, the European Union, although a relative newcomer to the world of international powers, is by default the intellectual heir to the Enlightenment government cause of First Consul Bonaparte. Before

[2] See https://ec.europa.eu/info/strategy/european-semester.

Brexit, the EU was the one intergovernmental organization where the former major colonizing powers of the world pooled their sovereignties in a union of the "civilizers" and "modernizers" of the past three centuries. Their empires may be long gone, but promoters of the Napoleonic Code and its administrative philosophy, of the human rights concepts of the Scottish Enlightenment, of Max Weber's impersonal bureaucracy and capitalist ethics are all still being produced by British, French, and German universities. The best and brightest are recruited by the European Commission or the development agencies and charities that are its subcontractors in the field. This is the world's largest accumulation of experience of the deliberate sponsoring of governance transformation abroad. Of course, few would wish to state that present-day development efforts have anything to do with the older attempt at "modernization" or "civilization," tainted as it is by its association with imperialism, its patronizing character and the overall lack of modesty of such endeavors. However, awareness exists in the most enlightened strata of the development community that playing the enlightened conqueror (or the "Raj") is the name of the game (Knaus and Martin, 2003). While it was a characteristic of the nineteenth century to set over-ambitious objectives and to consider that no barriers exist to science and rational thought, we can trace the same transformational aspiration with only short intermissions right up to our own days, when in place of empires we find the "EU" or the "international community" or other equivalent syntagma. The overall goal of bringing Western progress and enlightenment to everybody continues, its proponents undeterred by events of the past or any realization of the world's enormous diversity and the counter-reactions they provoke, such as the revival of Islamic fundamentalism. To the grand objectives that Napoleon himself proclaimed, such as the promotion of freedom, equality, and prosperity, even more ambitious ones have since been added – for instance controlling the Earth's climate.

The map of our inquiry is therefore quite extensive.

First, we examine the EU proper, where the common market and its level-playing-field competition policies, policed by the Luxembourg Court of Justice, are supposed to exercise an influence over control of corruption. More open competition has been alleged to lead to less corruption (Ades and Di Tella, 1999), and the EU's common market is a test case for that proposition. If it is valid, the most corrupt countries in the EU should have been the first to evolve, initially after their integration into the common market, and then after joining the euro and coping with the fiscal constraints imposed by it. In fact, the two cases that best fit this inquiry are Greece and Italy; other potential cases such as Portugal, Ireland, Spain, and Cyprus had far better corruption indicators long before they joined. Both Greece and Italy are also long-standing EU members, so that there has been sufficient time since they joined the common market for some impact to have materialized.

Second, we examine new member states and accession countries, in other words, countries that joined the EU after the 1993 Copenhagen summit, which first spelled out governance (in particular the rule of law) as a key condition for joining. Furthermore, specific conditionalities on corruption and independence of justice were specified for a number of accession countries, some of which joined later, for instance the Eastern Balkan countries (Romania and Bulgaria), the Western Balkan countries (of which Croatia joined), and Turkey. Those cases warrant attention.

Third, we consider the rest of the world where the EU offers development aid. Originally, the EU favored apolitical trade agreements and development aid in dealing with partner countries, based on the principle of noninterference in partner countries' systems. Like many of the other major suppliers of development aid, both individual countries and multilateral donors, from the mid-1990s the EU began to include the promotion of democracy and good governance as aims of its development aid. Before then those matters were sidelined in favor of economic cooperation (Kleemann, 2010). The 1992 Maastricht Treaty was the first to mention promotion of democracy as an explicit aim of development cooperation, but it was the Copenhagen Criteria that not only made liberal democracy a starting point for accession negotiations, but also provided the blueprint for much of what would later become good governance conditionality. Bolstered by the apparent success of democracy promotion in the context of the accession process, by the late 1990s good governance promotion was firmly established within EU development cooperation across the globe and within all of its agreements with the widely varying partner countries (Freyburg et al., 2009).

Of course, there may be important differences across regions. For instance, Eastern European and Mediterranean countries are the object of the European Neighborhood Partnership, which has a strong focus on good governance. More than seventy ACP countries have benefited from a special treaty with the EU, the Cotonou Agreement, which among its provisions includes good governance. While the requirements of good governance are weaker than for EU accession countries, they are still present, with dedicated aid programs or specific conditionalities, so I hypothesize that we shall find differences across the different groups according to the depth of their relationships with the EU.

Based on original research by the EU FP7 ANTICORRP project,[3] this book aims to shed light on contemporary practices of good governance promotion and their effects, by focusing on the EU's good governance promotion and its impact on old and new member states and countries of the developing world that receive EU aid. The collected data covers more than 120 net recipients of EU ODA between 2002 and 2014, for which most of the listed disaggregated data is available, and all EU member states for a common period of twenty years, or longer in certain cases. The sample of countries spans five continents and includes national populations ranging from fewer than a million to 1.3 billion. But while the data collection is probably unprecedented for EU assistance and anti-corruption policies, both at global and country level, this book also aims to provide analytical narratives of the interventions intended to change governance across borders. External intervention is only one part of the governance transformation story, and frequently only a small part. Unless we manage to fit the story of intervention within the broad national story, we shall not understand either why countries change or why they do not. Our aim here is to understand the EU's theory of change, the means and mechanisms of intervention and their final impact, if any. The earlier literature on conditionality and EU smart power was infused with an extraordinary optimism, which within just a few years was refuted by facts. The backsliding of Hungary and Poland, both early transition achievers; disappointment with Turkey and the Arab Spring countries; the persistence of corruption in countries ranging from Greece to Ukraine, let alone in more distant countries to which the EU is an important donor – all of these circumstances give a clear warning that ideology is detrimental to science and that even advanced statistics can be used to distort clear facts when the conclusions are foregone.

This book will now proceed as follows. First, I will discuss the concepts related to EU good governance promotion and establish my conceptual framework across time, strategies, and areas where there might be different understandings (Chapter 1). Next, I will operationalize that conceptual framework and establish indicators so that it will be possible both to identify the benchmark (good governance and control of corruption) and how changes to it can be traced over time (Chapter 2). Then I will look at the theories of change and their tools: in other words, at the strategies and instruments of EU good governance promotion (Chapter 3). That analytical framework will then be used across all the cases to show how good governance progressed over fifteen years of EU aid development, ending with the most recent trends (Chapter 4).

[3] See www.anticorrp.eu.

The second part of the book will be dedicated to analytic narratives, where selected case studies from the different geographical and political areas described will be analyzed in depth, trying to distinguish the impact – or lack of it – of Europe in the specific governance evolution narratives in those contexts.

2 The Concepts

So far, I have used the vague and generic term "good governance promotion." But what exactly does that mean, and how can we distinguish it among Europe's complex, manifold development interventions in the rest of the world? Let me give an example. In the summer of 2008, I was visiting Christian Orthodox monasteries in Kosovo that have been designated as UNESCO Heritage Sites. Because of the war and subsequent peace arrangements, the monasteries were now completely isolated from any Serb Christian Orthodox community and an international peace force was protecting them. Talking to the Italian officer in charge of the mission, I remarked on the impressive restoration work going on at one of the monasteries, to which he replied that this was only the last phase. He then explained that the Italian masons were in fact finishing and repairing the work of a previous generation, who had carried out extensive restoration at the same monastery during the Italian occupation of Albania in the Second World War. This was the sort of highly specialized work for which only a country with remarkable historical heritage would be likely to be able to muster the human resources. Remarkably, then, the restoration of the medieval Byzantine churches was funded and executed by two Italian missions more than sixty years apart during two quite separate interventions that were completely different in all other respects, one of them having occurred during a forcible occupation and the other the result of a UN peace and reconciliation mandate. The point that struck me, as I talked to the Italian officer, was that few interventions are simple, singular, and without history; and understanding their complexities even far back in time is important if we are to assess them properly. This chapter will thus review and revise the most frequently used concepts as far as European or, more generally, Western intervention is concerned.

2.1   Intervention

The concept of intervention is the first that needs clarification. In his history of the global Cold War, Arne Westad defines intervention as "any concerted and state-led effort by one country to determine the political direction of another country" (2005, p. 3). Westad's minimal definition fits both Soviet and US interventions during the Cold War, and indeed it also covers Napoleon's interventions in support of liberalization, as well as the Austrian contrary interventions in support of conservative regimes during the 1848 revolutions. But should we not introduce some further qualifications? One possible ground for qualification might be about *ends*: should we not differentiate between interventions that end with the democratic liberalization of a country, and those that end with the opposite? Another qualification might appropriately be applied to *motives*. Surely it is worth distinguishing between interventions based on the self-interest of the intervening power and those that are purely altruistic, in other words liberal or humanitarian interventions. The consequences of such different types of motivations (to suppress a revolution, as in 1848, as opposed to aiding it, for instance) vary radically. Another possible ground to be considered refers to *means*: should military force, diplomatic activity, and indeed simple assistance for development (economic aid, sharing of expertise) all be ranged under "intervention"? Henry Kissinger famously considered economic aid to be a type of intervention, and he boosted it to help countries in the developing world resist the Soviet Union (ibid., p. 35).

A clear specification of motives is not easy to add to any definition because motives for an intervention are often complicated to assess, and they might appear rather differently when judged retrospectively. The intervention of the French under the Directorate and Empire in Switzerland had ambiguous motives – exploitation, occupation, and political emancipation all at once. Indeed, historians in general and the Swiss in particular have continued to debate the pros and cons of that intervention ever since it occurred. Most literature, including in French, tends to see French interventions in Europe, from Italy to Russia, as being based on some geopolitical reason. Still, it is undeniable that, following the Revolution, Napoleonic governance deeply influenced the process of the modernization of European governments, consisting in centralization, bureaucratization, and the adoption of a civil code modeled after the French one. Intervention ranged from deeply transformative, whether successful or not (Naples, North Italy, Scandinavia, Prussia, Belgium), to superficial (e.g., Poland, Westphalia, and Spain), where French reform initiatives tended to be minimal (Davis, 2006). That did not prevent Napoleon's regime from exploiting those countries, which paid tribute in money and conscripts to sustain his wars.

The distinction between particularistic self-interested motivation and universalistic grounds for intervening in another country might be quite narrow when the ends are not specified and when the final goal is not conquest and indefinite occupation. While Immanuel Kant, in his "Fifth Preliminary Article for Perpetual Peace," argued that "no nation shall forcibly interfere with the constitution and government of another" as such an intervention would "violate the rights of an independent people" and constitute "an obvious offense and would render the autonomy of every nation insecure," he also argued that perpetual international peace depends on all states developing "republican" constitutions, and that all states have a duty to become "republican" (Kant, 1983 [1795], pp. 109–115). In other words, intervention is destabilizing for the international world order, and undesirable if a country has its own rule of law and constitutional ("civil") order. But if a country does not have that, and its neighbors and the global order itself suffer from the fact, that then opens the door to a certain interventionist logic. While the classical arguments for intervention are generally humanitarian (to stop ongoing atrocities or "genocide," from the intervention of the European powers in Ottoman Greece in the early nineteenth century to that in Kosovo at the end of the twentieth century), once an international legal framework was developed through United Nations conventions, the argument could be made that gross or brutal infringements of its principles in a country may destabilize the international world order. Civil wars, violent repression, and large-scale corruption are associated with mass migration, refugees fleeing to neighboring countries, and brain drain. Within a global world order and a globalized capitalist economy, the line between domestic and external is blurred and, in principle, negative externalities for domestic policies can always justify "interventions" in favor of restoring a decent constitutional order. In recent decades, where military intervention was under consideration, the argument has been made more often about terrorism and weapons of mass destruction; but in the civil intervention in Bosnia, for instance, the principal objective of the international community was the implementation of the Dayton constitutional reform agreement.

Motives, as well as means, have always been controversial and the nineteenth-century debate on intervention still resonates today. In the wake of the French intervention in Syria, John Stuart Mill wrote in *Fraser's Magazine* in 1859 that for the most advanced country in the world, as both he and nearly everyone else saw Britain at the time, "the declared principle of foreign policy is, to let other nations alone." But Mill's further reasoning traveled in the opposite direction, too, like Kant's:

Any attempt it [a country] makes to exert influence over them [other countries], even by persuasion, is rather in the service of others, than of itself: to mediate in the quarrels which break out between foreign States, to arrest obstinate civil wars, to reconcile belligerents, to intercede for mild treatment of the vanquished, or finally, to procure the abandonment of some national crime and scandal to humanity, such as the slave-trade. Not only does this nation desire no benefit to itself at the expense of other, it desires none in which all others do not freely participate. It makes no treaties stipulating for separate commercial advantages. If the aggressions of barbarians force it to successful war, and its victorious arms put it in a position to command liberty of trade, whatever it demands for itself it demands for all mankind. The cost of the war is its own; the fruits it shares in fraternal equality. (Mill, 1984 [1859]).

In other words, while intervention is bad generally, and especially if it is self-interested, intervention on behalf of ethical universalism is not only morally acceptable, but sometimes inevitable.

And what about the means of intervention? Can we introduce any qualifications here? The first pure "liberal" intervention by Europeans is universally considered to be the assistance given to the Greek rebellion intended to establish independence from the Ottoman Empire, which led to the defeat of the Turkish fleet at Navarino by an international coalition. That was followed by large-scale state-building after part of Greece had gained independence. King Otto of Greece, a Wittelsbach, took ship aboard the British frigate *Madagascar* and set out from his native Bavaria in 1832 with 3,500 Bavarian troops and three Bavarian advisors. His task was to build a modern Greek state, and he went on with the job until 1862, when he was evacuated from Greece on another British warship. However, he did leave behind a constitution, courts, and his own special creation, the University of Athens. That sequence, of military intervention on a humanitarian/pro-democracy rationale followed by state-building, was invented in the nineteenth century. It was attempted both when motives were more self-interested, as in the case of Napoleon Bonaparte's interventions, or more altruistic, as in the case of the Greek war of independence. Altruism was the rationale later in Syria, where weakening of the Ottoman state led to Islamic persecution of Christians so that Napoleon III could justifiably intervene with an international mandate to protect them. In that case, the French emperor dispatched his soldiers to "effect the triumph of the rights of justice and humanity" (Bass, 2008, p. 156). Meanwhile the overwhelmed but reform-minded Ottomans, forced to look on while a foreign power intervened to restore law and order in their territory, agreed that a complete overhaul of their institutions was needed in order for them to catch up with the more modern Western Europe (ibid., p. 191). The state-building repertoire deployed in those early interventions was indeed remarkable, ranging from original constitutional devices aimed at creating fair and nonconflicted representation (as in Switzerland and present-day Lebanon) to the introduction of a post office or mandatory vaccination. But still, it makes sense to differentiate between the military intervention at Navarino, after which things could simply have come to a halt as happened in many other military interventions, and the civilian intervention in which the Bavarians, supported by the British, attempted to build a modern state in the former Ottoman domain.

Undoubtedly, it is sometimes difficult to disentangle military from civilian objectives: they often come paired with each other, as in Afghanistan, Iraq, or the Balkans. It is equally hard to distinguish the self-interested from the altruistic, for example in the Allies' occupation of Germany at the end of the Second World War, followed by the Marshall Plan. All were in fact planned together with the sequential objectives of removing dictatorships and then instituting free elections, as in "regime change." Such difficulties are smaller, however, for the specific type of intervention that is the subject of this book. I call "intervention" the attempt, by another country or by an intergovernmental organization or foreign entity, to change governance in a country, with varying possible motives and means but with the self-avowed goal of the promotion or restoration of ethical universalism: the principle of equal and fair treatment of individuals by the state. According to the degree of development of the society where the intervention takes place, the goals might range from the abolition of slavery or feudal institutions, as in certain nineteenth-century interventions (some accompanying colonialism), to the restoration of constitutional order or the rule of law. The reforms accompanying such interventions also vary considerably, from land reform by the United States in Taiwan or South Korea to the European Union's attempt to build the rule of law and control corruption in the Balkans. By and large, such reforms have similar aims, namely the elimination of privileges, favoritism, and discrimination by authorities. Therefore, in the context of this research and book, I do not consider military intervention on either humanitarian or self-interested grounds, but only the attempt to effect decisive change to the institutional quality of a country to bring about more ethical universalism in government. Tools might include development aid, conditionality and sanctions policies, membership in trade alliances or offers of privileged trade status, and even direct government by external powers, as in Kosovo or Iraq. In the specific case of corruption, I look at the European Union interventions that have aimed to promote change in a country so that it moves from institutional or systematic corruption to a condition in which corruption is the exception. In fact, as I shall explain, corruption cannot be examined as an isolated issue but rather must be addressed in the context of the rest of governance.

2.2   Modernization and Westernization

Many of the attempts to change governance in developing countries are labelled "modernization," and long before American social scientists developed the concept as a dominant paradigm in development ("modernization theory") nineteenth-century policymakers and journalists used the term in reference to both advanced states and countries emulating them.

It is therefore important to delimit the concept and explain its use in the present research. In Victorian times, the term was used for societal and governmental change on the Western model, in other words, Westernization – and before the ascent of US global power, Europeanization. For example, the Ottoman Empire had to be "modernized" by taking up Western technology and institutions, or else it would not have been able to compete with Russia in the east (Bass, 2008, pp. 192–193, 348). In the twentieth century, Samuel Huntington gave a neutral but broad definition, seeing modernization as "a multifaceted process involving changes in all areas of human thought and activity" (Huntington, 1968, p. 52). However conceptualized – whether as industrialization, economic growth, rationalization, structural differentiation, political development, social mobilization, secularization, or some other process – modernization is fundamentally about the *transformation* of national states and societies. What they are transformed *into* is considered a closed question by those who believe in the linearity and unidirectionality of social change, but others see the question as an open-ended one. For example, although certain Gulf monarchies have undergone important changes over the last twenty years, Qatar or the United Arab Emirates could hardly qualify as "modern," despite being technologically advanced; for one thing, it is only a few years since the budget of the monarch was separated from the budget of the state in those countries. Modernization, then, is a transition, or rather a series of transitions: from primitive subsistence economy to technology-intensive industrialized economy; from subject to participant political cultures; from closed, ascriptive status systems to open societies and merit-oriented systems; from extended to nuclear kinship units; from religious to secular ideologies; and so on (cf. Lerner, 1958, pp. 43–75; Black, 1966, pp. 9–26; Eisenstadt, 1966, pp. 1–19; Huntington, 1968, pp. 32–35; Tipps, 1973,

p. 204). Such changes do not necessarily come together, and nor do they progress at the same pace, even when interconnected. For modernization theorists, this is no simple change, but one defined in terms of the goals towards which it is moving – in other words, it is an *evolution* (Tipps, 1973). With the export of nineteenth-century European sociology to the United States after the Second World War and the extraordinary process of new nation- and state-building connected with decolonization, the main policy message of modernization theory was that certain interconnected evolution processes replicating the European development sequence were bound to occur in the rest of the world. That belief quickly became the mantra of all development agencies, despite the presence of a more realistic approach showing that if societal development and economic development are out of tune, what might occur is not evolution but instability (Huntington, 2006, pp. 32–92). As Fukuyama puts it, according to modernization theory, by following the Rostow stages of growth everyone was supposed in short order to become Denmark, the prototype of European good government (Fukuyama, 2014, p. 47; Rostow, 1959). Indeed, significant ideas of modernization theory remain axiomatic today, particularly in the political development version illustrated by Seymour Martin Lipset. Individual economic development, which is generally associated with urban as opposed to rural social organization, is alleged to bring political progress. Furthermore, as modernization theory had a clearly actionable character, it managed to suffuse theories of change across development agencies. It did much to open the door to the idea that accelerated change could be engineered through various devices: foreign aid to provide capital and modern expertise; psychological manipulation to better motivate individuals to achieve and promote their personal integrity; and reform of legal and economic norms. There might equally be a combination of those things that would minimize both domestic and external path dependencies, such as the international context of modernization (Chirot and Hall, 1982). The ideal balance between endogenous and exogenous factors in determining national governance is still open to debate, hence the present book. Certain authors have laid greater stress on the endogenous nature of the change process (Rostow, 1959; Parsons, 1951) while others highlight the importance of exogenous factors such as the diffusion of values and the transfer of technology and institutions from advanced nations of the West to poorer nations in the developing world (Lerner, 1958).

When modernization is defined as transformation, it might be useful to distinguish three aspects: economic modernization; political modernization, which Lipset has framed as essentially the gradual extension of political rights and individual political autonomy; and institutional modernization. Institutional modernization refers to the transition from systems based on legal privileges, collectivism, and traditional loyalties to those seen in Europe as modern. Such systems feature individual private property, equality before the law and state, and autonomy of the state apparatus from private interests.

That type of *institutional modernization*, specifically the transition from closed, ascriptive status systems to open societies and merit-oriented systems, is what the present research addresses. Such transformation has remained unaccomplished in nearly all the states created after the Second World War, with fewer than ten exceptions having managed to closely approach Western benchmarks. Of course, modernization being so multifaceted, it is a challenge for scholars to disentangle that particular institutional transition from economic or political modernization, but it has already been examined (North et al., 2009; Mungiu-Pippidi, 2015b; Mungiu-Pippidi and Johnston, 2017). Even in the late nineteenth century, when no state was yet fully modern, the "ideal state" model was emerging in sociological literature and the aspiration and benchmarks of modernization had already been clearly defined:

1. social control over a nation's own territory (Weber's legitimate force monopoly);
2. independent judges appointed and paid by the state;
3. a treasury department raising both direct and indirect taxes that are seen as legitimate by citizens;
4. officials appointed only on the basis of competence (as early as 1824 in Denmark, one could not fill a government office without a law degree from Copenhagen university);
5. corruption, and trespassing for profit over the public–private border, seen as morally undesirable and punishable, not taken for granted (Osterhammel, 2014, p. 605).

How did those benchmarks come to be set? In the early twentieth century Max Weber advanced one theory, showing how a new type of authority, the rational–legal type, had emerged from the patrimonial and feudal struggle for power. At that time, various status groups in Western Europe had found the promotion of ethical universalism and government rationalization to be both in their own best interests and inherently just. The tool of modernization was bureaucracy, which replaced the earlier "sales of office" and direct payments to officials, whether in kind or (in the case of judges) by the interested parties. Weber argued in *Economy and Society* (Part 2, Chapter 11) that bureaucracy is defined by formal written rules of operation and organized by strict hierarchy and divisions of labor, with recruitment and advancement based on evaluation of skills and merit; furthermore, it is concerned with efficiency and, above all, operates in an impersonal environment that it creates itself.

Bureaucracy rationalizes government by the elimination of personalistic and particularistic features related to any private interest, making it, in other words, autonomous from any private interest. There arises a clear distinction between the public office and the office-holder as a private individual, with the crossing of those lines considered an offence. By contrast, the previous regime of patrimonialism had held such confusion to be the rule rather than the exception. Bureaucracy is inimical to favoritism, its interests being aligned with those of the state. Bureaucracy therefore operates by rules that are blind to the claimant's background, rather than by rules derived from personal connections or family loyalties, which had been the norm of previous forms of governance (feudalism or patriarchalism). While "bureaucracy" is frequently referred to in common parlance as "red tape," emphasizing its negative connotation, Weber's bureaucracy is positively connoted as a solution to the problems of societal anarchy, state inefficiency, and particularism. Accordingly, the construction of a secure and trained bureaucracy is supposed to enable constitutional and administrative rationalization. That ideal model was inspired by the example of French bureaucracy, whose emulation Napoleon prompted in the German states, from the Rhine valley to Prussia (Breuilly, 2003). The Central European bureaucracies that inspired Weber's ideal model, themselves largely a work of diffusion (through French exports or emulation of Enlightenment ideas by enlightened despots), thus became a prototype for the rest of the world.

The replication of bureaucracies in countries outside Europe has proved remarkably challenging, however. Of all the elements of "modernization," the impersonality and impartiality of bureaucracy or, to put it better, the state's autonomy to private interest (Migdal, 1988) has proved the most difficult element to achieve, despite the continuous growth of literacy and urbanization in recent decades. The evidence points rather to a lack of bureaucratic autonomy in most new democracies and autocracies, characterized by nepotism, patronage, and instability. In sub-Saharan Africa for many decades, only two countries, Botswana and Mauritius, have operated bureaucracies that qualified as reasonably autonomous from political influence, both at appointment level and subsequently throughout individual careers (Goldsmith, 1999, p. 540). In Eastern Europe after EU accession, except for the Baltic countries, politicization has continued to be the name of the game (Meyer-Sahling, 2011). Furthermore, evidence exists of collusion between politicians and bureaucrats in promoting "perverse economic policies, which while impoverishing most of society, provide concentrated and significant benefits to the national elites and interest groups" – in other words, rent creation (Mbaku, 1996). Early models of successful bureaucracies are associated with "enlightened despots" – for instance in Denmark, in Prussia, under the Habsburg Monarchy, or in Napoleonic France – where strong monarchs seeking greater social control, a better-performing military, and an extension of their taxation basis developed the merit system as a by-product (Mungiu-Pippidi, 2015b). Conversely, where free universal elections preceded the development of bureaucracy, as in the United States, modernization of the state took far longer – many decades in the American case – even when the rule of law was present. The reasons for such delays were the politicization of bureaucracy and the slow development of a merit-based system.

In the end, there is no clear sequence of institutional modernization, just as there are few, if any, purely endogenous evolutions. In Britain, for example, it was fear of a French-style revolution at home that prompted the modernization of the British voting system to make it more inclusive. Meanwhile France's revolutionary regimes, from the first Constitutional Assembly to the Directorate and then to the Napoleonic era, all took the greatest strides towards modernizing the state, despite a Roman Catholic society that was more resistant than certain Protestant ones. Napoleonic intervention in Europe then changed the paths of a variety of countries, although their transitions are sometimes presented as endogenous evolutions – in Sweden, for instance. So, we have nothing like the Rostow stages of growth to offer as a template for the evolution of institutions. Moreover, social sciences lack any equivalent of the hierarchical classification system of species invented by the eighteenth-century Swedish scientist Carl Linnaeus (1707–1778) with which we could rank governments as more or less modern – although corruption is actually a useful proxy measure. In fact, the Darwin-inspired presumption of modernization theorists that every society has to pass through similar stages is controversial today. Thus there is no agreed scale of modernity that we can use as a benchmark, and we find only partial correlations between progress in economic development, good governance, freedom, and human happiness, among others things.

Unlike Acemoglu and Robinson (mentioned in Chapter 1), modernization theorists believe in the primacy of economic rather than institutional development, with industrialization as the prime mover of social change. Earlier modernization scholars believed corruption was connected with positive evolutions in economic development (Leff, 1964; Leys, 1965; Nye, 1967), state-building (McMullan, 1961), and political development (Huntington, 1968; Scott, 1969). Samuel P. Huntington argued that "patronage from above ... has contributed directly to the building of the most effective political parties and most stable political systems" (Huntington, 1968, p. 70). James Scott argued that in most developing countries voting behavior is driven by "the desire for immediate, particularistic gains" rather than "class consciousness and ideological concerns" and therefore "in the short run, at least, competitive political parties are more likely to respond to the incentives that motivate their clientele than to transform the nature of these incentives" (Scott, 1969). Scott further argued that in environments where particularistic interests capture *de jure* policy formulation, corruption provides "an alternative means of interest articulation" that allows political demands originating outside elite circles to influence *de facto* policy implementation (ibid., p. 326).

However, since the late 1970s the idea of corruption serving a functional role in the modernization process has become unpopular. The first generation of nationalist dictators of the newly independent states that Huntington and Nye referred to had ruled with the support of bureaucracies largely left over from colonial times. They were followed by a generation of predatory kleptocrats who eliminated what was left of colonial bureaucracies and anything that could have given corruption any kind of positive connotation.

As to the evolution of corruption, these early scholars shared the belief that corruption is a natural aspect of the development process and would wither away as states reached more advanced stages of modernization. However, things did not go as they expected. In Western Europe the modernization of society, characterized by individualism and literacy, has generally preceded modernization of the state, at least in urban societies. Elsewhere, meanwhile, beginning with Peter the Great's Russia and flowing out in Eastern Europe and the rest of the comparatively underdeveloped world, the process of modernization of societies was programmatically *led* by the states copying modernity from the successful West. The more similar a society is to Western Europe – the more educated, urban, secular, gender equal, and oriented towards achievement rather than consumption – the more similarly it is expected to perform. After all, societies in Oceania and Canada, the successful colonies, were the most culturally similar to those in European metropolitan centers that influenced them. Otherwise, few societies in the world – Japan being a notable exception – came to resemble the Western original, even after a century of intervention (Fukuyama, 2014, pp. 184–186). More often than not, the result of "engineering" was only an increase in the distance between formal (modern) institutions, such as constitutions based on separation of powers, and informal ones, such as for example "telephone justice."

The tipping point, when one exists, seems to be the point of convergence where social structures, economic institutions, and culture align

sufficiently with the Western modernization template to make the definitive step towards governance based on ethical universalism. Drawing on
the World Values Survey, some scholars argue that human development
capacity is what converts nominal freedom into the capacity to steer
governance towards general rather than private welfare (Welzel et al.,
2003).

The view that corruption, and more generally particularism and parti-
ality, are in fact the main obstacles to modernity – indeed, that they
prevent modernity by their mere existence – is therefore relatively recent.
Certainly, few contemporary virtuous circles are on record. Jong-Sung
You, for instance, describes how extensive land reform initiated by the
Americans in Taiwan and South Korea led to the creation of a first
generation of middle-class land owners who chose to have their children
educated. Those children then became the students who took part in the
demonstrations of 1968 – demanding, among other things, jobs in the
cronyism-infested public sector. Their action indeed led to the introduction of a merit-based system and the eventual creation of a modern
bureaucracy (You, 2015). The time span of that particular institutional
virtuous circle was half a century, and the agency for change began as an
exogenous intervention. Taiwan and South Korea, where the intervention took place, progressed, while the Philippines, where such intervention did not happen, stagnated.

2.3   Civilization and Backwardness

If "modernity," either economic or institutional, can be seen as an unam-
biguous term that can be operationalized as "development" and bench-
marked against "development goals," then the process of modernization
is more than just "getting to modernity." In fact, due to its social
Darwinism, it is a conflict-loaded theory of change. If modernization
theory is correct, then one stage of development follows another, and
the later stage can be seen as superior to the earlier stage. Historian Alan
MacFarlane (1978) argues that Western development theory of change
(that of Marx, as well as that of Weber) is fundamentally flawed because
all its authorities, regardless of ideological persuasion, base their arguments on England, the world's first industrial nation. But, says
MacFarlane, England is an exception, and he goes on to present evidence
of an English institutional path totally different from that on the continent. MacFarlane argues that English individualism is far older than
previously thought; instead of the premodern transition that other
authors believed in and that we have tried to reproduce in the rest of the
world ever since, a much slower and less radical evolution had taken place

in England. When India and Britain met, it was not an encounter between countries at two different stages of development, the one being more primitive or backward and the other more advanced. Rather, they were *two different civilizations* that had previously coexisted on parallel paths. Turning India into England, the endeavor that inspired Kipling's poem *The White Man's Burden*, therefore, is not about bringing "civilization" to India but rather turning India into *another* civilization. And it may well be that this was why it did not work. North, Wallis, and Weingast similarly do not believe that the developing world is "developing" in the sense of becoming a Western-type open society (2009).

The opposition of "civilization" to "barbarity" can be traced back to ancient Greece or China and their encounters with less sophisticated but threatening groups. But it was not until the nineteenth century that the "civilizing mission" was embraced by the most advanced Western states and not just by missionaries. Such "civilizing" of the rest of the world was sometimes a companion to colonization and sometimes an independent trend, oscillating between hypocrisy and earnestness. Nevertheless, it is the indisputable ancestor of the normative globalization of the twenty-first century, when policies on human rights and even good governance (such as the United Nations Convention against Corruption) were adopted by most states of the world and became universal norms (Osterhammel, 2014, p. 818). The civilizing project was also adopted by many elites in the world, who embarked on "advancing" their own societies to norms of civilization the West itself had in some cases only very recently adopted. Such norms included disavowal of torture and cruel treatment generally, abomination of slavery, shunning of superstitions that created health hazards, and adoption of concepts such as individual rights and freedoms. From Napoleon's Egyptian campaign, the idea that societies can be made to progress *by design*, rooted in Enlightenment beliefs in universalism and education, followed an extraordinary trajectory, particularly in France and Britain (ibid., p. 830). Even liberal thinkers who were against intervention, such as John Stuart Mill, agreed that a fundamental difference existed between civilized people and barbarians. Mill, for instance, saw the difference in the barbarians' incapacity to grasp the concept of reciprocity (1859). Only a small number of thinkers shared the insight of Georges Clemenceau, the French journalist turned statesman. Clemenceau remarked that the French should be more reluctant to think any nation, in fact any civilization, "inferior" after hearing German academics proclaiming the French an inferior race following their defeat by Prussia in 1870 (Girardet, 1978, p. 92). While many Europeans considered actual colonization a bad idea, either on moral or economic grounds, the "duty" of spreading civilization

actually enjoyed wide appeal, and both fiction and anthropological academic literature successfully romanticized it. Rudyard Kipling sincerely
believed in the benefits to colonized nations of the "thankless" task of
building roads and schools for them, and he was by no means alone in his
views. Freud's suggestion in *Civilization and Its Discontents* – that the
civilizing process in societies through history resembles the maturation
of the individual – came out of a long and distinguished tradition (2005
[1930]). Adam Ferguson, in the introductory paragraph to his *Essay on
the History of Civil Society*, stated that "Not only the individual advances
from infancy to manhood, but the species itself from rudeness to civilization" (1995 [1767]). The belief in the universalism of Western values
such as human rights or gender equality survives today in the World
Values Survey and the Global Corruption Barometer, and that belief is
not without empirical evidence to support it (N. Ferguson, 2012, p. 146;
Headley, 2016).

Institutional reform was an intrinsic part of the civilizing mission, on
both idealistic and practical grounds. The obstacles they met should have
warned the civilizers of the difficulty of their task, but as they were either
unscrupulous adventurers or almost exact replicas of characters from
Jules Verne, many were undeterred. A core issue, then as well as now,
was that of property. The Western model proposes individual rights on
one hand and the taxation basis of an efficient modern state on the other,
and both depend on the concept of individual property. In order for
individual rights and taxation to be made possible, and to separate indigenous rights from the rights of colonizers, in many societies individual
property had to be invented because it was largely unknown. As Emperor
Napoleon III put it to the Duke of Malakoff, the governor-general of
Algeria: "We need to persuade the Arabs that we have not come to Algeria
to press and spoil them, but to bring them the benefits of civilization. And
the first condition of civilization is the reciprocal respect of everybody's
rights."[1] Furthermore, Napoleon III vetoed a bill that would have taken
land for Europeans at the expense of the Arabs. The emperor insisted that
Algeria was not a colony but an Arab kingdom, and that he was as much
the Emperor of the Arabs as he was of the French.[2] In the United States,
the Dawes Act of 1887 sought to end collective ownership of the reserva-
tion lands granted to native Americans, and pushed for individual allotments. The maneuver required arbitrary dispensing of Western names to
the "Indians" – for how else could the Americans tell them apart? – plus
a "family" name was required to pass on inherited title to land. Within
only a few decades this policy had proved to be a disaster for Native

---

[1] Extracts from letter of Emperor Napoléon III, February 6, 1863.   [2] Ibid.

Americans and would become a lasting nightmare for the American administration (Sandweiss et al., 1994). More than in Algeria, where the intention was to separate some land for colonizers and appease the fears of the rest by granting clear property entitlements, the Americans wanted, besides appropriating "excess" native land for settlers, to Americanize the "Indians": a gift of citizenship came with acceptance of allotments of land (ibid., 1994).

Civilizing others, therefore, had to be fitted into the straightjacket of individual property law, a reform that remains unfinished today, when competition among traditional gifts of land, government concessions, and the modern property market is still a problem. That is true for Nigeria, for instance, one of the difficult reform "cases" that Fukuyama discusses in his 2014 book and relates closely to the other civilizing dimension of governance: promotion of the rule of law.

For the French, education and high culture were important; for the British, the market economy and religion equally so. But no civilization was possible without constitutions, courts, a body of law, and a law-abiding population, and for the "civilizers" there lay great work ahead. The British seem to have done a better job, as a result of their more flexible attitude to local legal traditions and their inherent concept of the accountability of authorities and the protection of individual rights as enshrined in the procedures of English common law (Osterhammel, 2014, p. 833). Nevertheless, it is enough to look at Nigeria again to see that the modern justice system has not yet managed to convince; and it must compete with more traditional law systems such as sharia (Harnischfeger, 2004).

Just as the First World War diminished the stature of the white man in what was then still the colonized world, the financial crisis of 2008–2009 seems to have dealt a similar blow to the notion of Western institutional superiority over the rest of a world that is now independent. Popular titles such as *Are We Rome?* (Murphy, 2007; 41 million Google searches by mid-2017) or *Collapse: Europe After the European Union* (Kearns, 2018; 50 million searches) have therefore multiplied, while simultaneously the "business-as-usual" writers are still planning for global governance under Western leadership, or for an ever deeper and more successful European Union (Mungiu-Pippidi and Kukutschka, 2018). The commonality of the new gloom and doom literature lies in the primacy of the institutional explanation. In other words, what seems to be failing is civilization itself. The West, which has conquered the world due to its superior "inclusive institutions," as Acemoglu and Robinson call them, is now losing out both with those institutions and with the social fabric that generated them in the first place. Western elites now excel only at "fiscal optimization" and have lost their sense of duty to broader society, while leaders espouse a completely different set of values from those we identify as Western universalism. As Niall Ferguson argues, the West has entered what Adam Smith in *The Wealth of Nations* called "the stationary state," whereby "a corrupt and monopolistic elite" exploits "the system of law and administration to their own advantage" (N. Ferguson, 2014, p. 9). In that regard, traditional distinctions of the "West versus the rest" type have begun to matter less and less, as it seems the assumption that market-based liberal democracies would become the template regime following the demise of communism might have been no more than a delusion. The twenty-first century, when the new international mission against corruption began to promote Western governance standards to the rest of the world, coincided with the West gradually backsliding on those very standards itself (ibid., p. 19).

2.4   Corruption and Good Governance

For many scholars, good governance is little more than a fuzzy concept, invented by a few development professionals (read, "profiteers") to avoid using the politically dangerous "C-word" – corruption. In this book, however, I argue differently. Good *governance* is an indispensable concept when the level of analysis is the nation-state, and is superior to good *government* because it acknowledges that it is the society and its relationship with the state that matters, rather than just the state or the government as standalone entities. If we agree that governance is the set of formal and informal rules that determines who gets what in a society, "good" governance is that situation where the dominant rule of the game in government ethos and practice is ethical universalism – the norm according to which everyone is treated equally and fairly, and following which if universal welfare proves inaccessible, the outcome must be that the broadest possible social welfare is achieved. "Corruption" is not a macro concept, but an individual one. While its use is frequent as an adjective at levels above the individual – "a corrupt country," "a corrupt organization," "a corrupt practice" – too many qualifiers are needed for it to be especially useful at those levels.

The umbrella concept of "good governance" can be defined quite specifically, and its meaning has shifted surprisingly little across time, showing remarkable consistency. Even in antiquity, both Plato and Aristotle argued that the definition of a virtuous ruler is one whose government is dedicated to the common good, and not to self-interest (Plato, 2018; Aristotle, 2013). Righteous forms of government, according to Aristotle, are those under which "the individual, the few or the many govern with a view to the common interest: but the governments which rule with a view to the private interest whether of the individual, or of the few or of the many are deviations" (quoted in Mulgan, 2012, p. 30). Cicero best synthesizes Greek and Roman thought on the matter when he explains in his *De officiis* (*On Duties*):

> those who propose to take charge of the affairs of government should not fail to remember two of Plato's rules: first, to keep the good of the people so clearly in view that regardless of their own interests they will make their every action conform to that; second, to care for the welfare of the whole body politic and not in serving the interests of some one party to betray the rest. For the administration of the government, like the office of a trustee, must be conducted for the benefit of those entrusted to one's care, not of those to whom it is entrusted. Now, those who care for the interests of a part of the citizens and neglect another part, introduce into the civil service a dangerous element – dissension and party strife. (Cicero, 2006 [44 BCE], p. 66)

Those definitions of good government as *nonpartisan government* and of the good state as *a state autonomous from private interest* enjoyed a long and distinguished intellectual history (Mungiu-Pippidi, 2015b, Chapter 5). Max Weber introduced them into modern sociology with concepts such as universalism (as opposed to particularism) and impersonal treatment (in the case of bureaucracy) as opposed to patriarchal or patrimonial (when the public and private realms are fused) (1947). The name of the governance doctrine that succeeded in becoming prevalent with Western modernization is *ethical universalism* in public life, a political order based on the fair and equal treatment of citizens by the state. After the Enlightenment, universalism and individualism became generally agreed norms in the West without their being either natural or necessarily and invariably good principles. However, their origin is to be found in Catholic universalist doctrine. Thomas Aquinas developed and promoted Aristotle's and Cicero's doctrines of rights (Wilson, 1993). The Western tradition has always promoted the equality of rights – in other words, equality before the law – as fundamental to good governance. Since ancient times, corruption has always been defined in both the West and the East as government in the private interest of the rulers versus good governance, which is exercised in the public interest of all. The most common definition of corruption today, defined by Transparency International as the misuse of public authority for private gain, is in fact an Aristotelian definition on all counts, although it leaves the level of observation unspecified (Mungiu-Pippidi and Hartmann, 2018).

But how can we establish what is in the public interest of everyone? Starting with the nineteenth century and Jeremy Bentham's utilitarian doctrine that good governance is "freedom and effective drainage," the intervention of the government was supposed to be either minimal or benevolent, and thus no room for corruption would exist (1996 [1781]). Adam Smith put forth the liberal view of good governance by arguing that social welfare arises incidentally, as a by-product of pursuing self-interest: "By pursuing his own interest [one] frequently promotes that of the society more effectually than when he really intends to promote it. I have never known much good done by those who affected to trade for the public good" (2007 [1776], p. 293). In the classical liberal view, development and corruption are incompatible, and government favoritism necessarily develops out of government discretion, impeding merit as a basis of wealth development. As Ayn Rand put it:

when you see that money is flowing to those who deal, not in goods, but in favors – when you see that men get richer by graft and by pull than by work, and your laws don't protect you against them, but protect them against you – when you see corruption being rewarded and honesty becoming a self-sacrifice – you may know that your society is doomed. (1957, p. 413)

It was on similar theoretical foundations that the economist Daron Acemoglu developed an equilibrium model of the allocation of talent between productive and unproductive activities (such as rent-seeking), arguing that allocations of past generations, as well as expectations of future allocations, influence current rewards, and a society might become trapped in a rent-seeking steady-state equilibrium (1995). "Rent-seeking" is a concept coined by the economist Anne Krueger to indicate the situation in which firms compete for privileges bestowed by the authorities (for instance, import licenses) rather than in a free market (1974). The "public choice" school of thought also introduced the useful distinction between profit-seeking and rent-seeking, with the former based on merit (providing a product or service that consumers would be willing to pay more for than the opportunity cost of the resources used) and the latter based on coercion by preventing others from competing equally or by forcibly taking their wealth (Buchanan et al., 1980). Unlike profit-seeking by market means, rent-seeking by political means creates no wealth but merely transfers gains from one party to another. That actually wastes the resources used to acquire the rents, because those resources are invested to produce an outcome from which nothing of value is created. Furthermore, acquiring rents through political power distorts the operation of the market process, impinging on interest rates and the prices of goods and services. So rent-seeking of that kind actually destroys wealth (ibid.). Moreover, rent-seeking tends over time to create perverse incentives, as more people feel encouraged to engage in it, trying to acquire political power and gain advantages over the less powerful. Rent-seeking therefore subverts the rule of law, the concept of private property, and faith in government (Mungiu-Pippidi and Hartmann, 2018).

Looking at corruption as an institution or a rule of the game provides deeper insights. Institutions, as Douglass North defined them, differ from organizations, such as an anti-corruption agency (1991). They encompass formal and informal rules and norms and shape practices in a society. Dissent and minority behavior always exist, but institutions can still predict how most people will behave. Foreign capitalists arriving in a new country will wonder whether they will be expected to bribe the port captain or not: after all, if that is the local institution, anyone seeking to enter that market must be mindful of it, and with good reason.

North advanced the preliminaries of a theory of why development and corruption evolve in inverse progression. He argued that "as human beings became increasingly interdependent, and more complex institutional structures were necessary to capture the potential gains from trade," societies needed to "develop institutions that will permit anonymous, impersonal exchange across time and space"; however, their success in creating the *right* institutions varied because of diverse "local experience" (1993). Societies that do not manage to create open access and impersonal, merit-based institutions to govern both the market and the state–citizen relationship remain poor. Their economies remain privilege-based, and their states remain captured by particular interests. Such societies do not evolve to embrace ethical universalism. In a society of that type, even if competition exists both in politics and in the economy, the main stake of politics amounts to despoiling public resources to the benefit of particular groups (Mungiu-Pippidi, 2006a).

Of course, there are no ideal models to be found in reality, and as Krueger suggested (1974) evolution is a continuum extending from an economy completely regulated by particular interests, which monopolize authority to control economic rents, to its contrary, an open economy where freedom and the rule of law allow perfect competition. Some authors focus more on the processes defining the continuum, others on its outcomes; but in recent years we have found increasing agreement across disciplines that the capacity of a state to enforce public as against private interest is the major feature of good governance, shaping social allocation and consequently development. The set of opposites in Table 2.1 are evoked with remarkable consistency and should actually be seen more as complements of an emerging consensus across at least economics, historical sociology, and political science.

Table 2.1 *Governance orders*

Author(s)	Continuum "bad" extreme	Continuum "good" extreme
Anne Krueger on rent-seeking societies (1974)	Government restrictions	No government restrictions
Alina Mungiu-Pippidi on control of corruption (2006; 2015)	Particularism (favouritism and other forms of corruption)	Ethical universalism
Douglass North, John Wallis, and Barry Weingast on social order and violence (2009)	Limited access order	Open access order
Bo Rothstein and Jan Teorell on quality of government (2008)	Favoritism and its opposite, discrimination	Impartiality
Daron Acemoglu and James Robinson on prosperity (2012)	Extractive institutions	Inclusive institutions

Source: Mungiu-Pippidi and Hartmann, 2018

To understand corruption, we first have to grasp if it is manifested in isolated cases (corruption exception), so that we can deal with it at the individual level, or if it is a widespread practice (corruption norm), in which case we treat it as institutional corruption, which can be described as the systematic abuse of authority to divert *public* resources intended for *universal* use for the benefit of *particular private* interests. The separation of public from private is a modern European innovation. Previously, patrimonialism reigned, as described in Max Weber's work. The line between public and private did not exist or was not enforced, with the consequence that authority holders appropriated public office and its benefits for themselves and their cronies (Weber, 1991, p. 296–299).

Particularism, a concept developed by Talcott Parsons on the basis of Weber and that I have worked to develop further (Parsons 1997, pp. 80–82; Mungiu-Pippidi, 2006a), is a mode of exchange common to collectivistic societies. Particularism encompasses a variety of interpersonal transactions and transactions between individuals and the state. Such transactions include clientelism, bribery, patronage, nepotism, and other favoritisms, some of which imply a degree of patronage at the individual level. Particularism is defined as deviation from the universal ethical norm of social allocation. Ethical social allocation is defined by law, rules, and the modern principles of administrative impersonality, impartiality, and equality, as well as by market relations. If particularistic exchanges are the dominant mode in a society, and exchanges are carried out on the basis of status and connections rather than impersonal factors such as meritorious products, market prices, and rules, then markets may be trapped in a state of imperfect competition. Similarly, particularism of transactions between state and citizens makes democracy at best a façade, as its bureaucrats and rulers collude to despoil the public of their rightful resources and direct them towards their clients. The dominance of particularism thus limits access to public resources because certain applicants are favored while others are discriminated against, which results in unfair treatment. Particularism is a broader concept than corruption, as it includes both criminalized forms of corruption, such as favors in exchange for undue profit, and what Daniel Kaufmann labeled "legal corruption" (Kaufmann and Vicente, 2011). In its extreme form, in which most government transactions are particularistic, it can result in a state being entirely "captured" by private interest.

At the end of this brief review of the concept of good governance and corruption, it is important to note their strong developmental character. Social scientists increasingly agree that particularism, and not ethical universalism, is humanity's default condition. Particularism has overwhelmingly predominated as the most widespread institution of governance throughout human history. Societies based on open and equal access and public integrity, far from being some determinate historical endpoint, have in fact been very much the exception, and the rest of the world has engaged in more or less complicated state-building to catch up. By 2018, more than 160 countries had signed the 2008 UN Convention Against Corruption, pledging their allegiance to the ethically universalistic norm. Also, the sixteenth Sustainable Development Goal, part of a UN manifesto officially adopted by the United Nations and applicable from January 2016 with 2030 as its target date, states as objectives, "the provision of access to justice for all, and building effective, accountable institutions at all levels." Such "good governance" language has the merit of taking a developmental rather than a normative position, as it acknowledges that is not enough simply to repress corruption, as if the norm were already established and all that were needed would be to arrange punishment of deviation from it. Rather, accountability has to be created. The notions of "modernization" and "civilization," in the sense of building the norms of equal individual rights, citizenship, the rule of law, and government in the public interest, are extremely close to the European Union's current efforts to promote good governance. Today's efforts to convince national governments that they should take "ownership" – install themselves in the driver's seats of the assistance programs offered to them by external actors – are not a radical break from the past: over the last two hundred years, many efforts have been made to persuade the locals to internalize Western governance standards and implement them by themselves.

3   Theories of Change

Three basic questions underpin this inquiry. The first is what determines changes at a national level to the control of corruption. That means dealing with cases where corruption is a policy problem, and therefore aiming to build a society's capacity to control its office holders so that they act for the public and not the private interest. That is a system-building endeavor, and therefore quite different from controlling a few deviants, which would amount to "system maintenance." System-building calls for an empirical model of evolution towards control of corruption as the arrival point, from a departure point in a state where corruption is more or less widespread. In other words, what is called for is *a transition to a good governance model* or models, not just as an account of path dependencies explaining how a country got there (i.e., as the result of difficult geography, bad colonizers, and poor history in general, as many accounts by economists claim) but as an actionable model showing how it can change. As I have shown in my previous work, we have only a handful of such transition models, simply because in contemporary times only a handful of societies seem to have traveled far enough on that path.

The second question is whether governance *can* be changed by external agency, or how substantial the contribution of external agency can be to such change. The answer, again, is empirical and demands new questions. Any intervention intended to alter governance – modernizing the state, increasing accountability and control of corruption – might also have unintended consequences that must be considered. Indeed, every previous wave of "modernization" and "civilization" was plagued by such unintended consequences.

The third question is: if the answer to the second question is in the affirmative, then under what local and international circumstances and by what tools can governance be improved by external influence, or when do the desired effects outweigh the undesired effects of an external governance intervention? Switzerland worked but Naples did not, despite similar modernization intentions from the French. Samuel Huntington (1993) famously remarked that military occupation by a democratic "civilizing" power is a shortcut to successful democratization, but that logic was followed up in Iraq and Afghanistan with only very poor results. We need to decipher how international actors intervene in the control of corruption in another country, whether to provoke or steer improvement, and what contexts enable or subvert their interventions. What theories of change underpin or should inform such interventions, and do those theories of change vary with the specific context of each intervention?

3.1   The Evidence for Theories of Change

We have a large body of interdisciplinary theory to explain corruption and institutional quality, but very little to explain evolution towards control of corruption. The first obstacle is the minor variation in our dependent variable. There has been very little change in the world since our measurements of corruption were devised. More than twenty years have now passed since 1996, the first year of the most validated (but also most contested) perception of corruption measurements, but is that a long enough period for governance to change?

The expert scores aggregated in the commonly cited perception indicators of corruption[1] and the more recently developed objective indicators in the Index of Public Integrity[2] both show that control of corruption changes only incrementally, with stagnation being the rule. In 2017, for instance, the world (109 countries, more precisely) scored 6.64 on average in the Index of Public Integrity (itself made up of six different subcomponents from different sources), up from 6.57 in 2015 (the first year covered). Moreover, there was little significant change in any of the six components: judicial independence, press freedom, digital empowerment ("e-citizenship"), administrative burden, fiscal transparency, and red tape affecting trade (IPI, n.d.). If we calculate the average change over the last two decades, we notice that change is only incremental, with richer and higher-middle-income countries actually regressing, while poorer countries mostly stagnated (see Figure 3.1).

Why is there so little change? The main reason is that social allocation in a society is deeply embedded in its power balance – hence the more than 40 percent correlation of control of corruption averaged across years with the "power distance" concept of Geert Hofstede (see Figure 3.2). That makes a good proxy for Weber's status society, defining, in other words, the degree of acceptance of power inequality (status) in a society

---

[1] Transparency International's Corruption Perceptions Index; World Bank's World Governance Indicators, one of which is control of corruption (CoC).

[2] The Index of Public Integrity (IPI) is compiled by the European Research Centre for Anti-Corruption and State-Building and available at http://integrity-index.org

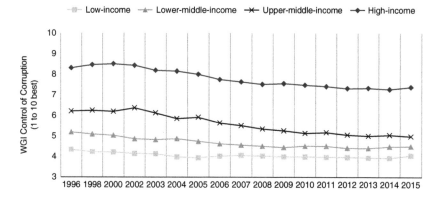

Figure 3.1 Evolution of the WGI control of corruption average by income group, 1996–2015 (sample of 180 countries)
Source: own calculation of World Bank Control of Corruption indicator (CoC), 1996–2015.

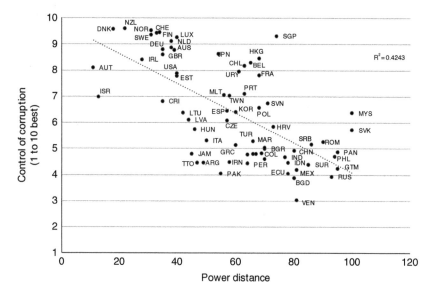

Figure 3.2 Correlation between control of corruption and power distance, 2015 (sample of 69 countries)
Source: regression of Hofstede power distance on World Bank CoC.

(Mungiu-Pippidi, 2015b, Chapter 4). Singapore and Venezuela are outliers in Figure 3.2, as obviously the first has too much power distance to match its good control of corruption and the second too much contestation to match its poor one. By and large, few political changes are followed by the kind of change in political and material status that would matter for corruption.

The second difficulty hindering the development of an effective theory of change is the disentanglement of the control of corruption from other elements of governance – political pluralism, the rule of law, and control of violence. Can a separate theory of change exist that is limited to corruption alone? The violence–corruption nexus is a central theme for North et al. (2013), as well as for Paul Collier (2011), after Joel Migdal had earlier centered the state-in-society model on social control (1998). The plain answer is that corruption problems come in two categories: some countries have corruption involving violence (such as vote rigging, arrest of opponents, and the like) and others have corruption without violence (with more or less impunity for incumbents). The explanation lies in the causes of violence, or the capacity for social control, not in corruption: corruption might in fact emerge as an alternative to violence, a bridge to transit out of violent predatory regimes. There is no need to kill opponents when elections can be bought (Collier and Vicente, 2014). The relation between violence and corruption is complex and not always intuitively evident. Violent environments, such as wars generating existential threats, have historically provided an incentive for leaders and ruling elites to introduce merit systems in the military and civilian bureaucracy (Rothstein and Teorell, 2012; Jensen, 2014; Mungiu-Pippidi, 2015b, Chapter 3).

This relationship is reflected in the close connection between corruption and human rights. Corruption is reasonably well predicted by the physical rights integrity index (cf. Cingranelli and Richards, 1999). By contrast, the legislative index of political competitiveness (rating competitiveness of elections for 177 countries as part of the Database of Political Institutions) is a poor indicator. Property rights, however, assessed by both the Heritage Foundation and the Economic Freedom of the World survey, are strongly and positively associated with control of corruption (ibid.). The association between Freedom House–Polity 2 integrated democracy measurements (measuring pluralism on a scale of 1 to 10, with 10 more plural) and the World Bank's Worldwide Governance Indicator (WGI) on control of corruption is also significant, but not linear. Moderate pluralism is associated with lower control of corruption, although only by a small amount, and only countries with an advanced democracy (pluralism scores over 6) become increasingly associated with greater control of corruption (Treisman, 2000; Jackman and Montinola, 2002; Sung, 2004). In other words, what matters to a democracy in terms of control of corruption is not elections as periodic mechanisms to select preferences but rather the permanent capacity to ensure that whoever is ruling respects individual rights and public property (Persson and Tabellini, 2003, p. 173; Mungiu-Pippidi, 2015b, Chapter 4). The policy answer, then, is that control of violence and promotion of human rights can certainly be disentangled from control of corruption, but they are undoubtedly synergetic with it. Political stability is the only WGI that correlates with the others somewhat less, indicating that it is more exogenous to governance than the other World Bank WGIs and its causes need separate attention. The other components of governance – rule of law, control of corruption, regulatory quality, government effectiveness, and voice and accountability (Kaufmann et al., 2011) – seem to measure one latent variable: governance defined as the set of formal and informal institutions determining who gets what (Mungiu-Pippidi, 2015b, Chapter 2). Their disentanglement is therefore neither possible nor even desirable. What is needed is a certain amount of hierarchy within the complex represented by governance, which can be structured like this:

Significant power asymmetry → State capture with preferential legislation and allocation in favor of powerful groups → Widespread particularism in public spending and service delivery (favoritism versus discrimination) → Unequal opportunities and treatment → Widespread cheating, law avoidance, and bribing → Corruption, both "legal" (privilege, rent) and illegal

Abuse of power is at the heart of corruption, and as Michael Johnston argues, corruption will persist and even be the rule rather than the exception until "deep democratization" enables citizens (the losers from corruption) to control their ruling elites (2014). The reverse also works or has worked in the history of corruption, as enlightened despots from Denmark in the nineteenth century to Bhutan in our own time have gradually eliminated privileges for themselves and built inclusive institutions. It is not difficult to see why elections are not significant in regression analyses of these factors. There may be elections, but the new winners could simply inherit and adopt the rents of the losers, as seems to be the case at present in many new democracies (Diamond, 2008). Then there might be unelected rulers, as in Singapore, who decide to end patrimonialism but without allowing full political pluralism. However, while most countries in the third wave of democracy barely cope with institutionalized corruption, enlightened despotism is also exceptional, with only four "not free" countries in the top fifty best-governed (Mungiu-Pippidi, 2015b, Chapter 2). From the point of view of intervention, this indicates that serious anti-corruption activity must be deeply political, and questions such as political violence and physical rights have to be addressed either before or at the same time as corruption: disentanglement is hardly practicable. In the case of Switzerland, Napoleon removed the main conflict factors by reorganizing the country and making it federal; by adding more cantons, he also removed a traditional conflict line while simultaneously eliminating privileges. Had the peace not held through those constitutional interventions, it is doubtful that the elimination of privileges could have held fast by itself.

A short review of statistical evidence on the main explicit and implicit theories of change returns ambiguous results. Glaeser et al. (2004), in an influential paper, examined a larger set of political institutions – some closely related to corruption control – and argued that poor countries escape from poverty through good policies pursued in many cases by dictators, and *subsequently* improve their political institutions. Glaeser et al.'s chief examples were South Korea and Taiwan, also two of the achievers in control of corruption over the past thirty years. Most literature by economists on institutional quality considers corruption to be a secondary phenomenon in discussions of security of property or executive constraints. Many economists, in fact, have no comprehensive definition of governance pertaining to the motivation of rulers, be those rulers autocrats or democrats. That is why economists continue to underestimate particularism as the one core concept explaining both imperfect markets and discretionary government in poor countries, and neglect its role in explaining all the other important institutions.

The hypothesis of modernization theorists that economic development takes primacy over institutional development is supported by only weak evidence in the recent past. The prosperity of the world has indeed grown since we have been collecting corruption data, but control of corruption has not caught up (see Figure 3.3). Education has been expanding for the past twenty years, while corruption control has remained flat. What makes a difference seems to be the active and long-sustained presence of "enlightened" citizens with a voice (in other words demand for good government) rather than education alone (Mungiu-Pippidi, 2015b, Chapter 4). The post-communist countries enjoy nearly 100 percent literacy, but that has not prevented former Soviet Union (FSU) countries, among them Russia, Ukraine, Moldova, and Belarus, from being more corrupt than the poor, illiterate sub-Saharan African countries; and that is simply because the capacity of ruling elites to control the population, a communist heritage, is even stronger in the FSU countries than in sub-Saharan Africa.

Djankov et al. (2003) and Glaeser et al. (2004) offer the clearest narratives consistent with modernization theory, insofar as they consider that each community and the set of institutional opportunities it faces are shaped by the human and social capital of its population. Institutions, as

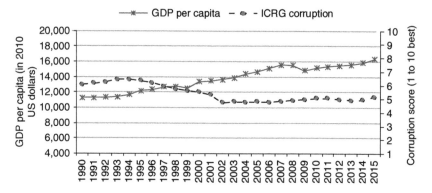

Figure 3.3 Trends in corruption and economic development (sample of 110 countries)
Sources: World Development Indicators (WDI); Public Risk Services' International Country Risk Guide (ICRG).

Glaeser et al. see them, are points on the graph of this opportunity set, determined by history, including colonial history. In other words, the potential of institutions improves as a country develops, but in fact that means that institutions are endogenous and therefore cannot be relied upon to initiate the necessary governance change – if a radical one is needed.

What does the evidence show about the association of corruption (proxied by the World Bank Control of Corruption (CoC) Indicator) with development? If we equate modernity with human development, using the Human Development Index (HDI; Anand and Sen, 1994), we find that human capital explains a little more than half the variation in control of corruption (Mungiu-Pippidi, 2015b). The association of CoC with HDI shows that in view of their human development some countries overperform on governance while others underperform, although in more than half the countries we find close correspondence (see Figure 3.3). Countries that seem to have managed to create the virtuous circle of development by political agency and favorable historical opportunities are New Zealand, Norway, Denmark, Singapore, Chile, Uruguay, Georgia, Estonia, Costa Rica, and Botswana. Countries that have under-performed are Venezuela, Argentina, Zimbabwe, Azerbaijan, Central Asian countries, Italy, and Greece. How an optimal balance was reached or was missed in such countries is a source of useful lessons (Mungiu-Pippidi and Johnston, 2017). The presence among the achievers of coun-tries with a poor fit to a classic modernization model at the time they

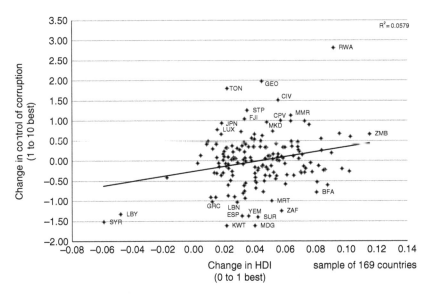

Figure 3.4 Change in human development and control of corruption, 2005–2014 (sample of 169 countries)
Note: bivariate regression with selected outliers featured.
Sources: United Nations Development Program, Human Development Index; World Bank CoC.

started their transformations (Chile, South Korea, Georgia, Botswana) also shows that despite structural constraints, transitions from one mode of governance order to another can be engineered and then steered, although that has not happened in many cases (ibid., 2017). Matching change in control of corruption with change in human development, we find disappointing results for modernization theory. Modernization of a society, as captured by the HDI (a mixture of education, health, and income improvement), does not seem to bring about improvement in corruption control for the limited time interval for which we have data (see Figure 3.4). An improvement in HDI explains neither Georgia, a top performer, nor Kuwait, a poor one; only a few countries (such as Zimbabwe) show a certain amount of connection between the two.

A separate variant within the institutional quality theory is modernization of the state (Mungiu-Pippidi and Johnston, 2017, Chapter 1). Proponents of the effects of this variant believe in some sort of primacy of public administration. They say, "Fix the bureaucracy and the rest of development will follow" (Rothstein and Tannenberg, 2015). The source of that belief is an influential paper by Evans and Rauch (1999) who used a scale of meritocracy in public service for a sample of 35 developing countries for the period 1970–1990 to find that "Weberian" bureaucracy enhanced prospects for economic growth, even when controlling both for initial levels of gross domestic product (GDP) per capita and of human capital. But is that a theory of change or yet another finding at a certain point in time? After all, was there ever any doubt that an autonomous bureaucracy – *once you have it* – is better for economic prosperity than a corrupt one? The problem once again is developmental, in other words *how to obtain* an autonomous bureaucracy. Bureaucracy is not exogenous to corruption, so, observing the trends over time, we were not surprised to find them tied completely together[3]. The only countries where bureaucracy has evolved in recent times are the Gulf monarchies, such as the United Arab Emirates, for example. Otherwise, the more room there is for political contention the less likelihood there is that bureaucracies will be autonomous, as predicted by Samuel Eisenstadt (1956). In new democracies, therefore, we can hardly expect a highly politicized administration or one riddled with cronyism to be able to direct a transformation to good governance.

However, at first sight those arguing for the primacy of institutional quality over development find just as little conclusive support. Few countries have improved CoC enough for that view to be supported; some countries, such as China, that have not improved their CoC have still experienced high growth rates. Of the few countries that have managed to make significant progress in their governance over the past thirty years, Chile, Uruguay, Costa Rica, Estonia, Georgia, and Botswana present clear evidence of the primacy of politics, as political reforms clearly preceded economic take-off (Mungiu-Pippidi, 2015b, Chapter 6); South Korea and Taiwan remain the most mixed cases.

Nevertheless, the countries with "bad" human agency, those below average for the rule of law or that are not free, have clearly regressed in control of corruption over the last fifteen years according to the World Bank CoC indicator (Mungiu-Pippidi and Dadašov, 2017). The more ambiguous results come from the fact that generally the free and partly free countries and those above average for the rule of law (according to the World Bank rule of law indicator) have registered only slight progress or have simply stagnated. However, that does not mean we find no factors associated with change, nor that any lack of association is a robust finding – only that such associations do not fall within classic modernization theory

---

[3] As estimated by Political Risk Services, a consulting group that publishes the International Country Risk Guide.

paradigms, state modernization paradigms, or the legal–normative hypothesis that characterises most current interventions. In other words, the hope of many in the development community, including those involved in the United Nations Convention against Corruption (UNCAC), is that if countries adopt the formal framework of public integrity then practice will accordingly follow (ibid.). Many anti-corruption agencies have tried, so far unsuccessfully, to reproduce the success of Singapore in new democracies and their governments stand accused of "implementation deficit." But it is unclear if such "deficit" would not be better described as a proxy for the inadequacy of legal tools where the rule of law does not exist. In such circumstances, neither adoption nor implementation have been realistic options from the beginning.

Given that there is a very close correlation between the rule of law and control of corruption (at over 90 percent in Worldwide Governance Indicators), wherever corruption is high the rule of law in turn tends to be inadequate. How then can legal anti-corruption approaches be expected to work, i.e., how can the solution be the same as the problem itself? Evidence shows that change in control of corruption in countries with an anti-corruption agency (ACA) but lacking the rule of law is on average marginally lower than in those that have introduced an ACA and have attained a certain level of rule of law (ibid.). The reasons are obvious, for regardless of how much emphasis UNCAC and the international anti-corruption community place on "autonomous" anti-corruption agencies, they can hardly be divorced from the context of the country (Doig et al., 2007; Mungiu-Pippidi and Dadašov, 2017). Cases will still have to be tried in domestic courts; the Guatemalan concept of a special anti-corruption court under international influence has been temporarily floated in Ukraine, but its sustainability even in Guatemala has meanwhile been cast into doubt. Anti-corruption agencies therefore work only when the political will to make them independent *precedes* the establishment of the agency, i.e., when political leaders are both not themselves corrupt and determined to fight corruption. An ACA alone can hardly succeed against a majority in parliament and the executive, even if supported by the international community, as in Indonesia, Romania, or Ukraine.

The existence of a judiciary independent from both government and private interests and able to hand down judgments impartially, fairly, and honestly is presumed to be an indispensable component of both the control of corruption and the rule of law. That is confirmed by statistical evidence, using different proxies (Ali and Isse, 2003; Herzfeld and Weiss, 2003; Damania et al., 2004; Mungiu-Pippidi, 2015b; Mungiu-Pippidi and Dadašov, 2016). Countries fighting corruption need a judiciary that is both independent and accountable, with a possible trade-off between the two in the short or even medium term. The problem is that the same factors prevent both the independence of the judiciary and the electoral accountability of the political elites who determine corruption. While an effective legal system is viewed as a key component of reducing corruption, researchers also found a significant interrelationship between legal effectiveness and various measures of corruption (Hertzfeld and Weiss, 2003). Furthermore, judicial independence is notoriously difficult to influence from outside a country, which explains the eagerness of donors to invest in autonomous agencies despite their lack of success. A survey of change over the twelve years for which data are available finds little progress across, for instance, Africa, the Middle East and North Africa, and Asia. Meanwhile, countries with the most active judicial anti-corruption systems in the world, Romania and Brazil, which have jailed dozens of politicians, have registered progress but still no more than 1 point on the 1–10 scale of the judicial independence component of the Index for Public Integrity (IPI, originally a Global Competitiveness Report survey item). For the world average, therefore, those countries' progress is too little to offset setbacks elsewhere in the world, for instance in common-law countries such as India.

The story is actually more complex. The quality and not the quantity of regulation matters, and that is not easy either to quantify or to test. First, there is evidence that *administrative simplicity* is closely related to good control of corruption, as classic liberal theory predicts (Mungiu-Pippidi, 2015b, Chapter 4). Clear evidence exists that regulation is shaped by rulers to fit their own interests and feed their rents, hence the close correlation between regulatory quality and control of corruption (Shleifer and Vishny, 1993). Rather than asking what regulation should be added by international intervention, the first question ought rather to be "What regulations should be removed?" as many existing regulations are designed to create barriers favoring connected (protected) companies against competition (Ades and Di Tella, 1999). Administrative simplification reforms worked miracles in Estonia and Georgia (Mungiu-Pippidi and Johnston, 2017). This refers in particular to the relationships between citizens, businesses, and the bureaucracy and is captured in the IPI in figures for administrative burden (the time it takes to pay taxes and to register and close a business) and trade openness (the time it takes to arrange imports and exports). The reduction of the administrative burden thus becomes a universal policy objective and indeed is pursued by the World Bank in many countries where that organization assists reforms. However, there is a caveat: *administrative simplicity* should not be confused with *deregulation*, decisions about which must be weighted by other criteria as well. For instance, where procurement is concerned deregulation might reduce bidding competitiveness, while where construction permits are concerned it actually reduces bribery (Fazekas, 2017).

Secondly, a deterrent to corrupt exchanges is their visibility, so *transparency* is the solution there. For instance, restriction to party funding is a sensitive area and is promoted heavily by the international anti-corruption community. However, the more regulation is adopted, the more corrupt a country becomes, probably because party funding then migrates entirely out of sight (Cingolani and Fazekas, 2017; Mungiu-Pippidi and Dadašov, 2017). Full transparency is therefore indispensable to the regulation of party finance. Because too many restrictions might increase corruption and lower access to politics rather than having the opposite effect, things should be adjusted to fit the specific problems within a particular society rather than being imported from elsewhere as a standard package.

Thirdly, evidence shows that no amount of regulation, even of the kind that we have found to have most impact, is efficient by itself, without voluntary contributions from some part of society to implement those regulations because they are in some group's best interest.[4] Control of corruption is therefore dependent on the *interaction* of the right policies with societal agency. The statistical interaction between factors reducing resources for corruption and those increasing constraints is highly significant (ibid.), showing that the most promising policy interventions include some form of transparency, monitoring, or feedback that can be used by civil society or media activism to change practices. If party finance legislation is ineffective by itself, once associated with judicial independence it becomes significant (Lopez et al., 2017). Similarly, transparent financial disclosures by politicians, which alone have a weak impact on control of corruption, become stronger when associated with free media (Vargas and Schlutz, 2016), while freedom of information legislation is effective only when combined with a strong civil society (Mungiu-Pippidi, 2015b, Chapter 4). Conflict of interest legislation is not significant in the absence of judicial independence (Mungiu-Pippidi and Dadašov, 2017), and newly developed ICT tools require civil society activism if they are to have any impact (Kossow and Kukutschka, 2017). For instance, such e-government services as are offered lead to progress only when there is participation in them (Mungiu-Pippidi,

---

[4] Three sources of data were used for this analysis. Those were the Public Accountability Mechanisms framework initiated by the World Bank, which covers 90 countries and reflects the extent of regulation as at 2012; the Doing Business database of the World Bank (190 economies); and the Political Finance Database of IDEA International (180 countries).

2013). Even the best anti-corruption tools, then, are not silver bullets; the tools must be fine-tuned to local stakeholders who will use them to promote change because change is in their best interest.

The top countries for control of corruption, for example Norway, Germany, or Uruguay, therefore seem outliers when we associate density of public accountability legislation with corruption, as their good performance in control of corruption is not based on extensive integrity regulation and was probably reached by other means. The countries historically successful at corruption control did not attain their optimal equilibrium through anti-corruption regulation. A degree of power-balancing came first, whereby ruling elites were forced to show more restraint. But what if a country is missing those conditions that enabled those earlier successful countries? What other enablers can we combine with regulation to correct the equilibrium? The right question becomes not "Which is the right tool?" but "What is the right complex of policies to fit the local agency in favor of ethical universalism?" And that might differ from case to case.

Some of the earliest academic papers by economists about corruption argued that in systematically corrupt countries, *policies and not lawyers* should be the solution to corruption problems (Ades and Di Tella, 1997). In a context of "weak governance" and poor judicial independence, the suboptimal governance equilibrium leading to corruption might need to be subverted as it cannot be attacked directly. If direct constraints on corruption cannot be increased, resources for corruption can perhaps be gradually cut (Huther and Shah, 2000; Mungiu-Pippidi, 2015b, Chapter 8), arriving in time at some disequilibrium, which can be the entry point for a change with the potential to lead to an optimal equilibrium.

Thus control of corruption emerges from an examination of this empirical literature as an equilibrium determined by opportunities (or resources) for corruption, such as natural resources, aid funds unaccompanied by accountability requirements, lack of government transparency, administrative discretion; and constraints, such as legal constraint (an independent judiciary) and normative constraint(the media, civil society, the international community). The theoretical model (Becker, 1968; Norad, 2011; Mungiu-Pippidi, 2015b, Chapter 4) is supported by a vast empirical literature, which was used to create the Index of Public Integrity (www.integrity-index.org). The index captures only the actionable factors on both resources and constraints, but as the model shows, these are grounded in a certain goodness of fit with modernity (Djankov and Glaeser's human and social capital). While a government can occasionally be pressed to cut red tape due to some external conditionality, increasing demand for good governance within a given society is a longer and more complicated affair. The mixture of actionable (to different

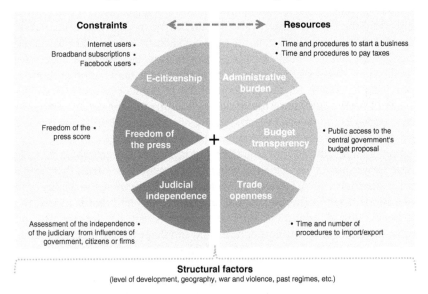

Figure 3.5 Control of corruption as interaction between resources and constraints in index of public integrity proxies
Source: Mungiu-Pippidi and Dadašov, 2016. See www.integrity-inde x.org

extents) interacting factors that are associated with control of corruption are the basis for the Index of Public Integrity (Figure 3.5), which serves as the main tool in this book.

How does this work in practice? Opportunities for corruption increase with the scope of the state and the budget allocated for discretionary spending (Tanzi and Davoodi, 1998). By contrast, funds for universal spending – pensions, scholarships, social aid – although they can all be abused corruptly, are far less correlated with corruption simply because of their universal dedication. The best-governed countries in the world, from Sweden to Botswana, enjoy large – not small – public expenditure, but as such expenditure is universally allocated and transparently spent, the amount expended is not a problem. Quite the contrary, in fact (Persson and Rothstein, 2015). The problem occurs when there are funds available that may be spent with greater discretion: greater than, for example, scholarships for high school students who do well at mathematics. Such funds might then be channeled towards particular interests, to privileged allocations such as preferential subsidies, concessions, infrastructure funds, procurement money, cash profits from natural resources, or foreign aid.

Societal constraints increase with education (Uslaner and Rothstein, 2016) and pluralism, but as resources also increase as the scope of the modern state is widened, resources may come to outweigh constraints. Equilibrium could then result, but it would be suboptimal. It is in fact through successive equilibriums that societies arrive at the optimal constraints upon authorities exercising discretion for the preferential use of public resources. Both elements of such equilibrium, the resources for corruption and the constraints on it, depend to some extent on the degree of societal modernization but also are – or can be – subject to international influence.

Foreign intervention is of course very attractive, as it seems to be the only clear exogenous factor with the theoretical potential to break the vicious circle (see Figure 3.7). Donors can work directly to improve the quality of fit with modernization (human capital, infrastructure), and that is indeed the scope of most development assistance. Donors can act directly also, on either resources or constraints or both, and can shape the balance. Of course, there are unintended consequences of intervention too, as donors might create false incentives or unwittingly increase resources for corruption by pouring unaccountable money into kleptocracies (Knack, 2001). The reason why so much potential has remained largely unachieved remains to be reviewed in the country-by-country analysis.

If we trace the individual components of the IPI (Figure 3.5) it becomes evident why corruption has not declined globally over the past twenty years compared to the previous interval in the 1990s, when it registered some improvement. First, freedom of the press, its main component, has been declining ever since the 1990s, while trade openness and economic freedom have stagnated. A certain amount of red tape has been reduced, but as Fazekas argues, the sort of red tape mostly conducive to government favoritism is not usually the first to be cut (2017). E-citizenship, defined as access to the internet combined with the number of Facebook users per country and considered a proxy for civil society autonomy, has increased, but electronic government in general (e-services offered and e-services used) still has some way to go in most countries. Some change has occurred, but is neither comprehensive nor deep enough to tilt the balance.

3.2   The International Factor

3.2.1   Trade and Globalization

Section 3.1 of this chapter showed that the most direct interventions, for instance in the form of anti-corruption legislation or agencies, have not reduced corruption to any significant extent. But the examination of international influence cannot be limited to those alone. Ever since Napoleon III changed policy to put into practice the Saint-Simon doctrine that freedom of trade is essential for development and that trade barriers hinder it, the free-trade factor has been at work, when not hampered by protectionism and other distortive government interventions (Spitzer, 1962). As early as the nineteenth century, free trade and corruption were seen by liberals in Britain and France as mutually exclusive. However, experience of the expansion of global trade has always been ambiguous, then as now. The present world is not the first to be confronted with the paradox of more globalization apparently creating more corruption. The first major corruption scandal of the modern world originated with the infamous East India company, which offered a fast track to enrichment in India not by trade alone but by corruption, and which was able to resist many parliamentary attacks at home in England thanks to its political protectors. A number of politicians profited directly as shareholders and therefore granted the company favors, ranging from immunity to publicly funded bailouts when bankruptcy loomed. But the East India Company was also the case that prompted Edmund Burke's argument that one cannot have bad government abroad without risking bad government at home (1783). That still holds today and informs the ideology of the Foreign Corrupt Practices Act and the OECD Anti-Bribery Convention: that international traders and the governments protecting them have to be consistent in their defense of free and fair trade, without violence, extortion, or corruption.

So how does globalization affect corruption, and can we rely on it to spread good institutions from the countries that have them to the countries that do not?

Corruption perception indexes, such as the ones developed by Transparency International and the World Bank, show large differences across countries. Certain exceptions aside, developed countries emerge as mostly clean, while as a general rule less developed countries are seen as corrupt. Less than a third of the world is in the upper third of a 1–10 scale for control of corruption, indicating that corruption is the rule rather than the exception in most of the world. There are few places where it is safe to trade when integrity is in question; even in the EU, many countries score highly on government favoritism in the annual Global Competitiveness Report. The paradox of international trade is that exchanges between countries perceived as corrupt and countries perceived as not corrupt do seem to lead to an increase in corruption and to negative spill-over. Companies working out of economies that are perceived as clean pay bribes to enter the markets

Table 3.1 *Top fines paid by international companies for bribing abroad*

Company fined	Amount, USD million	Year	Country of origin
Telia Company AB	965	2017	Sweden
Siemens	800	2008	Germany
VimpelCom	795	2016	Netherlands
Alstom	772	2014	France
KBR / Halliburton	579	2009	United States
Teva Pharma	519	2016	Israel
Och-Ziff	412	2016	United States
BAE	400	2010	United Kingdom
Total SA	398	2013	France
Alcoa	384	2014	United States

Note: Amounts represent top judicial fines imposed on companies for bribery abroad on the basis of the Foreign Corrupt Practices Act.
Source: FPCA blog.

of countries perceived as corrupt. Put simply, it is the story of the encounter of Britain with India all over again, with corruption blamed on a local "corrupt" culture, but actually fueled by the foreign country that is supposedly "clean." Over the years a more balanced language has emerged to refer to international corruption, with talk of "supply and demand" sides, both of which can be to blame. In a similar vein, most of the efforts of OECD and Transparency International went into increasing the costs to multinationals that pay bribes in poor countries, resulting in the development of a whole industry of "compliance" with anti-bribery laws.

Observation of the Foreign Corrupt Practices Act (FCPA), the world's oldest and best-implemented international anti-bribery law, shows the top offenders to be companies based in some of the "cleanest" countries in the world, starting with Sweden, for many years at the very top of every ranking for public integrity (see Table 3.1). Apart from the USA and Israel, all other fines were issued to EU-based companies. Telia, a company from Sweden, the world's least corrupt country, paid bribes in Uzbekistan, an authoritarian and corrupt country. This seems to indicate that corruption, rather than integrity, might be more likely to spill over in international transactions. However, the new international anti-corruption framework is more likely to harm Telia than Uzbekistan; trade and its related conditionalities have yet not managed to change much in corrupt countries. There is also the risk of recidivism on the part of international companies fined for paying bribes. Siemens, for instance, has allegedly continued to experience difficulties in many countries after pleading

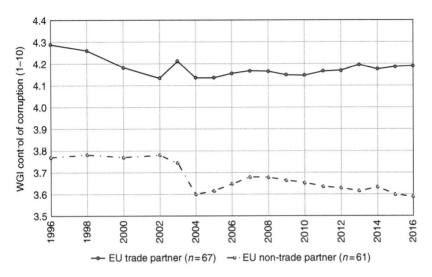

Figure 3.6 Average corruption across EU trading partners versus the rest of the world
Source: World Bank CoC.

guilty to charges of corruption (Kartner and Warner, 2015; Canter, 2015).

At first sight, simply avoiding dealing with the most corrupt countries might seem the easiest way to fight corruption. A company that chooses to invest in a country below the middle rank of Transparency International's Corruption Perception Index score knows what will be expected if it is to do business locally. As a British governor of the Straits Settlements aptly put it two centuries ago, if companies or individuals, "knowing the risks they run, owing to the disturbed state of these countries, choose to hazard their lives and properties for the sake of large profits that accompany successful trading, they must not expect the British government to be answerable if their speculation proves unsuccessful" (Ryan, 1967, pp. 122–123). Engaging with such countries has always been problematic. By 2017, the average perceived corruption of current EU trading partners, for instance, was lower than for countries the EU was not trading with (see Figure 3.6). But pressure has been growing to engage with countries perceived as the most corrupt, which are for the most part the poorest. Such countries are recipients of foreign aid, which brings significant procurement of interest for international companies, but the poorer countries need to develop and therefore seek foreign investment and lower tariffs. Excluding them from trade in order to avoid temptation is therefore increasingly seen as both morally problematic and practically difficult.

More international competition might bring the risk of more corruption, because countries where foreign competition is inhibited, perhaps due to natural resources or legal monopolies or protections, tend to be more corrupt (Ades and Di Tella, 1999). Shleifer and Vishny argued that governments also manipulate legislation to create rents in order to consolidate their own economic and power bases (2002), resulting in a vicious circle of corruption and protectionism. While an economy of that sort would be sustainable under certain conditions – for instance if the price of the rent-sustaining natural resources were to remain high (oil, diamonds) – in the long term the vicious circle of "extractive institutions" arises, leading to chronic underdevelopment, as described by Acemoglu and Robinson (2012). That is because any allocation not based on merit is harmful to any economy.

The possibility that control of corruption will increase in such situations is minimal: why would governments that sustain themselves by rent manipulation open up to competition from foreigners and endanger their rents (Leff, 1964)? The tension between domestic extortion and admitting international investors is an old one. Typical examples of corruption encountered by foreigners are the solicitation of bribes to obtain foreign licenses for exchange, import, export, investment, or production, or to avoid paying tax; although for international investors that sort of extortion amounts to an extra tax anyway (ibid.). Certain researchers have found evidence for negative effects of corruption on foreign direct investment (FDI) and for the hypothesis that corruption deters foreign investment by acting as an extra tax (Ades and Di Tella, 1997; Egger and Winner, 2006; Habib and Zurawicki, 2002). The effect varies, however, from developed economies to less developed ones and it may be that it decreases over the years (Egger and Winner, 2006). Ades and Di Tella found that corruption deters investment, but more so in an environment where red tape is low (1997). In other words, red tape is inherently detrimental to investment (see Figure 3.4). Other authors found a clearly positive relationship between corruption and FDI, with corruption appearing to act as a stimulus for FDI (Egger and Winner, 2006). Others found that corruption generally hampers international trade, whereas paying bribes to customs enhances imports, particularly in importing countries with inefficient customs services where long waiting times at the border significantly reduce international trade (Bogmans and de Jong, 2011). While very different samples, controls, and time intervals in these studies mean that results do not always agree on the impact of corruption on FDI, most reviews suggest that foreign investors generally avoid countries with poor

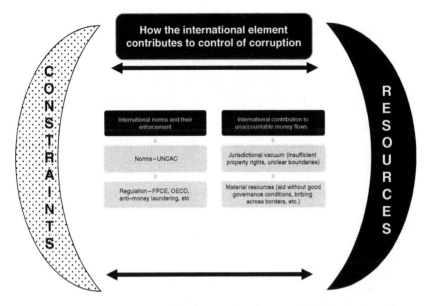

Figure 3.7 Desired and unintended influence of the international factor over control of corruption

institutions (Bénassy-Quéré et al., 2007; Habib and Zurawicki, 2002). However, the reason for that is not only corruption but high transaction costs more generally. For instance, one World Bank paper found that both corruption and export orientation explain why a country attracts FDI or not, showing the complex linkage between corruption, trade, and FDI (Jun and Singh, 1999). In the ANTICORRP project, we tested whether more globalization leads to more corruption within the framework of the corruption model that explains control of corruption as equilibrium, as in Figure 3.7. We captured globalization through two indicators that are part of the Swiss KOF index of globalization, one measuring the degree of economic globalization, which captures trade as well as financial openness, and the second the degree of social openness, based mostly on data on information flows and use of telecommunications services (Dreher, 2006).[5] The data cover the years 1996, 1998, 2000, and 2002–2010 and are from a sample of 113 countries.[6] Since the

[5] The KOF Index of Globalization is provided by the KOF Swiss Economic Institute and was developed by Axel Dreher (2006). For more information see http://globalization.kof.ethz.ch/
[6] We applied two standard estimation methods for panel data analysis: the random effects model and the fixed effects model. The latter we used additionally to account for potential

results may have been affected by the inclusion of developed countries, we also tested with samples from only middle- and low-income countries. The results confirm that power discretion and dependency on fossil fuel exports are associated with poor control of corruption. By contrast, economic openness, (in the form of lower trade and financial barriers), social openness, and press freedom positively influence control of corruption.

The close relationship between red tape and corruption explains why it is difficult to change corruption by regulation – it is because corrupt elites shape regulations in order to maximize their own rents. A way to break the vicious circle can hardly be endogenous, so it is better that incentives for change come from outside. While foreign aid does not penalize recipient countries for their corruption, private investors from clean countries frequently do (Alesina and Weder, 2002). Poor countries need both international aid and foreign investment, which might together provide the exogenous impetus that could stimulate competition and begin the unraveling of the vicious structure of an economy based on privileged connections. Adopting trade agreements might help level the playing field between domestic and foreign investors (reducing both tariffs and red tape) and change the vicious circle into a virtuous one. How would it work? It would weaken domestic rentier companies and show governments that a gradual loss of rents can be amply compensated by new resources gained through economic growth led by foreign investment. If a government accepted trade liberalization, its loss of very primitive rents in the form of favorite companies making corrupt payments to officials or the governing party might easily be offset by gains derived from growth. Such gains would enlarge the budget and could help ameliorate social unrest associated with systematic corruption. However, experience shows that rents do not vanish overnight; what tends to happen is that gradual transformation allows favored companies to become more competitive, as the mostly successful transformations of South Korea and Taiwan show (You, 2015).

We expect therefore that international trade agreements will help in the control of corruption in two ways:

effects of country-specific unobserved time-invariant factors such as political culture and tradition. Overall the models explain more than 70 percent of the differences in the level of control of corruption in our total data sample, most of which, however, result from the cross-country rather than the time variation. The full report, produced by Alina Mungiu-Pippidi with Roberto Martínez Barranco Kukutschka and Ramin Dadašov (Mungiu-Pippidi et al., 2014, pp. 54–58), may be seen at http://anticorrp.eu/publications/quantitative-report-on-causes/

1. by directly increasing competition due to the removal of tariffs, which diminishes the power of the rentier companies that influence regulation in their favor;
2. by contributing to a fairer business environment through transparency provisions; i.e., by reducing non-tariff barriers, generally used as an advantage to domestically well-connected companies.

Given the proliferation of trade agreements and the fact that we have available certain corruption measurements – although most are based on perception researchers have started gathering direct evidence. Recent studies highlight that improving transparency in trade agreements can result in effective gains for trade.[7] However, an OECD study found that countries with more democratic institutions and higher standards of governance are the ones more likely to include comprehensive coverage of transparency commitments, such as a fully-fledged transparency chapter in their regional trade agreement. Both effects are statistically significant at the 1 percent level (Lejárraga and Shepherd, 2013), suggesting that the vicious circle might continue unaffected in the more difficult cases. We do not yet have ex post evaluation research to show whether or not corruption has been reduced anywhere after the adoption of international trade agreements. For the past twenty years corruption has been largely stagnant everywhere in the world, so that any association that we could show between trade openness and corruption is largely of a structural nature. We can therefore be certain only that corruption and red tape are barriers to competition. It is to be hoped that the coming years bring less corruption, following the increased trade openness of the latest decades. But we are not there yet.

3.2.2 International Normative Pressure

Corruption was established as an international problem in the aftermath of the controversial Washington Consensus reforms in the last decade of the twentieth century, and it has grown exponentially ever since. The former World Bank president James Wolfensohn and the NGO founded by World Bank retiree Peter Eigen and his friends Transparency International managed to add to the agenda a problem that had been taboo until then. Increased awareness and individual agency of various

---

[7] A study of the Asia-Pacific Economic Cooperation (APEC) countries, for instance, found that improving trade-related transparency could increase inter-APEC trade by approximately USD 148 billion or 7.5 percent of baseline trade in the region (Helble et al., 2009). Other studies estimate that including transparency commitments in regional trade deals could generate an increase in bilateral trade of more than 1 per cent (Lejárraga and Shepherd, 2013; Jenkins, 2017, p. 4).

kinds were followed by the beginnings of an international normative framework and then the explosive development of an anti-corruption "industry." Undeterred by the poor performance of global anti-corruption activity, as shown by their own measurement instruments (Sampson, 2010; Norad, 2011; Cole, 2015; Mungiu-Pippidi, 2015b), anti-corruption professionals from all sectors have managed to institutionalize themselves into an anti-corruption industry worth hundreds of millions of dollars. That industry helps develop and implement policies, regulations, initiatives, conventions, and "compliance" of business with this rapidly accelerating regulatory avalanche. It offers training, monitoring of activities, and programs to enhance integrity and improve public administration, and it generally advocates for more of the same. Transparency International's positions on various issues are semi-official in G20 meetings and other top-level official gatherings. The theory of change is that the more awareness there is among top international actors and the more integrity legislation is passed and implemented, both soft (ethical codes, self-regulation) and hard (criminal legislation, for instance), the more corruption will be reduced. Evaluations starting from 1984 had so far found no sign of any such reduction, for the reasons explained above (Cole, 2015), but an international normative framework has nevertheless been created. Some of its tools have been implemented and might possibly be able to effect some change in the future. A brief menu follows.

3.2.3   Anti-Bribery and Anti-Corruption Conventions

The United States, with the Foreign Corrupt Practices Act (FCPA) of 1977, was the first country to declare it a crime for a domestic firm to pay bribes to foreign public officials. The passing of that law came in the aftermath of the Watergate scandal and was an exceptional occurrence, a real breakthrough, although it was some years before implementation was possible. The adoption of the FCPA, and ensuing concern at the creation of a comparative *de facto* disadvantage for US companies vis-à-vis competitors with no restrictions on bribery abroad, led to strong American advocacy that other industrialized nations should follow suit. Following a first proposal to the OECD in 1989, the USA deployed all possible diplomatic and other persuasive means, including informal use of media to "name and shame" reluctant partners (Abbott and Snidal, 2002). It took nearly twenty years from the adoption of FCPA (until 1996) for ministers of 26 industrialized nations to agree at an OECD meeting that bribes to foreign officials should no longer be tax deductible; in fact, they should be criminalized instead. That decision was then endorsed by a later G7 meeting (Pieth, 1997).

On 15 February 1999, the OECD Anti-Bribery Convention came into force, requiring signatory countries to adopt similar legislation. To date, 43 countries have signed. Cases of cross-border corruption have been alleged (see Table 3.1) and by the end of 2016, 43 individuals and 158 entities had been sanctioned in criminal proceedings for foreign bribery occurring since the convention came into force. An additional 121 individuals and 235 entities have been sanctioned in criminal, administrative, and civil cases for other offences related to foreign bribery, such as money laundering or false accounting, in 8 parties (OECD, 2017). A monitoring mechanism exists but it is based on peer review; and of course there are no sanctions. The OECD itself acknowledges that implementation is poor except by the United States, Germany, and the United Kingdom (OECD, 2018). As more bribery takes place where there is more investment, the lack of any cases in certain countries indicates low implementation rather than low corruption. The FCPA was later amended after the OECD's Anti-Bribery Convention was adopted, when implementation, too, increased. The US Department of Justice and the Securities Exchange Commission are the enforcing agents, and as Table 3.2 shows, they both have good records.

The acts forbidding bribery abroad thus originated in the American discovery after Watergate (and a handful of other scandals) that such dirty money can spill over in originating countries and infest domestic politics. The initial goals were to preserve the integrity of the country where the company or multinational was registered and to cleanse the international business arena. The concept that forbidding bribery in foreign countries would make those countries where bribery takes place cleaner has never been fully developed and is in fact based on uncertain logic, because Western multinationals paid to enter closed or semi-closed markets. In their absence nothing can prevent businesses from other countries or domestically connected firms to thrive from preferential treatment. Corruption is the abuse of power, so it is a misconception to presume that the foreign company is the one inducing corruption rather than simply aligning itself with existing corruption and then fueling it. If pressure cannot be put on local authorities to prevent all bribery, forbidding only businesses from developed countries from doing so can hardly help control of corruption in the "receiving" country. The 1999 OECD convention created serious costs for businesses in the form of a whole "compliance industry," complete with "integrity pacts" endorsed by Transparency International, whereby signatories to the convention agree neither to offer nor to pay bribes. But, as most businesspeople are aware, the error is in presuming that corrupt countries would be clean in the absence of international companies, and that

Table 3.2 *Membership and enforcement for main international anti-corruption treaties*

Legal act	Adoption year	Members to date	Number of sanctions
FPCA	1977 amended 1998	1, but wide jurisdiction	204 SEC, 312 DOJ (Stanford Law School)
OECD Anti-Bribery Convention	1997	43	58 entities sentenced; by 2018, 500 investigations under way in 29 parties
EU Convention against Corruption Involving Officials	1997	28	
United Nations Convention against Corruption (UNCAC)	2005	183 (140)	Peer review mechanism with no sanctions
United Nations Convention against Transnational Organized Crime and the Protocols Thereto (UNCTOC)	2000	188 (144)	Peer review mechanism with no sanctions
WTO – GPA	1996, last revised 2014	By 2018, 19 parties including 47 WTO member states	WTO Committee on Government
WTO – TFA	2017	All WTO members	Procurement WTO's binding dispute settlement system

Source: Mungiu-Pippidi 2018a.

by extracting pledges from foreign entrants not to engage in bribery it is more likely to clean up that market rather than effectively handing it over to the non-signatories of the convention. Accordingly, a recent paper based on a survey in Vietnam comes to the conclusion that signatories paid fewer bribes after implementation was stepped up, while non-signatories paid more bribes. The overall result was therefore the same amount of corruption but with fewer market actors (Jensen and Malesky, 2018). In short, the OECD Anti-Bribery Convention, even in the highly improbable event of ifs full implementation, has the potential to protect only foreign investors from corruption, and not the corrupt countries where those foreign investors had been planning to invest.

The United Nations Convention against Corruption (UNCAC) and Convention against Transnational Organized Crime (UNCTOC) (see Table 3.2), along with the Council of Europe Group of States against Corruption (GRECO), all address matters of corruption control with a focus on *procedures*. Countries are in effect asked to create anti-corruption agencies and adopt integrity regulation, although a more recent shift towards implementation is noticeable. The theory of change behind those acts is that international awareness and cooperation can socialize individual states into at least formally addressing the issue, with the hope that by their creation and periodic evaluation such institutions will become effective regardless of the original political will. UNCAC asks that:

Each State Party shall, in accordance with the fundamental principles of its legal system, develop and implement or maintain effective, coordinated anticorruption policies that promote the participation of society and reflect the principles of the rule of law, proper management of public affairs and public property, integrity, transparency and accountability. 2. Each State Party shall endeavor to establish and promote effective practices aimed at the prevention of corruption. 3. Each State Party shall endeavor to periodically evaluate relevant legal instruments and administrative measures with a view to determining their adequacy to prevent and fight corruption. (UNCAC, 2005, p. 9)

OECD evaluation reports are public by default, so at least where freedom of speech exists, they can be used to criticize a government if it is failing to reach targets. UNCAC reports are available only case-by-case. Although over the years progress has been made with implementation, treaties enforced by peer review pressure are not really generating breakthroughs anywhere. There is no case on record where UNCAC provoked a national destabilization of corrupt ways or even any major public debate on progress. A mid-term evaluation of the UNCAC's impact found that countries that had joined by 2014 had made no more progress than non-signatories (Mungiu-Pippidi, 2015b, Chapter 7), although it is true that, prompted by international pressure, many countries had adopted legislation and created anti-corruption agencies (Passas, 2010). The same kind of evidence exists in relation to the Extractive Industries Transparency Initiative (EITI), which is another important treaty intended to reduce corruption resources. Using the WGI control of corruption index, recent research found that EITI membership had not resulted in reduced corruption scores (Kasekende et al., 2016).

International anti-corruption enforcement varies greatly both in means and outcomes. Table 3.2 offers a synthetic view. In practice, however, variety is less impressive. The WTO has a dispute settlement system (DSB) that functions reasonably well in trade disputes, but is inadequate to deal with international bribery. The GPA, a procurement extension, asks all participating countries to open up their markets and establish independent "domestic review systems," i.e. mechanisms to review complaints to which both foreign and domestic suppliers may apply for correction of procedural errors. Hopefully, foreign suppliers from other, potentially less corrupt GPA parties would have stronger incentives and fewer inhibitions than domestic players to report collusion or corruption, both of which are likely to be major obstacles to their participation in procurement markets (Anderson and Müller, 2017).

Regional trade facilitation agreements (TFA) have increasingly featured transparency and anti-corruption provisions. They are enforced through both bilateral investor–state dispute settlements and bilateral dispute settlements between governments. As seen in Tables 3.1 and 3.2, the FPCA remains the most effective instrument and the recent practice of seeking claims on behalf of other countries promises more cooperation in future. Researchers found that FCPA enforcement increases with US investment in a country, and that the presence of bilateral mechanisms for cooperation in regulation and enforcement between the United States and a given host country is strongly associated with increased FCPA enforcement in the host country (McLean, 2012). The FPCA provides the means to intervene in far more situations than might seem plausible for legislation that has only one party, the USA itself. In fact, as the FIFA case showed, American jurisdiction can extend very far these days, even if there is only minimal American connection – such as the use of an American bank account, as in the FIFA case, or the existence of an American shareholder. The European companies fined most heavily for bribery abroad had paid bribes on other continents but they were caught by American FPCA enforcers.

The very recent Petrobras case shows another route to enforcement, with international investors seeking redress under US civil law. Hundreds of holders of Petrobras stock have begun to file "derivative suits" through which shareholders can sue a company's directors and officers for breaching their fiduciary duties to that company. For instance, in *In Re Petrobras Securities Litigation*, a group of shareholders allege that Petrobras issued "materially false and misleading" financial statements and "false and misleading statements regarding the integrity of its management and the effectiveness of its financial controls." They did so because Petrobras has publicly boasted of its code of ethics and corruption prevention program in order to attract investment. The claimants allege that as a result of price-fixing and cover-up, the value of Petrobras common stock fell by approximately 80 percent. In another case, *WGI Emerging Markets Fund,*

LLC et al v. Petroleo, the investment fund managing the Bill and Melinda Gates Foundation has alleged that failure by Petrobras to adhere to US federal securities law resulted in misleading shareholders and overstating the value of the company by USD 17 billion. The plaintiffs claim to have "lost tens of millions on their Petrobras investments" as a result (Young, 2016).

Monitoring mechanisms and collective sanctions are mentioned as enforcement means – but seldom implemented. Relying as they do on peer review evaluations, the UN conventions, GRECO, and the OECD completely lack any sanctions mechanisms. Indeed, it is unclear on what basis sanctions would operate, as those conventions focus more on instruments than on results. A country that might adopt conflict of interest legislation but not present any case for judgment would be safe in any event. The European Commission, too, has seldom exercised sanctions for corruption against member states or aid recipients, although a mechanism for cooperation and verification for Romania and Bulgaria served to monitor their capacity to control corruption, and EU funds were temporarily discontinued to those countries on corruption grounds. The same happened with certain African countries receiving aid (Mungiu-Pippidi et al., 2017). A monitoring mechanism with collective sanctions is included in the EU's "trade for all" strategy, but as it was never implemented in the Cotonou Agreement (only one country has ever been sanctioned) a solution has still to be found to unblock the collective sanctions instrument, despite that particular treaty's ample provision for sanctions.

3.2.4   *Factoring in Unintended Consequences*

This brief account has reviewed the presumed domestic and international theories of change that might positively influence corruption. But the issue of influencing corruption *negatively* from abroad has been touched on only marginally. In fact, most international anti-bribery regulation addresses the unintended consequence of international business, the "bribery abroad" phenomenon, and not domestic corruption. Aside from the unintended consequences of globalization, there are other ways the international factor can insidiously affect corruption in a given country, as the Panama Papers and Paradise Papers have clearly shown. Money laundered by criminals, assets stolen by corrupt rulers of countries, and "legally optimized" funds that firms and individuals in developed countries choose to place offshore rather than pay tax – all have negative effects. The estimated amount of money laundered globally in one year is 2–5 percent of global GDP, somewhere between USD 800 billion and USD 2 trillion.[8] Some of the best known offshore tax havens have even become so rich that they have actually made progress up the good governance charts (St Kitts and Nevis and other Caribbean countries, for instance) while breaking records for laundering other countries' money. Getting richer helps against petty corruption, so country analysts gave them better governance scores – even as *de facto* growth came from money laundering. That only goes to show the limitation of questionnaires that inquire only about domestic behavior. A theory of change in relation to unaccountable money flows – money belonging to criminals as well as money from tax optimization – is not so difficult. As Gabriel Zucman has shown in *The Hidden Wealth of Nations*, the required legal steps are no secret, as proposals have been around for many years (2015). The problem is global governance, which multiplies and aggravates collective action problems at national level. A proposal by Nigeria to freeze assets of corrupt leaders preceded even the UNCAC, and an extraordinary amount of energy and money is still spent on it, despite obvious limitations such as the requirement of a criminal conviction before assets may be seized. The question really is whether that is the right focus for Nigeria, and whether the amount embezzled since the original proposal by those who governed next is not a multiple of what expensive lawyers are supposed to retrieve in their international chase. In short, international tools are expensive and rather ineffective compared to what could be done domestically if leaders willed it.

The final category of unintended consequences not mentioned so far is international aid. The aid industry has itself been accused of being corrupt (Hancock, 1992) or of creating corrupt incentives by rewarding corrupt countries (Alesina and Weder, 2002; Kleemann, 2010). Its effectiveness, even with the best of intentions, has been proven wanting because of a different set of incentives ingrained in its organization from that of the people it is supposed to help (Gibson et al., 2005). Older evidence had found both that aid weakened the quality of institutions (proxied as corruption, bureaucratic quality, and rule of law) in direct proportion to its quantity (Knack, 1999) or that poor institutions, proxied by corruption, made development aid ineffective (Burnside and Dollar, 2000). In a review of evidence on the general effect of aid, William Easterly, one of the earliest voices to be critical of the aid industry, concluded that while the main goal (development) might remain elusive, aid could still help achieve piecemeal objectives. Failure was attributed

---

[8] Interviews at the European Chamber of Commerce, February 2018. For further information, visit the United Nations Office on Drugs and Crime (UNODC) website: www.unodc.org/unodc/en/money-laundering/globalization.html

instead to wrong theories of development, poor incentives for the development industry to learn from its own performance, and confusion about actors and ownership. That led in turn to extreme reliance on experts and a continuous game of blame-shifting (2007), a sequence of events that is certainly relevant for any specific type of aid, including that dedicated to good governance. More recent time-series panels find that multilateral (referring to EU) aid actually has a positive effect on governance and corruption control when contrasted with bilateral aid from either the US or individual EU member states (Charron, 2011; Dadašov, 2017). It is hard to say if the difference is due to the different time intervals, the methods, or, more optimistically, because after the first wave of negative results the aid industry became more aware of unintended consequences and corrected itself. That is improbable, however, as most of the critical literature did not refer to the EU, and US aid has still had no significant impact on corruption. On the other hand, in recent years fewer reports have come in that aid is actually producing corruption in the international arena, leaving just the literature on EU funds. The constant finding is that institutional quality renders the funds ineffective and that the funds in their turn do not improve institutions among EU member states (Ederveen et al., 2006; Beugelsdijk and Eijffinger, 2005; Mungiu-Pippidi et al., 2016; Drápalová, 2017).

The question of aid's unintended consequences was theorized first by James Buchanan as the "Samaritan's Dilemma." Buchanan showed that aid recipients might stop trying to help themselves if aid comes from the Samaritan (for instance, why plant grain if flour comes by the sack, for free?). In other words, the incentives created by aid make the aid recipients' lack of effort the obvious rational response (Buchanan, 1975). Aid should therefore be designed to create sustainable improvement – and that applies to everything from famines to the concept of having an internationally manned anti-corruption force arrest the corrupt. Elinor Ostrom and her team took things a step further when describing the depth and variety of collective action problems encountered in development, acknowledging that "[w]e need to help build institutions, but we cannot build institutions primarily from the outside. Yes, we can build the hardware, but in our resource studies around the world, we repeatedly find that hardware is only part of what is needed to achieve development. Without the software of institutions, projects do not do well or last" (2013, p. 33).

Where anti-corruption is concerned there is far less critical reflection. Anti-corruption is booming – it has become a bandwagon that everybody jumps on – and little learning exists despite a dedicated learning unit of the UN (U4) that produces excellent papers. In the words of one anthropologist, anti-corruption, like so many other industries in the sphere of development, might just be another therapeutic, feel-good industry, enjoying "doing something" and insouciant about whether it is actually doing any good and whether or not corruption is thriving in tandem with it (Sampson, 2010).

3.3   Studying Interventions for Control of Corruption

Many anti-corruption policies and programs have been declared successful, but no country has yet achieved control of corruption as a result of international assistance and its standard prescriptions, although a few have succeeded on their own. A number of cities in Venezuela, Russia, and Bolivia that declared successes fifteen or twenty years ago have meanwhile regressed because of general lack of evolution of their countries, as unfortunately the equilibrium described in Section 3.1 of this chapter refers to the national level – not regional, not local, and not international. Control of corruption is built at the level of the nation-state, as it is the core unit of both historical and current political evolution. What, then, can be considered success? "Success" can only mean a consolidated and sustainable dominant norm of ethical universalism and public integrity. Exceptions, in the form of corrupt acts, will always remain, but as long as they are so numerous as to make the dominant norm virtually indistinguishable, a country cannot be seen as an achiever. A successful transformation requires both the dominance of public integrity as the norm (such that the majority of acts and public officials are not corrupt) and its resilience against possible backsliding, as happened in some Eastern European countries after EU accession. Sustainably reducing corruption to the status of an exception thus defines a successful evolution (Mungiu-Pippidi, 2017). A few developing countries such as India, Brazil, Bulgaria, and Romania are struggling in a borderline area, where the old and new norms confront one another and where popular demand for integrity of leaders has increased substantially over the years. However, if we exclude tax havens, the list of contemporary achievers remains very short indeed. In Europe, Estonia is certainly a success story; to some extent so are Georgia and Slovenia, as are Chile, Uruguay, and Costa Rica in Latin America and Botswana in Africa. Taiwan and South Korea in Asia are still disputed but have definitely made great progress. As I have pointed out when dealing with those cases in detail, they are not successes of the international anti-corruption community nor are they "interventions," despite an international factor being present in certain of their transformations (Mungiu-Pippidi, 2015b, Chapter 5; Mungiu-Pippidi and Johnston, 2017). They are in fact evolutions of a domestic equilibrium in which control of corruption has moved towards the optimal point where corruption is no longer taken for granted and is no longer the social norm and majority practice.

The international factor can thus influence control of corruption both with desirable effects and with unintended ones (see Figure 3.7). The positive contribution to control of corruption is the creation of more constraints by the international normative framework (the norm being UNCAC, the externally induced regulation on transparency, anti-corruption, and money laundering). Additionally, the conditionalities created by international trade for a level playing field and equal treatment of businesses, as well as conditionalities derived from other international engagements, could increase constraints on corruption. The evidence so far shows that some such influence does exist but is at best weak. The negative international contribution to the control of corruption consists in the creation of further resources and opportunities for corruption through the blurring of jurisdictions as a result of globalization and the resistance to regulating it, through foreign businesses operating in corrupt countries paying bribes to obtain public contracts or to reduce their transaction costs, and finally through unaccountable development aid, the objectives of which are seldom subjected to broader consultation in society and for which spending is seldom transparent.

Any methodology for studying institutional change must therefore account for the dynamic evolution of these factors and their interaction at the same time. As estimates of corruption have existed only since 1984, the sole reliance on such perception indicators may fall into the trap that such indicators worsen precisely when more action than ever before is being taken against corruption (Cole, 2015). Any serious account of transformation must therefore rely on country-based and fact-based indicators and not expert scores. A "before and after" analytical framework for any intervention can be devised only on that basis. Having a general transformation model along with the indicators to trace it in time, we can perhaps factor in the intervention, deconstruct its theory of change, and assess to what extent expectations were achieved.

4 Doctrine and Practice

4.1 Europeanization's Many Meanings

In the new global normative order promoting good governance, the EU plays a unique role, less perhaps by what it does (although it is the world's largest donor when multilateral aid is aggregated with member states' bilateral aid) but rather by what it is. As good governance substantially overlaps with modernization (the development of a rational state autonomous from private interest) and civilization (rule-abiding citizens being required for rule of law as much as rule-abiding rulers), Europeanization is the oldest and most comprehensive attempt to encourage "good governance."

The concept of Europeanization has had many lives and several meanings, which raises legitimate questions about its utility. In its oldest, broad, cultural meaning, Europeanization signifies the adoption of European ideas, technology, and customs to displace autochthonous and traditional ones. More often than not, Westernization and Europeanization mean one and the same thing. In that sense, Europeanization is transformation according to a European blueprint: market economy, rule of law, secularization. But since the advent of the European Union, EU integration scholars have contrived a meaning of the word to refer to the internal transformation of European Union member states under EU impact, in terms of converging towards a standard, both legal and substantial. There is no consensus about whether the term should be limited to applying within the EU (as neighbor countries are often encouraged to "Europeanize," i.e., to adopt EU legislation) or if it should encompass means, as well as processes and outcomes, but by and large it refers to change within a member state whose motivating logic is tied to an EU policy (Börzel, 1999, p. 574; Radaelli, 2003, p. 30; Ladrech, 1994). Europeanization is furthermore largely seen as different from compliance, integration, convergence, and harmonization, although much debate exists across the large body of scholarship theorizing EU governance. Roughly speaking, Europeanization when referring to the member states takes place when there is a difference between EU integration requirements and domestic structures – and so adaptational pressures appears that lead to change (Green Cowles et al., 2001). The closer a country is to European good-ness of fit (for instance, if a specific EU policy is crafted after a German model), the smaller the changes needed for that particular country. Europeanization, in this meaning, thus refers to substantial transformation due to EU integration, the latter being a more formal process.

Like the United States, with which it has more in common than some-times publicly avowed (Zielonka, 2011), the EU has ambitions to change the rest of the world, too, not just its member states, by imposing a certain "normative agenda"; although, unlike the United States, mostly by civi-lian means – at least until recently. This is the "other" Europeanization, the changing of the world according to EU norms: in other words, to the latest "civilizational norms" that Europeans arrived at after much strug-gle, advanced as universal norms (Rosecrance, 1998, p. 22). In its claim to represent a normative power, is the EU so different from the old European "civilizing" empires? Some authors suggest that the EU spreads its norms and extends its power in various parts of the world in a truly imperial fashion, as it tries to impose domestic constraints on other actors through various forms of economic and political domination (Zielonka, 2008).

The broad normative basis of the European Union has been developed over the past fifty years through a series of declarations, treaties, policies, criteria, and conditions, included in the acquis communautaire and the acquis politique (Manners, 2002). Besides norms of peace and freedom, we find democracy, rule of law, and respect for human rights and funda-mental freedoms, all of which are expressed in the preamble and founding principles of the Treaty of the European Union, the development co-operation policy, the common foreign and security provisions of the union, and the membership criteria adopted at the Copenhagen European Council in 1993. Finally, and more recently, the norm of good governance, already implied by the rule of law, was launched in Romano Prodi's inaugural speech to the European Parliament as presi-dent of the European Commission (Prodi, 2000), further treated in the "White Paper on European Governance" (EC, 2001), and mentioned in nearly every strategic document related to EU accession and EU neigh-borhood and development policy. Just as each of these norms is grounded in a specific historical context, the norm of good governance also emerged in the aftermath of the resignation of the Jacques Santer European

Commission in 1999 on corruption grounds. There was a need to defend the European normative realm from accusations of double standards (Manners, 2012), and perhaps, in the words of David Miliband, to pose as a "model power" rather than a "superpower" (quoted in *The Independent*, November 2007). The grounds for Europe being a model power seem to reside as much in *what Europe does* (respecting human rights, upholding environmental standards, showing high integrity, etc.) as in *what Europe is* or perceives itself to be: "a global civilizing effort," transcending Westphalian norms and setting a blueprint for the rest of the world (Kristeva, 2000), "pioneering institutional practices far in advance of anything viewed elsewhere," and succeeding in "the spread of European integration in its region and of multilateral norms worldwide" (Moravcsik, 2009). The original, most successful campaign of Europe as normative power was to convince many countries around the world to abolish the death penalty: many other topics followed. At the end of the day, it is the belief in the universality of European norms (such as human rights) that is at the core of Europeanization, what some label as "soft imperialism" (Headley, 2016).

The topic of good governance was actually not even mentioned in the accession criteria as defined by the June 1993 Conclusions of the Presidency in Copenhagen: "stability of institutions guaranteeing democracy, the rule of law, human rights, respect for and protection of minorities, the existence of a functioning market economy as well as the capacity to cope with competitive pressure and market forces within the Union" (EC, 1993). Nevertheless, the "Copenhagen criteria" seem to be universally seen as the departure point of the EU's commitment to good governance, as the European Union had the strongest leverage in candidate countries and forged most of its rule of law and anti-corruption approach during the East European accession of the late 1990s. Corruption had not been a topic on the occasion of the earlier Greece accession, and it reached prominence only with the accession of Romania and Bulgaria in 2007, the two belated candidates from the "big bang" accession of 2004. Romania and Bulgaria had special provisions related to independence of the judiciary and corruption in their cooperation and verification mechanisms (CVM), the safeguard clause attached to the accession treaty that provided for potential membership suspension if conditions were not met.

Meanwhile the Lisbon Treaty has better defined the pillars of what the EU understands by good governance: participation in civil society and the strengthening of multilateral cooperation.[1] Since the European

---

[1] Treaty of Lisbon amending the Treaty on European Union and the Treaty establishing the European Community (OJ C 306, 17.12.2007); entry into force on December 1, 2009.

Commission presidency of Romano Prodi (1999–2004), significant emphasis has been placed on the promotion of good governance through civil society participation in order to encourage openness and transparency and to facilitate democratic participation, as specified in articles 21a and 8b (Manners, 2008). The treaty further suggests that good governance is to be achieved through as least three different practices involving participatory democracy, openness and transparency, multi-lateralism, and good global governance, as specified in articles 8b, 10a, 21a. The right to good administration is included in the citizens' rights title of the charter (Lisbon Treaty, 2007).

However, the European "goodness of fit" standard for good governance is not specified and cannot be, as in other areas, for each individual EU country, given that a large variety of practices and norms exist across enlarged Europe; and therefore, no treaty or document is able to spell it out. Even if EU member states as bilateral donors promote their national institutions models sometimes (specific organizational forms in the judiciary or administration, for instance), the EU promotes more general benchmarks included in international anti-corruption and money laundering treaties and conventions, as well as some objectives promoted by the United Nations Convention against Corruption, the Bretton Woods institutions (such as limiting budget deficits) or OECD (e.g. transparency of policy formulation). The EU also endorses the Council of Europe's Group of States against Corruption (GRECO), a peer review assessment mechanism of anti-corruption legislation (focusing on conflict of interest and party funding, among others), including Council of Europe members, whose number (forty-seven by 2018) far surpasses the number of EU member states. GRECO has developed standards of its own, which remain nonmandatory and have not been tested against outcomes. The countries that have evolved the most in its area of jurisdiction are, once again, countries such as Estonia and Georgia that had their own, domestically driven reform paths and did not change due to the implementation of external legal prescriptions.

Two years after Copenhagen, the 1995 Barcelona Declaration, dedicated to the Mediterranean sphere of influence of the EU (including some of the most corrupt countries in the Northern hemisphere), pledged to promote "the rule of law and democracy in their political systems, while recognizing in this framework the right of each of them to choose and freely develop its own political, socio-cultural, economic and judicial system."[2] By 2000, however – after the Santer Commission had stepped

---

[2] Barcelona Declaration, Barcelona, November 27–28, 1995, adopted at the Euro-Mediterranean Conference.

down on corruption grounds the year before and the Prodi Commission had been sworn in – the EU had arrived at a serious credibility problem. In the words of a then EU official, "Over the last decades, European external assistance gradually lost its overall unity of conception, action and structure (integrating the political dimension, trade and development cooperation). This explains, to a large extent, the loss of our capacity to produce added-value and impact" (quoted in Bossuyt et al., 2000). This led to the revamping of framework agreements that the EU had with various regions. For instance, the Euro-Mediterranean Partnership was replaced with the European Neighborhood Policy (ENP), which made good governance and rule of law a priority. It advanced a motivation sounding like a theory of change, stating that promotion of reforms in these areas is key to the ENP's objective of stabilization, an important goal in both Mediterranean and East European countries, which were plagued by conflicts.

EU interventions in other regions also took a while to arrive at good governance. In 1975, the former French, British, Belgian, Spanish, and Portuguese colonies joined forces to form what would become the African, Caribbean and Pacific Group of States (ACP), which evolved from an alliance of 46 states when it was set up to include 79 countries by 2003. The basis for their relationship with the EU was the Lomé Convention (1995–2000), which regulated trade and aid with some minimal political conditions. At the Africa–EU summit in 2000, EU officials stressed political aspects, while their African counterparts focused on trade and aid (Carbone, 2010). The result was the Cotonou Agreement (2000, revised 2005, 2010) with the whole ACP group (79 states: 48 African states, 16 Caribbean, and 15 Pacific). The agreement links preferential trade with development aid and explicit political conditions: democracy, human rights, rule of law, and good governance. The transition from the previous Lomé IV bis Convention to the Cotonou Agreement also meant that on top of the "essential elements" of the partnership between the ACP and the EC (defined as human rights, democratic principles and the rule of law, whose violation could lead to the suspension of aid), "good governance" becomes a fundamental element and the fight against corruption a priority for the first time. The theory of change was developmental: simply put, the development results under Lomé had been poor for African countries, and the EU sought to better govern aid, presuming that good governance conditionalities and dedicated aid would lead to more aid effectiveness and better development outcomes for the recipient countries (Carbone, 2010, p. 257). Critics were not convinced of the transformational vocation of the treaty, seeing it as a triumph of "realism over idealism." In other words, it was seen as an imposition arising from the EU's particular worries about security and migration and the supposition that improving governance was the key to solving these issues, notwithstanding the development community's concern that aid might become too tied to these issues (Farrell, 2005). "There was no big theory of change," a top official told me, "and we knew very well that implementation is a different matter altogether, but what harm was there in being aspirational, in spelling out the good principles for the first time? Nevertheless, the Treaty of Lisbon has changed the game altogether and now corruption is in many cases part of the interest-based political dialogue."[3]

The Cotonou Agreement outlines the EU's definitions of corruption and good governance. Article 10/3 states:

In the context of a political and institutional environment that upholds human rights, democratic principles and the rule of law, good governance is the transparent and accountable management of human, natural, economic and financial resources for the purposes of equitable and sustainable development. It entails clear decision-making procedures at the level of public authorities, transparent and accountable institutions, the primacy of law in the management and distribution of resources and capacity building for elaborating and implementing measures aiming in particular at preventing and combating corruption.

Article 33/2 furthermore states that "[t]he Parties shall work together in the fight against developing capacity in other critical areas such as: bribery and corruption in all their societies." The dispute settlement mechanism consists of "consultations" to reach mutual agreement about a "solution," with only "serious cases of corruption" constituting a violation. Article 97/3 furthermore stipulates that those measures shall be used "which least disrupt the application of this agreement" and that "suspension would be a measure of last resort."[4]

Furthermore, a joint statement by the European Council and the Commission in 2000 on development policy was followed by the European Consensus on Development (ECD) in 2005 (Hout, 2007), in which the European Council, Parliament, and Commission jointly agreed on prioritizing poverty reduction in the context of sustainable development, according to the principles of aid effectiveness and increased policy coherence (Michel, 2006). The EU reiterated its commitment to the promotion of good governance and democracy as well as institutional

---

[3] Interview with retired European Commission official, Rome, October 2018.
[4] The Cotonou Agreement, Cotonou, June 23, 2000, revised in Luxembourg on June 25, 2005, revised in Ouagadougou on June 22, 2010, and multiannual financial framework, 2014–2020.

reforms in partner countries. The ECD relies on an exceedingly broad concept of good governance as "the state's ability to serve its citizens."[5]

The EU theory of change has thus developed over time. Partner countries stand to gain from their relationship with the EU across all aspects – trade, aid, and knowledge transfer – and a smart mix of the three might confer "smart power" to the EU, i.e. power to convince partners to adopt EU values in exchange for mostly positive incentives. The attraction force that flows from the EU's prosperity, security, and open society should have the power to transform both countries that aspire to join and others striving to close the development gap even without joining. In the words of a former EU commissioner:

> Let me explain what I mean by "smart power." Essentially, it is combining soft and hard power better in the EU's external relations by using the whole spectrum of our policy instruments and economic resources ... [The] guiding principle to reinforce the EU's smart power is to project its values and interests in its own neighborhood more effectively in order to extend the European zone of peace and prosperity, liberty and democracy. In enlargement policy, this projection of the EU method and model has had a transformative power over decades in numerous countries, from Spain to Poland, from Greece to Estonia. It needs likewise to be reinforced in the EU's neighborhood policy.[6]

Aside from the documents mentioned here, there is no specific EU doctrine of good governance or any theory on why good governance itself (a different phenomenon from economic development) might happen, because EU has no such experience. Compared with either the IMF or the World Bank, which had by the 1990s already developed a whole intellectual infrastructure to deal with corruption (indicators, country diagnoses and theories of change), the EU was poorly equipped to handle corruption from the outset, as it was not a development agency but an intergovernmental organization designed to deal with cooperation across Europe. In all its previous expansions, corruption had not been a topic, which might explain the surprise at the fall of the Santer Commission on corruption grounds in 1999. Except for Euroskeptic British tabloids, hardly any news outlets cover EU corruption;[7] the most cited authors

---

[5] Communication from the Commission to the Council, the European Parliament and the European Economic and Social Committee – Governance and Development. (2003) EUR-Lex – 52003DC0615 – EN – EUR-Lex.

[6] Olli Rehn, EU Commissioner for Enlargement, "Europe's Smart Power in its Region and the World," speech at the European Studies Centre, St Antony's College, University of Oxford, May 1, 2008.

[7] Only very recently has Transparency International Europe, which had been a partner for the European Institutions (also heavily funded by them), also become a watchdog, a role that had simply been missing for decades. *See* Freund 2017.

on corruption in European Union institutions tend to be from the USA, New Zealand, or other distant places.[8] Even the disbursement of EU funds in countries with poor governance has failed to trigger much discussion, despite academics warning fairly early that the development goal of funds are not met when corruption is high (Ederveen et al., 2006; Beugelsdijk and Eijffinger, 2005). None of the Brussels think tanks deal with issues such as corruption, and the term "governance" is generally used in reference to the understanding of complex relations between EU institutions and aspiring member states. The quality thereof never manages to become much of a topic. Even in the aftermath of the economic crisis, most of the debate focused on the "democratic deficit" of the EU, in rather structural terms (grassroots EU versus intergovernmental EU) rather than on the core elements of governance, such as accountability or impersonality.

Where the promotion of good governance abroad is concerned, the EU's approach to the different categories of countries that I study – old member states, new member states, accession countries, neighborhood countries, and assisted countries – vary greatly in regard to specific conditions and expectations set up by the EU, albeit in the framework of similar general goals. The scarce literature that exists on the evolution of good governance under EU influence is therefore scattered across a wide range of publications, among the literature on Europeanization in Western Europe, on accession conditionality for Eastern Europe (the "transformative power" of Europe), on democracy promotion in the Mediterranean and Africa, and on development in the rest of the world.

4.2   Theories of Change

No special theory of change on corruption seems to have existed when the EU began its efforts to promote good governance. By and large, EU officials have presumed that a country would improve its governance given trade advantages and EU aid. Traditionally, aid for good governance relied on the assumption of good will on behalf of recipient countries and the premise that the only obstacle to their implementing reforms was a lack of funds: this led in the early 2000s to the use of budget support as a preferred aid modality (Hayman, 2011). As the recipient countries' appetite for governance reforms proved less than presumed, a later

---

[8] For instance, the oft-cited Shore (2005) "Culture and Corruption in the EU: Reflections on Fraud, Nepotism and Cronyism in the European Commission" or Warner (2007) "The Best System Money Can Buy: Corruption in the European Union." It may also be that European scholars, like the author of this book, are also funded by EU research funds, which may induce some self-censorship in criticizing the EU.

argument was made for empowering the citizenry, whose interest in the effective provision of public goods would drive them to hold their governments accountable (Booth, 2012). Despite some accommodation of both views ("supply" and "demand" driven) over time, government and civil society aid remain *separately* funded in EU aid designs; they seldom share program ownership, apart from perhaps a joint seminar or training session.

Conditionality has been the main theory of change when accession and neighborhood countries are concerned. Conditionality can be defined as an "incentive instrument in the relationship between two actors, in which one actor aims at changing the behavior of the other by setting up conditions for the relationship and by manipulating the cost–benefit calculation by using (positive and negative) material incentives" (Koch, 2015, p. 99). In the case of accession countries, there was an additional constituency made up of the EU's existing member states, some of which had never had a great enthusiasm for enlargement. Conditionality, in particular on rule of law, was meant to alleviate the concerns of these skeptical member states, although the European Commission itself worked to make enlargement successful, not to hinder it. The Copenhagen criteria would thus go on to serve as a template for the EU's more general understanding and use of conditionality, strongly influencing the design of the European Neighborhood Policy (Balfour, 2012, p. 15).

The standard form of political conditionality in the 1990s was *negative conditionality* related to violations of association or trade agreements. This allowed partners to take appropriate measures in case of a breach.[9] Its origin is in the partnership between the ACP countries and the EU, when in the 1970s the EU developed the so-called Uganda Guidelines in order to enable the suspension of agreements with partner countries in the event that they engaged in widespread human rights violations (Bartels, 2007a, p. 738). From 1995 onwards, such clauses became part of all new cooperation and trade agreements, and were transformed into essential elements of Lomé Convention IV and its successor the Cotonou Agreement in 2000 (ibid.). Since then, conditionality clauses have been integrated in the EU's autonomous instruments under which it grants financial aid to partner countries, including the Instrument for Pre-Accession Assistance (IPA); the European Neighborhood and Partnership Instrument (ENPI); the Development Cooperation Instrument (DCI), which includes

---

[9] See, for instance, EU–Egypt agreement, 2004: "A material breach of this Agreement shall consist of the repudiation of this Agreement not sanctioned by the general rules of international law or a grave violation of an essential element of this Agreement, creating an environment not conducive for consultations or where a delay would be detrimental to the objectives of this Agreement" (EU Council, 2004, 304 OJ L).

countries within the ACP group; and the Overseas Association Decision (ibid.). The spread of these formal requirements has not necessarily translated into substantive change.

European development aid after 2000 adopted an incentive-based system of *positive conditionality* favoring engagement and political dialogue and complemented by rewards for partner countries for their reform gestures. The "Agenda for Change" reinforced good governance as a priority (EC, 2011b). However, with the Arab Spring in 2011 it became evident that in the absence of enlargement, "carrots'" were insufficient to motivate good governance reforms. The EU adopted a stronger focus on positive incentives, as shown in the "more for more" approach. This meant that in exchange for progress on governance reforms, the EU offered incentives superior to the financial incentives that had proven inefficient in the past, for instance linked to market access and mobility (EC, 2011b).[10] Since 2008 the European Development Fund, which finances development assistance to ACP countries, has included an instrument called the "governance incentive tranche" by which additional funds can be allocated to countries that adopt or credibly commit themselves to governance reforms (Warkotsch, 2016). Similarly, the ENPI introduced a specific "governance facility" instrument in 2007 to reward countries for progress in good governance reforms.

Conditionality clauses have also been included within the EU's general trade agreements and within the instruments under which the EU grants trade preferences to developing countries. For example, the Generalized System of Preferences (GSP), which has granted preferential market access to developing countries since 1971, added both positive conditionality in 1991, related to Latin America's crackdown on drug trade, and negative conditionality in 1994–1995 related to forced labor (Portela and Orbie, 2014). In addition to the downgrading of trade preferences through the GSP system in case of noncompliance with norms in areas other than trade, such as human rights or labor rights, the EU can apply sanctions – so-called restrictive measures – in order to enforce the objectives of its Common Foreign and Security Policy (CFSP), including "common values" such as the promotion of democracy, rule of law, human rights, and good governance (ibid.).

Consultations on aid sanctions based on Article 96 of the Cotonou Agreement were initiated seventeen times in the first fifteen years of the agreement, with Liberia the only country sanctioned mainly for

---

[10] This showed in umbrella programs such as SPRING (Support for Partnership, Reform, and Inclusive Growth) for the southern neighborhood, and EPIC (Eastern Partnership Integration and Cooperation Programme) for the eastern neighborhood.

corruption.[11] However, other related elements (suppression of press freedom, election irregularities) do feature more often. Nonetheless, in Africa, "the biggest aid increases have not gone to the most reformist states" (Youngs, 2010, p. 70). In the words of an official at DEVCO (the EU directorate in charge of development and cooperation): "We are about cooperation, not about sanctions. We are not there to sanction them, but to fund them, primarily, we are there to help."[12] For the same reason, ENP action plans focus more on effective governance than democratic governance, favoring emphasis on efficient state institutions that help regulate the economy rather than on democratic issues and reforms (Börzel and van Hüllen, 2014). The priority on security and migration, as well as the rejection of interference in domestic issues by national regimes, especially in the Mediterranean, have often led to the *de facto* sidelining of political issues in favor of closer economic and security cooperation. The often formalistic approach of the EU, privileging rule adoption over rule application, has also led to an implementation gap in the ENP where good governance is concerned (Kleemann, 2010). Because there is general agreement that large-scale economic sanctions, such as those applied against the regime of Saddam Hussein in Iraq in the 1990s, unduly hurt the population of the target country, and are generally ineffective, the EU has been hesitant to leverage trade sanctions under the conditionality clauses embedded in its trade agreements; it has only resorted to negative conditionality in its GSP program in two cases (Bartels, 2007b). In case of the Cotonou Agreement as applied to Zimbabwe, for instance, the EU resorted to discontinuing aid with the government as main recipient, but transferred aid to civil society instead of completely suspending it. However, partner countries within the ACP group have been the object of most of the aid suspensions recorded, since in the ENP sanctions have been not been much used (Youngs, 2010, p. 70).

As Karen Smith has remarked, it is not easy to assess the impact of EU conditionality on political evolutions due to the difficulties of isolating the EU effect from other factors that determine a country's evolution/involution, and therefore most literature on Europeanization assesses the implementation rather than the impact (1998). A whole cottage industry of research on successful "rule transfer" developed (Schimmelfennig and Sedelmeier, 2004), identifying, for instance, "robust and strong effects of EU political conditionality on democracy in the neighboring countries" (Schimmelfennig and Scholtz, 2008) or explaining the "lack of backsliding" just at the time when backsliding was in fact accelerating

---

[11] Evaluation of the Cotonou Partnership Agreement, Brussels, July 15, 2016. (EC 2016c).
[12] Interview with anonymous official at DEVCO, June 10, 2018.

(Levitz and Pop-Elecheş, 2010). Only after 2010 did it become impossible to deny that even successfully "Europeanized" Poland and Hungary were experiencing major rule-of-law backsliding, and other countries in Central Europe (Czech Republic, Slovakia, Slovenia) had also regressed on governance alongside neighboring countries, leaving only the Baltics on a progress curve. The more recent research consensus has moved towards acknowledging that conditionality has not been an effective instrument in improving the policy framework of partner countries (Lavenex and Schimmelfennig, 2011; Killick, 2004; Dijkstra, 2002), due to the inconsistency of its implementation and other factors, mixing causes that are internal to donors (EU) with factors in recipient countries (Hayman, 2011, p. 682).

Additional frequently invoked reasons for the lack of effectiveness of EU development policies are related to the specific organization of EU aid. Firstly, there are coordination difficulties not only between different agencies within the European context but between the interests of member states, on the one hand, and between member states and EU agencies on the other (Warkotsch, 2016). Secondly, the instruments are flawed, with inconsistencies in the EU's theory of change as well as in the use of its instruments in promoting such change. In practical terms, the results are relatively cautious preferences for engagement over confrontation, for technical cooperation over overtly political cooperation, and for the side-lining of governance issues in favor of security and economic cooperation (ibid., 2016).

The continuing complexity of the EU framework for external action, the Common Foreign and Security Policy (CFSP), does not help the effective use of conditionalities. Tools and objectives under each institutional arrangement struggle with the consistency principle spelled out for the entire foreign policy (Warkotsch, 2016). The EU's policies toward developing countries illustrate this tension. Trade remains an exclusive EU competence, largely isolated from other policies. Development constitutes a shared competence between the EU and its member states. Foreign and security policy remains largely intergovernmental (Portela and Orbie, 2014, p. 63). The Treaty of Lisbon (2009) stated that European foreign policy should not undermine but rather reinforce Europe's development aims. It reshuffled the institutional configuration for decision making in the realm of external relations with the setting up of the European External Action Service (EEAS) with the goal of establishing a more coherent, visible, and effective union in its external relations (Tannous, 2013). The EEAS, under the authority of the High Representative (HR) situated between the member states and the European Commission, aims to combine the different elements of EU foreign policy – supranational, intergovernmental, and national – and the different foreign policy instruments into a more coherent framework (Balfour et al., 2015, p. 34). Instead of simplifying responsibilities and streamlining the external action process, the result has so far been rather an increase in complexity, with the different stages of the programming cycle now divided between the EC (DG DEVCO) and the EEAS (Tannous, 2013). The EC thus remains in charge of most financial instruments of external assistance, while the EEAS contributes to programming and implementation (ibid.).

This institutional arrangement unavoidably implies high transaction costs. It can only undermine policy coherence in general and impede a more consistent approach to good governance promotion in development assistance, especially when trade-offs appear between foreign policy goals and when partner country governments are reluctant to change their practices (Warkotsch, 2016). Thus, despite an increase in both rhetoric and funding for good governance reforms, the largest share of governance money has not necessarily gone to promoting political reform, having been devoted instead to issues of border management or, in the case of Central Asia, towards commercial law in connection with European investment interests (Youngs, 2010, p. 76). The consequences become visible especially when violations of good governance conditions occur. Sanctions require intergovernmental decision-making procedures, although their implementation is carried out by the European Commission (Börzel and Risse, 2004). This might further explain the reluctance to apply sanctions against partner countries where other interests of the EU or its member states, in the realms of economic or security cooperation, are at stake. The EU has more recently taken more decisive steps: for example, cutting budget support aid where there was evidence of corruption or malpractice and where the cuts in aid did not raise major strategic issues in the EU's relations with the country in question. This, however, creates double standards, with one set of sanctions applying to Turkey and another to Moldova, for instance; without such double standards, it is likely that EU influence would be even lower.

Doubts have been raised in the literature about the will of the EU and its member states to promote their values energetically when they may conflict with self-interest (Youngs, 2004). Direct infringement of EU rules and norms were reported on exports of arms (Erickson, 2011, p. 218), on China (Balducci, 2010, p. 51), and on oil-rich former Soviet republics (Amani, 2013). The end result is an EU that is seen rather as a "modest force for good" (Barbé and Johansson-Nogués, 2008), when not altogether failing to make target countries act as they would otherwise not have done (Diez, 2005, p. 616). The distance between the EU's ethical norms and the traditional interests of its member states is a significant limitation on the EU's normative power, but also Europe as a whole has interests, and not just values, that have to be considered.

If aid conditionality associated with the promotion of values was constantly plagued by such inconsistencies, budget support aid evolved over the years to cross the boundary to what is called in the literature "aid selectivity." Budget support involves direct financial transfers to the national treasury of the partner country. Its current overall philosophy is derived from the principle of ownership of aid by the recipient country as enshrined in the 2005 Paris Declaration on Aid Effectiveness,[13] which states that developing countries should set their own strategies to reduce poverty, improve their institutions, and tackle corruption, and that donor countries should align behind these objectives and use local systems (principles of ownership and harmonization). Critics have argued that this presumption does not hold, particularly for countries in need of aid, as they tend to have serious governance problems; and so the principle of ownership should rather be read as ownership by the broader society (or the poor, in the development agencies mission) rather than just the government (Rose-Ackermann, 1998; Mungiu-Pippidi, 2006a; Rothstein, 2011). The Paris Declaration aimed to counteract the demonstrated ineffectiveness of aid on the basis that it was largely due to poor governance. The solution to this apparent contradiction in terms – giving more ownership to corrupt governments so that they can clean themselves up – is an approach called "cash on delivery," an *ex ante* conditionality method requiring certain eligibility criteria for budget aid, the above-mentioned "selectivity." Long recommended by think tanks and scholars (Birdsall et al., 2012), and tried with limited success by the Millennium Corporation (Mungiu-Pippidi, 2015b, Chapter 7), selectivity crept into EU assistance through increased preconditions for budget aid: better financial management, macroeconomic stability, inclusive growth, and less corruption and fraud; sector reforms and sector service delivery; better domestic revenue mobilization and less aid dependency.[14] Critics questioned the suitability of good governance as an *ex ante* criterion for development assistance policies, arguing that good governance and control of corruption (CoC) cannot be preconditions because they are development objectives themselves (Hermes and Lensink, 2001; Pronk, 2001, p. 626). The persistence of budget support and its evolution is

---

[13] Paris Declaration on Aid Effectiveness, Paris, February 2005, followed by the Accra Agenda for Action, 2008.
[14] See the European Commission's "Budget Support and Dialogue with Partner Countries" page at www.ec.europa.eu

largely due to the lack of alternatives – no other incentives have been found to stimulate good governance reforms except the *ex ante* conditions. By 2016, budget support disbursements amounted to EUR 1.73 billion and accounted for 18 percent of all EU development aid (including neighborhood countries and the Instrument for Pre-Accession Assistance). Sub-Saharan Africa was the largest recipient of budget support in volume (42.5 percent), followed by neighborhood countries (29.2 percent), Asia (13.0 percent), Latin America (5.4 percent), the Caribbean (4.1 percent), overseas countries and territories (2.4 percent), the Western Balkans (2.3 percent), and the Pacific (1 percent). The major problem for European development assistance has become the risk of losing the countries, due to their backsliding on eligibility criteria, exactly when Brussels is refining such criteria to cover the agenda for essential human rights and good governance.

4.3   The Instruments of EU Aid

Between 2002 and 2014, Official Development Assistance (ODA) disbursement from EU institutions to developing countries tripled from above USD 5 billion to over 16 billion, with 12 percent of the total ODA funding in 2014 allocated to the government and civil society sector. [15] In fact, a considerable amount of this funding went to efforts to improve governance. In recent years the EU has created new development instruments using the principles of positive conditionality for allocation of financial assistance. The European Commission identified institutional indicators on democratic accountability, rule of law, control of corruption, government effectiveness, economic governance, and internal and external security as key factors for the evaluation and monitoring of countries' reforms in this area (Hout, 2013). The data used in this book covers more than 120 developing countries that are net recipients of EU ODA, and the period between 2002 and 2014, for which most of the disaggregated data is available.

4.3.1   Types of EU Aid

EU development policy can be categorized in a number of different ways: by sector, geographical region, type of aid, funding instrument grouping,

---

[15] In accordance with the open data policy of EU-funded research, I published a preliminary report of data reported in Section 4.3 on the Anticorrp.eu website, and it is publicly available. Some of the data and comment also featured in the Anticorruption Report Volume 4, a publication of the project with Barbara Budrich that I edited with Jana Warkotsch (2017).

the way aid is channeled to recipients, income grouping, and the relative size of aid to a country compared to its economy (see Figure 4.1). Differences across these categories may explain differences in governance outcomes and the effectiveness of aid overall. Empirical literature on foreign aid specifically emphasizes the importance of certain factors in analyzing its effectiveness: the sectorial allocation, and the types and channels of ODA (see, e.g., Wright and Winters, 2010). These instruments, however, overlap within our broader categories, such as "modernization," "civilization," or "good governance." For instance, education-dedicated funds fit all the three categorizations above.

Sector classifications track the share of ODA allocated to each specific purpose in a recipient country. The sector destination is assigned using the answer to the question "Which specific area of the recipient's economic and social structure is the transfer intended to foster?"[16] Sectors can be labeled with purpose codes for these specific areas.

The "type" of aid is presumed to impact on outcomes as well. The OECD started to collect data for the type of aid in 2010 to distinguish between the various modalities of aid.[17] Between 2006 and 2009, ODA was retroactively assigned to certain types based on an automatic mapping, based in turn on purpose codes. This means that for our sample years, aid type is partly uncategorized (2002–2005), partly categorized using a mapping formula (2006–2009), and categorized regularly (starting in 2010). According to the OECD, types can include (1) budget support, (2) "core contributions and pooled programs and funds," (3) project-type interventions, (4) experts and other technical assistance, (5) scholarships and student costs in donor countries, (6) debt relief, (7) administrative costs not included elsewhere, (8) other in-donor expenditures.[18] The first four types listed are the largest and the most relevant to this chapter.

Budget support means that the donor relinquishes exclusive control of its funds by sharing responsibility with the recipient. Budget support can be sector-specific but also simply a transfer to the national government's treasury. Funds for which the responsibility is shared with another stakeholder, such as NGOs, other donors, or multilateral organizations, fall under the "core contributions and pooled programs and funds." Project-type interventions are for more narrowly defined projects with

[16] See OECD glossary at www.oecd.org/dac/stats/dac-glossary.htm#Sector_Class
[17] See Query Wizard for International Development Statistics (QWIDS) at https://stats.o ecd.org/qwids/
[18] See OECD aid statistics at www.oecd.org/dac/stats/type-aid.htm

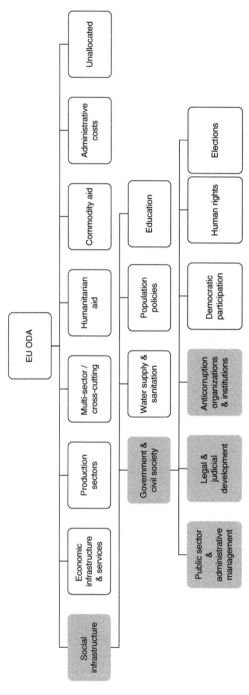

Figure 4.1 Types of EU overseas development aid (ODA)
Source: OECD 2018b – QWIDS Official Development Aid.

specific goals and outputs. The label "experts and other technical assistance" covers the provision of personnel, training, and research in private and public bodies, including university courses, exchanges, and publications.

Multilateral aid can also be categorized by channel. Channels include the public sector, NGOs and civil society, public–private partnerships, and multilateral organizations. The public sector includes not only national governments but also local governments and public corporations or "third countries" with delegated cooperation on a certain ODA project. NGO examples include Transparency International, the International Women's Tribune Center, and the African Medical and Research Foundation. In certain countries, government-operated organizations that mimic NGOs (GONGOs) are also recipients of ODA. Multilateral organizations may include such groups as UN agencies, the IMF, the International Organization for Migration, or the Nordic Development Fund.

In 2002, the EU allocated nearly one-third of its funds in the commodity aid/general program assistance sector, but by 2014 this sector represented only 7 percent. Other sectors receiving increased emphasis by 2014 were mainly "economic infrastructure and services" and "social infrastructure and services." Figure 4.2 shows sectorial differences between 2002 and 2014.

As a share of total aid within the social infrastructure and services sector (Figure 4.3), government and civil society allocation increased from 2002 to 2014, remaining the largest category within this type. In 2014, it occupied nearly half of all social infrastructure and services aid. Civil society itself was however a very small part of it, as figures per individual countries will show.

In 2002, "public sector policy and administrative management" received most of the aid labeled as government and civil society funding (see Figure 4.4), but in 2014 a much wider range of subsectors received funding, including decentralization, human rights, democratic participation, and legal and judicial development. Anti-corruption organizations and institutions are not recorded in 2002 as a recipient of government and civil society sector aid, and are relatively small in 2014 as well.

The ODA category is mostly composed of "project type" aid, increasing over the course of this timeframe. This is a highly relevant category, as it captures clear objectives that can be evaluated against the budget support type. Budget support itself increased from 8 to 12 percent in this interval, which made it just a sixth of the amount invested in projects for 2014, the last year in this evaluation. The category of "experts and technical assistance" appears first as a type of funding after 2010, varying

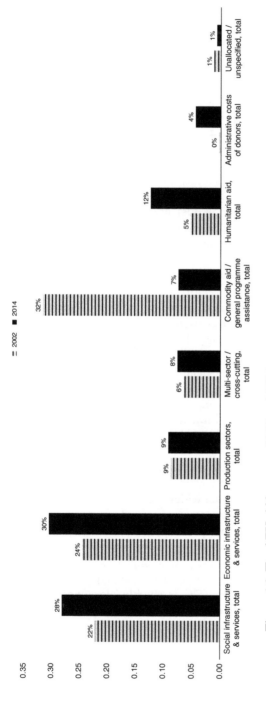

Figure 4.2 Total EU aid by sector, 2002 and 2014
Source: OECD 2018b – QWIDS Official Development Aid, ANTICORRP.

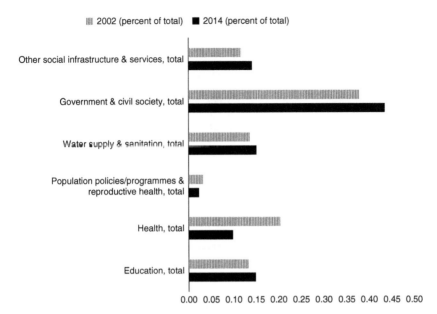

Figure 4.3 EU aid for social infrastructure and services, 2002 and 2014
Source: OECD 2018b –QWIDS Official Development Aid, ANTI-
CORRP.

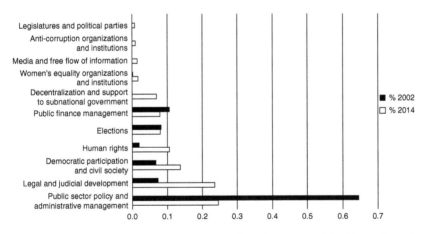

Figure 4.4 EU government and civil society sector aid, 2002 and 2014
Source: OECD 2018b – QWIDS Official Development Aid, ANTI-
CORRP.

Table 4.1 *Distribution of EU aid, 2006–2014 (127 countries)*

	Budget support		Project type		Experts/tech	
	USD mil	%	USD mil	%	USD mil	%
2006	843	8	5,117	51	0	0
2007	833	7	5,660	49	0	0
2008	825	6	5,516	43	0	0
2009	1,220	9	5,760	44	0	0
2010	2,309	18	7,753	61	1,285	10
2011	2,306	13	13,103	73	1,142	6
2012	2,253	12	13,180	73	995	5
2013	2,285	13	12,181	71	1,016	6
2014	2,221	12	13,333	72	929	5
Total USD mil	15,095		81,603		5,367	
Average %		10.3		55.5		3.7

Source: OECD 2018 – QWIDS Official Development Aid; author's own calculations.

between 5 and 10 percent of total aid. The "core contributions and pooled program and funds" category is missing from Table 4.1.

Recipients of EU multilateral aid can be classified in multiple ways. The focus of European aid over this period shifted a number of times, and its instruments changed repeatedly as well. Some ODA recipients physically closest to the European Union itself are candidates for EU membership. These countries, including Albania, Bosnia-Herzegovina, Montenegro, FYR Macedonia, Serbia, and Turkey, receive money through the Instrument for Pre-Accession Assistance (IPA). Immediately surrounding the EU and its membership candidates are the countries under the European Neighborhood Policy (ENP). These include countries to the south such as Algeria, Egypt, Jordan, Lebanon, Libya, Morocco, Syria, Tunisia, and the West Bank and Gaza Strip. To the east, Armenia, Azerbaijan, Belarus, Georgia, Moldova, and Ukraine also fall under the ENP instrument. The Africa, Caribbean and Pacific (ACP) instrument covers the most numerous and most geographically widespread recipients. Finally, Other Developing Countries (ODC) refers mostly to countries on the Asian continent outside of those already categorized. The instrument used might be relevant because research by Dadašov finds that the significance of multilateral EU aid in relation to governance varies by region, if outliers are excluded (2017).

Apart from "instruments," the World Bank uses a common regional classification that I also resort to. Europe and Central Asia (ECA) consists of the IPA countries, the East ENP countries, and the Central Asian region. The Middle East and North Africa (MENA) consists of countries

Table 4.2 *Recipients of largest amounts of EU ODA*

Country name	Total Aid (USD mil.)	Income group	Instrument	Region
1. Turkey	14,326.30	UMIC	IPA	ECA
2. Serbia	5,122.11	UMIC	IPA	ECA
3. West Bank & Gaza Strip	4,739.61	LMIC	ENP	MENA
4. Morocco	4,237.52	LMIC	ENP	MENA
5. Afghanistan	3,607.53	LIC	ODC	SA
6. Congo DR	2,963.63	LIC	ACP	SSA
7. Tunisia	2,814.33	UMIC	ENP	MENA
8. Ethiopia	2,801.91	LIC	ACP	SSA
9. Egypt	2,605.02	LMIC	ENP	MENA
10. Sudan	2,463.36	LMIC	ACP	SSA
11. South Africa	2,257.28	UMIC	ACP	SSA
12. Ukraine	2,238.82	LMIC	ENP	ECA
13. Bosnia-Herzegovina	2,183.02	UMIC	IPA	ECA
14. Mozambique	2,032.05	LIC	ACP	SSA
15. Tanzania	1,943.47	LIC	ACP	SSA

Source: OECD 2018b – QWIDS Official Development Aid; author's own calculations.

that are in the South ENP and other Arabian Peninsula states. South Asia (SA) comprises Afghanistan, Bangladesh, Bhutan, India, Maldives, Nepal, Pakistan, and Sri Lanka. Sub-Saharan Africa (SSA) refers to countries to the south of the MENA region on the African continent. The East Asia and Pacific (EAP) and Latin America and the Caribbean (LAC) are self-explanatory geographical regions.

The largest recipient of EU aid over the 2002–2014 time period (see Table 4.2) was Turkey. With USD 14 billion, it received more than twice the funding of the next largest recipient, Serbia. There are only three low-income countries in the top ten, and countries such as Turkey and Serbia fall within the upper-middle-income group.

More relevant is the fraction of aid in total income (GNI; see Figure 4.5 and Table 4.3). This makes Somalia the largest recipient: its 13 percent of aid relative to its GNI represents twice as much as the next highest recipient's, Liberia. All but three of the top fifteen receive aid through the ACP instrument.

Another interesting way to categorize ODA recipients is by their income group. Income groups differ from geographic or instrument groups because countries change groups over time. A country that is considered

Table 4.3 *Recipients of largest EU ODA as a percentage of GNI, 2002–2014*

Country name	Total aid (% GNI)	Income group	Instrument	Region
1. Somalia	13	LIC	ACP	SSA
2. Liberia	6	LIC	ACP	SSA
3. Djibouti	5	LMIC	ACP	SSA
4. Burundi	5	LIC	ACP	SSA
5. West Bank & Gaza Strip	5	LMIC	ENP	MENA
6. Guinea-Bissau	4	LIC	ACP	SSA
7. Kosovo	3	LMIC	IPA	ECA
8. Central African Rep.	3	LIC	ACP	SSA
9. Sierra Leone	3	LIC	ACP	SSA
10. Niger	3	LIC	ACP	SSA
11. Malawi	3	LIC	ACP	SSA
12. Afghanistan	2	LIC	DCI	SA
13. Eritrea	2	LIC	ACP	SSA
14. Haiti	2	LIC	ACP	LAC
15. Mali	2	LIC	ACP	SSA

Sources: OECD 2018b – QWIDS Official Development Aid; author's own calculations; http://concordeurope.org/2012/10/09/eu-aid-the-facts/

low-income in one year might be considered low-middle-income the next. For 2015, the World Bank uses GNI per capita (Atlas Method) to define low-income countries (LIC) as USD 1,185 or less, lower-middle-income countries (LMIC) as USD 1,026 to USD 4,035, upper-middle-income countries (UMIC) as USD 4,036 to USD 12,475, and high-income countries (HIC) as USD 12,476 or more.

The average ODA per region was less varied in 2002, increasing for all regions except for Latin America/Caribbean and East Asia/Pacific. By 2014, the ECA region had the largest average aid disbursements, followed by MENA. The gap remains, albeit less starkly, when Turkey is removed from the calculations for 2011, with the MENA region surpassing it thereafter. From 2010, Turkey received a far higher amount of aid than any other country.

Of the four instruments, the pre-accession instrument consistently received the most ODA. ODC and ACP countries remain below USD 100 million on average, and while the ENP received in 2012–2014 nearly double what it received before 2010, the pre-accession countries saw growth of over USD 500 million from 2010 to 2011, which decreased somewhat in the following years. If Turkey is removed from the group of

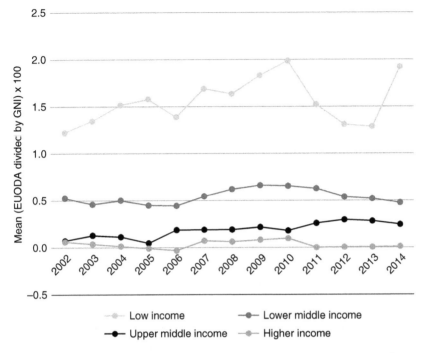

Figure 4.5 EU aid relative to GNI by income group (sample of 127 countries)
Source: OECD 2018b – QWIDS Official Development Aid, ANTI-CORRP, and author's own calculations.

pre-accession countries, however, the 2011 spike for IPA is not as pronounced.

When aid is calculated relative to GNI, a different picture emerges. IPA funding decreased from 2002 to 2008 but rose sharply thereafter. Aid consistently makes up around 1 percent of GNI for ACP countries and usually less than 0.5 percent of GNI for ENP and ODC regions. When grouped by region, aid makes up the largest share of GNI for SSA countries, and post-2008, the second highest share of GNI is to be found in the ECA region.

4.4 The Link between Governance Change and EU Aid

What indicators can be used to assess whether aid that is intended to promote good governance fulfills its purpose, when there are no fact-based indicators – either across countries or across years – to measure corruption? Both public opinion surveys and expert scores are subjective and difficult to use to assess a country's performance across time. They are also lagging. Looking at expert scores, as Daniel Treisman remarked, it is uncertain what sort of lags one should expect before political or economic changes influence perceived corruption, and moreover it's likely that changes in formal institutions would cause experts to expect changes in corruption, even if they do not observe them directly, and would therefore rate a country more favorably (2007, p. 220). The World Bank's Control of Corruption initiative (CoC) and Transparency International's Corruption Perception Index (CPI) are, in practice, more or less sophisticated averages of expert estimates. Comparing across averages may be seen as problematic in itself, in particular since the number of sources varies across countries: some countries have more experts rating them, others very few, which may present a bias (as in the case of Qatar, consistently rated better than Spain in the CPI in the years when corruption allegations over the World Cup and defense contracts bribes were coming out). Furthermore, new sources are added and others discontinued, and the CPI in particular should not be used across time but only across countries – earlier years were actually included as a baseline to calculate the scores for later years. The World Bank researchers Kaufmann and Kraay calculated transparently that about half the variance over time in the World Bank index results from changes in the sources used and the weights assigned to different sources (2002, pp. 13–14). Daniel Kaufmann et al. nevertheless argue that some changes over longer periods are significantly large (2006), and CoC has a confidence error built that basically measures the consistency across sources and checks for significant change. Using this measure corroborated with other indicators, I assessed in my previous work that only about ten cases have passed the threshold to reasonable control of corruption (the threshold being over 6 on a 1–10 scale!) since the CoC came into existence in 1996 – only a few more if we include fiscal paradises such as St Kitts and Nevis (Mungiu-Pippidi and Johnston, 2017).

To assess change or stagnation in this book, I will therefore use several sources, with CoC only as the departure point and using individual country surveys wherever available. On each country, I resort to country-specific indicators that are facts, and not based on perception. And even if the Index for Public Integrity is only three years old, most of the components of the resources-versus-constraints model (except fiscal transparency) go further back in time and can be traced back in order to understand how the equilibrium changes or persists.

What I present in this section is therefore just an elementary mapping of change, or rather lack of change, on the basis of CoC, the best existing perception indicator. Some limitations therefore apply to these trends and cross-sectional evaluations presented here. The confidence error per country does not appear, as the mapping shows averages across countries; each individual case can be checked on the World Bank website for its particular confidence error. The only region in the world where the average change is significant is South-Eastern Europe (SEE), where the Pre-Accession Instrument is in operation; meanwhile ACP countries have, on average, regressed. No statistically significant change was registered for the ENA, and other developing countries report, on average, a small progression (see Figure 4.6). The SEE group includes the Balkans and Turkey, and it will have a dedicated chapter (Chapter 6) on the profoundness of changes and their causes.

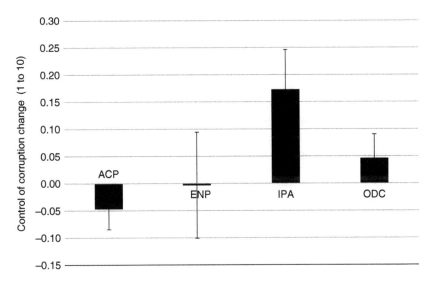

Figure 4.6 Corruption evolution across instruments

ACP = African, Caribbean, and Pacific partner countries

ENP = European Neighborhood Policy, which covers cooperation with south Mediterranean countries (Algeria, Egypt, Lebanon, Libya, Jordan, Israel, Morocco, Syria, Tunisia, and the West Bank and Gaza Strip) and east neighborhood countries (Armenia, Azerbaijan, Belarus, Georgia, Moldova, and Ukraine)

IPA = Instrument for Pre-Accession Assistance provides assistance to countries directly in line to become members of the European Union (such as the former Yugoslav Republic of Macedonia, Turkey, and Croatia) and the Balkan countries (Albania, Serbia, Kosovo, Bosnia-Herzegovina, and Montenegro)

ODC = Other Developing Countries, referring mostly to countries on the Asian Continent

Source: World Bank CoC

Upon examination of the largest aid recipients (Table 4.4), and their progress on control of corruption (CoC) and judicial independence (JI), only IPA countries seem to have registered some progress. The table does not account for the recent backslide in Turkey, as the data covers only the twelve years up to 2014. Turkey therefore wrongly seems the only significant achiever in this list of the largest recipients. That leaves only Serbia and West Bank/Gaza with a positive sign of change, even if that change is small. These two countries also rose up from very low departure points in 2002, when our aid data starts; so, they are still far below the threshold beyond which corruption becomes clearly an exception.

Most of the countries receiving specialized aid did not register any significant progress on control of corruption (CoC) or freedom of the press (FoP) (see Tables 4.5, 4.6, and 4.7). Egypt, Ukraine, Colombia, and South Africa regressed, and some IPA countries – Montenegro, Albania, and Serbia – progressed by around half a point on a 1-to-10 scale (which is not a big change, but that's what is driving the regional average up) on both judicial independence and anti-corruption. Macedonia and Algeria also progressed. Kosovo, with a staggering 35 percent of aid share for governance reforms (public sector and civil society combined), Ukraine (16 percent), and Bosnia (15 percent targeted aid) have really not managed to take off.

The list of top aid recipients in Tables 4.4–4.7 is thus quite different from the list of top achievers on governance progress (see Table 4.9), with only Serbia featuring on both lists. In Figure 4.7, countries in the upper

Table 4.4 *Recipients of largest EU general aid and their CoC and JI performance, 2002–2014*

Country	Total aid (USD mil.)	Change in CoC	Change in JI
Turkey	14,326.30	1.06	−1.24
Serbia	5,122.11	0.50	
West Bank & Gaza Strip	4,739.61	0.72	
Morocco	4,237.52	−0.14	0.34
Afghanistan	3,607.53	0.18	
Congo DR	2,963.63	−0.05	
Tunisia	2,814.33	−1.15	−2.03
Ethiopia	2,801.91	0.54	0.84
Egypt	2,605.02	−0.54	−1.23
Sudan	2,463.36	−0.77	

Sources: OECD 2018b – QWIDS Official Development Aid; World Bank CoC; World Economic Forum; author's own calculations.

Table 4.5 *Recipients of largest EU public sector aid and their CoC, FoP, and JI performance, 2002–2014*

Country	Aid (% GNI)	Aid (% ODA)	Change in CoC	Change in FoP	Change in JI
Somalia	0.34	2.55	−0.94	0.09	
Guinea-Bissau	0.24	6.53	−1.19	−1.80	1.17
Djibouti	0.21	3.98	0.40	−0.54	
Comoros	0.19	10.58	0.61	−0.18	
Afghanistan	0.18	7.81	0.18	0.27	
Mali	0.16	8.10	−0.34	−1.17	−1.02
Burundi	0.14	2.90	−0.45		−0.31
Kosovo	0.10	2.58	0.20		
Malawi	0.09	3.66	0.45	0.36	5.50
Sierra Leone	0.09	3.44	−0.36	0.90	3.71

Note: Changes in freedom of the press recorded for 2005–2014; changes in judicial independence recorded for 2006–2014.
Sources: OECD 2018b – QWIDS Official Development Aid; World Bank CoC; Freedom House and World Economic Forum; author's own calculations.

Table 4.6 *Recipients of largest EU legal and judicial aid and their CoC performance, 2002–2014*

Country	Aid (% GNI)	Aid (% ODA)	Change in CoC	Change in FOP	Change in JI
Kosovo	1.09	0.20	0.20		
Moldova	0.08	0.18	0.18	1.08	2.43
Afghanistan	0.07	0.18	0.18	0.27	
Albania	0.07	0.56	0.56	0.09	−0.16
Rwanda	0.07	2.32	2.32	0.54	6.83
West Bank & Gaza Strip	0.05	0.72	0.72		
Georgia	0.05	3.38	3.38	0.81	2.41
Guinea-Bissau	0.04	−1.19	−1.19	−1.80	1.17
Eritrea	0.04	−1.66	−1.66	−0.27	
Malawi	0.04	0.45	0.45	0.36	5.50

Note: Changes in freedom of the press recorded for 2005–2014; changes in judicial independence recorded for 2006–2014.
Sources: OECD 2018b – QWIDS Official Development Aid; World Bank CoC; Freedom House and World Economic Forum; author's own calculations.

left corner progressed the most while receiving little aid. Turkey, the top recipient, first progressed on control of corruption, but in more recent times it regressed on both CoC and judicial independence; it received the

Table 4.7 *Recipients of largest EU anti-corruption aid and their CoC performance, 2002–2014*

Country	Aid (% GNI)	Aid (% ODA)	Change in CoC	Change in FOP	Change in JI
Liberia	0.039	0.70	0.70	0.54	
Guinea-Bissau	0.018	−1.19	−1.19	−1.80	1.17
Montenegro	0.014	0.67	0.67		4.55
Kosovo	0.010	0.20	0.20		
Burundi	0.006	−0.45	−0.45		−0.31
Albania	0.003	0.56	0.56	0.09	−0.16
Comoros	0.002	0.61	0.61	−0.18	
Bosnia-Herzegovina	0.002	0.13	0.13	−0.45	−3.92
Mozambique	0.002	−0.45	−0.45	−0.18	0.01
Cameroon	0.001	−0.11	−0.11	−0.09	0.92

Note: Changes in freedom of the press recorded for 2005–2014; changes in judicial independence recorded for 2006–2014.
Sources: OECD 2018b – QWIDS Official Development Aid; World Bank CoC; Freedom House and World Economic Forum; author's own calculations.

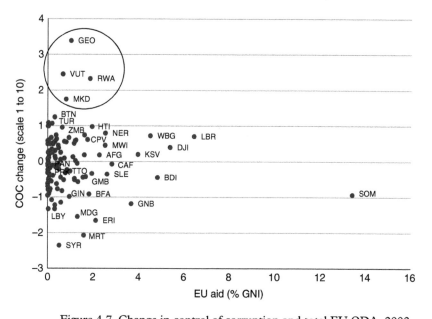

Figure 4.7 Change in control of corruption and total EU ODA, 2002–2014
Sources: World Bank CoC and OECD 2018b – QWIDS Official Development Aid.

Table 4.8 *Types and percentages of government aid for selected cases, 2002–2014*

Country	From	Income group	Total aid (USD mil.)	Total aid (% GNI)	% governance aid in total
BIH	IPA	LM/UM	2,183	1.11	14.80
Egypt	ENP	LM	2,605	0.12	4.02
Ghana	ACP	L/LM	1,033	0.32	10.58
Kosovo	IPA	LM	1,587	2.88	34.94
Tunisia	ENP	LM/UM	2,814	0.58	4.41
Ukraine	IPA	LM	2,238	0.14	15.92

Sources: OECD 2018b – QWIDS Official Development Aid; World Bank CoC; Freedom House and World Economic Forum; author's own calculations.

largest amount of aid for JI in the world. Georgia and Rwanda progressed the most, disproportionately to the aid received, driven by domestic factors (leadership in particular). At around 10 percent progress, we also find countries such as the Maldives, Senegal, Côte d'Ivoire, Laos, Bhutan, and Korea. Tunisia registered a spectacular improvement on freedom of the press, which has also driven control of corruption positively, but far less than expectations, and far less than its potential – it has the best goodness of fit when modernity is concerned (high education). The cases we look at more in depth in this book are listed in Table 4.8. They have all received consistent governance aid and therefore some progress should be expected.

The top governance achievers do have some EU funding, but it is disproportionate to their progress on control of corruption. This is the case for Georgia, Rwanda, Macedonia, Vanuatu, Uruguay, Indonesia, and Chile (see also Figure 4.7, circled). Others, including Mauritius and Zambia, do not have governance-dedicated aid, but a considerable part of their budget comes from donors. The latter countries thus contribute, next to IPA countries, to the globally weak association that we find between EU aid and control of corruption. When associating aid as a percentage of GNI with progress on corruption the finding is confirmed that the biggest recipients have not progressed the most. How much aid the progressing cases received is shown in Table 4.9.

Comparing performance in governance improvement across countries that receive more *total aid* than the others, we find no significantly better performance on the CoC indicator (see Figure 4.8). Given that aid recipients' performance declined, on average, in both major constraints (legal independence of the judiciary) and norms (freedom of the press,

Table 4.9 *Achievers on control of corruption and their EU aid, 2002–2014*

Country	Change in CoC	Average of total aid (% GNI)	Average governance aid (% GNI)
Georgia	3.38	0.91	0.19
Vanuatu	2.45	0.82	0.14
Rwanda	2.32	2.15	0.15
Macedonia	1.75	0.87	0.15
Bhutan	1.24	0.35	0.06
Uruguay	1.08	0.03	0.01
Turkey	1.06	0.16	0.02
Belarus	0.99	0.03	0.01
Indonesia	0.99	0.02	0.00
Haiti	0.97	1.88	0.14

Sources: OECD 2018b – QWIDS Official Development Aid; World Bank CoC; Freedom House and World Economic Forum; author's own calculations.

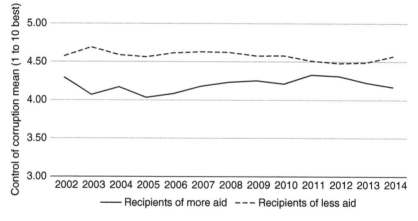

Figure 4.8 Progress on control of corruption by aid, 2002–2014 (recipient of below- versus above-average amount; sample of 120 countries)
Sources: World Bank CoC and OECD 2018b – QWIDS Official Development Aid.

where IPA and ODC countries are, in fact, regressing at alarming rates), and that even in broadband subscriptions they trail behind lesser aid recipients (due to poorer original conditions), the resulting control of corruption cannot be expected to have improved much. Some

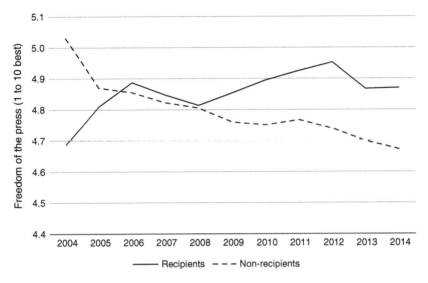

Figure 4.9 Comparison of press freedom in recipients (30 countries) and nonrecipients (89 countries) of EU anti-corruption aid, 2004–2014
Sources: Freedom House – freedom of the press and OECD 2018b – QWIDS Official Development Aid.

improvements exist only in the reduction of red tape and the expansion of internet connections, which have been growing globally, but with no difference across recipients of more or less aid. On judicial independence, only ODCs seem to have progressed significantly.

Similarly, when comparing countries receiving *anti-corruption aid* from the EU compared to countries that do not (see Figure 4.9), no significant progress is shown. The number of recipient countries for this sample is just twenty-two, with registered disbursements from 2009 to 2014. Countries receiving anti-corruption aid seem to perform even *worse* on CoC on average, but the difference between recipients and nonrecipients and the change from 2002 to 2014 are not significant at the 95 percent confidence interval. However, when checking for targeted aid's influence, we find that countries receiving anti-corruption aid actually do better on average than those not receiving it on two crucial items: judicial independence and freedom of the press (see Figure 4.9).

Budget aid countries deserve a special mention, as among our sample they appear closer than the rest to having progressed significantly, although there are also significant outliers. A 2017 report by the European Commission, drawing on the experience of implementing

263 budget support contracts in 88 countries or territories for a portfolio of EUR 12.7 billion and payments amounting to EUR 1.7 billion in 2016, is also rather positive.[19] The report shows better results in this group of countries on poverty, health targets, and disparities between urban and rural areas. Good governance, public finance management, and budgetary transparency have stayed stronger in countries where the EU provides budget support, and there was also some improvement in control of corruption among this group compared to the rest (ibid.).

A review of this data thus has some mixed, but not ambiguous results. What do we know?

- Multilateral total EU aid does have some small positive effect on governance, whereas aid from either the USA or individual EU member states shows no association at all with governance progress (Charron, 2011; Dadašov, 2016). This finding should be taken with reservations as long as we do not have any successful cases to confirm it. So far, the countries performing best are far from having received the most aid, and they are not the ones associated with EU projects on corruption. If anything, this finding should argue in favor of full donor coordination or even joint management when control of corruption is concerned, since bilateral funds seem not to produce any effect at all.
- Dedicated project aid for good governance and control of corruption have not yielded results on overall corruption reduction. This type of aid largely includes projects in support of integrity in the public sector, anti-corruption agencies, and the like. However, we did find that dedicated support on projects and *ex ante* conditions help progress in judicial independence and freedom of the press,
- Support for civil society is so small and so entirely disconnected from any theory of change on how civil society can improve governance that it is nearly impossible to assess. EU funds in this area should move towards sponsoring interactions between transparency/e-government tools and society, empowering civil society as a stakeholder capable of monitoring and auditing public services and holding them accountable. This should be done consistently and as an integral part of all aid projects and activities, rather than separately as just civil society aid. Simply put, a social accountability component should be included in any aid project. While including civil society consultations on budget support conditions is a step forward, more could be done to demand that the governments who benefit from such support must fund civil

---

[19] *Budget Support: Trends and Results 2017* from the Directorate-General for International Cooperation and Development and Directorate-General for Neighborhood and Enlargement Negotiations.

society audits or consumer surveys for government programs and donor projects. This might work better than official oversight agencies, which have so far proved ineffective.

Finally, the EU has signaled the will to switch some development support to market actors rather than focusing exclusively on classic government-organized development (approaches such as investment facilities or "blending" [Bilal and Große-Puppendahl, 2016]). This approach might mitigate the unintended consequences for governance of frontloaded aid for which governments are not held accountable, which are a partial element of the poor results so far. Aid should rely on natural monitoring and oversight of the beneficiaries (conceived as the representatives of the poor, not the kleptocrats), and if the aid goes by design to private entities acting in their own interest, results might be better. However, this approach cannot replace *ex ante* conditions, political dialogue, civil society, or technical assistance as components of the support for good governance, simply because the business community that the EU relies upon to participate needs some support to handle local corruption and is wary, under OECD anti-bribery conventions, to assume so many new costs along with the old risks of confronting domestic government favoritism.[20] For example, investment in India, where the business community followed the EC call to invest, was assessed as a failure by my interviewees at the European Chamber of Commerce precisely due to corruption and red tape. Hence the need that *ex ante* conditions, technical assistance, and civil society projects stay focused on cutting red tape, increasing transparency, and creating the right conditions for businesses to consider it profitable, and not a political burden, to follow the European Commission's lead.

---

[20] European chamber of commerce interviews, February 7, 2018, Brussels.

5   Old Europe: Stagnation and Decay

5.1   What Subverts Trust in Elites in the European Union

In the aftermath of the euro crisis in Europe, a Spanish bank called Bankia went bust unexpectedly in 2012, after announcing a return to profit – in part due to patriotic, small-amount investments from ordinary people who had been called upon to save it, and the euro along with it, a few years before. This was "the biggest financial debacle in Spanish history," as the newspaper *El País* put it (Barrón and Pérez, 2016), which led to a bailout by the Spanish public and the EU to the tune of EUR 46 billion. Those small investors lost close to EUR 2 billion (Koch, 2016). An internal email from the bank was leaked to civil society activists, who had rallied to fight the bank's executives and expose the system that had made Spanish banks so unaccountable for so long.[1] The email's author, a respectable public figure (he had even been a spokesperson for the Spanish royal court) in charge of the bank's corporate social responsibility, was writing to his top executive to inquire if in that particular year, as in previous years, "gifts" from the bank would go to the governing party, opposition parties, union leaders, and top media editors and opinion leaders, in a descending order of proportion.[2] The depiction showed a perfect particularistic system, where "gifts" were spread across the board according to present and potential future influence. It explained why Spanish bank executives got away with millions in daily allowances and gifts, while the bank had faced economic difficulties for years – not exactly a meritworthy achievement. Furthermore, here was one main reason – alongside EU funds and other golden opportunities – that the main Spanish political parties had all ended up with troubles over illegal funding, to the

---

[1] See Wikivisually page of activist Simona Levi at https://wikivisually.com/wiki/Simona_Levi

[2] Author's interview with Simona Levi from Xnet, the organization that disclosed the email and later sued on behalf of small investors, Berlin, January 2016.

extent that in 2015–2016 alone over 1,500 officials faced corruption charges (*Politico*, 2017). The system crashed due to a major problem: millions, if not tens of millions, of people ended up paying to cover the losses, many of them not even Spaniards. The Brussels-based *Politico* newspaper headlined "Spain's Never-Ending Corruption Problem," underlining that even after the Spanish democratic transition – during those glorious EU years when the country led the platoon of successful entrants with Portugal, Ireland, and in theory even Greece – Spain's corruption problem had not gone away at all (Ibid.). If anything, it has grown worse.

The question then arises whether European promotion of good governance should not show results first in Europe itself, in particular since the good governance crusade started with Roman Prodi's 2000 speech on good governance and the subsequent "White Paper on European Governance" (Prodi, 2000; EC, 2001). European countries – in particular the EU–15, the older and richer member states – are reputedly at the top of good governance charts, leading on rule of law, control of corruption, democracy, and government effectiveness. Their performance has always been uneven across countries, with Italy notoriously corrupt and Scandinavian countries famously honest. But has Italy become more Scandinavian due to joint membership in the common market, the euro, and the European legal space – or rather the other way around? Has the unification of Europe brought better quality of control of corruption across member states, starting, of course, with those where corruption was a problem from the outset? To answer this, this chapter will first review the evolution of Europe as a whole and will then focus on two "old" member states, Greece and Italy, that had always been seen as European outliers on governance quality, investigating whether their EU membership has helped them achieve better control of corruption. The time frame is data dependent, as time series governance data is scarce, but fortunately the expert and public survey data does cover the interval 2000 to the present, and even a few years before Prodi's speech (since 1996). For more fact-based data, the country examples will hopefully suffice.

Despite the resignation of the entire Santer Commission on corruption grounds in 1999, corruption has hardly ever been a salient topic in Europe. Eva Joly, a Norwegian-born French prosecutor, narrates the harassment that she and her team had to face from politicians using secret services and the media once they started to investigate corruption (Joly and Beccaria, 2003). By that time, corruption in Western Europe had become "no longer … a marginal or exceptional problem, [but rather] a kind of meta-system which is equally effective in operation as the official state-apparatus to which it is attached and which nourishes it" (Della Porta and Mény, 1997, p. 4). The kind of corruption that Joly started to unravel – a corrupt linkage between publicly owned companies such as the French energy giant Elf, the country's political parties, and top officials including the foreign affairs minister Roland Dumas – is all too familiar in developing countries. One would not expect it, however, in France, the first historical promoter of good governance abroad, from Montesquieu's separation of powers to Napoleon's administrative and legal codes. Similarly, the ending of the story, with Ms. Joly returning to Norway and the charged minister Roland Dumas basically walking away, is all too familiar in developing countries where the EU is trying to promote good governance – and is not a happy ending.

The eventual successful convictions of some top politicians in France and Italy in the 1990s have not managed to shake the belief that something has gone fundamentally wrong in Western Europe. Eva Joly herself attributes the decay of ethics in the West to the oil crisis in the seventies and the need of European companies to recover from the vast increase in costs: unlike the United States, they had no such resources. Starting in 1977, European governments began allowing their companies to declare publicly the bribes they paid abroad and to claim tax exemption on them, at exactly the time when the Americans were adopting the Foreign Corrupt Practices Act (Joly and Beccaria, 2003, pp. 264–268). "This goes against the general interest and against ethics, but it can be seen in a narrower sense as in the interest of the enterprise," according to an official opinion on the French bill authorizing the tax exemption presented to the National Assembly (ibid., p. 266). While the 1997 OECD anti-bribery convention eliminated such exemptions, the failure to implement the convention allowed the same corrupt patterns to continue. Yves Mény attributes the decay to a shift in values in France and more generally among the Western capitalist class in the seventies, with the replacement of the old, strict rule-based behavior in entrepreneurship with a trade-off mentality (1996). Globalization and its deregulation further empowered such types of capitalists, no longer characterized by an "inner worldly asceticism," as Max Weber famously described purveyors of modern European capitalism (1968, pp. 542–546). The lessons from the Elf affair in France and the Clean Hands (*Mani pulite*) campaign in Italy were not properly drawn: transparency increased only in very visible areas of the public sector, but not in banks or privatized utilities, and the politics–business networks have proven highly resilient to this day. Some non-European scholars even questioned whether the sophisticated and highly transactional system created in Europe by European Union governance was not itself conducive to ever more corruption, the "best system that money can buy" (Warner, 2002; 2007). Meanwhile, as the European Union enlarged – allowing entry to countries such as Romania and Bulgaria, which by all standards were "developing" and not developed – a new, more visible sort of corruption emerged. This consists of a large spectrum of symptoms, from informal payments to poorly paid doctors or clerks to top-level officials' undue profit owing to unregulated conflict of interest. The new member countries' corruption captured most of the attention (and sanctions) of the European Union after the 2004–2006 enlargement (Vachudova, 2005; Innes, 2014). They also provided an extraordinary alibi for the older half of the continent. In an attempt to create a pan-European corruption report, for instance, the European Commission's Directorate-General for Migrant and Home Affairs (DG Home) fell into the expected trap of strongly criticizing new member states, Bulgaria and Romania in particular; while Luxembourg, the country that Eva Joly first exposed (with some endorsement from the Council of Europe) and that was then shown in the LuxLeaks scandal to be systemically corrupt in its manipulation of legal rules, got only a few lines in the report, mostly praise (EC, 2014b).

After the euro crisis, however, with its unpopular austerity policies and accompanying digital leaks (LuxLeaks, Panama Papers, Paradise Papers), doubts about the older half of the EU arose with a vengeance (Heywood, 2014; Freund, 2017), on top of more general questioning whether even the most advanced democracies are free of government favoritism (Rajan and Zingales, 2003; *The Economist*, 2016). And recent scandals have plagued nearly all European countries, even in what used to be unassailable areas. The British parliament, a historical contributor to good governance, was engulfed in scandal over fraudulent benefits; the German car industry, the country's greatest pride and source of competitiveness, has turned out to thrive on unethical behavior; top IT companies in the Netherlands, Finland, and Sweden became engulfed in bribe scandals in Eastern Europe; preferential public contracts or publicly owned companies in France and Spain turned out to have funded political parties systematically; and Luxembourg, after having built into its tax system a European tax avoidance scheme, sentenced the very whistle-blower to a suspended jail sentence for revelations on tax optimization schemes. In 2018, Denmark, the world's absolute good governance benchmark, joined the platoon: it turned out that during the process of digitization of its tax authority one person alone was left in charge of approving reimbursements on double-taxed dividends, with the result that the budget was swindled out of EUR 2 billion, or EUR 3 million per hour for as long the scheme lasted (Segal, 2018). The EU had long been the benchmark for the rest of the world where rationalization of governance is concerned, but is this still the case? Has the EU managed to socialize its most poorly performing members on public integrity and so help them to catch up during their membership, or has the center of the EU itself rather lost something of its shine?

Several Eurobarometer surveys (2011, 2013, and 2017) have highlighted the fact that the majority of Europeans believe that corruption is a major problem for their country. In 2017, more than two-thirds of respondents (68 percent) believed that corruption was widespread in their own country. More than half of respondents thought that corruption was widespread among political parties (56 percent) and among politicians at national, regional, or local level (53 percent), notably in Greece (96 percent), Lithuania (93 percent), and Portugal (92 percent). On the other hand, only one-fifth of respondents in Finland (21 percent) and Denmark (22 percent) thought that corruption was widespread. A quarter of Europeans (25 percent) have stated consistently since 2013 that they are personally affected by corruption in their daily lives. The highest proportion of respondents with this opinion lives in Romania (68 percent), Croatia (59 percent), and Spain (58 percent); the lowest live in the Netherlands (4 percent), in Denmark, and Finland (5 percent each). Only about one in ten Europeans say they know someone who has taken or offered bribes (12 percent), and only 7 percent of Europeans say that they have been victims of corruption personally.

The business surveys commissioned by DG Home (EC, 2013e; 2015b) also tend to indicate that poor governance has become a European standard. The surveys show France and Germany, EU's "motor," both on the wrong side of the norm. In Germany, over half of businesses in the sample believe that procurement deals in Germany are either inside deals or prearranged as a rule. A similar percentage declared that favoritism towards friends and family was widespread in the German business community. Likewise, 50 percent of French businesses complained that favoritism towards family is widespread in the public sector (and 52 percent found it so in the business sector); 42 percent reported tax evasion and VAT fraud as very common; and 37 percent considered that the practice of granting favors to businesses in exchange for campaign contributions is rife. In estimating the extent of nepotism, French businessmen rated France at a score between Romania and Bulgaria (EC 2013e, p. 374; EC 2015b, p. 428).

Regionally, we see great variety across Europe (see Figure 5.1). Northern Europe (the Scandinavians) do far better on ethical universalism than the rest. Everywhere else, people seem to agree that particularism is the norm in both the public and the private sector, a highly surprising result. Clearly Southern and Eastern Europe perceive

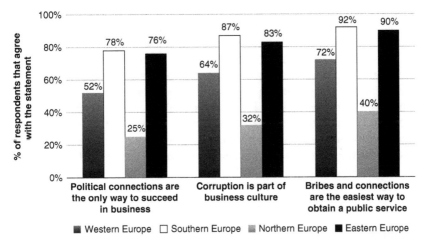

Figure 5.1 Perceptions of corruption and particularism in the EU by region
Source: EB, 2013

widespread particularism and corruption, and there is little difference between younger EU members in the east and the older Mediterranean members: longer socialization within the EU seems hardly to have mattered). Strangely, Western Europe shows strikingly high agreement with "Corruption is part of business culture" (64 percent), "Bribes and connections are the easiest way to obtain a public service" (72 percent), and even "Political connections are the only way to succeed in business" (52 percent). This region includes France, Germany, Netherlands, and the UK – the quintessential modernization benchmark countries. Newcomer Estonia has already surpassed France in the Corruption Perception Index and the Index for Public Integrity.

If a cross-sectional picture thus reveals a Northern Europe that is fairly distinctive from the rest of the continent, a Western Europe where the ethical universalism norm seems challenged, and Southern and Eastern Europe (with the exception of Estonia) with particularism perceived as rife, the longitudinal trends in Europe show a more uniform picture. Stagnation is the name of the game: from 1996, since we have data, European member states have hardly changed. Within the confidence margin of 5 percent on control of corruption (CoC), Mediterranean countries actually regressed, suggesting that more competition and tighter EU fiscal rules have not managed to trigger any improvement. Italy – a member since 1958, so for more than half a century, and a eurozone member since 1999 – and Greece – a democracy since 1974, an EU member since 1981, and a eurozone member since 2001 – are perceived not to have evolved at all. In both cases, rule of law is perceived to have declined sharply, while control of corruption experienced some backslide. Spain and Cyprus also regressed on CoC, while Estonia and Croatia progressed. By and large, the little existing progress was made by East European members, while decline marked Mediterranean members. Most countries, however, have simply not changed. A process tracing of surveys shows that perception deteriorated after the economic and euro crises, which started in 2009 and led to national scandals about rationality of spending and corruption. Before that, analysts had rated all Mediterranean countries favorably. The decline perceived is at the limit of a confidence error of 5 percent, but it looks rather marked against the perfectly flat line of OECD countries' group during the same interval.

The Eurobarometer questions offer a snapshot into governance and people's perception of where their country is on the particularism–ethical universalism continuum. In other words, they show us the outcome of the equilibrium: more or less control of corruption as perceived by the population at a given moment in time (see Figure 5.2). The trends in time reveal the constancy of this situation, i.e. whether the equilibrium is stable or not, and the existence of any contestation to the current rules in governance. An additional indicator shows the public's evaluation of the government's response to corruption, and it can be compared before and after the deterioration of corruption perceptions after the crisis. And again, here the regions are not internally consistent: Austria, Belgium, and Netherlands are closer to Scandinavia with higher approval rates for the political will of their governments, and so are Estonia, Poland, and Romania among the East European countries, where citizens evaluate that their governments are trying to fight corruption in earnest (data from EC, 2017g). The approval rate is 40 percent in Northern countries, compared to 33 percent in Western Europe, 29 percent in Southern Europe, and 26 percent in Eastern Europe. The regional variation thus covers only 14 percent, although the distance between the highest approval (Austria, 47 percent) and the lowest (Latvia, 11 percent) is far higher. Between 2009 and 2017, support for anti-corruption policies has grown in Romania (the largest approval in EU) and in Hungary and Poland (showing why, among other reasons, voters there support their leadership), but also in Ireland and Cyprus, two countries seriously affected by the crisis.

It is far more difficult to assess the perceived integrity of European institutions themselves, as European citizens are notoriously poorly

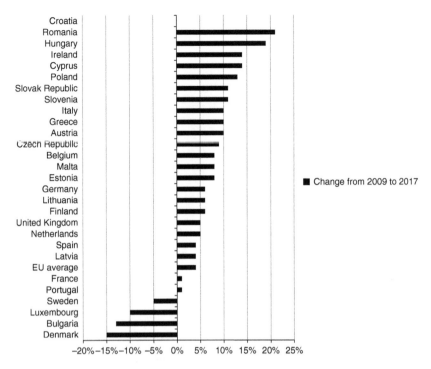

Figure 5.2 Perceived effectiveness of governments' anti-corruption efforts (change from 2009 to 2017)
Source: Eurobarometer 72.2/2009 (QB5), Eurobarometer 79.1/2013 (QB15): "Please tell me whether you agree or disagree that the government's efforts to combat corruption are effective"

informed about the European Union (Anderson, 1998; Karp et al., 2003; Mungiu-Pippidi et al., 2016) and trust in Europe is grounded in national trust, so it is not exogenous. At a low level of awareness, attitudes are not worth reporting. What we do know objectively is that control of corruption equilibrium is built at national level. We see this in the consistent pattern of corruption in procurement, where both EU funds and national funds have similar patterns per country, despite more protective rules against fraud in the use of EU funds (see Figure 5.3).

The use of noncompetitive tenders (single bidding) is a fact-based indicator, which draws on a proven correlation between single bidding practices and fraud in public procurement (Fazekas and Toth, 2014). The indicator is quite consistent with the Eurobarometer results, with the most competitive tenders in Northern countries and the least competitive

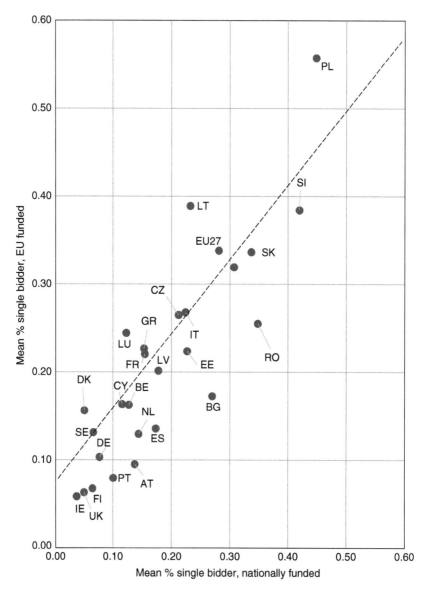

Figure 5.3 National consistency in patterns of corruption in procurement across EU and national budget allocations
Note: Single bidder shares of EU and nationally funded public procurement contracts per country, EU 27, 2009–2013
Source: Fazekas and Tóth, 2017.

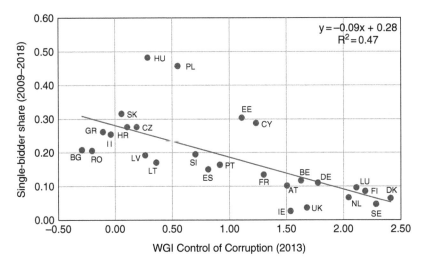

Figure 5.4 Association between perceptions of corruption and single bidding

Note: Single bidding: EU's Tenders Electronic Daily, data released by DG GROW of the European Commission (EU TED); Corruption Perception Index (TI CPI, 2013)

Source: Fazekas and Tóth, 2017

in Eastern Europe. The results should be weighted with transparency – there is a great deal of variation in available data across countries, which partly accounts for the surprise cases of Poland and Estonia (both lead in single bidding but are also the most transparent). This fact-based indicator correlates at 0.67 percent with expert scores of from Transparency International's Corruption Perception Index (CPI) and at 0.69 percent with the World Bank's CoC indicator (Mungiu-Pippidi et al., 2016) – obviously outliers such as Poland and Estonia account for the rest. Figure 5.4 illustrates the association between expert score CPI and single bidding.

Politicians tend to discard results of public opinion surveys as completely subjective and as driven by scandal-prone media and populists. However, perceptions are grounded in experience, as already pointed out (Mungiu-Pippidi and Kukutschka, 2018); people with bribery experience perceive significantly higher corruption than the rest of the sample. Additionally, people with regular access to the internet are *less* likely to believe that corruption and particularism are defining trends of their countries' governance regimes (see Figure 5.5). The biggest difference between these two groups is in regard to the importance of political

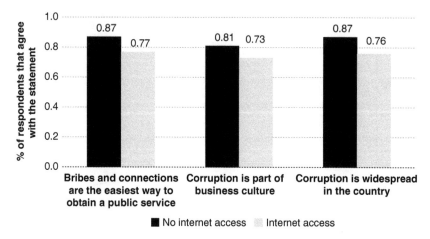

Figure 5.5 Perceptions of government favoritism and of private and public particularism by internet access
Source: Mungiu-Pippidi and Kukutschka, 2018

connections for succeeding in business. While three-quarters of respondents without internet access believe that this is a problem, only 63 percent of respondents with access to the internet share this opinion. Despite clear differences between the two groups, it is important to highlight that very strong majorities in Europe see the governance regimes in their countries as characterized by traces of corruption and particularism regardless of media exposure (ibid.). Of course, surveys have important limitations (Luxembourg citizens' definition of corruption may differ from that of the Finns or the Greeks), so there is definitely some variation due to country mentality. But seeing the overwhelmingly critical attitude of all European citizens, one can safely state that tolerance of corruption has reached a historical low in most places.

The Index of Public Integrity (IPI) allows us to classify European member states by their public integrity framework, showing who has more versus less corruption risk at the national level (see Table 5.1). Apart from judicial independence, the components are based on objective data; this is the closest we can get to an objective and neutral assessment, comparing every country both with the rest of Europe and with its income group. A mix of Northern and Western countries thus appear in the upper-left-hand quadrant with the lowest risk (low opportunities and sufficient constraints), another mix in the lower-right-hand quadrant with the highest risk (Greece, Romania, Bulgaria, Latvia, and Poland) and two groups in an intermediate position.

Table 5.1 *European member states classified by public integrity risk*

		CONSTRAINTS			
		High		Medium	Low
RESOURCES	Low	Finland Netherlands Denmark	France Estonia United Kingdom	Lithuania	-
		Sweden	Ireland Belgium		
	Medium	Luxembourg Germany Austria		Latvia Portugal Spain	Hungary Greece Slovenia	Italy
	High	Malta		Cyprus Slovak Republic	Poland Czech Repupblic	Croatia Romania
						Bulgaria

Note: Risk increases from upper left quadrant to lower right quadrant
Source: Index of Public Integrity (2018, www.integrity-index.org)

Cyprus, Estonia, Lithuania, and Hungary are at risk due to greater opportunities created by EU funds (or other funds, in the case of Cyprus), although they impose sufficient constraints. At the opposite extreme, insufficient constraints exist in Italy, Portugal, Slovakia, Slovenia, and Spain, but their opportunities are lower also, because they receive less EU funding, have sufficient transparency, or both. The first three years of IPI show some progress for Greece, Romania, and Latvia, for example, and regress for Hungary. However, neither on the basis of subjective nor from objective data can a positive convergence be observed in the quality of governance within united Europe. There is no evidence of that.

We should at all times keep in mind the limitations of this analysis. First, there is the limitation of national borders – nothing prevents a company from the low-risk quadrant behaving corruptly in an environment of high risk across borders (for example, Scandinavian companies offering bribes in Eastern Europe), behavior which would escape these kind of national indicators. Second, not all countries are equally homogeneous across their internal regions; and third, there is no evidence of a correlation between *public* corruption and *individual* infringements of integrity, in the form of legal rent-seeking behaviors (such as tax "optimization"), which are still deviations from ethical universalism. This being said, however, the exercise captures the capacity of each national society to constrain rent-seeking and indicates what to expect as default behavior in that given society.

5.2   The European Influence

How could the European Union have affected the quality of governance? Returning to the model of change presented in Chapter 3, two substantial influences could be theoretically disentangled:

1. EU could influence governance *negatively* as an unintended consequence by providing resources for corruption through EU funds, which are known for their associated red tape and difficult (highly specialized) access, factors that we know to be corruption risks.
2. EU could influence governance *positively* as an intended consequence by policing a level playing field for business in the common market, by promoting rule of law, and through the political conditionalities arising from the Copenhagen summit. Although the Lisbon Treaty is dedicated to the accession members and not the member states, its Article 7 carries an article that allows the EU to act in case of default on rule of law and European values more generally:

On a reasoned proposal by one third of the Member States, by the European Parliament or by the European Commission, the Council, acting by a majority of four fifths of its members after obtaining the consent of the European Parliament, may determine that there is a clear risk of a serious breach by a Member State of the values referred to in Article 2. Before making such a determination, the Council shall hear the Member State in question and may address recommendations to it, acting in accordance with the same procedure. The Council shall regularly verify that the grounds on which such a determination was made continue to apply. ... The European Council, acting by unanimity on a proposal by one third of the Member States or by the European Commission and after obtaining the consent of the European Parliament, may determine the existence of a serious and persistent breach by a Member State of the values referred to in Article 2 after inviting the Member State in question to submit its observations. (OJ C 306, 17.12.2007)

The values alluded to are defined in Article 2 as "liberty, democracy, respect for human rights and fundamental freedoms, and the rule of law." As a country's voting rights could even be suspended, Article 7 is probably the EU's most powerful tool in this context, although it is unclear whether corruption itself could ever be considered a sufficient threat to rule of law to trigger Article 7. In 2018–2019 the debate in the European Parliament surrounding Romania's revision of anti-corruption legislation occasionally touched on Article 7. But the final requirement of unanimity makes its application impractical, as the 2017–2018 Hungary/Poland crises show.

Other EU tools that could contribute to increasing constraints on corruption have emerged in recent years: a directive to allow the recovery of assets from corrupt proceedings (Directive 2014/42/EU of the European Parliament and of the Council of 3 April 2014 on the freezing and confiscation of instrumentalities and proceeds of crime in the European Union); the introduction of a European prosecutor to prosecute fraud involving EU funds, instead of sending such matters to national prosecutors, as the European Anti-Fraud Office had done for many years (Council Regulation EU 2017/1939 with 22 EU MS joining by 2018); and a unified European legal framework on whistleblowers (under adoption as of 2018 [EC, 2018c]). Furthermore, to rein in public spending and allow a rationalization of governance, selected member states signed a Fiscal Compact (the 2012 Treaty on Stability, Coordination and Governance in the Economic and Monetary Union, TSCG). Implemented in 2013, it requires that a balanced budget be maintained in domestic legal orders. Out of the twenty-five contracting parties to the TSCG, twenty-two are formally bound by the Fiscal Compact (the 19 eurozone member states plus Bulgaria, Denmark, and Romania). The compact is monitored by a annual report known as the "European Semester," which looks at both fiscal and governance indicators and makes recommendations to countries. Finally, the Luxembourg Court, the European Court of Auditors, and the European Ombudsman all deal with good governance and implicitly with corruption in various ways. Additionally, the EU endorses the Council of Europe's GRECO initiative against corruption, which makes periodic assessments of both legislation and the implementation of anti-corruption laws and cooperates closely with the OECD's SIGMA and Integrity Initiative programs.

An examination of evidence, scarce as it is, shows that EU funds do seem to increase corruption risks (Fazekas et al., 2014; Dimulescu et al., 2013; Drápalová 2017; Fazekas and Toth 2017), despite this phenomenon going rather under-reported before the accession of former communist countries. It was only after the financial crisis that scandals erupted and some judicial follow-ups took place in Italy, Spain, and Greece. More than one-third of the EU budget is spent on the so-called Cohesion Policy, largely aimed at fostering regional convergence; yet clear evidence exists, consistent before and after the economic crisis, that EU funds do not manage to change pre-existing institutional quality, reaching their development objectives only where, in the terms of Acemoglu and Robinson, inclusive institutions precede them (Ederveen et al., 2006; Beugelsdijk and Eijffinger, 2005). But if some evidence exists on unintended consequences of EU accession, and even on cohesion funds as a resource for corruption, far less attention has been paid to the impact of EU-induced constraints. Of course, we know the end result – little to no impact – but this arises from a mix of factors that cancels out the intended constraints. The vast research work on compliance with EU law, for instance, is very formal and refers only to the implementation of EU directives. There is very little work on the impact of the European Court of Justice (ECJ) on corruption. Some evidence on the reverse effect has been published: corruption at national level impedes compliance with ECJ rulings, but not the other way around (Mbaye, 2001). The European Court of Auditors audits only EU institutions, not member states. It is the only EU office with clear demonstrable anti-corruption impact, as it made a whole European commission (Santer) resign. The European Anti-Fraud Office (OLAF) was created in 1999 to defend against EU budget fraud. It had a staff of 421 and recovered EUR 901 million in 2014, its best recent year, after a low of EUR 194 million in 2012 (the EU's yearly budget was roughly EUR 145 billion in 2015; EU, 2018). OLAF was born from the restructuring of a previous agency and was itself restructured in 2012: the new European public prosecutor is further tasked with correcting what is perceived as lack of effectiveness in policing and recovering defrauded funds. As to the implementation of the Fiscal Compact, the Bruegel think tank estimates that "overall implementation of recommendations by EU countries has worsened in the last few years, in particular when it comes to recommendations addressed to countries with excessive macroeconomic imbalances" (which are also the ones where corruption is a problem; Efstathiou and Wolf, 2018, p. 1).

The absence of tough sanctions, such as a more functional Article 7, is only one aspect preventing the European Union from more strongly constraining the behavior of member states. The inherent tension between national state governments and the supranational EU institutions is paramount. On one hand, the latter are seen as less representative of the citizens (except the European Parliament or the Council of Europe's Parliamentary Assembly). On the other hand, they are staffed by the same national elites, even if supranational. So how much different can they be? And are elected officials indeed more accountable than appointed ones? Scandals about discretionary expenses and lack of transparency at the European Parliament had been legion, and OLAF has always complained of the difficulty of searching its premises in the event of a corruption complaint. Elected officials are strongly protected by political immunity. In 2017, for instance, the Council of Europe had to add to its usual annual warning against corruption a reference to its own internal corruption scandal involving the Council of Europe's Parliamentary Assembly (the so-called "caviar diplomacy" – bribes and perks to encourage its members to lobby for corrupt but oil-rich Azerbaijan; Radio Free Europe, 2016). The scandal had dragged on for some years until some sanctions were finally enacted (GRECO, 2018). How much authority can the Council of Europe, whose GRECO recommendations to member states are also endorsed by the European Commission, command when its own situation is so ambiguous? The first report of Transparency International dedicated to EU institutions in 2017 found that more than 50 percent of ex-commissioners and 30 percent of ex-members of the European Parliament (MEPs) left politics to join organizations on the EU lobby register (Freund, 2018). The European Ombudsman strongly criticized the European Commission in 2018 for failing to sanction the commission's former president, José Maria Barroso, for joining Goldman Sachs, a controversial investment bank due to its behavior preceding the 2016 crisis (European Ombudsman, 2018). In an answer to the Ethics Committee to whom the European Commission deferred the case, it turned out that the meaning of "integrity" is unclear, since the European Court of Justice has never had the opportunity to define it (ibid.). Why the European Union does not exercise sufficient constraints on old member states and its own commissioners or MEPs (who have less scrutiny and conflict of interest regulation than most member states' national parliaments) is easily explained: on top of poor instruments to constrain EU member states into good behavior, there is just not sufficient political will for the European institutions to lead by example, as compellingly argued by both Ombudsman O'Reilly and Transparency International. And the promotion of good governance in Romania, Bulgaria, and Greece fails to be "Europeanization," because in order to produce domestic change, the European-promoted institutions should *precede* change, Europeanization being a process of institutional adaptation through socialization and other mechanisms (Radaelli, 2006). But there is no Europeanized good governance shown in any unitary good governance standard: neither in law nor in practice. The nearest proxies are the European procurement and concession contracts directives, although these are only partially regulated at European level (Directive 2014/23/EU; Directive 2014/24/EU). Their implementation began only after 2015 in practice, indicating that some benchmarks might emerge – in the future.

The whole European Union, therefore, is still looking ahead for some meaningful Europeanization in this area. As for the past, the European integration process simply had to proceed alongside national corruption, which sometimes even put integration at risk, notably in Italy and Greece.

5.3   Italy: From the Clean Hands to the Five Stars

In 2019, the sought-after prize of European Capital of Culture went to the town of Matera, in Basilicata, one of the poorest Italian regions in the extreme south. For over half a century, the region had borne the stigma of a label placed by an American anthropologist, Edward Banfield, in 1956. The Basilicata he described was the quintessential home of "amoral familism": a place of stagnation and distrust, the absolute opposite of ethical universalism, where people cluster only around family and clan ties, seeking their welfare often at the expense of others. With so many free-riders and widespread social envy preventing association, public goods tend to be in undersupply in such places. Thus Banfield's Basilicata very much resembled Switzerland before Napoleon, with no decent roads to interconnect its settlements. But Basilicata had had roads thousands of years before, and ports too. Matera – a place where people are sometimes described as still living in caves – has Byzantine frescoes and superb museums (*The Observer*, 2017; 2018). Down on the coast, one encounters Magna Grecia, the southern rampart of Greek and Trojan colonies, where among the still-standing columns Pythagoras is said to be buried. On the northern border of the region, the Constitutions of Melfi were promulgated on 1 September 1231 by Emperor Frederick II Hohenstaufen. Historian Ernst Kantorowicz referred to that new legal code for the Kingdom of Sicily as "the birth certificate of the modern administrative state" (Kantorowicz, 1957). Little has been achieved, however, from this promise of the "modern administrative state" over centuries, as inhabitants deeply felt by end 2018, when doubts were growing that the EUR 400 million earmarked by Rome and Brussels would be at least spent in time for the town's inauguration as European Capital of Culture 2019, if not spent meaningfully.

A walk through Basilicata on its capital cultural eve captured this paradoxical state of affairs – perhaps telling for more than just this southern region. The head of the region was arrested on corruption grounds, threatening the already problematic deadline for the public works needed to open by 1 January 2019 to the European public. Next to the Greek ruins, the splendid beaches at the Ionian Sea were full of empty beer bottles and cans – a reminder that Italy has long topped the list of infringements of EU directives on environment issues. The road infrastructure, praised a few years ago (Venanzi and Gamper, 2012), still had that air of unpredictability that the corruption scholar encounters from Brazil to Andalusia. The roads strangely either double one another or make long detours, allegedly due to connections of landowners who profited from expropriation. Southern Italian good governance may have existed in pre-pre-modern times, based on rule of law, albeit thin, but it did not make it to modern times. While for the rest of Western Europe modernity meant the triumph of impersonality and legalism, here informality and particularism have flourished.

Italians in central or northern Italy might be outraged to hear the whole of Italy compared with Basilicata. But the small and charming Southern region does capture the two interrelated challenges that the Europeanization of Italian governance has to confront. The first is the inability of the unified Italy, whether under the Savoy monarchs of Piedmont or later regimes, to build modern *national* good governance despite *local* islands of good governance having existed since the Middle Ages (in Italian northern cities, for instance: see Mungiu-Pippidi, 2015b, Chapter 3). The second is to make the development of rural southern Italy catch up with the north. The two are closely interlinked, and when wandering on the Ionian beach – recycling bins nowhere to be found – one is left wondering if the bottles left on the beach prove a lack of development, or a lack of civic culture, or both. It took another non-Italian after Banfield to point to the cultural explanation. Robert Putnam argued that the low-trust culture of the south reflected an inability to associate around common goals and that this resulted in poor governance, itself responsible for the ability of the region to catch up with the north (Putnam et al., 1994). Empirical tests on the determinants of corruption in Italy in the period 1963–2001 using statistics on crimes against the public administration at a regional level found some support for this thesis (Del Monte and Papagni, 2007). But while the Mafia used to be mostly in the South, the practice of offering kickbacks (*tangenti*) on public works that became notorious as *tangentopoli* was first identified in Lombardy and was clearly a national phenomenon.

Italy, a founding member of the European Union, is a country where elites have consistently and deliberately sought to resort to Europe or to external factors more generally to help improve the country's governance. This began with the end of the Second World War. Italy is a negative outlier in Europe and the world, as it has the largest disproportion between good human development and poor quality of governance. The poor ratings of Italian governance reflect a mix of three different streams feeding Italian "corruption":

1. *A lack of modern governance* associated with rural and poorly developed southern Italy, similar to that in developing countries (corruption as unfinished modernization, as in St. Augustin's "good is the absence of evil" paradigm), which had an important impact at national level by providing a stable vote basis for corrupt politics and a low-trust environment in which the Mafia survived (Gambetta, 1996).

2. *An organized crime/private protection industry with historical roots,* which even Mussolini's heavy-handed tactics could not disrupt (Gilmour, 2011, pp. 316–317). This industry has changed shape over time to adapt to opportunities and constraints, proving extraordinary resilient. Between 1983 and 2009, Italian mafias succeeded not only in resisting in their traditional strongholds but also developed a significant presence in the central and northern provinces, as shown by the Mafia Index (an indicator based on a combination of mafia-type associations, mafia hits, city councils dissolved for infiltration by organized crime, and assets confiscated). Thus the Mafia is no longer merely a southern, but a national problem (Calderoni, 2011).

3. *A modern state capture syndrome* with various status groups (of very diverse backgrounds) aiming to capture rents (most of them legal) and reduce competition, thereby also reducing meritocracy. Rent-seeking groups use diverse organizations in Italy to advance their interests (Freemasons, for instance, as well as ordinary trade unions). But what makes Italy exemplary is the historical instrumentalization of political parties as the main hierarchical vehicles of particularism, with the resulting syndromes of *partitocrazia* (division of the public sphere strictly across parties: see for instance Pasquino, 2006) and *lottizzazione* (division of management positions within public organizations among parties, notably within public media and the judiciary: see Mancini, 2009). While this syndrome in its very visible form looks like political corruption, the participation and in fact the agency of diverse groups in broader society where connections (*raccomandazioni*) rule over impersonal exchanges should not be underestimated, as it explains why such diverse political parties have behaved so similarly over the years (Hooper, 2015). The deep penetration of politically organized particularism into the public sector subverted the development of an autonomous bureaucracy and created a class of "partitocrats." These corrupt actors colluded regardless of election results in a country that had a tradition of manufacturing majorities by switching political allegiances (*trasformismo*), which led in time to a decline of electoral turnout in the most corrupt regions. This "competitive corruption" syndrome draws on the basic competition for resources that can be used to buy votes. Originally it was driven by intra-party competition among ruling Christian Democrats, but these behaviors remained unaffected by increased challenges from other parties and repeated changes of electoral system (Golden and Chang, 2001). Political competition has not been as effective as expected in the control of corruption, in part due to political

fragmentation.[3] At a deeper level, cross-party agreement has emerged on the practice and justification of legal particularistic allocations and illegal acts (such as kickbacks) as the means whereby parties fund their participation in the democratic processes and reward their constituencies (Della Porta and Vannucci, 2005).

5.3.1   How Corrupt Is Italy, Still?

The question of how much Italy's governance has progressed during its EU integration years is the source of much controversy. Transparency International's Corruption Perception Index claims that Italy has either stagnated or regressed during its EU years. Hard as it is to believe that Botswana (and more recently Namibia) are doing better than the developed country, just 11 percent of Italians think the country is better off now than before the *tangentopoli* cleanup, according to the pollster DEMOS (DEMOS 2017).The Eurobarometer also measures Italians' perception of corruption as going up rather than down (97 percent claimed that it was "widespread" in 2014 compared with 84 percent in 2007), but their direct bribery experiences are very low: only 7 percent knew someone who paid a bribe, and only 10 percent had ever been victims of corruption, according to the 2017 survey (EC, 2017g). From 2008 to 2017, 10 percent more Italians passed favorable judgment on how their government handled corruption, bringing the total of approval to over 30 percent (EC, 2017g). But disapproval was still the majority opinion. Businesspeople are more critical than ordinary citizens, with 49 percent considering corruption a problem for business and 48 percent complaining of nepotism in the public sector (Flash EB, 2013). The perception of the main corruption device exposed during the *tangentopoli* scandal, kickbacks (*tangenti*), is down to 7 percent, but tax evasion and VAT fraud are perceived as widespread by 51 percent of businesspeople (ibid.). Businesspeople are strongly skeptical that the anti-corruption campaign has managed to clean up politics, with 91 percent of them considering that bribery and abuse of power for private gain are widespread among the political class, 92 percent considering that corruption hampers business competition, 90 percent that bribery and personal connections make public services function, and 64 percent believing that business also works this way (ibid.). The expert panel behind the institutional ratings in the Global Competitiveness Report (GCR) is also

---

[3] Interview with Jean Monnet, Chair in European Studies, and Professor Sergio Fabbrini, LUISS, Rome, November 20, 2018.

fairly negative.[4] In fifteen years Italy has not budged from an average score of 3.5 on institutions (with 7 the best). While business protection and audit capacity are somewhat better rated (>4), expert judgment remains critical of government favoritism for companies, administrative burden, diversion of public funds due to corruption, and the inability to use the legal framework to change arbitrary administrative decisions – all scoring around 2 (GCR 2017) By and large, Italy has not gained in competitiveness since the GCR was first created, despite having reasonable ratings for health, education, and infrastructure and recently increasing its rating on innovation capacity as well. In a way, Italy proves that a country can develop beyond its poor institutions. Were economic stagnation and overindebtedness not such a problem, the lack of institutional quality might not even be an issue.

Some progress can be observed in a few fact-based indicators, even if it remains unacknowledged by popular perception. In 2009, 16.74 percent of Italian public procurement procedures were allocated without a call for tender, as registered by Tender Electronic Daily (TED) and recorded on Opentender.eu, an oversight procurement portal. By 2014, unadvertised public contract tenders had fallen to 7.69 percent. Moreover, in 2009 risky procedures employed in public tenders amounted to 18.6 percent, recorded in TED, while by 2014 they had declined to 10.3 percent, according to the same sources. The Italian National Anti-Corruption Authority (ANAC) reports that the number of procedures regarding "corruption for an act contrary to due diligence" decreased significantly from 769 in 2006 to just 14 in 2014. Similarly, the number of procedures regarding "corrupt behaviors of public employees" fell from 206 in 2006 to only 3 in 2014 (ANAC, 2014). OLAF also lowered the number of its investigations into improper Italian use of EU funds, from 13 in 2006 to 8 in 2016.[5] Similar declines had also been reported ten to fifteen years ago, however, and might be explained either by the shifts from one to another type of corruption over time, or by changes in the legislation, rendering

---

[4] The *Global Competitiveness Report* ranking is based on the Global Competitiveness Index (GCI), which was introduced by the World Economic Forum in 2005. Defining competitiveness as the set of institutions, policies, and factors that determine the level of productivity of a country, GCI scores are calculated by drawing together country-level data covering twelve categories – the pillars of competitiveness – that collectively make up a comprehensive picture of a country's competitiveness. The twelve pillars are institutions, infrastructure, macroeconomic environment, health and primary education, higher education and training, goods market efficiency, labor market efficiency, financial market development, technological readiness, market size, business sophistication, and innovation. The 2017–2018 report is available from the World Economic Forum at http://repo rts.weforum.org/global-competitiveness-index-2017–2018/press-release/

[5] *European Anti-Fraud Office*, European Commission website, https://ec.europa.eu/anti-fr aud/homeen

time series on corruption offences rather misleading, as Alberto Vannucci has remarked (2009).

The objective indicators on Italy's public integrity framework on Europam.eu shows that the country is above the European average on public procurement regulation and political funding regulation, albeit just slightly. It is also roughly on the average for politicians' financial disclosures, conflict of interest regulation, and freedom of information. In the Index for Public Integrity, Italy is not behind Namibia or Romania as in the Corruption Perception Index, but occupies the steady rank of twenth-seventh with a score of 7.89 (on a 1–10 scale). This implies, nevertheless, that during its EU years Italy has registered far less progress than a newer member state, Estonia, which ranks tenth with a score of 8.93. With the exception of trade openness, where Italy has reduced red tape and does very well, its scores for administrative burden and fiscal transparency are worse than its peers in Europe and its income group (IPI, n.d.). When Romano Prodi, Italian's reform-minded prime minister and European Commission chief, declared in 2013 that Italy still dealt with "Italian public administration and corruption" problems, he missed the connection between the two: poor regulation remained due to its potential to feed privileged access to rents (Della Porta, 2004). GCR respondents also complain of administrative burden and shifting regulations.

The capacity of the Italian media and civil society to constrain corrupt behavior is ranked at 24 to 26 out of 30 European countries surveyed. In other words, Italy presents a paradox: it ranks poorly on the causal determinants of public integrity for European countries, while its integrity itself is overregulated. Some have bravely attempted to reduce administrative discretion, notably the Monti government, which slashed ten of thousands of useless laws and regulations in an attempt at legislative simplicity (Gilmour, 2011). The IPI 2018, however, reflects the situation after many years of pro-business (Berlusconi) and technocratic (Prodi, Amato, Monti, Letta, etc.) governments (see Table 5.2). The moderate score on independence of the judiciary, despite Italian magistrates being notoriously "activist" against politicians, is due to the GCR's defining of independence of the judiciary as being "towards private interest." While the Italian magistrates' activism is acknowledged, allegations have always existed of partisanship and corruption. Notable critics from throughout the system admit that independence gets privileged above accountability in the design of the Italian magistracy (Di Federico, 2004). Furthermore, historical accounts of the fight against the Mafia have always highlighted, alongside stories of heroically fulfilled duty, collective action problems within the Italian judiciary: it is worth noting that Giovanni Falcone, the internationally famous anti-Mafia judge, has never managed to win a vote

Table 5.2 *Italy's public integrity framework compared*

Components	Component score	World rank out of 109	Regional rank out of 30	Income group rank out of 40
RESOURCES				
Administrative burden	8.90	39	23	28
Trade openness	10.00	1	1	1
Budget transparency	8.71	20	10	13
CONSTRAINTS				
Judicial independence	5.34	55	24	32
E-citizenship	6.85	36	26	35
Freedom of the press	7.53	32	25	31

Source: Index for Public Integrity

on the Superior Council of Magistracy (Italy's self-ruling supreme body for magistrates), either for his promotion or becoming a member (Stille, 1995, Chapter 18).

5.3.2   Where Could the EU Have Changed Italy (and Did It)?

Italians have bravely starting fighting corruption in the 1980s, and organized-crime-related corruption twenty years earlier – although only at local level and without much success. Policemen, magistrates, politicians, priests, and journalists fell victims to the fight – the modest scale of progress shown by the objective indicators and the pessimism of the subjective ones tend to obscure this effort. Moreover, part of the Italian elite consistently sought European Union integration over the years precisely as the means to bring about the government rationalization and modernization that Italians had somehow not managed by themselves (Ginsborg, 2001, pp. 240, 265, 306; Loughlin, 2004). But the process of "Europeanization" and "civilization" is deemed incomplete still.[6]

There are many reasons for this. The main one related to Italy is that the country arrived at anti-corruption tangentially rather than by grand design. When finally unfolding, Italian anti-corruption was excessively based on repression and not on broader reforms, as GRECO critically observed in its first review (GrecoEval1/2Rep[2009]2E). In particular, reforms needed to curtail legal privileges and to simplify a legislation meant for profit gatekeepers proved very hard to enact. In time, the

[6] Interview with Sergio Fabbrini.

activism of magistrates led to a counter-reaction from politicians (led by Silvio Berlusconi) and a true conflict between state powers. Legislation against corruption came out enfeebled. In part due to the failure to streamline the Italian judiciary's trial length and resolution procedures, public interest in the conflict between legislators and prosecutors has waned (Della Porta and Vannucci, 2007). Legislators apparently lost the immunity that had characterized their *casta* before the Clean Hands campaign (half the parliament was indicted, but most of the politicians arrested were never jailed). Thus the political party lost its role as a vehicle for organizing influence-peddling, but this might be only because more subtle and hidden vehicles emerged in the form of less obvious brokers (Della Porta and Vannucci, 2007). Once entrepreneurs politically instrumentalize anti-corruption from whatever quarters (media, politics, judiciary), its efficiency is lost (Sberna and Vannucci, 2013). By the end of 2018, a young deputy prime minister without any anti-corruption credentials, Luigi de Maio, was leading the anti-corruption camp, not some leading magistrate who had starred in the *tangentopoli* investigation – some of whom had meanwhile faced corruption investigations themselves. Populist parties, the Lega Nord (Northern League) and the Cinque Stelle (Five Stars), won in 2018 with a strong anti-corruption agenda, yet they are the Euroskeptic parties.

There are also EU-related causes to help explain why its influence was so weak in this area. The European Union could hardly have fought corruption *directly* in Italy, a founding member. Even for its own financial interests, the EU did not create a legal basis or agencies until quite late in its existence. The Audit Court, though founded in 1977, became empowered to supervise all EU funding only after the Treaty of Amsterdam, some twenty years later.[7] It policed the finances of the European Commission in particular, and with some impact, as its reports to the European Parliament provoked crises in 1984 and 1999 leading to the resignation of the Santer Commission. Corruption scandals also led to more empowerment of the Anti-Fraud Coordination Unit (UCLAF, created 1988), which later became OLAF (1999). UCLAF worked alongside *national* anti-fraud departments and provided the coordination and assistance needed to tackle transnational organized fraud. The lead role fell to national law enforcement agencies, though. The EU began to police its own funds more seriously only *after* the great Italian cleanup (Mario di Chiesa's arrest by di Pietro in 1992), which shook all of Europe.

---

[7] Treaty of Amsterdam Amending the Treaty on European Union, the Treaties Establishing the European Communities and Certain Related Acts. European Commission, signed 1997, entry into force 1999.

In fact, the corruption scandals of that time convinced the union that at least the appearance of an anti-corruption policy had to be established.

In 2003, the European Commission issued a report to the Council, the European Parliament and the European Economic and Social Committee "On a Comprehensive EU Policy Against Corruption" (COM [2003]317) and adopted the definition of corruption used by the United Nations' Global Programme Against Corruption. This included "abuse of power for private gain," which was and remains inadequate for understanding systematic corruption of the Italian type. The report's conclusion states for the first time that the fight against corruption should be the object of "a strong political commitment at the highest level," that both EU member states and EU institutions should develop and improve skilled staff to defend both national and EU budgets, and, finally, that anti-corruption should be linked with trade policies and accession of new members or special agreements (through political dialogue). As late as the end of 2018, the EU had still not adopted the recommendations that the European Community adheres to the Council of Europe's conventions on corruption and participates in its monitoring mechanism, GRECO, on one hand, and that similar integrity administrative standards be put in place across all EU public administrations. So, the EU could not have had a direct influence on Italy in this arena, even in theory. The rise of Silvio Berlusconi in the aftermath of *Mani pulite* created an unfavorable environment regardless. Despite many discussions in the European Parliament and constant negative European press coverage of his leadership, the Italian electorate had spoken and no legitimacy or tools existed at the time to intervene in the affairs of a member state.

Indirectly, however, the EU could have played a large role on both sides of Italy's suboptimal equilibrium. And it did, only this influence was more ambiguous and less consistent than needed. On the reduction of resources for corruption, for instance, Italian leaders insisted on Italy's participation first in the fixed current exchange system. Then the EMU arguably led to the rationalization of public expenses, drying up resources for clienteles at regional level and perhaps even triggering the unraveling of the anti-corruption spiral (Ginsborg, 2001, p. 252). From the end of the Second World War, there were individuals in every generation of Italian politicians who sought to include Italy in any form of European cooperation as a means to reform the country, from classic figures such as Sforza or De Gasperi to contemporary characters such as Romano Prodi or Mario Monti. Individuals among the Christian Democrats, socialists and technocrats, plus a consistent group at the Bank of Italy, have always used Europe as the main driver of change in Italy (Ginsborg, 2001). Their efforts produced some advances on administrative reforms, for instance on transparency, but got lost in the constant Italian belief that formal changes somehow condition substance as well – and therefore that only deep constitutional reform could change Italy (Bull and Pasquino, 2007). Italy is the world's number one example of incessant reform of the electoral system and of party funding – indeed, everything tried in Eastern Europe later on the advice of Europeans had been tried in Italy first. But the discarded institutions have existed in other EU countries without Italian-level corruption, which should have argued against a causal link and a fix by way of continuous institutional reform. Mario Monti, a former European trade commissioner, then prime minister, who enacted an anti-corruption law 190/2012 (COM[2014]38, (known as law Severino after Paola Severino, the then justice minister), arrived only after many years at this conclusion: "I gradually convinced myself that Italy's problems don't depend so much on the constitutional reform or the electoral law, but a few fundamental traits: tax evasion, corruption and a political class that uses the money of tomorrow's Italians as a barrier against its own unpopularity" (*Financial Times*, 2016). Although actions to reduce red tape and increase tax effectiveness have not exhausted their administrative potential (Business Anti-Corruption Portal, 2017), the difficulty of getting a majority around any legislative steps still tempts Italian politicians to turn to constitutional reforms aimed at solving collective action problems once and for all (Ceccarini and Bordignon, 2017). In fact, the anti-corruption legislation has never been optimal; given court inefficiency and defense lawyers' strategies, even by putting much emphasis on repressive anti-corruption Italy has not managed to make it effective.[8] After being elected in 2018, the populist Northern League–Five Stars coalition sought a shortcut by freezing the statute of limitations for corruption crimes at the level of first instance. Nothing else was deemed able to deliver results in a reasonable interval of time.

Despite increased European Commission intervention since the 2012 Fiscal Compact, controlling Italy's public debt also has remained an uphill battle – not due to bribes or other visible forms of corruption, but to the incapacity of arriving at optimal taxation and a reduction of the informal economy (the highest among old member states, although average as compared to new members [Medina and Schneider, 2017; IMF, WP/18/17]). The European Semester 2018 made three recommendations for Italy that covered direct corruption (statute of limitations, whistleblower protection), administrative reforms (on lagging regions in particular), and business environment improvements (recommendations 15–17, COM [2018]411). In 2013, immediately after the Fiscal

---

[8] Interview with Alberto Vannucci, Rome, November 12, 2018.

Compact was signed, corruption appeared for the first time in the recommendations (under number 11), alongside court effectiveness and the usual concern for the stability and growth pact indicators (COM [2013] 0362). Austerity did not deliver more public goods versus targeted ones, as Italy's politicians have great skill in directing funds to facilitate their reelection.[9]

Beyond keeping expenditures under control, which had little to do with corruption after the euro crisis, European integration actually brought supplementary resources for a problem that Italy had already tried to solve with money, unsuccessfully: the underdevelopment of the south. Italy's famous "Mezzogiorno problem" became the syntagma for failed development in economic textbooks. How much of the problem is due to specific history determining the present "culture," which in its turn determines economic performance, is still up for debate. Surely, when passing his "advanced" reforms, Frederick II also generated long-term negative consequences, for instance discouraging autonomous cities, which led to the urban underdevelopment of the south compared to the north (Kantorowicz, 1957). But as we cannot make right the past, our interest is rather in what EU funds could do to correct this situation or at least to avoid aggravating it. Much of the literature argues that administration is the channel through which institutions ("culture") determine economic outcomes. This leads to a vicious circle. Regions with clientelist culture and poor administrative capacity cannot absorb the highly bureaucratic EU funds. Funds then only profit regions with high-quality institutions (Becker et al., 2013; Ederveen et al., 2006; Beugelsdijk and Eijffinger, 2005), and act as a "resource curse" for the others (Del Monte and Papagni, 2007; Brollo et al., 2013). The evidence shows that administrative quality strongly mediates their effect on development (Milio, 2007). Italy set a pattern with its behavior with EU funds, being the first member country to display in full the poor institutional quality syndrome: a vicious circle of improvised planning and poor management leading to poor absorption (below Greece in many years) and endless scandals related to EU funds (Ginsborg, 2011). Poor capacity cuts across the state and does not refer to the executive alone: for instance, the length of civil trials in the southern region of Calabria is four to five times that of trials in developed northern regions such as Veneto (SWD [2017]132).

While some politicians see a beneficial EU effect in the creation of a bureaucratic elite capable of handling EU funds,[10] this capacity apparently

---

[9] Interview with Economics Professor Guido Tabellini from Bocconi University, Rome, November 27, 2018.

[10] Interview with former prime minister Enrico Letta, Paris, March 27, 2018.

varies according to the *initial* administrative performance of the regions. Thus, Basilicata and other southern regions profited less from EU funds due to poor absorption. A report of the Directorate-General for Regional Policy in 2017 on "lagging regions" singles out those regions as "low growth" rather than "low income," finding that Basilicata has not progressed significantly on competitiveness, from scores on the Program for International Student Assessment (PISA: skills mismatch, poor science attainment scores) to the share of its exports continuing to lag behind those of its southern neighbors, let alone the rest of Italy. This is clearly attributed not to poor investments (as roads have been built by now) but to investment "returns." The commission writes:

> Low-growth regions which have witnessed limited improvement in the quality of government, have not been capable of making the most of development and Cohesion Policy intervention and, as consequence, have also grown less and have been more exposed to the negative consequences of the crisis ... A sustained effort in order to address barriers in terms of government effectiveness, transparency and accountability is needed if the low-growth regions are to experience both sustainable levels of development and greater convergence to the rest of the EU." (SWD [2017]132)

With this clear conclusion, one would expect some *ex ante* conditions to unlock the obstacles that have so far prevented a judicious use of funds in such regions. Instead, a report textbox announces that Italy will devote EUR 828 million of cohesion funds to "address the quality and efficiency of the public administration at national, regional and local levels and of the judicial system," by reducing regulatory burdens, increasing transparency and access to public data, and improving administrative procedures through online services and digital inclusion. Another EUR 378 million will target the lagging regions Basilicata, Calabria, Campania, Puglia, and Sicilia to support the public administration in its fight against corruption and organized crime, for instance IT systems for public procurement, as if it had been the lack of money that had posed the main obstacle to transparency and enabled government favoritism so far.

Since its creation OLAF has conducted many investigations related to EU funds in Italy, but far less than press reports had called for, ending with the country eventually paying back the EU in some of the most notorious cases. For instance, EUR 420 million for the A3 Napoli–Salerno highway has been recuperated. Anecdotal evidence abounds on funds granted to Sicily or Calabria and used by local mobsters in cooperation with local politicians to secure reelection and launder money through green energy or other trendy projects. Yet evaluations of such funds come out positive on the whole, as they focus mostly on growth and job creation, not "institutional quality." However, the problems that surrounded various Italian projects – Expo 2015 in Milan, the Mose project that was supposed to protect Venice from rising waters of the lagoon, and the G8 summit in 2009 – could not be blamed on the South; they were all projects where kickbacks were paid, and they ended with huge scandals, demands to lift immunity of top politicians, and eventually arrests.

The explanation for why EU funds have not succeeded in breaking the vicious circle of the Italian south lies in the poor fit between theories of development underpinning EU funds and theories of institutional change needed for control of corruption. The connection between the two has always been loose – if any – and remains a source of much controversy. As EU funds are matched by co-funding by national or local authorities, a political establishment that is used to patronage as the default distribution mode gets even more resources and political leverage at its disposal through EU funds, and thus EU funds risk perpetuating pre-existing vicious circles. In building good governance, the south missed out primarily on civil society and collective action. EU funds did not help increase corruption constraints on local government; only where business communities managed to get their acts together to ask for effective and clean government were EU funds put to good use (Drápalová, 2016). But in most places, this did not happen. Quite to the contrary, the south has always had problems in creating a critical mass for civic action, due to massive brain drain and migration (to richer Italian regions). Despite awareness of this constant problem, counter-policies have never existed (Bonifazi and Heins, 2000). By and large, then, EU funds reinforced local power arrangements, and so indirectly they did not contribute to good governance at all, whatever other direct effects they might have had.

On the corruption constraints side, perhaps some indirect influence of the European Court of Justice ought to be mentioned. Italy has always trailed behind the union on all stages of the infringement proceedings, taking the longest time to transpose EU directives on average, a fact attributed to its being a powerful member state with limited bureaucratic capacity and a home to strong domestic veto players or plain corruption (Mbaye, 2001; Börzel et al., 2012). Many infringement cases touch on corruption in areas such as discrimination against foreigners, excessive length of legal settlements, and undue state aid. Italy was sentenced twice for noncompliance with a court verdict *after* losing the initial case. Its resistance may not be singular among big countries, but its persistence was rather exceptional: The European Court of Justice had to issue six rulings against the country in favor of teachers from abroad claiming labor discrimination (Hooper, 2015, p. 222). No substantive compliance from

Italy has been forthcoming, and a walk on Basilicata's beaches also reminds one that law enforcement should not be taken for granted. However, both private and public sector companies have become more transparent in time: when companies are publicly listed it becomes more difficult to use them as resources for party funding.[11]

Scrutiny of judicial independence and anti-corruption performance came mostly via GRECO, due to the lack of competence of other European institutions on the matter. Italy joined GRECO in 2007, only after many essential battles had already been fought. Its fourth evaluation round, launched on 1 January 2012, deals with "corruption prevention in respect of members of parliament, judges and prosecutors, after dealing with independence of the judiciary (round one), the executive branch of public administration (round two), and political financing (round three)" (GrecoEval4Rep [2016]2). The European Anticorruption Report of 2014 shared the view that Italian anti-corruption actors had staked everything on judicial repression; the report recommended corruption prevention instead, as the repressive approach had reached its limits and even provoked counter-reactions (EC, 2014b; Savona, 1995). In its most recent review, GRECO noted some progress, due mostly to the Monti government, with more repressive measures (harsher penalties, broader scope of corruption offences, stronger guarantees of more expeditious trials) complemented by comprehensive prevention mechanisms (freedom of information, addressing conflicts of interest, a national anti-corruption plan). ANAC became the coordinating body for purposes of corruption prevention and transparency of public administration. GRECO expressed some reservations towards the politicization of magistrates. However, it expressed its faith that the judiciary was governed by a very solid legislative framework enshrining its independence, both for judges and prosecutors, despite some controversies about their effectiveness (GrecoEval4Rep [2016]2).

Also, on the side of corruption constraints, the EU had almost no instruments to help the Italian media, except through political statements during Berlusconi's time. The European Parliament tried, but to no avail: a resolution condemning media concentration and lack of freedom was voted down in 2009.[12] The deeper reason why the Italian public did not resent Berlusconi's quasi-monopoly of commercial channels was its long-time resignation to *lotizzazione*. Although, arguably, several partisan sources are better than one dominant partisan source (Mancini, 2009),

---

[11] Interview with economics professor Guido Tabellini from Bocconi University, Rome, November 27, 2018.
[12] See www.ft.com/content/41f9a84c-be59-11de-9195-00144feab49a

once the public gets used to the concept that the media does not even aspire to objectivity, the condemnation of partisan media becomes more problematic. Also, unlike non-Italians, Italians knew very well that most politicians were alike.

The EU had several projects supporting e-government and digitization of Italian public services, but they remain significantly below the European average in this regard. Italians download official forms less and write fewer requests online, despite the creation of many roadmaps for an Agency for Digital Italy and despite countless initiatives by the commission and for the Open Government Partnership (EC, 2015a). The web page for public expenses transparency, Soldipubblici.gov.it, is directly relevant to the capacity of digital citizens to control corruption and quite a step forward, but expenses are not presented by invoice or contract, as they are on Opentender.eu or the Slovenian expense tracking portal. One can find out only aggregated information, e.g. how much Basilicata spent on public transportation contracts (*contratti di servizio di trasporto pubblico*) in 2018 compared to 2017. The absence of transparent public procurement data is a major obstacle to tracking Italian progress over time and therefore adjusting policy. A dedicated Italian think tank alleges that one contract in two might be corrupt, in view of the exorbitant cost per kilometer of railroad-building compared to other developed countries and the wild variation in costs across regions.[13] Costs allegedly still vary from EUR 47.3 million per kilometer between Rome and Naples, to EUR 74 million between Turin and Novara, to 79.5 million between Novara and Milan, reaching EUR 96.4 million between Bologna and Florence. They stand out compared to EUR 10.2 million per kilometer for high-speed rail links between Paris and Lyon, EUR 9.8 million between Madrid and Seville, and USD 9.3 million between Tokyo and Osaka, though it is not clear that sufficient controls were added to make these figures comparable (Ansa. it., 2016).

As GRECO has stressed in more than one of its evaluation reports on Italy, combating corruption has yet to become a matter of culture (GrecoEval4Rep [2016]2). The commitment to an open access society was not yet very visible as of 2018 in all sectors of Italian society. Nonetheless the unprecedented, though uneven, mobilization against the mafia over the last thirty years shows what a long way Italy has come. Populist parties, not civil society, reinvigorated the topic of

---

[13] CSAC is the Centro Studi Europeo sull'Antiriciclaggio e Antocorruzione, www.csac.it. On the specific costs, see the Italian news agency's report "Corruption 40% of Italy large-scale public works contracts" (ANSA.it, 2016).

corruption, showing that public discontent has not abated in the aftermath of the Clean Hands movement (Morlino and Tarchi, 1996). The Cinque Stelle won in 2018 with a radical anti-corruption program: e.g. reopening the question of statute of limitations for corruption crimes as a weapon against the old political class (although it is not clear if it was that policy, rather than their promises of cash delivery, that endeared them to voters). European media, exposing also the informal views of EU officials, expressed the hope that they would not be elected or not be able to govern. In the summer of 2018, Jean Claude Juncker, the commission's president, provoked an outrage by recommending Italians to work harder and be less corrupt (Horowitz, 2018).

However, by 2017, Italy's top Forbes capitalists were its post-war industrialists and traders, not the Corleone family and their like. Berlusconi was the only notorious political name among brand names such as Ferrero, Armani, and de Longhi (*Statista*, 2018). The technocrats who had worked on the anti-corruption legislation pinned their hopes on ANAC, although they were aware the agency was not strong, while broader civil society involvement seemed to sink in the populist frenzy. The main lesson learned from Italian anti-corruption is that the judiciary alone can hardly create an open society from one based on particularism; on the contrary, to attempt to do so would risk raising the worse populist instincts against any representative democracy. The Brazilian elections in 2018, after Judge Sergio Moro and his colleagues emulated the Italian Clean Hands campaign with their Car Wash operation, provided another confirmation: the anti-corruption majority turned to a right-wing general to be their president.

Europe has been the main incentive for and supporter of Italian reformers, even if the euro itself might not have been a blessing for Italy. Furthermore, Italy has progressed within Europe, although less than its reformers had hoped. The mix of intended and unintended consequences of EU integration did not prove a strong enough cocktail, however, to overcome some of Italy's chronic collective action problems – forever wrongly addressed as principal agent problems – thus playing again and again into a vicious circle where politicians, bureaucrats, and voters ended by supporting the status quo (Golden, 2000). One has to recall that Tomaso di Lampedusa warned us, in his *Leopard*, that everything changes only in order to stay the same in Italy.

5.4 Greece: A Missed European Opportunity?

In the summer of 2018, Donald Tusk, president of the European Council, tweeted to Greek citizens: "You did it! Congratulations Greece and its people on ending the program of financial assistance. With huge efforts and European solidarity, you seized the day" (*The Guardian*, 2018). For many Greeks and external observers, the message was quite cryptic. What day did the Greeks seize? What does this success consist in? Leaving aside the partial repayment of debts (many contracted to repay the original debts), have the inbuilt structural problems in the eurozone, for which Greece has only limited responsibility, really gone away (Rodrik, 2010)? Have Greek institutions – for which Greeks were shamed in the eyes of the entire world as an irresponsible people who nearly brought down all of Europe – really improved? Has Europe managed – at the price of Greek GDP dropping to a level matching that of fifty years ago – to "modernize" and "Europeanize" the Greek state? Was it Greece that was saved, or only the euro?

To answer these questions, we need to go back in time considerably. We may look back to the year 2000, when Greece, an EU member since 1991, was preparing to join the eurozone and was busy organizing the forthcoming Olympic Games. It used lavish EU funds (as well as its own) to build subways, airports, and soccer stadiums. In 2000, a deposit of 250,000 German marks was made into a Swiss bank account to support the reelection of the Greek minister for transport and communications, a member of PASOK (the Panhellenic Socialist Movement party). It was just part of a payment scheme undertaken by the German technology company Siemens to get public contracts in Greece in the run-up to the 2004 Olympics. This was no isolated incident. According to the German media, even Deutsche Bahn had to pay bribes to get a share in the infrastructure preparations in Athens (*Der Spiegel*, 2010). The transportation minister and the local Siemens representatives were among the few sentenced (years later), after acknowledgement of their faults, a guilty plea, and a legal settlement by Siemens. In reference to the same year, 2000, the European Anti-Fraud Office's activity report mentions Greece only once in 51 pages and 19,769 words, thus: "Bananas mainly entered the Community via Belgian and Italian ports, although similar operations have been identified in Spain, Portugal, Greece and Germany." Nothing else from Greece was deemed worth reporting by OLAF in 2000–2001.

And yet the warning signs were there. An economist educated in a top American university held, for one term, a top management job with a government agency distributing lavish EU funds and discovered that preferential contracts were the rule and not the exception. There were no rules whatsoever against conflict of interest, and a few known party brokers intermediated all the contracts.[14] At about the same time, a

---

[14] Interview with anonymous source, Athens, March 12, 2018. Confirmed from two additional sources.

young lawyer at a publicly owned company received a handwritten note from the wife of a top government official, indicating who should win a public contract.[15] The economist even tried to call OLAF, which flatly refused to investigate. Being Greek, however, he remembered he knew a countryman who was in the international anti-corruption business and called him. The latter called the then boss of OLAF, who finally obliged by opening an investigation. By the time the investigation had been completed, the whistleblower was no longer in charge of the agency. OLAF made no conclusions on the operating mode and only recommended that the brokers be pursued by local prosecutors. A long domestic investigation began. Meanwhile, the whistleblower found a bomb under his car, and the police proved unable to find the culprit. He became completely isolated as the person who tried – unsuccessfully – to denounce a lucrative system, which had met with no local complaints before. He sold his properties to pay for his family's security as years went by and the investigation dragged on. Eventually, Greek prosecutors decided that the systemic character of the problem required that more people needed to be pursued. They therefore extended the investigation to the entire boards of the agency during the years in question, including the whistleblower himself. As of 2018, the by then enormous investigation had stalled.

This story may seem more coherent with hindsight than it looked for its actors in its early days, and yet again a timely warning was present. Writing in the first round of the GRECO evaluation report in 2001, the Council of Europe found that fewer than five final sentences had been passed for corruption-related crimes in a year, and argued that "implementation of the relevant international instruments [e.g. the OECD Anti-Bribery Convention] cannot *per se* constitute an effective strategy for fighting corruption" in Greece. The GRECO experts found that little indeed was known or could have been known about corruption in a country where court statistics were not transparent and no evidence existed on how many corruption offences had been prosecuted, investigated, or sentenced, let alone on how many took place (GrecoEval1Rep [2001]15E). Furthermore, not even the number of civil servants was known, let alone the number of those working in the areas of control, auditing, or handling corruption in any way.

But it was not only the Greek authorities who were unconvinced of the existence of systemic governance problems in 2000. The European authorities also turned a blind eye to the warning that Greek statistics

---

[15] Interview with anonymous source, Athens, March 9, 2018. Evidence was shown to the author.

showing the country's readiness to join the newly introduced common currency, the euro, were improving a bit too spectacularly. As the BBC reported in 2012, some magic had made inflation and public deficit vanish away, raising the alarm among well-informed bank analysts, among others. How did it work? For instance, "the Greek state railway ... was losing a billion euros a year [and] had more employees than passengers. A former minister, Stefanos Manos, had said publicly at the time that it would be cheaper to send everyone around by taxi ... The [railway] company would issue shares that the government would buy. So, it was counted not as expenditure, but as a financial transaction" (*BBC News*, 2012). As such, it did not appear on the budget balance sheet, so Greece fulfilled the Maastricht Criteria and was admitted to the eurozone on January 1, 2001.

In 2016, I asked one expert in charge of good governance in the "troika" – the informal name by which the international intervention into the Greek crisis is known (including the EC, the International Monetary Fund and the European Central Bank) – whether the quality of governance had improved in Greece during the bailout years and, specifically, whether corruption had decreased.[16] As the main integrity-related activity at that time consisted mostly in organizing ethics training for public servants (as if their ethical ignorance was to blame for Greece's corruption), and because no indicators on public integrity had been monitored since the start of the troika's intervention, nobody could answer whether Greece had changed for the better or not. Yet EUR 288.7 billion later (the cost of the bailout) we should be able to answer this question.

To understand the impact of the EU's intervention in Greece, three elements should be considered:
1. the nature and extent of the corruption problem in Greece before it joined the EU and the eurozone;
2. the EU's influence in full, with its intended and unintended consequences, of which the EU intervention on good governance and the quality of institutions was only a small part;
3. the extent to which Greece had changed by the time of Mr. Tusk's congratulations at the conclusion of the Greek bailout.

5.4.1   How Corrupt Was Greece, Actually?

By the time of its eurozone accession, Greece had passed 6 on the 1–10 recoded CoC scale (an increase of 0.50 on its original scoring), so it was a

---

[16] Focus group in Athens organized by ELIAMEP and conducted by the author, March 2016.

borderline country approaching good governance (see Figure 5.6). From 1998 to 2000 it was even upgraded. But then with the scandals related to its statistics manipulation, the mishandling of public contracts in the run-up to the Olympics, and finally the crisis, the score only went down. To be certain, the Greek case shows how much perception indicators lag. Neither experts nor politicians complained about Greek corruption loudly, despite anecdotal evidence abounding prior to 2000. But when the crisis hit, it was like a boxer whose powers have been overestimated and whose entourage thrives on fixed match bets, and who, wanting to keep his rating high, one day picks an unfixed game against a far stronger opponent. That was Greece's eurozone entry, which could still have worked had the global crisis not exacerbated the euro's structural problem of large differences in competitiveness across members. It was a knockout for Greece, and afterwards, post factum over-explaining flooded the world. The experts who had given good marks to the PASOK government in 2000 were quick to slash them, exactly when better governments were trying to fix the mess. Many experts recalled that Greece had defaulted five times in modern history, starting with 1826 – so it must have been doomed to fail. But Spain had defaulted twice as many times, as had many other countries. The independent Greek state had indeed been born indebted to foreign powers who had supported Greek independence, but only with an interest. Such loans plagued the small country all through the nineteenth century, when other explanations than corruption were far more plausible for its economic difficulties (Clogg, 2013). Greece had a poor fit for modernization from the outset, as it became independent with the poorest rural areas inhabited by Greeks, but leaving the great Greek trading cities in the Ottoman Empire. Had the situation been otherwise, its economic development might have been an altogether different story. However, as Barrington Moore Jr. remarked, the explanation for the politics of small states in southeastern Europe lies mostly outside their own boundaries (1966). Nevertheless, the literature on Greece, including by the Greeks, abounds in historically determinist explanations that trace the contemporary default back to that of 1826 and see everything in between as a consequence of poor governance. As Loukas Tsoukalis reasoned: "Nobody can seriously argue that Greece was caught in the storm as an innocent victim. Its vulnerability has been the product of numerous mistakes and failings. And perhaps unavoidably, Greece has received a great deal of international attention, much of it negative and often undeserved" (2016, p. 4).

In 2000 the Eurobarometer still did not deal with corruption at all. Corruption was perceived as largely a non-European problem, confined to the developing world. Transparency International Greece, however, had commissioned a survey that the first GRECO review report quoted at

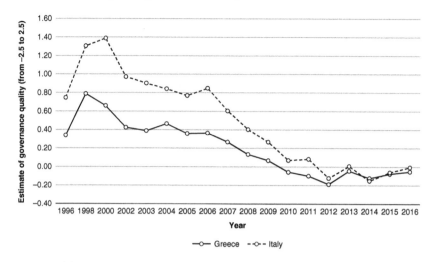

Figure 5.6 Evolution of control of corruption in Italy and Greece, 1996–2016
Source: World Bank Control of Corruption indicator 1996–2016.

length. Their February 2001 opinion poll showed that 45 percent of the 920 respondents admitted to having given a bribe or "backhander" and 18 percent to having taken advantage of "connections." Of the former, 42 percent said that if they had not bribed, their application or request would have been unsuccessful; 39 percent claimed to have answered a solicitation for a bribe; 23 percent claimed they had bribed out of fear of adverse consequences; 38 percent said they had conformed to what they were told was common practice or a "certain form of obligation." The practice affected mostly hospitals and the tax department, but no sector was free from bribery. People bribed utility services, general administrators, and law enforcement officials as well. GRECO commented that the "backhander" was quite universally perceived as an indispensable element of cutting through excessive red tape.

Being deprived of data and defining corruption mostly as bribery, the GRECO report saw only the tip of the iceberg (the Greek government rejected the Transparency International survey as unscientific). Illegal corruption of this type was grounded in particularism as a widespread behavior, in an economy with extensive rent creation and a society that was far from open. For one thing, nepotism penetrated politics and the administration to a very high degree. It appeared normal that political parties were often run by dynasties, and the political class was nearly a caste, "an oligarchy in all but name" (Eleftheriadis, 2014). For another, the administration was so highly politicized that one could hardly speak of an autonomous bureaucracy. In ADEDY, Greece's single confederation of civil service unions, in 2010 the share of collateral organizations that were party-led was 45 percent for PASOK, 28 percent for center-right New Democracy, 11 percent for Syriza, and 10 percent for KKE (communists), which left practically nobody independent of a political party (Sotiropoulos, 2018, Table 4). No private competition was allowed for places in the notoriously closed and nepotistic higher public education system (Mitsopoulos and Pelagidis, 2007) and needless restrictive regulation created an abundance of rents, benefiting such diverse groups as taxi owners, university professors, manicurists, lawyers, and truck drivers. These gatekeepers and rent-seekers enjoying legal "privileges" were accused of Viking-like behavior, mining the budget for their own short-term benefit and forming ad hoc alliances to resist any change (Mitsopoulos and Pelagidis, 2009). Getting a building permit took more time in Greece than anywhere else in Europe (198 days) and paying taxes required 19 payments per year and 264 hours, according to the World Bank's Doing Business survey.[17] Government activity was notoriously opaque: despite widespread internet use, there was no public disclosure of government spending on procurement. Information on the allocation of EU funds was not accessible online either, and, due to the absence of effective freedom of information legislation, it was difficult to obtain it even on paper. Courts did not publish any opinions and public audits were confidential, not public. As in all societies where particularism reigns, the state functioned mostly for the benefit of those who had connections or money for bribes (Mungiu-Pippidi, 2015b) – the rest took refuge in the shadow economy, where Greece has always been an outlier among the EU-15. The dark side of the economy was therefore at the same time a substitute for corruption and a complement to it, limiting the development of the official economy (Katsios, 2006). Estimates show that the Greek shadow economy *rose* from 22.6 percent of the official GDP in 1990 to 28.2 percent in 2004, the highest among OECD countries, Italy's shadow economy being 22.2 percent of GDP and Spain's 19.8 percent. In comparison, the United States had 7.8 percent and Switzerland 8.3 (Schneider, 2010). The inverse link between the quality of institutions and the strength of the shadow economy is very strong. Poor regulation, abundant red tape, and high tax burdens, on top of discriminative treatment by the state authorities, are the main determinants for individual entrepreneurs deciding to engage outside the official economy (Schneider, 2010).

---

[17] Historical data for Doing Business, results aggregated 2004–2008 (World Bank, 2018a).

On top of the above, huge EU funds and the boom created by the Olympics provided large resources for corruption around the time of Greece's euro accession. Greece in 2000 was atypical for a corrupt country, as it had been growing and apparently catching up to the EU economic average despite its poor governance and significant ongoing rents. Drivers of its growth were easy access to credit and EU inflows, which financed consumption, but productivity did not catch up and Greece did not become more competitive. The rapid growth of the 1990s "has made the extraction of rents even more lucrative in this environment of weak institutions and weak governance" and may ultimately explain why the interest groups did not try to obstruct the credit market reforms for euro accession: they did not perceive the changes as fundamentally threatening their rents (Mitsopoulos and Pelagidis, 2011).

The Greek economy therefore represented a paradoxical environment of strong crony capitalism where government regulations shaped the rents but without social loss, due to economic growth and incoming EU funds. Does this also mean that there were no losers from this system of economic privilege? This is hardly possible. Obviously, the losers would have been many, as access to so many opportunities was strictly controlled. But patterns of protest in Greece have never displayed a universalist agenda. Rather, protests both before and after 2000, and in particular after 2009 when they reached a climax, were associated with the preservation of group rents and not the universalization of some public good. In other words, the society had always been structured on the particularistic lines of interest groups who were vertically integrated by means of mass patronage parties, primarily PASOK since its assumption of power in 1981 (Mouzelis, 1986). Party patronage today is no longer the benign means of increasing political participation that it was in the nineteenth century. It is now the core structuring device for particularistic allocation of public resources. It is also the main factor for the subversion of administrative capacity, in that it prevents meritocracy in the selection and promotion of personnel. Societies structured as competitive groups of clients do not enjoy any advantage from elections, because only the winners change but not the rules of the particularistic game (Mungiu-Pippidi, 2006a; Piattoni, 2001). Greece is a notable case, in that the main constraints to corruption – civil society and enlightened voters – did not function: patronage delivered the goods to the population and kept voters mobilized within pyramidal structures based on self-interest. In the words of a top intellectual, "civil society in this country has always been about gaining more for oneself,"[18] with consideration of public interest coming second. A

---

[18] Interview with law professor Maria Gavouneli, University of Athens, member of the European Commission DG Home expert group, March 9, 2018.

broad alliance has never materialized around an ethical universalist agenda, despite instances of brave attempts at reform (e.g. a merit-based civil service reform bill, brought in 1994 by minister Anastasios Peponis and later spoiled by tens of amendments; or the creation of an ombudsman office). Those seeking change either lost morale or chose the "exit option" that attracts the best and brightest: Greece has always had very high brain drain. "Civil society in the Western sense does not exist here because there is no market for it," a Greek economist told me. "We have a lot of protests because people have learned that direct bargaining in one's own interest works better than changing the rules of the game for everybody. There are no successful examples of the latter."[19]

The mass media in Greece appears very much captive to this particularistic setting: Freedom House rates it as free, but the dominant approach is hardly the provision of objective information as in the Anglo-Saxon media model. The Greek media strictly covers the interest of its owners and the groups sponsoring them, among whom are individuals whose fortunes came from the usual mix of privileged access to the energy market, golden concessions, and public contracts (Eleftheriadis, 2014). Media outlets offer support for governments who protect their privileged access. The Greek media "trade their ability to guide the opinion of the uninformed public in exchange for favors they receive from the executive, legislature, and administration" (Mitsoupoulos and Pelagidis, 2009, p. 409).

One of the key constraints needed for control of corruption, the judiciary, is deemed generally free in Greece, but its freedom is severely limited by the magistrates' partisanship, by corruption, and by *de facto* immunity for top politicians. It has also been strikingly untransparent. The GCR rates Greece's judicial independence the lowest among the EU-15, with a score of 5.5 on a scale of 1–10, in line with its score on corruption control (see Figure 5.7). In its first round of reports from 2001, GRECO commented that the suspending of immunity for government members by parliament (because they too had been members of parliament) did not really work. There were also few convictions for corruption.

The final diagnosis by 2000 was therefore that Greece was a country where particularism was the norm, rife with connections and legal rents (privileges) that even outweighed bribery. Most corruption was "legal," as laws abounded with rules that in fact restricted competition and granted privileged access to the beneficiary interest group. Illegal corruption functioned mostly as a way to facilitate access or equalize market advantage. Greece's good control of corruption scores in CPI and CoC were based on a restrictive definition of corruption as mere bribery. This

---

[19] Interview with Michael Mitsopoulous, Brookings Institution, Athens, March 11, 2018.

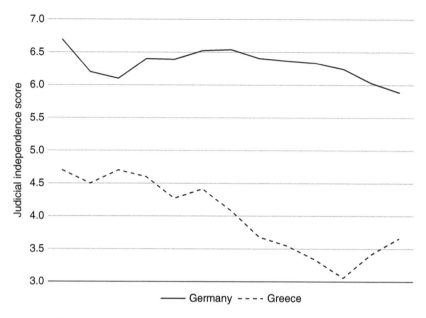

Figure 5.7 Evolution of Greek judicial independence compared to that of Germany, 2001–2014 (expert score of 1–7 with 7 the best)
Source: Global Competitiveness Report, World Economic Forum

was revised only after the crisis, when it turned out that particularism itself could generate social loss of catastrophic proportions. The system was a suboptimal equilibrium, fairly stable, and uncontentious, as high economic growth and EU funds prevented those marginalized from perceiving great loss due to constant political intervention in social allocations. While gains were very unequal and generally not merit-based, the losers did receive some compensation (for instance, no crackdown on the taxation of small businesses/professions or on the subcontracting of EU funds to SMEs from large companies). And henceforth Greece seemed to do well and even converge with developed Europe. It was all based on a complete misunderstanding of what corruption is (seeing it as just illegal bribes) and how it manifested itself in Greece in particular, a paradigmatic case of competitive particularism.

5.4.2   How Did the EU Contribute?

The EU's good governance intervention in Greece was partial and belated, and it must be understood in the context of overall EU influence over Greece. A donor-dependent country since its creation through loans from the great European powers, Greece is the center of a vast body of literature dealing with "Europeanization." The best of it has always discussed in earnest the fact that Greek society needs to "catch up" with modern Western Europe and that governance remained a challenge even after Greece joined the EU (Mouzelis, 1986; Featherstone and Papadimitriou, 2008). Still, no actual EU "intervention" for good governance would have come about had Greece not joined the Economic and Monetary Union (EMU) in 2000, based on a number of criteria such as inflation rate, budget deficit, public debt, long-term interest rates, and exchange rate, and using 1999 as the reference year. Joining the EU but not the eurozone would have probably spared Greece from confronting its particularistic governance. In principle, adopting the EMU comes with some requirements on quality of governance as well (on the fiscal and financial management side). But because all the legislation related to the EMU bypasses regular channels (e.g. consultation, studies on feasibility and impact), such requirements went almost unnoticed – so they would have never managed to change much.[20] Aware of the difficulties of respecting the criteria even after adopting the euro, the incoming New Democracy government commissioned an audit in 2004. It revealed that differences in methodology with Eurostat as well as some cheating practices (pioneered in Italy and other countries by Goldman Sachs and other banks) had beefed up the indicators, showing Greece as being fitter for the euro than it actually was (Eurostat, 2004; Piga, 2001)

Joining the EMU was not the first strain on Greece's capacity since its entry into the European Union. The absorption of EU funds has also been a major hurdle, to such an extent that the impact of the funds was relegated on the second plan for many years (ELIAMEP, 2013). For decades, average EU transfers ranged from 2.4 to 3.3 percent of the country's annual GDP. Since 1981, Greece has been a major beneficiary of EU funds (European Regional Development Fund, European Social Fund, Cohesion Fund, and structural support for agriculture). The EU's structural aid – about EUR 15.3 billion for 2014–2020 – has financed thousands of projects all over the country in almost every sector, from road infrastructure to human resource training (Liargovas et al., 2016). And yet the funds and their management were a mixed blessing at best. Greece's institutional framework could hardly absorb funds that had very high bureaucratic requirements, not all of them unnecessary – environment or geological evaluations, for instance. Since the structural fund's fundamental objective is to support economic and social cohesion across

---

[20] Interview with Michael Mitsopoulous, Athens, March 11, 2018.

and within the member states, the EU's evaluations have generally been positive, finding that the Greek projects do lead to job creation and other palpable benefits. A policy and administrative network was created within the Greek administration to absorb the funds. It has evolved due to various policy shifts at the European level and improved impact with the help of Brussels. But these structures never managed to improve the Greek administration's transparency, planning, or management capacity. Instead, they functioned in parallel as an archipelago of superior-capacity islands within traditional administrative behavior (Andreou, 2010). To manage absorption, a lot of corners were cut (e.g. having a fair and meaningful process for awarding building permits), and those corners represented exactly the governance areas in need of reforms. OLAF has never had much impact (a handful of investigations in total) in a country where the wife of the top party leader passed out slips of paper designating winners of major public works contracts. In fact, evidence abounds that OLAF deliberately refrained from intervening, even when whistleblowers did everything to push for it (*Spiegel Online*, 2013). Corruption schemes with EU funds in Greece took both legal forms (preferential "public" contracts) and illegal guises (fake research, for instance, or politicians' wives teaching hundreds of well-paid hours of "vocational" training during their holidays). The European Court of Auditors produced some occasional, critical reports on wasted money. But these were all in line with its mission focusing on individual cases, so it could not compensate for the absence of a systemic approach. "First there was boom, and nobody in Brussels wanted to hear about governance, absorption and catch up were the problem," a local analyst explains. "And then the bust came, and the recovery of the debt became the priority, with governance completely sidelined again." The lavish spending of EU funds also meant that "Everybody got a rent, who was not connected enough to get a public contract got a sub-contract from somebody who was connected, or a job, or a consultancy. It was not raining, but pouring with EU money, and that the money was distributed on the old system of connections did not seem important to anybody."[21] "Europe is fed up with Greece," one of the regulars from the Greek counterpart of the troika told me. "Now when the final bailout term is up, what they want to do is call it a success, unplug the life supporting systems and show that the person who came on a stretcher to the emergency room now walks out on her own legs. We're not going to look more closely, because the goal is to release her from the hospital to her own care."[22]

---

[21] Focus group in Athens organized by ELIAMEP and conducted by the author, March 2016.

[22] Interview on March 12, 2018; source chose to remain anonymous.

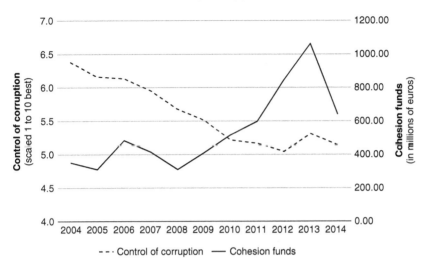

Figure 5.8 EU cohesion funds and control of corruption, 2004–2014
Source: OECD – QWIDS Official Development Aid and World Bank
Control of Corruption

European funds, in conclusion, were a tremendous resource for corruption in Greece, and the modernization of the administration that they
were supposed to provide pales in comparison to the many wrong incentives created by the regulatory shortcuts, the excessive red tape, and the
lack of transparency in their allocation. An illustration of the perverse
relationship between EU funds and the quality of governance can be seen
in Figure 5.8.

The economic crisis, however, should have brought important opportunities for reform by boosting constraints and cutting resources for corruption. The twofold intervention – from the crisis itself, causing resources to
dry up, and then of the troika, through the bailout program – was massive.
The first Economic Adjustment Program for Greece laid out detailed
conditions in the form of a full economic and financial program in
exchange for stability support to Greece via bilateral loans centrally pooled
by the European Commission (EC, 2010c). The main goals of the program
were, as expected, to restore confidence and maintain financial stability, to
enhance fiscal consolidation, and to reassure markets on the determination
of the authorities to do whatever it takes to secure medium- and long-term
fiscal sustainability. Consolidation, the EC appreciated, should rely on
measures that generated savings in public sector expenditure and improved
the government's revenue-raising capacity. It was clearly stated that the

program should also address the *causes* of the crisis by dealing with public administration reforms and measures to fight against corruption and tax evasion, under the title of "structural policies." The original document had 104 pages and mentioned the word "corruption" only twice. The subsequent memorandum of understanding went deeper to include not only important reforms against narrowly defined corruption but also measures to prevent rent creation and rationalize the government. For instance, take its words on the "modernization" of public administration: "Fragmented employment practices will be reformed by reorganizing recruitment procedures and finalizing the single payment authority for wages. A simplified remuneration system will be introduced, in a cost saving manner that will cover basic wages and all allowances that apply to all public sector employees. Procurement practices would be strengthened to generate efficiency gains and ensure transparency" (EC, 2010c, p. 48) The health care system, which had major expenditure overruns, was supposed to be overhauled through reforms in management, accounting, and financial systems. Below the central government level, a reorganization was planned to reduce the number of local administrations and elected/appointed officials. The government and the EC pledged to launch an independent external functional review of the public administration at the central government level. These reforms were aimed at prioritizing government activities and strengthening the fight against waste and corruption throughout the public administration. Furthermore, another objective was "[i]mproving the business environment and bolstering competitive markets." This objective proposes that

[t]he government will shortly adopt legislation establishing one-stop shops for starting new enterprises to cut procedures, costs and delays. Legislation will be introduced to cut licensing and other costs for industry. The government will fully implement key steps of the EU Services Directive in 2010, especially in priority areas such as tourism, education and retail. Over the course of next year, restricted professions will be opened by reducing fixed tariffs and other restrictions in the legal, pharmacy, notary, engineering, architect, road haulage, and auditing professions. The role of the Hellenic Competition Commission (HCC) will also be strengthened. Network industries will be progressively liberalized, especially in the transport and energy sector while strengthening regulators in these sectors in line with EU policies.

And finally, for another crucial area, state-owned enterprises, the document stated that "these need to be subject to greater transparency to increase efficiency and reduce losses. As a first step, 2009 financial statements audited by chartered accountants of the ten largest loss makers will be published on the internet. A time table and action plan for improving the financial performance of main loss-makers, most notably in the railway and public transportation companies will be produced" (ibid., pp. 48–49). European Funds were not forgotten, although the stress was, as usual, on absorption: "The government will work closely with the EC to raise the absorption rate of Structural and Cohesion Funds" (IMF, 2010).

These provisions made a great deal of sense. They went to the root cause of the problems and could, if implemented, have reduced opportunities for corruption considerably. But how many of them were implemented in fact? Since the publication of this document, Greece has had four rounds of reviews, compliance reports, and renewed commitments. While some local analysts have voiced criticism for the marginalization of structural reforms in favor of fiscal policies and tax collection (to pay debts), several reforms should have had a quickly noticeable impact: a central digital procurement page, an automatic invalidation of unpublished tenders, a centralization of procurement and of competition for jobs in the public service, some administrative simplification cooperating with OECD, etc. What the troika soon learned, however, was that "the most corrupt republics have the most laws," as the Latin saying goes, and that changing Greece fast would be impossible – if any change could be effected at all. Important reforms required more legislative changes by parliament. Constitutional reforms were needed, as were ministerial orders and even lower-tier regulation or implementation decisions. For instance, going after the "Vikings" by liberalizing entry into certain semi-closed professions proved to be a very complicated legal affair. One law was passed – and nothing changed. More specific legislation was needed, and then yet more specific. Year after year passed and nothing was really implemented. To the European Commission's credit, its experts followed up on the topic. Nevertheless, on this and most essential reforms, the EC had to adopt a decision to activate an "enhanced surveillance framework" for Greece after the "successful" conclusion of the ESM stability support program on August 21, 2018. In the end, most of the reforms, even those enacted, were at best taking their very first steps.

In the latest (third) compliance report of March 2018, only one activity in a list of 110 (number 108) referred specifically to corruption. It says of political finance: "The authorities will amend legislation to fulfil all GRECO's recommendations on the funding of political parties and electoral campaigns in light of its October 2017 report." The report states this as completed, as authorities amended the legislation on political party financing with article 65 of law 4509/2017. But most activities in Section V, "A Modern State and Public Administration," were either packed into an "omnibus bill" or still in the stage of launching calls or passing regulation. The organization of the fight against financial crime (prosecutor orders), which asked that the new system of cooperation between justice and tax administration be made fully operational (activity number 12), was reported as "done," although the Greek government had barely passed legislation (law 4512/2018). So, in reality, there was no way the system could be operational. Activities 59–62, on the liberalizing of professions (from private medical clinics and engineers to manicurists and chauffeur services, as everything had been restricted before), were also wrapped up in the omnibus bill to be passed at the very end. So, by 2018, nothing had been implemented. The reforms of key institutions, such as revenue administration and the Hellenic Statistical Authority (ELSTAT), were also still up in the air. The situation was better on the reduction of administrative burden, as there was a special section dedicated to it.

As part of the comprehensive agreement reached in the Eurogroup statement of June 22, 2018, the Greek authorities made commitments to continue the implementation of all key reforms adopted under the ESM program and to sustain their objectives, as well as to complete certain key structural reforms initiated under the ESM program against agreed deadlines. On this occasion, Greece returned to the European Semester framework of economic and social policy coordination and therefore reentered a system of normal monitoring alongside the other EU member states that were signatories of the Fiscal Compact.

Due mostly to the unpopularity of the austerity policies, the troika operated in an environment of great hostility and massive protests, from street rallies to paralyzing strikes. Despite growing attention to language that stressed Greek "ownership" of the reforms, the Europeans did not enjoy any mass support for their intervention. Furthermore, they relied on the old establishment – the one blamed for the crisis – whose response was nevertheless more rational and less populist. Then came the backlash. The direct political consequence of the crisis and the European intervention was the wiping out of the old political establishment and the rise to power of a populist party, Syriza. Afterwards, pushed by bare necessities, the new party gradually turned less anti-European and came around, in the end, to agreeing to play the European game. But they did not make in-depth changes to governance practices.

5.4.3   How Corrupt Does Greece Remain after EU Intervention?

The crisis and its management both strongly raised awareness of corruption in Greece. In the aftermath, both citizens polled in the Eurobarometer and experts whose assessments were averaged in the CoC or CPI rated Greece as being worse off than in 2000. But from the height of the crisis to 2017 some redress was also noted by the respondents. Those who claimed

Table 5.3 *Greece's public integrity framework compared*

Components	Component Score	World Rank out of 109	Regional Rank out of 30	Income Group Rank out of 40
RESOURCES				
Administrative burden	9.06	24	16	20
Trade openness	9.28	33	27	25
Budget transparency	6.54	77	27	33
CONSTRAINTS				
Judicial independence	5.34	52	23	31
E-citizenship	7.18	29	22	28
Freedom of the press	5.21	63	30	35

Source: Index for Public Integrity

that they were personally affected by corruption decreased by 17 points, making those unaffected the majority (from 46 to 53 percent in Eurobarometer 470). Only 9 percent of Greeks claimed to have personally witnessed or experienced a corrupt act, and 7 percent of Greeks, in comparison to the European average of 4 percent, said that they have been asked or expected to pay a bribe in the past year (EC, 2017g).

A systematic review of the objective indicators in our model through the Index for Public Integrity allows us to investigate more in depth, however (see Table 5.3).

Greece ranks thirty-eighth of 109 countries in the world in the Index for Public Integrity, on a par with Croatia and Bulgaria, so well behind the rest of the EU-28 (see Table 3.5). Its worst performance is on freedom of the press, which started to decline in 2005 and collapsed after 2011, and for which it ranks last among EU member states. Greece's media is still captive to private interest and unable to fulfill the role of objectively informing public opinion. Alongside the various private interests are those of the government. Among the means of controlling the media are hidden ownership, preferential advertising, and legal harassment due to poor regulatory quality. The attempts to correct this, in particular through regulation, never went all the way and therefore did not achieve much effect. This does not mean that among the media and journalistic professions there are none who perform as they should. The falsification of the whole media landscape, though, as is often the case in particularistic countries, reduces the impact of objective voices. The media can hardly mobilize people following corruption investigations, for instance. According to Freedom House, press freedom collapsed in Greece from the start of stabilization reforms (2012): it dropped to the level of press freedom in the former Yugoslav states and has not recovered since (Freedom House 2012; 2018), due to poor police protection of journalists against violence, tough defamation laws, and a temporary closing of the public broadcast service.

Judicial independence has also regressed, with Greece being surpassed by Romania in South-Eastern Europe by 2017 and ranking 23 out of 30 European countries covered by the index (including Norway and Switzerland). Anecdotal stories on the Greek judiciary are altogether scary, such as judges who lose trials on Article 10 (freedom of expression) in the European Court of Human Rights and then are promoted to management positions in Greece's supreme court. Two former top judges went into politics; the union of magistrates closed ranks against the EU during the crisis. The government enjoys the constitutional privilege of having the final say on top judicial appointments, and there was little to no European reaction to the quality of nominations (including from the European media, which prefers to focus on Poland or Romania, for instance). Top prosecutors in charge of anti-corruption have recently stepped down, while prosecutions of top officials have not really progressed. As reported from the third round of GRECO reviews, between 2001 and 2010 demands were made to parliament to suspend immunity for 137 ministers and 137 deputies. For ministers, 5 demands were discussed but none granted. For other members of parliament (MPs), 108 were discussed and 15 were granted (GRECO 2010, p. 21).

The Greek parliament has continued to defend its legislation, claiming it does not grant immunity. What it does grant is discretion to a committee in the parliament that has always endorsed a very narrow definition of corruption to prevent cases from being investigated and going to justice. In a response to GRECO, the Greek authorities explained that under Article 83 Paragraph 3 of the Standing Orders the only reason for not lifting parliamentary immunity is in a case where the conduct attributed to the MP was carried out in the course of his/her parliamentary or political conduct (or if it is deemed that the prosecution has political motivation) (GrecoRC4[2017]20). According to them, the Committee on Parliamentary Ethics, which handles petitions to lift immunity, established the practice of not considering acts of corruption to lie within parliamentary or political conduct. The committee does not debate the substance of the political or financial implications of such alleged conduct, but only whether criminal conduct is alleged (ibid., p. 8). If this is the case, the MP's immunity gets lifted. Accordingly, in the period 2015–2017, the committee received 1 request to lift parliamentary immunity regarding unjustified pecuniary benefit, which was granted. Another 7 requests concerned political decisions and their economic effects or repercussions. The committee then debated the detrimental consequences of these decisions to the public finances; 2 requests were granted and 5 were denied. The authorities stress that in some of these cases, the MPs concerned were members of collegiate administrative bodies issuing decisions challenged as detrimental to public finance. From October 2015 to 2018, a total of 44 requests for lifting immunity were discussed and 14 were granted. In the previous legislature (February 2015–August 2015), 11 requests were discussed and 4 were granted (ibid.). The risk of political harassment through corruption prosecutions without merit is evoked frequently. The whistleblower case reported here is enough to show how prosecution can be highly inefficient, even on the pretext of investigating more in depth. The result can be gross injustice. Also, the case of indictment of EC Home and Justice Commissioner Dimitris Avramopoulos and other former ministers was widely seen as a political investigation orchestrated by the Syriza government, especially after Prime Minister Alexis Tsipras called for the lifting of his immunity. According to several sources, the case refers to favors traded between Novartis and individual public physicians, who had great latitude over orders. In the FPCA file on Novartis, the Greek politicians are not even mentioned (SEC, 2016).

Finally, civil society still does not manage to exercise sufficient constraints in Greece, because there are too few civil society institutions based on ethical universalism facing too many particularistic interests. The country ranks 22 out of 30 European states from the EU on e-users of government services, according to Eurostat. That simply means that there should be enough economic autonomy for Greek civil society to exercise some constraints on rent-seeking groups. But that does not seem to be the case. There are very few NGOs dealing with corruption; Transparency International had no office in Athens by 2018, just in Thessaloniki. No recent, fact-based TI report exists on either corruption or integrity. While the foreign media widely covered the story of a website reporting bribes, bribery is not and has never been the core corruption issue in Greece. There are no associations within professions to promote ethical universalism, such as alternatives to associations of lawyers, journalists, or medical professionals. Austerity measures and the anti-Greek stereotypes that have spread across Europe and the United States have only served to demoralize Greek civil society even further. The scarce attempts at reform or denunciation of corruption go unacknowledged. The governments ruling Greece after the demise of the military regime have not been equally corrupt, and some of them had members who tried in earnest to solve these problems. There were a few integrity champions in both establishment parties. But the European Union had no strategy to help them retain power. Rather, the EU treated the Greek ruling class as entirely responsible for the disaster. "They were only interested that whoever comes to power respects the signature of the previous government and pays the debts," a man familiar with troika business told me in Athens. "And this is how they ended up with partners who did not even tell them that it's not enough to pass a law to kill the Vikings, who *de facto* dragged their feet on most reforms, waiting for it all to pass, even subverting them." In other words, the European Union never embraced a political economy approach, and so it has never sought to empower those whose best interest was to change Greece. By 2018, DG Just was promoting a European directive on whistleblowing, but the troika could have installed a mechanism to encourage and protect Greek whistleblowers long ago. The media has not managed to distinguish even a few integrity champions. Therefore, Greece lacks much of what you can find in other countries where corruption is a problem: national or at least city-based civil society anti-corruption coalitions, as in the likes of Ukraine, Mexico, or Brazil. The anti-corruption discourse was confiscated by populists, who used it during the last elections against the old ruling elites. But it stopped there, insulating the "people" from the critics.

In Greece, however, not only elites profit from rents. Most of the elite respondents to my questions on how the crisis had changed the winners and the losers of particularistic arrangements were very pessimistic. Some top politicians paid the price, with a handful going to jail, but the patronage structure remained intact (Eleftheriadis, 2014). A process of gradual transfer to the new political winners ensued. Some new oligarchs managed to catch up with the old, but the structure of opportunities has not opened enough. Greek society after the crisis has not significantly progressed on openness. On the contrary, the crisis and the subsequent austerity drove away hundreds of thousands of well-trained young people and replaced old bribes for privilege to doctors (for instance, to get in front of the queue) with bribes for access, as access diminished.[23]

By 2018, Syriza was accepting in its ranks many of the old PASOK cadres who originally had been part of the vertical pyramids of patronage. So the odds are down that a culture of integrity, even if painted in some excessive red, might become the new norm of Greek political elites. On the contrary, the Syriza-dominated parliament was gradually reinstating the old privileges by 2018, removing some of the barriers to public sector growth put up during the crisis (since the new parties also have clients hungry for public employment), and allowing the relaxation of some harsh measures for the oversight of spending (such as a digital prescription mechanism for doctors). Greece was the EU champion of reforms

---

[23] Interview with Maria Gavouneli.

from 2014 to 2015 in the Index for Public Integrity (1.50 progress on a 1–10 scale), but from 2015 to 2017 the progress lurched (7.25 up from 7.10, with the same global rank, 38) (IPI, n.d.).

An examination of Greece's public accountability equipment (see europam.eu), which is only a partial sample of the reforms needed brings further insight, shows that Greece is now doing better than the European average on political finance legislation (where GRECO efforts were concentrated). It is close to average on public procurement and financial disclosures for politicians (behind East European countries), but only scores 26 of an average of 40 in Europe on conflict of interest, and 37 of an average of 56 on freedom of information (EuroPAM, 2018).

Constraints to corruption may not have really taken off after the crisis, but we should expect resources for corruption to have been cut, since the crisis itself should have dried up unaccountable funds used for patronage. The evidence is paradoxical, however. First, the World Bank Regulatory Quality expert average assessment shows a constant *decrease* of regulatory quality, not an increase. This should have raised a red flag for the troika: it decreased on a par with the closely correlated control of corruption. The administrative burden, the target of so many reforms, has risen to 7.9 against the EU-28 average of 8, but is still behind the reform poster-country, Estonia. Following the impressive rise on IPI prior to 2015 (see Figure 5.6), progress slowed down. In 2017, Greece still ranked 16 out of 30 on administrative burden, 27 out of 30 European countries on import–export red tape (trade openness), and 27 out of 30 on budget transparency. This is not a good performance by any account, and these areas are directly and closely correlated with control of corruption. Nominally, many have been addressed, but in practice they need secondary legislation to be implemented and many reforms have not been. It took Estonia, under Prime Minister Mart Laar, less than two years to move from the cumbersome Soviet legislation to a modern one, with the state fully reorganizing itself in the early 1990s. For Greece, the years since 2000 have not brought sufficient change due to entrenched aspects of Greek legalism and formalism, with informal practices nearly always violating or ignoring formal rules and often-conflicting regulations resulting from client–patron relations (Spanou, 1996, 2008; Sotiropoulos, 2004). It was bound to be difficult for the troika to navigate this regulatory labyrinth without any guiding thread.

Spokespersons of the European Commission sometimes express concern that too much backtracking from agreed-upon policies is connected to the politically correct formulation of weaker "ownership" of reforms (Chrysolora, 2018). No "ownership" of good governance reforms seems to have materialized in the bailout years, although traces could be found during a few previous New Democracy governments and even PASOK ones (under Costas Simitis and George Papandreou). And here lies the core of the problem: the human agency behind these reforms. As in the Balkan countries, the real driver of reform in Greece has been the EU itself, but the EU's good governance interventions on record are poorly connected with real local political agendas. The interventions occur in a parallel existence of their own. The question arises as to whether EU intervention does not actually depress and disincentivize instead of supporting domestic agency, by imposing a formal, top-down, and bureaucratic good governance agenda, which becomes the sole official agenda. The few countries that have been successful in progressing towards good governance in our times have had their own political dynamics and their own good governance entrepreneurs: politicians, lawyers pursuing strategic litigations, investigative journalists, and finally good governance coalitions that win elections on such programs. A good governance alliance in Greece would have written its own good governance "omnibus bill" by now, like the one into which unkept promises to the EU were squeezed at the very last moment. It could be sponsored by business associations, by political parties, or, even better, by a broad civil society coalition. There is no indication of such a bill appearing in Greece. In its absence, reforms remain scattered, fragmented, not locally "owned" or driven by any group whose interest good governance would serve. Meanwhile, the groups opposing change are articulating their views well. Such a situation largely precludes potential tipping points when maximum impact could be had. This is because those who have the relevant knowledge either do not seem to cooperate or complain there is nobody to cooperate with. Greece's genuine good governance congregation has yet to coalesce.

5.5   Conclusion

The cases of Greece and Italy show how "Europeanization" can co-exist with poor control of corruption for quite a while before serious tension arises between the European integration process and the quality of governance. These tensions have only occurred in Italy and Greece due to fiscal convergence processes: otherwise, despite early signs such as low absorption of funding or corruption scandals related to EU funds, the two countries could have continued to be in the EU without much institutional change. While a pro-European and competent political elite has gradually grown in numbers in both countries, European integration did not empower integrity champions, who were few and fought mostly in isolation. Domestic anti-corruption agency was not explicitly coopted when the EU finally intervened (in Greece) and remains scarce in both countries. Eventually, as the EU pressed on the implementation of fiscal rules regardless of the governments in power and their commitment to good governance reforms, populists in both countries managed to set the agenda on anti-corruption themselves and take the political initiative. Whether populists will achieve anything substantial in building integrity remains to be seen in both cases. What is beyond doubt is that European intervention, either in its very weak (Italy) or strong (Greece) form, has not managed to make a substantial contribution towards increasing control of corruption in the two countries in the form of deep institutional changes, although many formal changes did take place. These two special cases thus confirm what indicators have pointed to for all EU-28: a lack of evolution in control of corruption during the decades of EU integration, with the genuine positive developments (such as the OECD anti-bribery convention) largely due to international (US) and not internal EU factors.

"You have damaged Croatia's reputation," a Croatian judge told former prime minister Ivo Sanader when sentencing him to eight years in prison in 2012; "[b]ecause you were a top state official, this verdict is a message to those engaged in politics that crime does not pay" (Bilefsky, 2012a). Although the judge also made the odd remark that no foreign entity had influenced his decision, EU pressure did play a large role in this particular conviction, as the director of the Croatian office of Transparency International acknowledged to the *Herald Tribune* (ibid.). It is one of the EU's proudest moments in its promotion of good governance, alongside the sentencing of former Romanian prime minister Adrian Nastase in the same year (Bilefsky, 2012b). Croatia had applied for EU membership in 2003, received candidate country status by mid-2004 and finally joined in 2013. Mr. Sanader had been managing most of Croatia's EU stabilization and accession process successfully, until he was charged with accepting bribes from Hungarian and Austrian firms that wanted to gain important assets in Croatia's privatization process. The Central and Eastern European Countries (CEEC) invited to join the EU at the Helsinki 2000 summit differed from earlier entrants as they were mostly ruled by leaders of neoliberal persuasion, who had privatized their countries' utilities and opened their procurement markets to Western European countries even before joining the common market. It seemed to be a win–win situation to accept into the EU even countries of ambiguous integrity credentials, such as Croatia, Romania, Bulgaria, or Slovakia, as their inclusion was a necessity for the stabilization of the South-Eastern European border. And profits were obviously to be had for EU companies: as a case in point, according to *Politico.eu*, the price of tap water in the Romanian capital, administered by the French company Veolia, has reportedly shot up by more than 1,400 percent since 2000. The company's revenues meanwhile increased from less than EUR 6 million (USD 6.8 million) in 2000 to EUR 167 million (USD 190 million) by 2014. Prosecutors eventually charged Veolia's Romanian subsidiary Apa

Nova with bribing nearly the entire Bucharest city council to manage this, but the company has not lost the contract (*Politico*, 2018).

Enlarging Europe thus used to be good business on both sides. Aside from the general security advantage (belonging to the safest and most prosperous supranational club), EU accession reportedly brings significant direct and indirect economic advantages to a country invited to join, priming it as a successful transformation, and so encouraging foreign investment on top of EU funds (Bevan et al., 2001; Gligorov et al., 2004). EU scholars also believed for a long time that the EU played a positive role in inducing democracy, in particular preventing the access to power of autocratically-minded populists, such as Slovak Vladimir Meciar, or civilizing illiberal leaders, such as Romania's Ion Iliescu (Kubicek, 2003; Vachudova, 2005). What has been less studied, however, is whether joining the EU really leads to an improvement in the institutional quality of a country. Do the constraints brought by the accession process and then membership balance the extraordinary opportunities that made Sanader and Veolia give in to corruption? The post-communist EU member states (which joined after 2004) are indeed doing better on control of corruption and rule of law than their neighbors in the Balkans or the former Soviet Union (see Figure 6.1), but this is hardly an accession effect. On one hand, they are both geographically and historically closer to Western Europe than other former Soviet Union countries were (and did not experience the trauma of the Balkan civil war); and on the other, they were invited to join *after* they had already proven successful. That indeed was the logic of accession: to invite the "regatta" champions, the best-prepared countries. The question is whether the EU's "transformative power" acts to help accession candidates evolve *if they are not ready* (as in the cases of Turkey and the Balkans) and whether accession negotiations and the mix of EU conditionality and socialization accompanying them can sustainably change the institutions of candidate countries (and afterwards new member countries) so that they do not backslide after joining the EU. For instance, Malta and Cyprus (which acceded in 2004) both started as EU members with high trust in government and low perception of corruption, only to be shown in a much worse position by Eurobarometer 2017. But if the lapses in Malta and Cyprus can perhaps be explained away by a mix of economic crisis and corruption opportunities provided by an overflow of EU funds, the limits of the EU's influence in Central and South-Eastern Europe, where strong conditionalities related to rule of law were imposed, need more explaining. Most of the literature looks less at corruption and more at the EU's promotion of rule of law in the context of democratization reforms (Börzel and Risse, 2004; Baracani, 2008; Freyburg et al., 2009; Wolff, 2009; Pech, 2012;

Kochenov and Pech, 2015; Burlyuk, 2015; Dietrich, 2017). This section analyzes EU intervention on control of corruption, with its intended and unintended consequences, which involve judicial independence and broader rule of law issues. While canvassing all the accession countries, I focus in particular on cases that were subject to the strongest EU intervention: the Eastern Balkans, in particular Romania, which enjoyed the transient reputation of a success case; Turkey, which had the longest accession time in history; and the two exceptional cases where conditionality mixed with direct EU rule, the regions of limited sovereignty of Bosnia-Hercegovina and Kosovo.

6.1   Europeanization Meets Transformation in the East

Control of corruption is inseparable from rule of law. They are both equilibria and are closely linked, with correlation between these two corresponding governance indicators at over 90 percent in the World Bank evaluation (Mungiu-Pippidi, 2015b, Chapter 2). Their common basis is the norm of ethical universalism (via the Cicero/Roman law heritage), which twins them and makes them indispensable to one another. Rule of law is the ethical universalism principle applied to law; control of corruption is ethical universalism applied to the allocation of public resources. We cannot have rule of law without controlling for corruption, or the most corrupt groups will twist the law in their favor; and the other way around is also impracticable – without equality in front of the law, the most powerful groups will divert public resources to their cronies. And rule of law matters: in the words of Daniel Kaufmann, "an improvement in the rule of law by one standard deviation from the current levels in Ukraine to those 'middling' levels prevailing in South Africa would lead to a fourfold increase in per capita income in the long run" (2004).

While this applies wherever international donors promote public integrity, it is nowhere as crucial as in the EU integration and accession process. In the EU's approach, rule of law is the major political benchmark and is privileged over control of corruption. As there is no word on corruption in the treaties, in practice it is rule of law that serves to advance the fight against corruption. On one side, the EU treaties highlight the rule of law as one of the transversal guiding principles of the EU's foreign policy, which must not only be respected but promoted abroad (Art. 21 TEU). And on the other, the rule of law is a formal accession benchmark for any country wishing to join the EU (Art. 49 TEU). The Copenhagen political criteria for accession do not specifically refer to judicial independence or corruption. However, the political criterion of ensuring "stability of institutions guaranteeing ... the rule of law" would be inconceivable without an independent and impartial judiciary.[1] For post-communist countries, the European Convention on Human Rights enforced by the European Court of Human Rights (ECHR) became part of the acquis as well. Domestic rule of law is thus required as a precondition to invitation, both to ensure that a country can safeguard EU law and because rule of law is a founding value of the EU club.

The existence of a judiciary that is independent from both government and private interests and is able to judge impartially, fairly, and honestly is an indispensable component of both the control of corruption and the rule of law. Not surprisingly, judicial independence has often been reported as having a significant effect on the extent of corruption (Ali and Isse, 2003; Herzfeld and Weiss, 2003; Damania et al., 2004; Mungiu-Pippidi, 2015b; Mungiu-Pippidi and Dadašov, 2016). But little is known about how to build such judiciaries or establish rule of law more generally. Furthermore, it is difficult to separate EU intervention from the broader context influencing the desired policy outcome. What determines rule of law? A consensus seems to exist that, as Rodrik, Subramanian, and Trebbi argued, "there is growing evidence that desirable institutional arrangements have a large element of context specificity, arising from differences in historical trajectories, geography, political economy, or other initial conditions" (2004). In the Eastern European context, legacies mean communism, and most institutions are rooted in the past decades. Linz and Stepan, for example, pointed out the important differences between the nature of transitions, opposing post-totalitarian and post-authoritarian regimes; considerable path dependence is presumed to exist in post-communist settings, rendering institutional reforms difficult (1996). We can therefore presume that a country remains further from the rule of law ideal the longer the time it spent under communism and the more deeply based was the communist regime. These factors influence especially the *political economy* of rule of law reforms. "Law is a tool of power," as Stephen Holmes noted insightfully (2002). A third explanatory category, the constitutional one, is the most focused on in the monitoring reports of European organizations (the Venice Commission, GRECO, the European Commission), as these organizations largely presume that judicial independence is internal to the judiciary and therefore certain types of judicial organization, their logistics, and public integrity or legal infrastructure are conducive to better performance.

---

[1] See the European Council's Conclusions of the Presidency (EC, 1993).

The rule of law background in the post-communist region is common among these countries. Post-communist governments had to rule on the basis of communist legislation due to the inability to replace it all overnight. It could have been canceled, but the agreement was that "the umbrella principle of upholding the law meant that however bad or inappropriate communist laws should continue to apply until revoked or amended" (Millard, 1999). Poor court logistics and a culture of informality accompanied the inherited poor regulation. Over the years, the training and payment structure of the judiciary improved: by 2014, the more corrupt an EU country was, the more disproportionately magistrates were paid compared to the average income.[2] The specific organization of the judiciary (who appoints judges, the presence of a judicial council, who controls budget of courts), as documented in the Council of Europe's European Commission for the Efficiency of Justice (CEPEJ) data, does not explain the variation in judicial performance across Eastern Europe (measured in Freedom House Nations in Transit data), with countries with longer communist regimes and less democracy having worse scores. This only fits the general rule that *de jure* judicial independence is a poor predictor for *de facto* judicial independence (Hayo and Voigt, 2007; Gutmann and Voigt, 2017), and a gap exists between the technical aspect of building rule of law from the political aspect (Frye, 2010). As suggested in a widely quoted Carnegie Endowment review of rule of law assistance efforts after the first decade of transition: "Rewriting constitutions, laws, and regulations is the easy part . . . Rule of law reform will succeed only if it gets at the fundamental problem of leaders who refuse to be ruled by the law" (Carothers, 1998). The indispensable element to understanding reforms' success is thus the coalition behind the reforms, as well as the defenders of the status quo. For instance, Daniels and Trebilcock divide countries into three categories (2008): those where politicians, legal professionals, and the public all support reform (Central Europe after the fall of communism, South Africa after apartheid); those where politicians support reform, but lawyers and the police do not (Chile and Guatemala); and those where lawyers want change, but politicians do not (Pakistan).

The communist legacy varied across countries, but in all of them, ample resources for corruption were provided by poor regulatory quality, excessive red tape, high administrative discretion, and poor transparency. The common prescriptions and the implementation of Washington Consensus reforms had to some extent aligned all accession countries by the time of EU integration, despite the original differences between

---

[2] Author's own calculation on the basis of CEPEJ data.

gradualist, radical, and reluctant reformers over the sequence and dura-
tion of original reforms, and in particular the control of elites over economic reforms (Stark and Bruszt, 1998). While Estonia and Poland led
the group that liberalized without the reformers seeking to generate rents
for themselves in the 1990s, the other countries, most notably Slovakia,
Romania, and Bulgaria, were far more hesitant. Due to their deep economic reforms, which drastically cut resources for corruption, the countries associated with more enhanced market reforms in the 1990s were
doing far better on corruption by accession year 2004: Poland, Hungary,
Estonia, the Czech Republic, and Slovenia. Estonia emerged as the most
sustainable performer in the end, describing a veritable virtuous circle
where governance reforms drove economic prosperity (see Figure 6.1).
Estonia practically closed down the judiciary inherited from Soviet times
and reinvented it under a new constitution. By the end of 1994, the
judicial body had undergone a 67 percent renewal (Mungiu-Pippidi,
2011). Out of all CEEC cases it was the closest to the Eastern German
model. In the former East Germany, higher court judges were "lustrated"
by a Western German commission. The whole judiciary body was evaluated and purged. As in the other successful cases, in Estonia fast and
deep democratization preceded the invitation to join the EU (Laar,

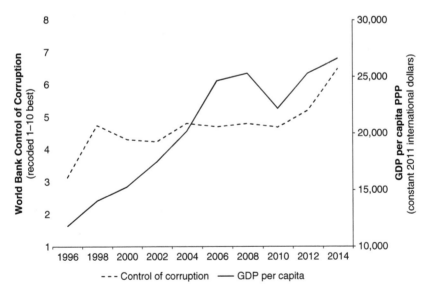

Figure 6.1 Estonia's progress on corruption and development
Source: Mungiu-Pippidi and Johnston, 2017

2008). As the process tracing of Estonia's road to good governance shows, reforms might have been driven by emulation and the desire to join the EU at some point (EU enlargement was not even a distant prospect at the time), but they were certainly not driven by conditionality; anti-communism and the desire to part with the old regime were the touchstone of Estonia's success (Kalniņš, 2017).

By the end of transition, Slovakia and the other Baltics lagged on reforms, and Romania and Bulgaria, the poorest countries of them all, were in the "red" area of systemic corruption. However, the overwhelming public support for EU integration drove even the regions' worse kleptocrats to seek EU accession and start some reforms (Vachudova, 2005), while geopolitical considerations forced the European Union to enter accession negotiations.

Over the years, an improvement in transparency (transparency has never been included in EU conditionality, but it was a NATO accession condition) and gradual economic development with better pay for administrators solved petty corruption to a great extent, leaving only particularism in public resources allocation as the major problem (Mungiu-Pippidi, 2007). The vicious mechanism worked similarly everywhere, though in various degrees and to a lesser extent in Estonia and Slovenia: politicization with a reshuffle of top civil servants after each election to ensure that party loyalists controlled all the rents, followed by preferential allocation of public contracts and the other rents (O'Dwyer, 2006; Grzymala-Busse, 2007; Meyer-Sahling and Veen, 2012). What varied was the extent of extraction (whether on every transaction or just a portion of them) and the kickback value, but even these differences across Central Europe were underestimated, with government favoritism a plague everywhere (Mungiu-Pippidi, 2015a). Figure 6.2 shows the fluctuation in numbers of civil servants after elections in Croatian public administration and publicly owned companies. The hiring of party clients swallows the public sector employment in electoral years; then it decreases gradually as clients of the elections' losers leave or are forced out, with the cycle restarting every election (see Figure 6.2).

The historical differences on the side of corruption resources have created their own national path dependencies, but EU accession also brought commonalities, imposing some alignment. For instance, these countries were flooded with EU funds, both before and after accession, and there was an increase in EU-related red tape (Jacoby, 2006; Mungiu-Pippidi, 2007). Unlike Italy, a rich country, Eastern European countries were poor and EU money became the largest stake to capture. Figure 6.3 shows the significance of EU funds over the years in Bulgaria, the poorest country in EU-28, as EU funds gradually surpass and replace national

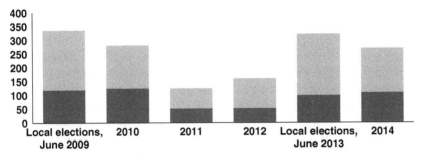

Legal persons and sectoral contracting authorities co-owned by two or more regional and/or local governments

Legal persons and sectoral contracting authorities co-owned by one regional or local government

Figure 6.2 Politicization in Croatia: flexible public employment associated with elections, 2009–2014
Note: Management reshuffling of contracting authorities owned by regional and local government, 2009–2014; sample of 95
Source: Podumljak and Barett, 2015

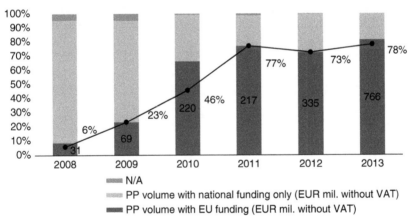

N/A
PP volume with national funding only (EUR mil. without VAT)
PP volume with EU funding (EUR mil. without VAT)
Share of EU funding from total procurement volume

Figure 6.3 High stakes: growth of EU funds in the turnover of top Bulgarian construction companies, 2008–2013
Source: Stefanov and Karaboev, 2015 (in Mungiu-Pippidi, 2015a)

budget funds for infrastructure. In just a few years, exactly as in Greece before, EU funds became the main rent disposed of at the discretion of authorities.

On constraints to corruption, such as judicial independence, the regional situations differed significantly. Democratization drove the initial reforms: the success of anti-communist parties in the first free ballots in Central Europe after 1989 helped these countries achieve judicial independence early in the 1990s. Despite a later start, the Eastern and Western Balkans followed in granting life tenure to judges (Anderson and Gray, 2007). In the post-transitional period – the time of democratic consolidation – the political elites' impact was gradually reduced as the newly created institutions became "more robust and resistant to change" (Magalhães, 1999). While political elites continued to be crucial for successful rule of law reforms, in the most advanced countries the judicial caste itself increased in importance (magistrates, prosecutors). EU accession was initiated in this context. Public opinion surveys have consistently shown that the public does not perceive people to be equal before the law in these regions (Mungiu-Pippidi, 2015a). The Global Competitiveness Report finds only one consistent positive outlier in the quality of the judicial process, Estonia. Respondents of this business survey find otherwise little difference between Romania and Bulgaria, on one hand, and the theoretically more advanced Central European countries (WEF, 2017).

Beyond constraints due to judicial independence, it was civil society that varied wildly across Eastern Europe (see Figure 6.4), explaining why

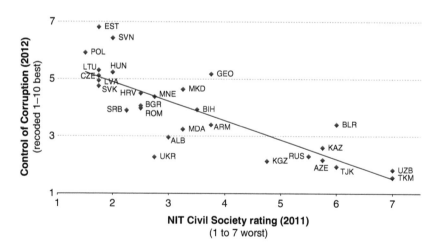

Figure 6.4 Civil society as constraint on corruption in Eastern Europe
Note: Linear regression, association significant at p = 0.05; NIT civil society coded 1–7, with 7 worst, and CoC coded 1–10
Source: Based on World Bank and Freedom House Nations in Transit rankings 2011

Central Asia and Central Europe drifted further apart on control of corruption than even geography would have predicted. Historically, developed Poland, Estonia, and Slovenia and poorer Georgia performed even better originally on corruption than their civil society rankings would have predicted (and Ukraine worse). For the rest, the strength of civil society predicts almost by itself the level of corruption control achieved. And EU accession or neighborhood policy measures have not changed this picture: EU funds can hardly be said to have gone for civil society development, indispensable to control of corruption (with the exception of Estonia, which organized itself differently for after the accession), but civil society development never became a goal in itself (Börzel et al., 2008). Furthermore, the retirement of other donors following the accession of Central European countries, on the erroneous presumption that the EU and the countries themselves could now take care of the NGO sector, may account for the backslide experienced in Central Europe, where major funding problems appeared thereafter (Mungiu-Pippidi, 2007).

During accession negotiations with the EU, reforming the judiciary and fighting corruption were crucial issues, despite the absence of clear standards and acquis. How does one promote the "European legal model" when Council of Europe report simultaneously warns readers that Europeans do not have one and might never have one (Bergel et al., 2015)? Still, some EU external instruments and other EU publications sketched a "substantive/thick" rather than a "formal/thin" understanding of the rule of law (Pech, 2012). Therefore, the EC, with the help of other international organizations, invested a considerable amount of assistance, monitoring, and coaching in the area. Conditionality was also strong, particularly for the "laggards" (Slovakia, Romania, Bulgaria). The action plans on home and justice affairs submitted in 2005, before the signing of the accession treaty of Romania and Bulgaria, became part of the mandatory acquis (under the penalty of treaty safeguard clause activation). The main instrument of monitoring was the regular EC report, issued twice a year, with some variation (see also Mendelski, 2012). The reports monitored the "benchmarks," the targets that the two countries were expected to reach (anti-corruption and judicial independence for both, in Bulgaria even asking for constitutional changes for better guarantees). Assistance accompanied conditionality: the total EU allocation for administrative and judicial capacity reforms between 1998 and 2006 (the last year before EU accession) amounted to EUR 452 million for Romania and EUR 260 million for Bulgaria, notwithstanding the considerable domestic expense, as budgets were raised repeatedly (ECOTEC, 2006).

2018 is a particularly good standpoint from which to discuss the EU's influence over quality of governance; most early literature on EU accession saw conditionality as a great triumph and so missed all the early warnings (Pridham, 2003; Jacoby, 2006; Haughton, 2007; Mungiu-Pippidi, 2007). Caution had nonetheless been spelled out clearly: "The day after accession, when conditionality has faded, the influence of the EU vanishes like a short-term anesthetic. Political parties needed to behave during accession in order to reach this highly popular objective, but once freed from these constraints, they returned to their usual ways. Now we see Central and Eastern Europe as it really is – a region that has come far but still has a way to go" (Mungiu-Pippidi, 2007). And confirmation came swiftly, as Poland and Hungary experienced major backsliding; street protests brought down governments in Romania and Slovakia over the issue of corruption; the Czech Republic and Slovenia were also shaken by corruption scandals and plagued by disappointments; and so the European Commission had to create a special mechanism, the Rule of Law Framework, to deal with successful former accession countries now turned into relapsing EU member states (Kochenov and Pech, 2016). From examples of successful transitions, the Central European countries turned into seminar cases on backsliding after EU accession.

There is simply too much literature on the positive effects on good governance of EU conditionality to be cited here, particularly since it was already not fitting facts well at the time it was written. Most of this widely cited literature focused on the formal transposition of EU acquis, rather than on substantive matters such as rule of law (for instance, see Schimmelfennig and Sedelmeier, 2004). The formal monitoring of "rule transfer" presented in academic literature should have been weighted to take account of the general capacity for aligning formal rules with informal practices, an older problem of East European societies. As of December 1, 2017, the European Single Market Scoreboard showed Spain, Germany, and Portugal on top of the "pending infringements" ranking, with Montenegro and Latvia at the opposite extreme. Shouldn't this indicate some missing variable rather than leading to the conclusion than Montenegro is more Europeanized than Germany?[3]

The stress on formality is understandable, but it has a strong development bias. It comes from countries with strong rule of law and low informality that have still to learn how the rest of the world works. Nobody in Brussels or elsewhere had learned the Greek lessons by 2004, the year of the "big bang" enlargement. If anything, Greece was then considered a success story and the Greeks in the European Commission were actively encouraging new Balkan

---

[3] European Commission Single Market Scoreboard: Infringements (EC, 2018).

candidates. As the core identity of the united European Union is mainly a body of laws and the commitment to enforce them, the enlargement was mostly about the formal adoption of the acquis by parliaments and governments of candidate countries, with the substance being relegated to the background (Jacoby, 2006). Awareness existed, however, that the capacity of a new EU member country to enforce EU law was paramount to successful EU integration. Therefore, besides the largely formal process of adopting the acquis, the applicant countries had to engage in a flurry of reforms meant to increase the overall capacity of their legal systems.

What did this effort amount to? The indicators we can use to assess progress leave much to be desired. Only from 2005, the Council of Europe (through the CEPEJ program) started collecting data on the judiciaries in the region, unfortunately based on questionnaires answered by countries themselves. Residents in countries that are parties to the European Convention on Human Rights can also appeal to the European Court of Human Rights (ECHR) when all domestic appeals are exhausted, a source of fact-based data alongside expert indicators such as the World Bank's indicators on rule of law and control of corruption, or the regionally dedicated Freedom House Nations in Transit. Table 6.1 and Figure 6.5 present a synthetic view of this data, leading to these brief observations:

- The essentials of the equilibria (rule of law and control of corruption) were in place *before* receiving the invitation for accession (by 2000), and have since then mostly stagnated (in Turkey they declined). Membership itself has not helped improvement on corruption ratings (if we observe change after 2004 for the Central European countries and 2007 for Romania and Bulgaria) and even the incentive of joining (change 2000–2007) led to rather unsustainable gains. Croatia progressed the most because it started from exceedingly low scores after the Yugoslav Wars, and it is still trailing in judicial independence and control of corruption.
- Romania is the only case to have progressed on the control of corruption indicator (over the whole twenty-year "transition" interval, however, not since accession), except for Estonia's earlier progress, although not on rule of law. It started far beyond Bulgaria and surpassed it, but remains below a rating of 6 out of 10. Romania's progress on CoC is worth examining because its judicial independence has improved, but only slightly, and it is the worst offender in EHCR lawsuits – with nearly one thousand pending, almost a fifth of the total forthcoming cases – and over 400 convictions on "right to a fair trial" violations, the highest per capita among the convention's signatories (by 2018).
- Poland, Hungary, Romania, and Turkey, which have all generated more headlines on backsliding on the rule of law in recent years, have in fact

Table 6.1 *Main indicators on rule of law and public integrity for former CEEC accession countries plus accession country Turkey*

Accession country (different waves)	Total violations up to 2017	Right to a fair trial violation	Pending 2017*	Judicial independence component IPI 2017, scale 1–10	Evolution on CoC before and after EU accession (1998–2018)
Bulgaria	588	90		4.05	Stagnant
Croatia	301	99		4.22	Progress
Czech Republic	186	66		6.30	Stagnant
Estonia	41	15		8.36	Progress, before accession
Hungary	448	41	3,550	4.24	Stagnant, recent regress
Latvia	110	19		5.58	Stagnant
Lithuania	116	19		5.84	Stagnant
Poland	958	108	1,400	5.22	Stagnant, regress after accession, then some recovery
Romania	1,202	436	9,900 (17.6%)	5.49	Progress
Slovak Republic	321	39		3.73	Stagnant
Slovenia	329	19		5.18	Stagnant
Turkey	3,988	878	7,500 (13.3%)	4.12	Stagnant

* Evolution reported only beyond the 5% confidence error
Sources: European Court of Human Rights statistics on "Pending applications allocated to judicial formation" and "Violations by Article and by State 1959–2017" (2018); Judicial Independence GCR, recoded for Index for Public Integrity IPI, see www.integrity-index .org; author's own calculation of CoC World Governance Indicator (World Bank)

always and more consistently had rule of law violations. The number of new cases filed with the EHCR only indicates that this has not dropped after the EU accession of the three newest members. The other countries are far below the threshold, so doing significantly better. Indicators in the graph and table are quite consistent regarding their evolution.

- Except Estonia and the Czech Republic, judicial independence has remained under 6 on the 1–10 scale for all former and present accession countries, with smaller than expected differences across cases. The bottom countries are Turkey and Slovakia, the Baltics are on top, and Central Europe is regressing.
- The evolution of "democracy" and of good governance are poorly correlated. Slovakia used to be the textbook example of EU influence;

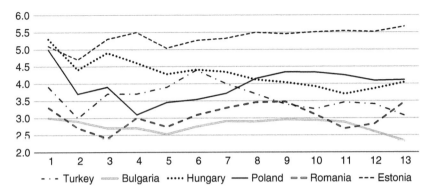

Figure 6.5 Evolution of judicial independence in selected CEEC cases, 2001–2014
Source: World Economic Forum Global Competitiveness Report 2017

despite populist Vladimir Meciar's party winning a relative majority in 1998, the EU's signals that his government might hinder the country's admission to the EU prevented him forming a government. Yet Slovakia has not progressed at all, either on judicial independence or on corruption, after this "success." After Slovakia joining the EU in 2004, populists remained strong, although more "European" than expected on fiscal and economic policy, but clearly EU influence has not managed to improve Slovakia's rule of law performance.

Figure 6.5 displays the judicial independence indicator over time separately (for selected cases only, due to space reasons; none with a positive evolution was excluded). The figure shows Estonia only on an ascending trend after EU accession, following its previous positive reform dynamic. The decline of Hungary and Poland on rule of law goes further back than the recent headlines would suggest, coinciding with accession. On the two countries with the strongest conditionality, Romania's progress is minimal, as its upward curve by 2009 is followed by a downward one; Bulgaria registers only a slight decline. For Turkey, Hungary, and Poland, updated indicators would show an even bigger decline.

This evidence thus indicates that EU influence over judicial independence, rule of law, and control of corruption in new member states is actually quite limited. If these are the plain facts, submitting them to refined statistical treatment in some inferential time series analysis cannot return valid and robust conclusions to support the opposite conclusion. Academic papers reaching such conclusions for quite some years before 2015 were simply wrong.

6.2   How Successful Is the Romanian "Success Story"?

In 2006, just a few months before Romania and Bulgaria joined the union, top EU officials were still trying to postpone their entry by one year, as their treaties allowed, to give them more time to "prepare." One official from the Directorate-General of External Relations explained to Romania's justice minister, Monica Macovei – the person who had done the most to satisfy the EU's conditions and create a strong anti-corruption framework – that the first act of the Romanian parliament after EU entry would be to fire her. Intelligence was already there that the country's MPs were upset at having to publish online the longest and most detailed financial disclosures in Europe (in which they had to publicly declare family possessions, jewelry, and paintings, along with real estate and bank accounts). Ms. Macovei refused. She was concerned that, due to growing enlargement fatigue, accession a year later might become indefinite postponement.[4] Indeed, in the spring and summer of 2007, referenda in France and the Netherlands halted enlargement for many years, by which time Romania and Bulgaria had already joined – and Ms. Macovei, according to expectations, had been forced to resign.

On January 1, 2007, the day that Romania and Bulgaria joined – the last from the Central European group – the European Commission established a cooperation and verification mechanism (CVM) to assess the commitments made by these late entrants in the areas of judicial reform and the fight against corruption and organized crime. An important role of this "safeguard mechanism" was to alleviate the reluctance of many member states to admit Romania and Bulgaria to the union. Central European states had also signed on to three-year safeguarding clauses, but these were not related to corruption. In 2009, an EC assessment said of Romania that "more needs to be done to deliver convincing results in judicial reform and tackling corruption, while for Bulgaria in the fight against organized crime was still seen as unconvincing" (EC, 2009b; 2009c). After the three-year clauses expired, the commission therefore decided to keep the CVM active: "The CVM ... should only be removed when all the benchmarks it set have been satisfactorily fulfilled ... The CVM is a support tool in this endeavor; it is not an end in itself nor can it replace commitment that ... authorities need to make in order to align the judicial system and practice with general EU standards" (ibid.). In time, as some benchmarks were fulfilled (an effective prosecuting agency for Romania), others were added (eliminating corruption, both petty and grand). This is how an unprecedented situation arose: the two countries

---

[4] According to private statement by Monica Macovei to the author in December 2006, Bucharest.

each came to hold the council presidency in 2018–2019, having been in the European Union for more than ten years, with the conditionality "safeguard mechanism" still active.

Romania is seen generally as a CVM success, and Bulgaria as a failure – at least according to the EU's institutional literature, yearly reports, and a 2018 European Parliament assessment, which found that Romania had managed to reach most of the benchmarks set by the commission but Bulgaria had not (Directorate-General for Internal Policies of the Union, 2018). The reason was that Romania's courts had issued jail sentences to eighteen ministers, including a prime minister, and had indicted most of the family and entourage of even its "anti-corruption president," Traian Băsescu, Ms. Macovei's former leader. Bulgaria, on the other hand, had not indicted any top politicians, and consequently the European Commission's reports had been extremely critical towards it for some years. However, in 2017–2018, while Bulgaria managed to stay out of the news, street protests in Romania, whose sentiments were largely echoed by Ms. Macovei (by now a European MP) in Brussels, prompted many European media headlines on Romania's "backsliding." Despite chairing the European Council in 2018 and 2019 respectively, Bulgaria and Romania have remained in the lower tier of member states, joining neither the euro nor the border-free Schengen zone (EC, 2017b; 2017c). As the conditionality mechanism was however identical for the two countries, it is likely that the difference in their performance (if confirmed) is due to a factor present in Romania but absent in Bulgaria, and not to the identical CVM (Mungiu-Pippidi, 2018b). As it is agreed that Bulgaria made little progress, the question remains whether Romania's governance really improved after joining the EU, and whether its experience offers lessons for other countries.

The two countries started with systemic corruption in the form of advanced particularism. In the early 2000s, they barely managed to get "functioning market economy" status, a precondition for EU accession, just in time to join. In Romania's early transition (prior to 1996), its governments had tried to control privatization on the model of Ukraine and Russia, which meant limited access for external players and the creation of a local class of oligarchs. By 2008, the cumulative wealth of the richest 300 Romanians had reached nearly EUR 40 billion, which at the time amounted to 32.5 percent of GDP. Of this wealth, 45 percent was concentrated in the hands of the 100 richest, with eight individuals holding fortunes worth more than EUR 1 billion each.[5] Most of the people at the top of the new economic structure had connections with the communist-era Securitate (the secret police) and *nomenklatura,*

---

[5] Author's own calculation on the basis of Forbes' annual list of top millionaires. See Romanian Academic Society Annual Report 2018 for more details, at www.sar.org.ro/en/

although not with top figures: rather, they had been petty money-changers in Securitate shops, official translators or guides for foreigners, and sons-in-law of various officials. Their main expertise was in converting political influence into wealth. They were the big winners from energy privatizations, land concessions, and trade monopolies, as well as owners of the new private media. There was not one retailer or manufacturer among them (Romanian Academic Society, 2018). In the year of the economic crisis, "favorite" Romanian construction companies made 30–50 percent profit rates from public contracts when the construction sector was contracting nationally by similar percentages (ibid.). Bulgaria was not much different, with a selected group of companies whose turnover came mostly from public contracts, and profits far above the average (Stefanov and Karaboev, 2015). Such contracts were obtained through connections, and winners were paid kickbacks as a rule, of which a percentage went to the governing party of the time.

Both Romania's post-communists and anti-communists were supportive of European integration. However, due to strong public opinion in favor of the joining of all East European countries, and after a formal statement of unity of purpose in 1996, the invitation to join was launched by the European Union at the 1999 Helsinki summit (Phinnemore, 2006). A transition that could be best described as a "democratization without decommunization" was then followed by a similar Europeanization process, which had to accommodate what was largely an unfinished transformation (Mungiu-Pippidi, 2006b). It was against this backdrop that the EU asked Romania, its accession date hanging in the balance (2006 versus 2007), to create an anti-corruption agency and adopt tough anti-corruption regulations. It was also under these exceptional political circumstances that the Romanian civil society association known as the Coalition for a Clean Parliament (CCP) was created in 2004. The coalition's goal was to prevent the post-communist PSD party, which had already governed for ten of the fourteen years of transition and was responsible for the rise of crony capitalism, from winning yet again in the 2004 general election and endangering Romania's EU accession. The successor communist party (Social Democrats, SDP) was leading in the polls at the campaign's outset. After agreeing with the major parties on criteria, the CCP publicized a list of parliamentary candidates involved in corrupt activities. This action, and the process of removing unfit candidates, raised corruption to the top of the political agenda and helped challenger Traian Băsescu pull ahead in the presidential vote. Furthermore, in December 2004, the European Council conditioned Romania's entry on an audit and a revamping of its anti-corruption strategy – a condition to which no other country, not even Bulgaria, had been subjected. This is when Romania started down its distinct path.

To fulfill this requirement, Băsescu appointed one of the leaders of the anti-corruption campaign, Monica Macovei, as justice minister. And Macovei in turn appointed two very young chief prosecutors, the first in Romanian history not to be fully politically vetted, but to advance by an ad hoc channel. A strengthening of anti-corruption legislation and anti-corruption agency organization during Macovei's tenure as justice minister (2004–2007) on the basis of the EU-ordered audit was the final ingredient that enabled the next anti-corruption prosecutions. After 2008, the anti-corruption agency (NAD, National Anti Corruption Directorate) began to charge top-ranking officials. The bulk of the sentencing came after 2010, when courts started to deliver verdicts with a stunning conviction rate of over 90 percent. Between 2010 and the end of 2017, 4,720 final corruption sentences were passed involving top officials, an average of nearly 600 convictions per year (Romanian Academic Society, 2018). Those convicted include generals, ministers, and members of parliament from every political party. By the time of the 2016 local elections, more than half of the heads of county councils (counties are Romania's main territorial division) had been indicted, as had countless mayors and *all* the presidents of the traditional parliamentary parties.

In the only objective time series evidence existing on particularism in Romania – open favoritism in public construction contracts, where the largest stakes are – a drop-off was registered from 52 percent to 39 percent during seven years of anti-corruption crackdown: a reduction, in other words, by 25 percent from 2007 to 2013 (Doroftei, 2016; see Figure 6.6). Public contract awards to companies openly connected to politicians fell to under 20 percent (ibid.). A correlation of 79 percent exists between convictions per county and procurement indicators such as awards to politically connected companies or agency capture, which measures whether over 50 percent of awards of one single public agency goes to a single private contractor (ibid.). However, by the end of 2018 the procurement scorecard of the EC's DG Grow, which monitors contracts in Tender Electronic Daily (a different population of contracts), seemed to indicate that single bidding was on the rise again and Romania was in the red on several procurement indicators.[6]

Half the top ten oligarchs, in particular those who owned media, went to jail during the crackdown years. Many EU firms have won public contracts in Romania (Romanian Academic Society, 2018), a country that has also privatized most of its utilities and some natural resources, making them available to many European companies. An open

---

[6] The European procurement scoreboard is published at http://ec.europa.eu/internal_mar ket/scoreboard/performance_per_policy_area/public_procurement/index_en. htm#maincontentSec2

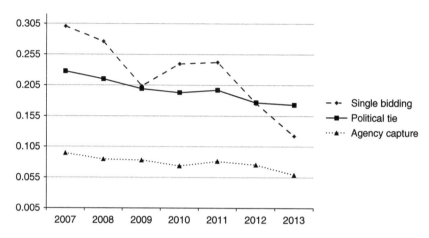

Figure 6.6 Romania: decline of political favoritism (ANTICORRP index) in public contract awards during crackdown years
Source: ANTICORRP.

privatization policy, together with arrests of top Romanian businesspeople, is largely accountable for increasing market competition, including in the public contracts market – although it is not clear that corruption decreased due to that. Some European companies that entered the market have also been indicted by prosecutors, as they paid bribes to win tenders and fix utility prices as eagerly as domestic companies did before them.

Romanians rank first in Europe (68 percent) in declaring themselves personally affected by corruption, but also first in judging that enough successful judicial pursuits have taken place (55 percent; the European average was 33 percent in 2017). On the other hand, 54 percent believe that efforts to combat corruption remain ineffective (compared to 39 percent who believe the opposite). The European average is 56 percent skeptical to 30 percent confident (Eurobarometer, 2017g). Reports of direct experience with bribery have fallen sharply in Romania, with the same survey showing that only 13 percent of Romanians are acquainted with someone who gave or took a bribe (the European average being 12 percent), which puts Romania in the fourteenth place (ibid.). Only 3 percent have experienced any kind of corruption in the last six months (rank 17). Romania ranks 30 (out of 109 countries) in the Index of Public Integrity, being trailed by EU members Croatia, Bulgaria, and Greece.

As it turned out later, this efficiency came with some costs for the rule of law. Firstly, then President Băsescu decreed corruption a threat to national security, and through a succession of secret acts made the secret service, the heir to Ceaușescu's feared Securitate, the *de facto* decision maker in corruption investigations. The Romanian Information Service (RIS, the official Securitate heir – Serviciul Român de Informații, SRI) started to work jointly with the NAD.[7] According to reports presented to parliament by RIS, 250,454 wiretap warrants were issued between 2005 and 2014, growing from 3,849 in 2005 to 44,759 in 2014 (eleven times as many), with 99 percent approved by the courts (Mungiu-Pippidi, 2018b). For 2015 alone, the last date when an RIS report was made public, "national security" warrants outnumbered those related to corruption by four to one, with evidence being leaked from security warrants into prosecutors' files. The total number of wiretaps was sixteen times more than the FBI's in the same year (in a country whose population is under twenty million people; Diac, 2016). Furthermore, over 4,000 wiretapping requests were approved between 2010–2015 by the supreme court, whose competence includes only top officials, which basically means that the whole government, parliament, and top courts were wiretapped during this period (Mungiu-Pippidi, 2018). Addressing a constitutional exception raised in a private trial, the constitutional court ruled in 2016 that RIS should no longer be empowered to organize wiretaps for the NAD and other judicial authorities, which should organize their own[8]. This left plenty of material to be used for blackmail in the hands of the secret service, as the prohibition is not retroactive. Now former President Băsescu, who had escaped jail himself over a couple of public real-estate abuse-of-function charges only due to immunity first and prescription later, and who, after his fall from power, saw most of his close relations and family imprisoned (or indicted), acknowledged that this had gone too far. He explained that he could not have won against the oligarchs without the secret services, but that his second term ended before he was able to put them under proper civilian control. However, he claimed that he had never authorized the manipulation of evidence that also allegedly took place (Mungiu-Pippidi, 2018b). The 2018 MCV report rejects this whole area, which is highly relevant for the rule of law and due judicial process, by stating that "The operation of the intelligence services is not a matter for the EU and falls outside the CVM benchmarks."[9]

---

[7] Answer of National Defense Council to the Union of Judges in Romania on the basis of a freedom of information petition by Union of Judges, available in Romanian at http://www.unjr.ro/wp-content/uploads/2017/01/CSAT-raspuns-UNJR-16-feb-2016.pdf

[8] The full decision of the Court (in Romanian) is available on its website at https://www.ccr.ro/files/products/Decizia_51_2016.pdf .

[9] https://ec.europa.eu/info/sites/info/files/progress-report-romania-2018-com-2018-com-2018–851_en.pdf, p. 2

The second problematic aspect of Romania's wave of corruption sentences is that many of Băsescu's anti-corruption "heroes" were apparently criminals themselves: two of the main prosecutors who sentenced oligarchs also ended up in jail, and other NAD prosecutors faced disciplinary procedures. The first head of the National Integrity Agency (Horia Georgescu), the head of the Anti-Organized Crime Unit (Alina Bica), and the main businessperson close to RIS, who denounced targeted oligarchs (Sebastian Ghita), were all arrested under the next president. Either Băsescu's anti-corruption force was a gang of criminals who targeted the other gangs, in typical post-Soviet fashion (their appropriation of numerous public contracts and other spoils is well documented in several official investigations), or they were the political victims of Băsescu's successor regime. In either case, one would expect to see some concern expressed in the EC's regular reports on anti-corruption processes when yesterday's integrity warriors become tomorrow's criminals, and when the "anti-corruption President" appoints his lady friend in charge of all EU funds, to the delight of the Western media (Schiltz, 2019). Furthermore, Romania saw some of its most successful anti-corruption convictions – reported as successes in EU commission reports – challenged by the revelation that the special High Court section judging top politicians had been in fact acting unlawfully, as not all its judges had been randomly assigned as in most courts.[10] But no mention of the above appears in the regular EU reports, only praise of the activity of NAD or the other agencies required by the EU during accession.

By end of 2017, most of the powerful corrupt actors of a decade ago had already served their sentences and been freed. Meanwhile, their operations (in media, politics, and business) had continued largely unaffected through changing hands to friends or family. A whole industry of reducing time in jail for corrupt top-level individuals has developed, too, with the contribution of many judges and nearly half of Romania's public universities, which vouched for the academic work written in prison by former top politicians (who had never been academics before; some did not even have a degree) and so helped their early pardon (*The Economist*, 2018). Romania's notoriously inefficient tax authority has not managed to recuperate the embezzled assets even in the few cases where courts could ascertain them. Furthermore, TV stations associated with defendants managed to publish quite daunting evidence on prosecutors threatening judges or fixing evidence, leading to the suspension of heads of two provincial NAD offices in 2018–2019.

---

[10] The Constitutional Court decision on this can be read at https://www.ccr.ro/files/pro ducts/685_cu_opinii_separate.pdf

Romania's anti-corruption example has been promoted in the Balkans, Ukraine, and Moldova by the European Commission due to its high number of top-level convictions. Romania's courts have convicted eighteen ministers since 2012, including a former prime minister. More than half of the county heads and mayors had been indicted for corruption by the 2016 elections, creating a critical mass of politicians asking for some judicial redress. In 2012 and 2016, the SDP and their allies, sworn enemies of anti-corruption legislation, won absolute parliamentary majorities (after their government had been pushed to resign in 2015 under street pressure) and most of the county and mayoral positions. This new majority in the parliament has used every opportunity since its latest victory to tame the threatening anti-corruption legislation. They started with vulnerable articles in laws (those questioned by European Court of Human Rights, for instance), to mount after 2017 a comprehensive legislative review meant to reduce what they claimed was unaccountable power of the judiciary. While the practically irreformable 1994 constitution[11] guarantees that the Romanian judiciary is fully independent – starting with a constitutional court, which frequently rules against the government, and continuing with a judicial council mostly elected by magistrates – the organization of the judiciary can be can operated on a merge of power and accountability, and here a battle ensued. The SDP and its allies tried to increase the rights of defendants in corruption trials and narrow down the "function abuse" article, the basis for many convictions in Romania. Supported by Facebook-based civil society and opposition parties (including the directly elected 2014 non-SDP President Klaus Iohannis), the anti-corruption prosecutors then tried to indict the politicians for seeking to dilute the anti-corruption laws. The politicians retaliated by trying to fire the prosecutors indicting them.

While the firing of General Prosecutor L. C. Kövesi in summer 2018 (nominally by President Klaus Iohannis, but at the request of the government) was largely perceived in Brussels as a setback for anti-corruption, the act was only part of a larger chain of events that led to the political instrumentalization of the anti-corruption agency under Ms. Kövesi (all three challengers to President Iohannis for the next presidential elections in 2019 were indicted by her, with two partially cleared by the courts in 2018) and the mobilization of the parliament against NAD. Between 2016 and 2018, the constitutional court was called to arbitrate several

---

[11] Attempts to change the Romanian constitution have failed for the past fifteen years due to requirements for a referendum following a vote in the parliament. The latest attempt in 2018 (to prevent gay marriage) failed to get the required (and *de facto* impossible) turnout. A proposal to organize a referendum on justice reforms would also not meet the current threshold, which is a guarantee of constitutional stability.

times, ruling that ministers cannot be indicted for the act of issuing legislation and that the president's appointment of top prosecutors is largely ceremonial, with the government having the upper hand. But the constitutional court also cut half the modifications to the Macovei legislation attempted by the SDP. Protests against the SDP, labeled as "criminal," became an everyday occurrence in 2017–2018 in downtown Bucharest, but their participants remained limited to traditional opposition voters.

To conclude, the NAD could not by itself have turned corruption from norm to exception in ten years without substantial regulatory and administrative reforms. And those were sidelined in favor of purely criminal justice, which became more and more politically instrumentalized. The remaining rents after privatization did not disappear due to arrests; they only shifted to Mr. Băsescu's entourage between 2005 and 2014, and then back again to the SDP after 2012. Ministers who replaced colleagues fallen on the anti-corruption front came with the same mandate: to produce income for the parties behind them. A new political class has not emerged meanwhile, and those lost to anti-corruption were replaced by family members, lower-rank party figures, and even chauffeurs, who remained proxies in the December 2016 elections and successfully defended constituencies for the SDP and other local "barons" from the other parties. Some mayors were elected while under preventive arrest (Mungiu-Pippidi, 2018b). The joke in Romania was that both corruption and anti-corruption had reached unprecedented heights during the anti-corruption years (ibid.). New parties created after 2014 seemed to be from the outset plagued by secret service connections, either opposing more control of the secret service in parliamentary committees, or using a Sercuritate-connected law firm for their own official registration. It remains to be seen whether they will manage to emancipate themselves from such tutorship.

While administrative corruption decreased due to privatizations and simply the doubling of income between 2000 and 2018, the unique judicial stress on anti-corruption may actually have hampered judicial reform itself. Romanians remain the main suppliers of new lawsuits filled at the European Court of Human Rights and due process violations (see Table 6.1; ECHR, 2018), with important financial and political implications as well. The country is ahead of Russia and Turkey on convictions per capita on the basis of Article 6 of the Convention of Human Rights, the right to a free trial, which also accounts for half of Romania's convictions. The MCV lacks basic indicators on the performance of the judiciary itself and judicial statistics, which were always poor, have not evolved since 2004, and are indeed not a policy tool. In the same interval, bankruptcies became quite corrupt (judges are appointed who preside over preferential returns of debts, sometimes towards the companies owned also by the debtor), and contract and property litigation rulings remained arbitrary (perhaps corrupt) without any effort to find a remedy, much to the unhappiness of businesspeople. The spotlight is only on criminal cases of political importance, preventing any structural reform.[12]

Corruption and anti-corruption combined took their toll on political stability and government effectiveness in Romania. The country's politics show a high degree of contestation, with two attempts to suspend a president (2007, 2013), two changes of government under street pressure (2012, 2015) and two contests due to shifting majorities within a regular term (2007, 2012), not to mention the no-confidence motions and government changes due to regular elections. Between 2007 and 2017, Romania had changed its education minister seventeen times and its finance minister fourteen times (three former finance ministers went to jail). This situation could have been alleviated if Romania had had a second layer of professional bureaucracy autonomous from political patronage and capable of ensuring continuity (Mungiu-Pippidi, 2018b). But frequent political appointments, by shortcutting or defying civil service legislation (with subsequent redress sought in courts and compensations paid), deter the creation of such a bureaucracy. Changes occur mostly after elections, but also within each mandate (and mandates in Romania after 2004 were all shorter than four years), leading to high instability. During the first government of PM Emil Bloc (right wing), six changes of top civil servants occurred each month, and during the first cabinet of Victor Ponta (left wing) the figure rose to eight changes per month (Volintiru, 2016). The civil servants' agency, which was part of the acquis, was gradually sidelined.

The European Commission was not idle or indifferent in relation to Romania and Bulgaria. Twice a year it issued warnings and recommendations in relation to the fulfillment of the benchmarks, and the MCV assessment teams frequently visited the two capitals. The EC resorted to other sanctions beyond the special safeguard clauses: encouraged by negative media in EU member countries towards corruption in new member states, the European Commission cut Bulgaria's agriculture and structural funds in 2008 after having pushed for the resignation of key stakeholders in the government (Reuters, 2009). In the case of Romania, funds were cut in 2011 and reinstated only after the country managed to convince EU regional policy officials that proper controls of EU funds were put in place. The EC's President José Maria Barroso

---

[12] Interview with head of main business association, AOR, July 2018, Bucharest.

summoned Romania's Prime Minister Victor Ponta to report to Brussels when a majority in the parliament tried to suspend Mr. Băsescu in 2012 and asked for guarantees on anti-corruption and rule of law. On top of this, several roadmap strategies to fight corruption were put in place and updated following each of the EC's monitoring reports, with each recommendation answered in full. In time, as some benchmarks were fulfilled (an effective prosecuting agency), others were added (eliminating corruption, both petty and grand), including in 2018. While scripting such generalities, the EC missed raising many important questions: on the secret service; on the prosecutors of the oligarchs, who themselves ended in jail a year later; on the extreme politicization of the administration, which went against the acquis; on the constant and sometimes headline-making misuse of EU funds by top political figures; or on the RIS itself (while the rest of Europe was adopting data protection, the RIS was trying to get reimbursed by the EU for interconnecting all personal data databases in Romania; *Erective*, 2018). By and large, the EC has always been perceived in Bucharest as an advocate and promoter of the NAD alone and entirely influenced by Ms. Macovei and her team: in other words, as politically partisan, an argument also endorsed by some scholars (Mendelski, 2012).

Romania's anti-corruption backsliding, as perceived by European institutions, is due precisely to the nature of the anti-corruption activity itself, which has made its sustainability doubtful from the beginning. The focus on "big fish" that the European Commission demanded for Romania's anti-corruption policy led to an extreme politicization of anti-corruption on the Italian model, with constitutional conflicts between various branches of government. The majority in the parliament has used every opportunity to tame the threatening anti-corruption legislation, and each election won by SDP was perceived as a green light for its MPs, who started with the vulnerable articles in law (those questioned by ECHR, for instance) to then mount after 2017 a comprehensive legislative review meant to reduce the power of the judiciary. Arguably, the CVM created its own political dynamics, empowering some local anti-corruption officials and the politicians supporting it. But through its own existence, it may have subverted the creation of local pro-reform coalitions with a broader and more substantial agenda, which at least in Romania, if not in Bulgaria, existed to start with. Romanian "anti-corruption" should therefore not be made an example of for countries such as Ukraine or Moldova and can be saved solely through depoliticization and broad political consensus around the next steps towards good governance.

6.3 The Travails of the European Raj Revisited: Bosnia and Kosovo

Ten years after its creation, in summer 2018, the EU's rule of law mission in Kosovo, EULEX, handed over responsibility for judicial affairs to local authorities. EULEX had been established in 2008 to take over the task of establishing a democratic state and the rule of law from the unpopular United Nations Interim Administration Mission in Kosovo (UNMIK), following the unilateral declaration of the independence of Kosovo from Serbia. Its parting heritage consisted in a backlog of over 800 cases, almost no convictions for corruption of top officials, a string of corruption scandals involving its own staff, and a Freedom House/Nations in Transit corruption rating that had not budged for ten years from 5.75 (7 is worst). A local newspaper commented on this inglorious exit (partial, as they would still be around for monitoring), after UNMIK had spent almost EUR 1.5 billion to build rule of law in Kosovo, with the immortal head-line: "Instead of Europeanizing Kosovo, We Have Balkanized EULEX" (*Exit*, 2017). Kosovo was the most expensive externally led state-building project in the world. In 2005, the country received 25 times more money and 50 times more troops per capita than Afghanistan. After becoming independent in 2009, the country still received an influx of USD 345 per capita aid on governance alone, as compared to USD 62 in Afghanistan and USD 41 in Iraq.[13]

The situation of control of corruption in the other former Yugoslav splinter where international peace-building was followed by an EU intervention, Bosnia Hercegovina (BiH), is not much better. Since the first year of its corruption assessment, 2009, by Freedom House NIT, its corruption score has worsened from 4.50 to 5; additionally, Bosnia's judicial independence score worsened to 4 from 4.75. If in Kosovo accusations were of collusion with local top politicians on the part of EULEX, in Bosnia the Office of the High Representative (OHR), which had been in charge of Dayton Agreement implementation since 1995, came under fire in 2002 for summarily suspending every single judge and public prosecutor in the country, "pending the restructuring of the judicial system." For many years, "the OHR [has been] working towards the point where Bosnia and Herzegovina are able to take full responsibility for its own affairs," its website proclaims (OHR, 2010), but meanwhile it has made unrestrictive use of its "Bonn powers" to fire elected or appointed local politicians or civil servants – perhaps for good reason, but this only indicates the extraordinary strength of this intervention. All top heads of

---

[13] OECD, 2014. Query Wizard for International Development Statistics. http://stats.oecd.org/qwids/

OHR, a mission established on the basis of a UN mandate, have been Europeans. Even though the Parliamentary Assembly of the Council of Europe, which BiH joined in 2002, has voiced complaints against the international intrusion in local democracy, asking for a transfer of powers to the Bosnian authorities as soon as possible (back in 2004[14]), anxious local protests led to the continuation of deep European involvement, also based on the assessment of the powers engaged in the peace process. The entrenchment and sustainability of rule of law are among the many conditions needed for a final closure of OHR and total transfer of sovereignty to the local entities.

The cases of Kosovo and Bosnia are similar, but not identical. They are both former Yugoslavian, post-conflict societies in which the main group, which perceives itself as a victim of previous state arrangements, has managed to obtain limited sovereignty. To stop the Bosnian civil war, warring parties were offered an agreement that largely respected their territorial gains from the war. While universally seen as the golden "Switzerland opportunity," post-war Bosnia entered on a path dependent on the Dayton Peace Agreement[15] and the multicultural design of a state with three constituent "nations" (Mungiu-Pippidi and Krastev, 2004). Each corresponded to a territorial entity: the Muslims, the Serbs, and the Croats, the latter two with their affiliations across borders (to mother nations Serbia and Croatia), which extended to them protection and various rights (for instance passports). Kosovo suffered a massive population displacement, which, unlike in Bosnia, convinced the international community to bomb the perceived aggressor, the Serbian army. Bosnia's post-war central state was weak due to this tripartite design and the poor investment of other groups than Muslims in the central state. Kosovo's state-building started at an even lower point, as the region had been deprived of autonomy under Slobodan Milošević and most of its institutions had to be rebuilt entirely. It also received only partial international recognition, so the problem of its status has always been embedded in its state-building, affecting, for instance, the freedom to travel. Bosnia signed its Stabilization and Association Agreement (SAA) in 2008, but although ratified in 2011, it did not enter into force until June 1, 2015. Kosovo signed its SAA in 2015. In both countries, sovereignty has come only gradually and has been only reluctantly transferred from the "interventionist" external UN- or EU-controlled organizations to the domestic authorities. Issues of transitional justice, reparation, the protection of

---

[14] See http://www.assembly.coe.int/nw/xml/XRef/Xref-XML2HTML-EN.asp?
fileid=17232&lang=en

[15] The General Framework Agreement for Peace in Bosnia and Herzegovina, AKA Dayton Peace Agreement (DPA), Dayton-Paris, 14 December 1995.

minorities, and the creation of ethnically neutral authorities remained major problems in both countries, traumatized as they were by civil wars and their legacies, which ranged from problems around the proper repatriation of people and property to war crimes. It took a while for corruption to rise to the number one problem on the agenda. Critical popular perceptions and the need to have more effective EU aid finally pushed corruption on to the public agenda.

Corruption in both Bosnia and Kosovo is firmly based on particularism, and in their cases, the usual party particularism has an ethnic connotation as well. Two ethnographic studies commissioned by ANTICORRP (in Bosnia during a protest in Sarajevo against local corruption, in Pristina in a normal everyday setting) found similar features to the rest of the Eastern and Western Balkans. Public services are not easily accessible by virtue of citizenship (as a right) but only through connections (and, in their absence, through "gifts"). This is not an absolute, and more self-assertive individuals manage to get public services without either. But the expectations are still that particularism rules. The root of the evil is seen as the intense politicization (and sometimes ethnicism and nepotism) of the administration and public services, which do not behave as autonomous bureaucracies but act as gatekeepers to services rather than as impartial distributors. The judiciary, police, and local governments enjoy very little trust. Otherwise there are differences between the two countries where health and education are concerned, resulting from their different histories. The overwhelming conviction of people is that grand corruption, for instance connected with privatizations, is manipulated to benefit those organizing them (Lofranco, 2014; Duli-Sefaj, 2014). The need to create a different, "European" way is something that people are aware of, but they are also rather skeptical, since most of the phenomena they describe have coexisted with international/European rule for some time now. In Bosnia, because most important parties are ethnic, the usual partitocracies, as seen in competitive particularistic regimes of the Italian kind, become ethnocracies.

In short, Bosnia and Kosovo, as multi-ethnic, post-conflict societies and new states, had tremendous opportunities for corruption on top of their common communist heritage. These can be ascribed to four categories fitting the general model in which control of corruption is evaluated by looking at resources versus constraints. These categories are (1) ethnic particularism and multiethnicity; (2) power discretion due to parallel or competing authorities; (3) large amounts of aid combined with poor oversight and transparency; and (4) excessive regulatory ambition.

1. Ethnic particularism and the multiethnic character of the state: it is well known in empirical literature that ethnic or any form of sectarian fragmentation of a society creates more opportunities for corruption,

because competition among particular groups and intragroup favoritism leads to systematic particularism and discrimination (Fearon and Laitin, 1996). That finding has been empirically confirmed (Mauro, 1995) and still holds true. In multivariate models with development controls, we find that metalinguistic and religious fragmentations are stronger determinants of corruption than ethnic fractionalization, but the mechanism remains the same: sectarian-based particularism (Mungiu-Pippidi, 2015b, p. 85). Fragmentation of a society into factions or nations results in competition among groups to gain benefits from the central state, thereby greatly favoring particularism based on ethnic, religious, or linguistic qualifications, as opposed to ethical universalism as an allocation principle blind to any group affiliations. Due to uncertainty of status and competitive state-building, the ethnic groups in these two countries remained high on particularistic trust (what anthropologist Edward Banfield called "amoral familism," 1958) and captive to their own group elites due to the perception of existential threats from rival groups they had fought in the civil war. While there were some constitutional checks and balances with the aim of securing ethnic cooperation, the system developed resembled an "ethnocracy," especially in Bosnia – rather than the textbook consensual (consociationalism) regime of the classic type described by Arendt Lijphart for the Netherlands and transferred to Lebanon (Howard, 2012; Hulsey and Stjepanović, 2017). The international community struggled for many years against local resistance to the Dayton constitutional arrangements, but to no avail; and thus the potential of Napoleon-like engineering (for instance, of canton reorganization to favor cooperation and not conflict) was largely lost.

2. Power discretion due to parallel or competing authorities multiplied the administrative burden on one hand, while confusing accountability on the other. By 2013, independent Bosnia had 13 governments, 143 legislative assemblies, and 260 appointed ministers – for a population of fewer than 3.8 million people (Podumljak, 2016). Kosovo is also on record for the highest number of independent agencies, many created on donor money to take care of some particular problem. A summary of agencies linked to ministries prepared by the Office of the Auditor General showed by 2016 the existence of 68 agencies, lacking clarity on status and structure, with only 22 filling out annual financial statements (OECD Sigma, 2016). In 2014, excluding ministries and constitutional bodies, 30 agencies reported directly to the parliament or the prime minister. The picture was completed by different governance arrangements for 17 central and 43 local publicly owned enterprises (OECD Sigma, 2016, p. 28).

3. The large amount of aid combined with poor oversight and transparency: Bosnia and in particular Kosovo featured for many years among the top most aid-dependent countries in the world. Although Kosovo's dependency declined from over 15 percent before 2009 to roughly 6 percent by 2016, according to the World Bank, at one point it received the world's highest per capita aid from the EU (World Bank, 2018c). After the Thessaloniki summit, the two countries moved from stabilization to "Europeanization" funds. The EU Instrument for Pre-Accession Assistance (IPA) was created to provide assistance to candidate and potential candidate countries in their preparation for accession. IPA I corresponded to the 2007–2013 programming period and IPA II, designed to deliver financial assistance under a longer-term sector approach, covered the period 2014–2020. Both stressed rule of law as one of the key priorities of the enlargement process and made it necessary for beneficiary countries to tackle issues such as judicial reform and the fight against organized crime and corruption. According to data provided by the Delegation of the EU to BiH, the total value of the EU's financial assistance to BiH through IPA for 2007–2013 amounted to approximately EUR 594 million, implemented through around 300 projects. Rule of law received around EUR 220 million, or 37 percent of the total, divided between democracy and governance (EUR 110 million and 34 projects) and rule of law and fundamental rights (EUR 110 million and 75 projects; Podumljak, 2016). Almost EUR 1.5 billion (USD 1.7 billion) in European Union funds were shelled out for the rule of law mission in Kosovo alone.[16] Of the total amount committed to Kosovo through projects, those related to the rule of law, anti-corruption, and good governance amounted to roughly 25 percent of the total allocated aid (Dodbiba and Duli, 2016). In 2012 and 2013 in Kosovo the subsector that received the most aid was the judiciary. In 2014, rule of law received support from 16 donors implementing 86 projects. The EU was the largest donor. While this could have provided leverage for the external donors, it seems in fact to have created irresistible resources for corruption. The operation of procurement in aid-dependent countries was aptly described by Balkan journalists as "tenders of endearment," attracting both local and international suppliers (*BIRN*, 2016). Agency capture is reportedly very high, but the sheer volume of procurement in the spending budget indicates a massive resource for

---

[16] See https://www.dw.com/en/eu-ends-kosovo-rule-of-law-mission-amid-criticism-over-results/a-44229405.

favoritism itself, and corruption spared neither international companies nor domestic ones (ibid.).

4. Excessive regulatory ambition served only to dilute the transformative potential of relevant reforms. Since the signing of the Stabilization and Accession Plan (SAP), Kosovo's regulatory quality has not progressed – rather the other way around, in World Bank estimations. While some scholars praise the logic of EU accession for providing incentives for the applicant countries to carry out reforms, what Balkan Europeanization seems to have brought is plans rather than incentives, a mechanism reminiscent of command economy rather than a market where supply and demand meet. The plans (also called roadmaps or strategies) range from "Europeanization" (adoption of EU legislation and standards, to be fit for accession) to anti-corruption. For these two countries – even for Kosovo, who has not submitted a formal EU application like Bosnia – EU accession means that, besides struggling with substantial political processes and rebuilding their own rule of law and economies, they are simultaneously flooded with laws and rules to make them closer to European goodness of fit in all areas. The 2018 EU report on Kosovo, for instance, and the previous one for Bosnia – after exhausting the major problems of borders, relations with neighbors, rule of law, human rights, and the economy – goes on to monitor progress on Europeanization. This roughly refers to legislative progress in the 26 acquis chapters, including fisheries, intellectual property law, and phytosanitary policy. The theory of change is generous in its intent: working with Kosovo on chapters of the acquis (without a being a candidate country, Kosovo is on the European "track" and was included in the invitation to join extended to the Western Balkans at the 2003 Thessaloniki summit) signals European good will and may make the country better fit for a future European integration. But it also shows a lack of prioritization in institutional reforms and of understanding of the need to build systems (rule of law and functional state operations) before adopting all this legislation, which would not be easy to digest even in a more mature country. In Bosnia, there has been some progress in the last ten years on regulatory quality, as efforts were made to better integrate the country, but they should be seen as merely corrections to the institutional mess from before. Bosnia's regular reports also have lengthy section on European legislation. These should not be seen as impositions by the EU: Bosnia has been one of the most frustrated Western Balkan countries in terms of the perceived slow pace of EU accession. It applied formally in 2016, and since then it has been engaged in answering the EU's "questionnaire" of preparedness. Accession countries are keen to be allowed into the EU, and this formal

and cumbersome process is given priority to their institutional transformation, of which it is seen as part or complement, without much (or any) reflection on the *interaction* of these processes, which are not always synergetic and even more rarely help one another in the early phases. While in recent years it has become topical (after most developing countries adopted lengthy regulations on conflict of interest, whistleblowing, and party finance, with little change of practice) to discuss an "implementation gap,"[17] the EU theory of change creates the implementation gap by design. The European Union works on the premise that countries that apply for membership do so voluntarily and therefore admit that there are a number of obligations to fulfill. Political will, present or future (as accession is an instrument of stabilization, offering countries a very long time to "prepare"), is therefore taken for granted; and the vast apparatus of aid, technical assistance, and political dialogue is meant to create the necessary legal and institutional conditions for EU acquis and for coming into line with European standards. These tools are created to be readily at hand when the domestic political agency becomes ripe to implement reforms.[18] The main rationale of the Europeanization of the Balkans has always been geopolitical, with the goal of stabilizing the European backyard through exporting democratic values and prosperity – or, in the words of an EU commissioner, "exporting stability to prevent the import of instability" (Hahn, 2015).

An excess of opportunities for corruption exists in these two countries, therefore, due to the combination of their state-building and Europeanization projects. One could have expected, however, that this would be offset by the unprecedented power of the EU in these two countries: in other words, by the increase in constraints to corruption created by the mighty EU intervention. So how much did EU matter, directly as well as through its influence on the general constraints, judicial independence, freedom of the press, and civil society?

The EU's *direct influence* in Bosnia and Kosovo was indeed very strong. In Bosnia, the Bonn powers were frequently used and the judiciary often reshuffled, together with ministers who were deemed unfit or corrupt. In Kosovo, arrests of members of government happened more than once, and even prime ministers were indicted for war crimes. But direct arrests of members of a government that a donor supports (for corruption or war crimes) subvert ownership, and in both countries a trade-off existed between doing the morally right thing and allowing some local ownership of reforms to take shape. Furthermore, Western intervention in both

---

[17] The concept is especially promoted by the World Bank and Global Integrity, after giving up the Global Integrity Index, which aggregated good governance legal equipment.

[18] Interview with EU official, summer 2018, Sarajevo.

countries has only opened the door to nation-building, and the process was in full swing when the EU started providing assistance for establishing rule of law and controlling corruption. In many cases, the current rulers were yesterday's nationalists whose fight had brought freedom for their peoples. They were natural patrons, and they used the state-building process to consolidate their client basis, which should only have been expected. Reformers in the region, of the likes of the Serbian prime minister Zoran Dindic (assassinated) or the Romanian justice minister Monica Macovei (dismissed after two years in office), were not easy to come by to start with: their fate discouraged others. Ownership of the rule of law process remained nominal during the accession years, with the whole process of building rule of law and corruption control treated bureaucratically by the EU and entrusted to the nominal local authorities, regardless of their commitment, rather than to some more change-committed alliance of stakeholders. In Kosovo, there were accusations of complete fusion between EU-led authorities and the Thaci government, with the consequence of letting some former Kosovo Liberation Army fighters turned government officials get away with murder (*The Guardian*, 2014).

Apart from these factors, conditionality was also subverted by poor strategy, competence, and organization on the EU side. Hardly any connection between rewards and achievements can be discerned. In Kosovo, by October 2015, when the Stabilization and Association Agreement was signed, there had been no contractual agreement between Kosovo and the EU, so while a record amount of funding was allocated to Kosovo no conditionality framework operated in practice (Dodbiba and Duli, 2016). Additionally, there were no indicators or baselines against which to measure progress. On one hand, EU funds in Kosovo are managed by the EU delegation in Kosovo (EUIK) and are disbursed mainly for technical assistance. Instruments that rely heavily on mutually-agreed-upon indicators and that require prior baseline studies have been discussed, but had not in fact been used by 2016 (ibid.). The existing conditionality was rather qualitative and general – for instance, related to a visa liberalization regime in Kosovo – and therefore did not tie reforms to funds. An additional challenge has arisen from the fact that the Program and Political Sections of the EU report to different Directorates at the EU level (DGDEV and DGNEAR), resulting in a lack of coordination between the development and political agendas of the EU (ibid.).

Furthermore, in Bosnia, the national IPA coordinator has been subordinated to entity-level political and administrative actors, exposing policies and actions to the risk of veto by ethno-political power groups (Podumljak, 2016). In addition, the complex structure of the federation increased transaction costs to arrive at common or consistent positions in dealings with the EU, which seldom materialized. The provision of financial assistance to Bosnia is formally conditional on progress in satisfying the Copenhagen Criteria and in meeting the specific priorities of the European Partnership (EU Council, 2008, 80 OJ L). Progress is monitored through mechanisms established under the SAP, notably through annual reports produced by the European Commission, which assess Bosnia's progress against the Copenhagen Criteria. However, although these reports monitor progress against defined tasks, they are not directly linked to decisions about whether to continue or withhold funding (Podumljak, 2016).

In Kosovo, the leading "plans" formulating prescriptions for reform were the yearly EC Progress Reports and the European Partnership Action Plan (EPAP). The EPAP of 2008 contained 79 priorities on the rule of law, but as the European Court of Auditors noticed, these were broad policy concerns, not linked explicitly to the IPA annual program, which contains targets of a technical nature (ECA, 2012). The progress reports primarily stress the need for amending the legislation to align it with the acquis, and the corresponding need to improve legislation. What is missing is the theory of change on how rule of law or control of corruption comes about and the sequencing of a mechanism to enable them. Instead, a collection of abstract notions and checkboxes are stacked on top of one another. Despite an extraordinary number of consultants (hence most money was spent on technical assistance and building a main courthouse), one cannot find a European official or master document to outline the vision and steps of state-building in Kosovo. In the vacuum, in Bosnia, interns and bureaucrats in EU delegations got quite creative, as Knaus and Martin have detailed (2003), with the result of a multitude of poorly informed, loosely contextualized, and mutually disconnected institutional imports. The next generation of bureaucrats added to the objectives: "streamlining," or the elimination of institutions introduced in the first years. In plainer terms, if indicators of progress on governance were lacking for so long, it was because the vast mass of technical consultants and bureaucrats from the EU had a good idea of how rule of law works in a "normal" country – but no idea of how to get there. The concepts could hardly have been operationalized even with competent staff, since they were altogether missing. This ignorance on the international side, combined with a vast amount of power and money, met the locals' desire to survive and not be left outside Europe (Chandler, 2000). In turn, domestic proponents of reform became either opportunistic or plainly uninterested, considering the rule of law discussion a price to pay for not being left out in the cold. Conditionality worked better when clarity existed on both the measures required to deliver and the incentive, for instance in the home office field, where the major incentive of visa liberalization (a palpable benefit for all, to travel and work in the EU) made governments in both countries adopt and implement the safeguards required by the EU (Podumljak, 2016; Dodbiba and Duli, 2016).

Successive evaluations of rule of law and anti-corruption programs in the Balkans have all struggled from the outset with two aspects: first, to find the grounding of the work in some programmatic document (some took it to be the chapters in the acquis devoted to home office and justice, but those refer to Europeanization *after* rule of law was created); and second, to assess any link between the programmatic documents, general and vague as they were, and the programs and funding allocations themselves (ECA, 2012; Berenschot and Imagos, 2012).

This failed because the policy frameworks on which actual priorities are negotiated at country level are not based on a theory of change, or, in the words of evaluators: "The [planning documents] do not provide the strong guidance needed in terms of what the program should focus on for what reasons (resource allocation criteria) or what are desired or expected achievements (results criteria, target values)" (Berenschot and Imagos, 2012). The fact-based indicators are missing because the concepts that they are supposed to measure are missing, and therefore even when some indicators were introduced, they were vague (for instance an "increased" number of corruption cases or financial crimes detected, prosecuted, and judged). Other indicators added in more recent years include the World Bank's Worldwide Governance Indicators, the World Justice Project's composite indicator Access to Justice (survey-based), and the World Economic Forum's Judicial Independence indicator (survey-based), signaling some shift towards performance assessment. But objective indicators are missing, and those offered by ECHR, for instance, are insufficiently used. By and large, the existence of sound judicial or administrative statistics by country is in itself the main progress indicator of an area: if no such monitoring instruments exist, monitoring only the carrying out of prescriptions is irrelevant. This is precisely what all evaluators on rule of law seem to find when innocently reporting that, despite adopting relevant legislation, corruption has not changed.

The EC Progress Reports over the period 2007–2014 find that Kosovo has made some progress in the fight against corruption, but many challenges remain. Under IPA I, the Support to Anti-Corruption Institutions in Kosovo project received major backing. The European Court of Auditors judged, however, that the project's impact had been limited (ECA, 2012). The audit concluded that EU assistance to the rule of law had been ineffective, unable to meet all its objectives, subject to delays, and dubious in terms of sustainability of results. As for Bosnia, a 2015

evaluation of all the Western Balkan countries and Turkey is unambigu-
ously negative: IPA support for the fight against corruption provided
unsatisfactory results. The evaluators rated projects as having "(serious)
deficiencies" (Berenschot and Imagos, 2012: 30). The lack of proper
outputs was blamed on the complex and highly politicized and fragmented institutional structure of BiH – which constrained collaboration
between beneficiaries in the various administrative units – as well as the
lack of involvement of beneficiaries in project design, weakness in the
conditionality, and poor donor coordination. The same evaluation rated
Kosovo as "satisfactory"on the overall performance of assistance related
to efficiency and effectiveness of anti-corruption, but saw the overall
assistance performance nevertheless to be "compromised by unsatisfactory impact and sustainability … due to low-level follow-up of the
projects recommendations, i.e. out of 35 proposals made on the Law on
Anti-corruption Agency and [Kosovo Anti-Corruption Agency (KAA)]
restructuring, the Kosovo authorities accepted only 14." This is a pre-
scription-based evaluation again, as there no way of knowing if prescriptions would have had any impact even if implemented. Evaluators saw the
most important threats to the achievement of long-term results to be a
lack of independence of the key investigation institutions – in the "lack of
authority of institutions such as KAA and the Central Electoral
Commission, and a lack of ownership among key institutions such as
KAA and the High Secretariat on Anti-corruption" – and ineffective
cooperation between preventive and investigating agencies (Berenschot
and Imagos, 2012). This means that the essentials of the integrity framework were not working at that point.

Where the two missions succeeded better was in simply building some
judicial and legal infrastructure and capacity. And these are worthwhile
development goals. Judges and prosecutors had to be appointed, court-
houses (in Kosovo) built and ICT equipment installed, and procedures
such as an electronic system of case allocation introduced for the first
time. These clear-cut benefits were less controversial compared to the
hard-to-pin-down "judicial independence" or "control of corruption."
The latter stagnated – and in light of the ethnic particularism in both
countries, it is hard to imagine that the new judicial elites would easily
turn against the new political elites simply because of international pressure. Out of all the indictments in 2016–2017 in Kosovo, 67 percent
failed in the courts, many of them in the first instance (i.e. they never even
took off). This trend suggests that some indictments against high-profile
cases are not well enough substantiated – pressed ahead only because of
international pressure (Western ambassadors frequently demand high-
profile convictions) or from fear of crimes coming close to violating

prescription terms (Kosovo Law Institute, 2017). Voters upset with *partitocrazia* reacted, instead, with the constant losers of party particularism explaining the rise of Vetevendosje as the single largest party in parliament. This rising radical nationalist party does have a strong pro-integrity agenda and made its debut in public life by smashing up EULEX cars in 2009 (Marzouk, 2009).

The EU's theory of change in these cases, to the extent that one existed, was that jailing some high-profile "big fish" would have a deterrent effect and dispel the culture of immunity from prosecution. Croatia's Ivo Sanader, the prime minister who successfully negotiated accession, and Romania's Adrian Nastase, the last prime minister from before accession, were both given jail sentences for corruption by their own judiciaries immediately before accession, perhaps to convince the EU of the good will of the two countries. But in Kosovo EULEX, which had direct powers of prosecution, had no similar high-profile case. What had succeeded in Croatia and Romania, because it was practically an *ex ante* condition and was executed by sovereign domestic agents, did not work in Bosnia and Kosovo, two nations still being built and with far greater sensitivities, despite the EU having at some point unlimited judicial power.

Aside from fighting immunity culture, with more or less success, the building of an impartial judiciary and bureaucracy were new, uncharted areas for EU delegations. Evaluators of IPA programs or of EULEX all complained of the poor quality of the international staff, but incentives are also to blame: one could hardly expect much from a crowd of competent Europeans available to take the job of building rule of law in Kosovo and Bosnia on a high daily consultancy fee for years, with zero accountability and very little guidance to go on. And while many quality people did pass through as part of academic or civil society events, there were not enough people brought into key positions who had succeeded in doing something similar before, from Estonia or Georgia, for instance. Incidentally, the reform of the police was judged to be both ineffectual and lacking domestic ownership in both Kosovo and Bosnia (ECA, 2012). According to a whistleblower who had a top position within EULEX, this failure partly reflected the difficult context, but the main causes were internal – incompetence, weak management, and a lack of loyalty to the mission's mandate (Capussela, 2015a; 2015b). Furthermore, in late 2014, the mission faced major allegations of corruption among its own high-ranking officials (EULEX, 2014; *The Economist*, 2014). This prompted the launch of a review in early 2015. It concluded that, considering the state of Kosovo's judicial system, the mission was not equipped to meet the challenges of corruption and organized crime, and so it had failed to create the foundations of a system capable of fighting corruption (Jacqué, 2015). Additionally, both the European Court of Auditors (2012) and the Jacqué report (2015) criticized the low quality of staff deployed to EULEX. The ECA's report states that some of the staff members were unqualified and that member states do not properly assess candidates prior to their deployment. The Jacqué report also considered that training of staff was inadequate. Expectations had been very high regarding EULEX's contribution in Kosovo (EUR 111 million p.a., separate from IPA) towards prosecuting high-ranking corrupt officials or criminal gang leaders.

The performance on judicial independence is, then, at best mixed. The next factor important to constrain control of corruption – freedom of the media – was far less the object of EU intervention. Kosovo and Bosnia have a vibrant media environment, although corruption (through both hidden and overt political ownership) and ethnic particularism created a model of *lotizzazione* as in Italy and typical of corrupt countries, in contrast to the information-oriented and advertisement-funded Western media (Mungiu-Pippidi 2015b: Ch 5). Pluralism in such a media land-scape comes from the plurality of sources, each highly partisan, and reporting of corruption may range from heroic to pure defamation (*kompromat*), but is highly selective according to source. The main problem in the Western Balkans, where many qualified journalists work in dedicated networks of investigative journalism, is ownership of the media. Citing unfair competition from local oligarchs and corruption in the advertising market, Western investors (even the less reputed ones) have gradually left (Siebenhaar, 2010). The identities of media owners are not transparent, and those known are local politicians, vested interest groups, or PR companies that deliver good or bad press to the highest bidder. While the EU's regular reports show an awareness of the importance of media freedom, the EU accession project has done little or nothing for the media, whose freedom has gradually declined on the average in the Western Balkans over the past ten years. Bosnia and Kosovo are below the region's average concerning freedom of the press, so behind Serbia and Croatia, although not so far from Greece. There is no dedicated aid or action for the media, and only in 2017 did the problem attract enough attention for the EC to organize an event dedicated to this issue in in Tirana (EC, 2017f). The newer digital media platforms should theoreti-cally help, but in view of the rural poverty of the Balkans it is not surpris-ing that a whole town in Macedonia "got rich" on fake news, working as a troll factory to support Donald Trump's campaign (BBC News, 2016).

If the EU's support for media freedom is minimal, aside from some political mentions in regular reports, civil society does not fare much better in terms of dedicated budget lines in IPA programs, despite being the other important constraint on corruption. The money for rule of law and anti-corruption is going entirely to the public sector, part of a broader pattern in the region, with practically no funds for social accountability or any state–society anti-corruption designs (such as consumer audits or evaluations of public service delivery). The few existing watchdogs receive EU funding, and those acting in cooperation with the media have some impact, but the absence of civil society accountability at the community level is striking and costly for control of corruption. In Bosnia's IPA I funding cycle, for example, the government was the recipient of 98 percent of the total amount, with the 48 civil society projects receiving only EUR 8.4 million. Figure 6.7 shows that control of corruption went only slightly down when the volume of EU funds in the total income decreased – but then it caught up again.

In conclusion, the most recent EU reports on Bosnia-Hercegovina and Kosovo acknowledge the limited progress on rule of law and control of corruption, despite their vague language on "some preparedness" in the fields of judicial independence and corruption. Failure is also admitted on

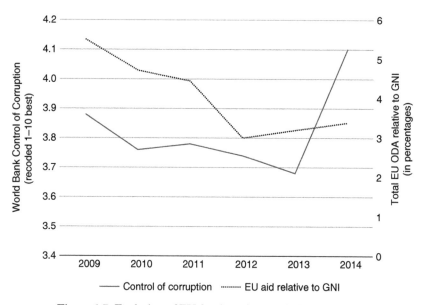

Figure 6.7 Evolution of EU funds and control of corruption in Kosovo, 2002–2014
Source: OECD – QWIDS Official Development Aid and World Bank Control of Corruption

administrative reform, especially due to politicization; progress, where it does exist (Kosovo registered some progress in reducing red tape and improving the business environment), is viewed cautiously. Locals and many of their supporters in the think tank community criticize the European shifting of "goalposts," showing that many objectives were, after all, fulfilled and this criticism is just meant to keep these two hardly constrained countries at bay.

It is difficult to do a counterfactual on Bosnia and Kosovo to test the EU's influence on corruption. While government favoritism would have probably not been much different without EU intervention, it is unlikely that the normalcy experienced in the two countries would have been the same. Also, despite impunity still existing in control of corruption, many major war criminals were indicted, which would also not have happened without the EU. The goal of stabilization was achieved, and it seems likely (as Mr. Capussela accused) that for Europeans this was the primary goal. Local politicians and experts have always suspected a lack of realism in the "zero tolerance" approach to corruption and the impossibility of attaining judicial impartiality in only a few years within an ethnically divided society. But they played along because this was the way to advance their EU accession cause – and to keep the aid money flowing in. The lack of ownership (called lack of "political will" in EU evaluations) is an important cause for these countries' not meeting goals on institutional reform. Money that went into hard infrastructure and the reconstruction of the region was indispensable, although it also stimulated corruption. However, a public spending structure that pays public servants little and commissions expensive projects is a bad and lasting legacy of EU intervention and a permanent resource for corruption (Belloni and Strazzari, 2014). Only a counterfactual on stability, and not on control of corruption, would thus shed some favorable light on the EU's intervention.

Stabilization therefore came with a price: in practice, and in spite of EU efforts, the main story of post-conflict was national, not state-building, with the success going to nationalist elites in crafting states that are far from the ideal of ethical universalism. We know from literature on nationalism that this is generally the case for new nations becoming states for the first time. Bosnia and Kosovo were candidates unlikely to resemble Switzerland, and the EC intervention was based on less local knowledge and wisdom than Napoleon employed in his Swiss intervention. Nevertheless, ethnic particularism will always subvert good governance, as it is fundamentally against ethical universalism. The United States and the European Union fought to prevent this phenomenon in both countries, but failed. In Bosnia, it might have been guilt over Srebenica and the failure to intervene, and in Kosovo, the NATO bombing, which convinced the Serbs that the intervention was biased; but the result was that in both cases later state-building assistance could not overcome the fact that the main outcome of the war was the *de facto* empowerment of ethnic elites to build national states (Mungiu-Pippidi and Krastev, 2004). In many ways, these cases confirm the failure of liberal interventionism, this experiment in social engineering that involves transplanting Western models of social, political, and economic organization into war-shattered states in order to control civil conflict (Paris, 1997). Furthermore, democratic elections in such places often reinforce the separation of the parties rather than facilitating their reconciliation. While the EU accession perspective may have stabilized the Western Balkans, its good governance approach (formal plans with stress on UNCAC, formal institutions, abundance of EU funds, vague conditionality) merely created a formal and bureaucratic process with limited perspective for changing institutions in a substantial and sustainable way.

6.4   Back to the Future: Turkey's Rule of Law Evolution

At midnight on January 7, 2014, in Turkey, the governing Justice and Development Party (Turkish acronym AKP) published a decree removing 350 judicial police officers from their positions, including the chiefs of the units dealing with financial crimes, smuggling, and organized crime, following a corruption probe targeting people close to the government (BBC News, 2014). The minister of European integration was among those targeted by the investigation, as was the son of Prime Minister Recep Tayyip Erdoğan. Three cabinet ministers resigned after their sons were detained in the raids, and the prosecutor in charge of the case was also dismissed. Mr. Erdoğan, later president of Turkey, described the corruption investigation as a "judicial coup" by his former allies in the Gülen movement. When still allies a few years before, they had managed a mortal blow to the old political order against a secularist, pro-American army, which traditionally had checked inefficient and corrupt politicians by staging coups, followed by constitutional rewrites and then returns to free elections (Stone, 2017, pp. 160–177). In 2007, following a statement from the army in which it pledged to be an "absolute defender of secularism" in a veiled threat of yet another coup, the government launched a massive crackdown against ten army generals and hundreds of other officers, as well as various journalists and professors, for allegedly seeking to undermine the government – by a conspiracy known by the mythical name of Ergenekon, a foundational legend of the Turkish nation. The indictments and trials were marked by clear breaches of due process and judicial procedure, years of pre-trial detention, and obvious inconsistencies (Rodrik, 2011; Freedom House, 2017b). In September 2013, 275 defendants were convicted, including the former chief of the armed forces, with the alleged collaboration of judicial figures in the Gülen network (Freedom House, 2017b). The sentences were annulled in 2016, when Mr. Erdoğan broke with his former allies, but by then the essential had been accomplished: Turkish *de facto* judicial independence, which had ranked fourth in the world in 2003, was brought under political control following years of reforms aimed at aligning it to the European acquis (Rodrik, 2011; Hayo and Voigt, 2007). The good score that Turkey had received in 2003 on expert indicators for *de facto* independence had resulted precisely for policies like not removing prosecutors or judges from ongoing cases, and the difference between its *de jure*, constitutional independence rank of only 34 showed that by 2003 Turkey's judicial practice was superior to its constitutional arrangements (Hayo and Voigt, 2007). Amazingly, a decade later, between EU accession on one side, with its legal alignment, and internal political dynamics on the other, the reverse came about. In the same interval, political intervention affected media freedom. When two top newspapers, *Hürriyet* and *Milliyet*, gave extensive front-page coverage of a German corruption court case accusing some top AKP figures of embezzling tens of millions of dollars from a Turkish charity, their publisher Doğan Media Group became the target of official persecution, which culminated in a USD 2.5 billion tax fine and the market capitalization of four-fifths of the entire company, leading to the selling of the two newspapers to another holding company with strong ties to the government (Freedom House, 2017b). The two essential elements of control of corruption, freedom of the press and judicial independence, had thus collapsed even before the final confrontation between AKP and their former Gülenist allies following a poorly staged coup by some air force officers. The crackdown after the coup brought down most of thise who were left and prompted Freedom House to degrade Turkey to nonfree status in 2017 (ibid.).

Corruption has been a pervasive problem in Turkey for many years, yet a distinct anti-corruption policy appeared only in the aftermath of the 2001 financial crisis at the prompting of international donors, the EU among them (Soyaltin, 2017). Turkey under the AKP seemed to have what only Romania, among the Balkan states, had briefly enjoyed: domestic agency for change. The AKP government made anti-corruption one of its three policy priorities, after winning a landslide victory in the 2002 elections (ibid.). A year after the elections, the new government established a parliamentary investigation committee and adopted proposals to open investigations into corruption allegations against a former prime minister, as well as several other ministers of the previous government (BTI, 2016, p. 23). They also beefed up anti-corruption legislation (Soyaltin, 2017), but it has soon become clear that their opponents alone would be targeted by these laws. Still, Turkey's performance looked like "a textbook example" of the EU's transformative power, despite some fluctuations over time (Kirişçi, 2011; Soyaltin, 2017).

Corruption has been a traditional problem for Turkey, with its Ottoman features changing shape but not disappearing in modern history (Baran, 2000; Buğra, 1994). However, the twentieth-century Ataturk dictatorship had a strong modernizing and developmental character, and as such it managed to make bureaucracies (in the civil service and the army) more autonomous vis-à-vis private interest and with a more universalistic ethos than under the Ottomans, for all their late reforms (Stone, 2017). The 1960 coup d'état in Turkey by a "new middle class" composed of managerial bureaucrats, army officials, and the intelligentsia also resulted in a regime friendly to capitalism. Although Turkish capitalism has always had a pronounced "crony" character, relying on the patronage networks that had been part of Turkish society historically, the combination of a powerful bureaucracy with the ascent of modern capitalism did get Turkey to improve on control of corruption. Democracy brought its usual paradox, with freedoms of the press and association being offset by the increase of particularistic politics throughout the 1980s and 1990s (Güneş-Ayata, 1994; 2002), and an institutionalization of complex networks of reciprocity enjoying government favoritism (Soyaltin, 2017). After the military handed power back to the elected leadership in 1983, then Prime Minister Turgut Özal, a former World Bank executive inspired by the Pinochet neoliberal approach to the economy, introduced further liberal reforms with the paradoxical result of the rise of what would later be referred to as the Anatolian bourgeoisie or the Anatolian tigers (Stone, 2017), who had previously been no match for the established businesses of Istanbul. Corruption featured as a salient problem in surveys of the public at that time (Adaman et al., 2001), and Turkey did poorly in the Corruption Perception Index published by Transparency International.

The evolution of Turkey's control of corruption has thus been a complex and nonlinear affair, but the bureaucracy (including the military one) and the entrepreneurial class succeeded in making Turkey a more successful economy than others in the Middle East or the Mediterranean, despite weaknesses of civil society and a great inequality across regions. While Turkey's democratic evolution has always been on the EU's radar, the understanding of control of corruption and rule of law and therefore their monitoring had always been poor. Due to Turkey's particular history, for instance, the EU has always feared the Turkish military and Kemalism more generally, and could not see any positive element in their influence (on universalism and the bureaucratic ethos, for instance) on the likes of what Sam Huntington had described in his controversial but classic book on civil–military relations (Huntington, 1981). Meanwhile, the rise of Islamism, as a new powerful identity based in doctrine, was seen rather positively, like some sort of "Calvinism" (Knaus, 2005) – when in fact, the Islamists seem to have had an overt design not to disrupt the existing rents in the economy but to take them over. Thus an important outcome of the neoliberal reforms of the 1990s was the consolidation of new elite cartels and the evolution from a state-centered to an oligarchic form of capitalism (Karadag, 2010). In doing so, resources for corruption were basically reorganized during EU accession. For instance, although a Public Procurement Law was put in force in 2003 with the objective of improving competition, transparency, and integrity and aligning better with EU directives, the post-2002 incumbent government party repeatedly changed it, prompting frequent exemptions (Emek and Acar, 2015). Dozens of public contracts were removed from its jurisdiction by being moved to other types of allocation, leading to the shrinking share of Turkish public procurement in GDP (e.g. 5–6 percent), well below the EU equivalent (15–16 percent on the average). The use of noncompetitive tender procedures, such as direct procurement and restricted procedure, has steadily risen in this interval, while the use of competitive open procedure has declined (ibid.). Procurement as a main tool of particularistic allocation thus gradually declined during the AKP's rise, with an increase in public–private partnership (PPP) contracts, which in Turkey have not been submitted to competitive procurement regulation as the EU's best practice would have required. PPP has increased over the years to become the preferred method for large-scale infrastructure investments. This trend produced losers (foreign participation in public tenders decreased, after having never been important in Turkey; Emek and Acar, 2015) as well as winners. Connections do play a large role again in explaining the economic success of the "Anatolian tigers," who proved not to be so Calvinist after all (Karadag, 2013), with the new champions of Anatolian capital shown to have ties to the government via both their religious–political identity and direct personal linkages (Buğra and Savaşkan, 2012). They also gained significantly from particularistic privatizations processes: for example, managing to acquire a large part of what used to be independent media with the support of public banks, as in the sale of the ATV-Sabah media group that fell, also in a controversial manner, to the Çalık Group in 2008 (Karadag, 2013).

Accession negotiations with Turkey had been opened in October 2005 after it had received official candidate status at the Helsinki summit in 2000. An association agreement between Turkey and the then EEC (later EU) originated in December 1964, and Turkey and the EU formed a customs union in 1995; 38 percent of Turkey's total trade is with the EU, and almost 71 percent of foreign direct investment in Turkey comes from EU member states. Despite Turkey being a big country, several conditions were thus assembled for the EU to play an influential role. The EU also provided financial support aimed at strengthening the capacity of state agencies to cope with the reform agenda (Soyaltin, 2017). Under IPA, Turkey received EUR 4.87 billion, an average of EUR 608 million p.a. between 2007 and 2013. The EU allocation for Turkey under IPA II for the 2014–2020 period is planned to be EUR 4.45 billion (EC, 2013c). Together with the funds provided under the Turkey Pre-Accession Assistance until 2006, the IPA funds make Turkey the largest recipient of EU aid, with over EUR 13 billion.

By 2013, after many years of stagnation, Turkey was getting good marks on EU accession conditions, implementing a list of steps that had been aptly called the "positive agenda." Corruption or politicization of the judiciary did not appear as particular problems, with Northern Cyprus still getting most of the attention. Under the headline "Fight against corruption," the EU 2013 Regular Progress Report noted in typical fashion that "Implementation of the National Anti-Corruption Strategy continued," praising the newly created institution of an ombudsman. The EU did not prompt the actions against the corrupt ring that ended in the prosecutors' dismissal; the Obama administration did, through its somewhat belated effort to enforce sanctions against Iran and dry up terrorist money in the Middle East. The dismissal of prosecutors investigating the government is noted in the EU report as a "risk" to the capacity of prosecution, as well as a rule of law "threat," but no serious consequence is envisaged:

The response of the government following allegations of corruption in December 2013 has given rise to serious concerns regarding the independence of the judiciary and separation of powers. The widespread reassignments and dismissals of police officers, judges and prosecutors, despite the government's claim that these were not linked to the anti-corruption case, have impacted on the effective functioning of the relevant institutions, and raise questions as to the way procedures were used to formalize these.

Nevertheless, the same text says candidly further down that "High Council of Judges and Prosecutors continued with the implementation of its 2012–16 strategic plan, broadly promoting the independence, impartiality and efficiency of the judiciary" (EC, 2013c).

Finally, secular Turkish civil society is either too weak or too dependent on the government to exercise serious constraints (TESEV, 2014). Islamic civil society has not shown much concern for corruption, despite the AKP's original anti-corruption platform, and its independence towards the government was dealt a serious blow when the rift with Gülen occurred. The media sector is largely controlled by businesses with particularistic ties to the government and was subjected to heavy persecution after the failed coup of 2016 (Freedom House, 2017b). In the Index for Public Integrity, the media freedom score is 3 out of 10, with Turkey ranking 94 out of 109 countries (see Table 6.2). Turkey's performance on media and judicial independence accounts for its poor performance on integrity (on the other components it is doing far better), showing that the problem is mainly a democratic one, i.e., political and unlikely to be fixed by technical means, training, or the usual integrity toolbox.

The original EU plan was generous, although excessively focused on material support, without reflection on the unintended consequences of simply flooding Turkey with money and setting no *ex ante* conditions or monitoring mechanism (see Figure 6.8 for a comparison of funds evolution versus control of corruption, showing the tendency towards recent regression as well as the progress made prior to the invitation to start talks). The pre-accession funds were planned at 50 percent for structural

Table 6.2 *Turkey's public integrity framework compared*

Components	Component score	World rank out of 109	Regional rank out of 14	Income group rank out of 28
RESOURCES				
Administrative burden	8.89	40	9	7
Trade openness	7.73	65	12	17
Budget transparency	8.07	33	5	10
CONSTRAINTS				
Judicial independence	4.12	83	9	19
E-citizenship	5.99	51	5	13
Freedom of the press	3.02	94	10	23

Source: Index for Public Integrity

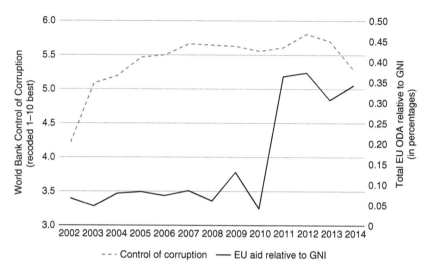

Figure 6.8 Evolution of EU funds and control of corruption in Turkey, 2002–2014
Source: OECD – QWIDS Official Development Aid and World Bank Control of Corruption

and sector reforms aiming in particular to harmonize Turkish legislation and practices with the EC acquis in close coordination with the IMF and the World Bank on structural policies. The other 50 percent of the appropriations were meant to finance other measures promoting Turkey's integration into the EU – for instance, to help Turkish administration and institutions develop the capacity to implement the community acquis (through institution-building); to assist Turkey in mobilizing investments needed to align its industry and infrastructure with European Community standards (through investment support and regional/rural development); and to support Turkey's participation in programs and agencies of the European Community (EC, 2003c). The European Court of Audits evaluated the effectiveness of EUR 3.8 billion in pre-accession assistance in the areas of the rule of law, governance, and human resources. It found that "mainly due to a lack of political will and because the Commission has made little use of conditions," the effectiveness of EU funding was "limited," as it had "insufficiently addressed some fundamental needs and the sustainability of results is often at risk." This thorough report is in fact highly critical and identifies general problems of EU intervention in this area, from poor conceptualization and absence of a theory of change ("What is a public sector approach and why is it supposed to give results?" the ECA asks), to the complete absence of project conditionality or any conditionality allowed by the legal assistance framework (the ECA reviews it carefully), to the only nominal support of some areas. The court notes aptly that "[h]owever, despite the importance of external audit and civil society organizations in the accession process and their role in the fight against corruption and organized crime, the IPA did not address the reinforcement of external audit and dealt too little with Turkey's capacity to engage with civil society." Projects have no performance indicators attached and therefore cannot be assessed. Regardless of events, there was no enforcement on any conditionality at any level. While the ECA conceded that the IPA objectives had been well designed by the commission, in particular because they "properly identified the requirements necessary to progress towards EU accession and made conclusive sector approach assessments," in practice "the IPA funds spent insufficiently addressed some fundamental needs in the rule of law and governance sectors, where some critical reforms are overdue." Only in areas where there was more cooperation from the government, such as customs, employment, and taxation, did the ECA state that "IPA I projects have contributed to aligning Turkey with the acquis and strengthening its administrative capacity – but there also sustainability was a concern due to domestic political developments" (ECA, 2018a).

But how realistic are Audit Court recommendations to get tough on delivery? If the EU has not managed to condition its aid for Turkey when there was more commitment and more democracy in Ankara, how could this happen after the crisis of refugees gave Turkey the keys to Europe's front door? By the end of 2018, the Europeanization language was already being replaced by reciprocal accusations and even open threats (Osborne, 2017). The transformative power of Europe did not succeed in keeping Turkey on the European path, and the deterioration that started even before the rise of ISIS and the Syrian war was largely endogenous to Turkey. It was just one more country whose key Europe did not manage to find before times turned from good to bad, and the window of opportunity had closed.

6.5   In Lieu of Conclusion: The Next Accession Generation

The next generation of would-be EU members in the Balkans, although less populous, do have one extra feature worth adding to the stories in this chapter: their learned ability to game the EU accession indicators. For instance, Montenegro, a Western Balkan country with less than 700,000 inhabitants, which succeeded in staying intact through the Yugoslav wars and in breaking off in time with Slobodan Milošević, was among the world leaders when Global Integrity was still doing an index based simply on formal rules and the existence of agencies (Macedonia, as it was named at the time, was the other champion in this). Montenegro also surpasses Germany on some EU compliance scoreboards. Montenegro applied for EU membership on December 15, 2008. The Commission delivered a positive opinion on October 12, 2011, and recommended the opening of accession negotiations. At its meeting on December 16–17, 2010, the European Council agreed to give Montenegro candidate country status. Montenegro has been an accession country since 2010 and is the only country in the world to have adopted the euro unilaterally. The country enjoys an economy where, besides tourism, smuggling and money laundering have been the top activities, and a politics where the Democratic Party of Socialists (DPS) has managed not to lose power since a multi-party system was established in 1990 (they had been governing under the name of League of Communists of Montenegro from the times of Josip Broz Tito). The DPS largely controls all public sector positions, the bureaucracy, the police and security apparatus, and the media. Freedom House degraded Montenegro to partially free in 2016 (Freedom House, 2017a), and Reporters Without Borders ranks them below the global average concerning journalists' rights (2018). Still, the old-time communist leader Milo Ðukanović has managed the extraordinary performance of maintaining his rule, even staging a temporary "permanent" retirement for the EU's benefit, after which he returned (in Putin-like fashion), and has simply convinced both NATO and the EU that only he could defend European interests in Montenegro against Russia (Farmer, 2018). This worked despite the fact that in its Montenegro Country Report 2018, the European Commission raised concerns over the independence of Montenegro's anti-corruption agency, citing "personal ties between its management and the political elite" (EC, 2018a). By mid-2018 Transparency International was writing desperate letters to the Parliament of Montenegro, urging MPs not dismiss their chapter director from the Council of the Agency for the Prevention of Corruption, the final act for the government to gain full control (TI, 2018). The end of 2018, however, saw Montenegro managing to appear to be both set on a successful EU accession path and locked hopelessly in its past practices. The government controlled both public and private media through state advertising, and tough anti-corruption and anti-crime regulations were being used mainly against opponents and investigative journalists (Bechev, 2018; RSF, 2018).

The EU objectives of geopolitical stabilization and of promoting control of corruption thus seem hardly compatible in the Balkans, where stabilization was achieved at the price of systemic corruption (Bulgaria,

Serbia, even Croatia), ethnocracy (BiH, Kosovo), and even the pro-Western and pro-EU semi-autocracy of Montenegro. In Central Europe, where successful enlargement led to eight new member countries, there were divergent paths, with only the Baltics remaining on a progress path even after integration (as the Russian threat has always made EU integration a first-order strategic necessity for them). Meanwhile, governance throughout Central Europe regressed after accession and in particular after the 2008–2009 crisis. Finally, accession country Turkey, where the Kemalist bureaucracy, American support, and pro-European business have all pushed for its Europeanization, backslid spectacularly towards more typical Middle-East-like institutions. The EU has not managed to empower the pro-European alliance in Turkey and has not really sought to. The EU's biggest impact remains arguably in the triggering of the convictions of prime ministers Ivo Sanader in Croatia and Adrian Nastase in Romania, two strongly pro-European leaders who thought they enjoyed impunity but who were actually used to signal to others that their corrupt practices were no longer acceptable. But as Sanader and Nastase were not just individually corrupt but the top of political pyramids deeply rooted in particularism, this spectacular success has not led to deeper institutional change so far – or else Croatia's judicial independence would not still be, in 2018, less than half Estonia's.

7   The Quest for the Rest

Speaking in 2011, as North Africans were rebelling against their long-time neopatrimonial dictators, EU Commissioner Štefan Füle said: "Europe was not vocal enough in defending human rights and local democratic forces in the region. Too many of us fell prey to the assumption that authoritarian regimes were a guarantee of stability in the region. This was not even Realpolitik. It was, at best, short-termism – and the kind of short-termism that makes the long-term ever more difficult to build" (2011). The Middle East and North Africa were not the only ones stirring in the vicinity of Europe at the time. In Ukraine and Moldova, local civil societies have also shown in recent years both their wish for democratic governance and their attachment to Europe. A long-time European wish built into the foundation of the European Neighborhood Policy (ENP), "common values" shared with neighbors thus came to the forefront as an objective. Europe had to do more for these countries, as obviously there was local demand for such "common values."

On paper, the aim was already there. The European Commission communication "Wider Europe," adopted in March 2003, had already listed among "common values" the commitment to rule of law and effective governance (EC, 2003d, p. 16). These values were meant to ensure the right framework for foreign investments. Still, a 2010 academic assessment of the influence of the ENP on the EU's impact on governance had found the impact "limited" (Kleenman, 2010). Governance indicators simply failed to show improvements in most of the partner states where the EU gave significant aid under ENP (see Figure 7.1 for an updated ten-year evolution starting in 2006). Where we did find significant improvement (see Georgia in Figure 7.1), there was ample evidence that domestic rather than EU influence had been the driving force behind reforms. Furthermore, frontloaded aid in massive quantities rewarded countries that had progressed the *least* (ibid.).

Why was that? By 2011, Europe was surrounded by a circle of poor, highly corrupt countries without any enlargement perspective. They

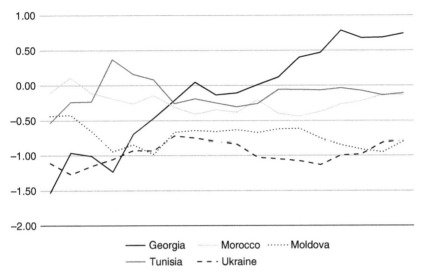

Figure 7.1 Corruption evolution of selected aid recipients under ENP and Cotonou, 1996–2016
Note: Original scores, −2.50 to +2.50 maximum good governance
Source: World Bank Control of Corruption

differed across many dimensions that mattered for the EU: their potential for geostrategic destabilization (through refugees and migrants, terrorism, violent conflict), specific exports, and common history (former colonies, with all the connections deriving from that status). European policy towards them was shaped by all these variables. The EU's political influence beyond the accession countries was relatively much weaker, and the EU's transformative ambitions were far smaller, too. Only when it turned out that the people in the boats arriving in Europe were actually coming from Tunisia and the deserts beyond did the need to address governance also in these remote countries come to the forefront.[1] On paper, it was an old objective, part of the Cotonou Agreement. As with the ENP, however, it had been dormant. Just as Russia's resurgent power in the east reminded everyone how important it was that Ukraine should not fail as a state, Mediterranean migration renewed the attention to the quality of governance in the south.

Jurisdiction for the "rest" of the world, where the EU also imposes good governance conditionalities in exchange for aid, is split. There is the

[1] Interview with Prime Minister Enrico Letta, Paris, May 14, 2018.

European Commission's Directorate-General for Neighborhood and Enlargement Negotiations (DG NEAR), which wields the European Neighborhood Policy. The Directorate for Development and Cooperation (DEVCO) covers the ACP countries, the Gulf countries, Asia, Latin America, Central Asia, and other parts of Africa. The ENP governs the EU's relations with sixteen of its eastern and southern neighbors. In the south this means Algeria, Egypt, Israel, Jordan, Lebanon, Libya, Morocco, Palestine, Syria, and Tunisia. In the east it includes Armenia, Azerbaijan, Belarus, Georgia, Moldova, and Ukraine. Within this area, a distinct group is made up of democracies in the EU's neighborhood that have European aspirations (Moldova, Georgia, and Ukraine) and that have signed some type of association agreement with the EU pledging ambitious governance reforms. By their own wishes, the EU treats them more like former accession countries (although they are not formally candidate countries). The rest of the ENP countries, which are either not democracies or are flatly denied EU aspirations on grounds of geography, are treated differently. In the end, this makes three groups of countries where some EU good governance promotion is attempted: the former Soviet Union, the Mediterranean, and the ACP countries. This chapter will attempt to review the most significant evolutions in each.

7.1   Desert of the Tartars

According to Samuel Huntington's scenario, a civilizational line cuts between Catholic/Protestant Western Europe and Orthodox Europe to the south and the east, including Croatia but not Serbia, and cutting Ukraine and Romania into two cultural halves (1993). Such presumed borders might also indicate differences in quality of governance. Blaming Greece for belonging to the wrong "civilization" might be tempting to some; however, the backslide of Catholic central Europe is a strong argument against simplistic cultural inferences. An alternative scenario, the "end of history," seemed for a while plausible in Eastern Europe (Fukuyama, 2006), if nowhere else. Here the triumphal tale was told of the only world region where the Washington Consensus reforms had worked across the board, ending in accomplished modernization: a transformation model for the rest of the world that Western policy-makers and development agencies would seek to transplant to the broader Middle East and other places. The Baltics are the best case in point. They started with Soviet-style governance and aligned with the EU in ten years or less. If such patriotic elites are to be found further to the East – who opt for Europe rather than Russia and for good governance over kleptocracy –

and are also ready to take advantage of any window of opportunity, why discourage them from joining? This was the logic of association agreements offered by Europeans to countries such as Moldova, Georgia, Ukraine, Armenia, and Azerbaijan, even after it became clear that the EU would not enlarge beyond Croatia in any foreseeable future. However, for the "end of history" scenario to work, an ideological alternative to liberal democracy should not exist. Then all that Europe would need to do is to help any willing country make progress along the path of reforms until it comes close enough to EU standards on all counts, economic and political. Integration would then follow as a logical consequence, and every country has an equal chance on the basis of merit (Verheugen, 2003). And even if the "civilizational border" scenario may be more realistic, should Europe not (on security grounds) still extend its border as much as possible? Shouldn't it offer any means to associate, if not enlargement itself ("everything but institutions"[2]), to any willing country, just to push enemies further away? Would that not be the ideal way to stabilize Europe, as well as those countries themselves, as former German Foreign Minister Joschka Fischer once argued (2000)? Such is the logic that the EU is bound to operate on, and therefore it cannot turn its back on local demand – when it manifests itself so strongly and heroically, as during Ukraine's "revolution for dignity." As a Georgian official once put it: "We know that the door [for enlargement] is closed. What we ask is just that you do not lock it, and by our own merit we shall throw it open someday."[3] This implies, however, that without having plausibly won the good governance battle in Italy, Greece, Hungary, or the Balkans, the EU needs to fight it in the most difficult places of all, beyond Romanian borders, in the territory that travel writers made famous under the name of "Desert of the Tartars."

Both the association agreements with ENP countries (and their corresponding action plans agreed with the countries) and the deep and comprehensive free trade agreements (DCFTAs) cite the fight against corruption as a general objective in the context of promoting the rule of law (Articles 3 and 22 in the Ukrainian agreement, for example), referring to relevant issues for the fight in specific sectors (although public financial management is strangely considered a separate issue). It is nearly by design that the anti-corruption approach to this region is copied (or imported by the same staff who worked on it and who have meanwhile been posted in ENP countries) from the previous enlargement

---

[2] More details on this approach in this Romano Prodi speech: http://europa.eu/rapid/press-release_SPEECH-02-619_en.htm

[3] Interview by the author with Georgian think tank leader, September 4, 2017, Tbilisi.

experience, without much consideration to domestic agency or will to change. Furthermore, there is no comprehensive theory of change applied to the post-Soviet context and these difficult transitions. The EU cooperates with the World Bank and the IMF, and each institution's approach has varied with the changing intellectually dominant paradigms of the times.

The former Soviet countries represent a mix between Michael Johnston's "oligarchs and clans" and "official moguls" corruption types (2014). The variation applies not only across countries but also across time in every country, depending on the capacity of the heads of state to enforce a single pyramid of extraction versus a more competitive corruption system. Ukraine illustrates the latter. The power balance among the key Ukrainian oligarchs (representatives of big business with strong political influence) shift after each major political upheaval, but without so far affecting the rents' structure or the oligarchic system *per se* (Kononczuk, 2015). Two revolutions have happened, not counting independence. "How many Orange revolutions does one need to do?" a young anti-corruption activist asked me a year before Maidan, when I was helping organize an anti-corruption civil society coalition meant to blacklist corrupt candidates for parliament (which materialized under the name of Chesno). While Azerbaijan has a ruling clan on the Central Asian model, Ukraine and Moldova have oligarchs who got rich from lucrative monopoly capitalism or state subsidies (i.e. could purchase cheap gas or electricity from one part of the state and resell it to another at tenfold the price); additionally, criminal cooperation is common, with criminal networks embedded in law enforcement, the secret services, and the judiciary. Although their businesses have diversified and even become more international over the years, one can always find at their roots an original "scheme," the key word designating pure embezzlement strategies. Money laundering from the former Soviet empire through Western European banks also remains a common practice among post-Soviet oligarchs, creating a particularly dangerous linkage between systemic corruption and organized crime (Shelley, 1998). The "nice" Baltic states next door, and even Western banks, are not immune: money has been laundered massively through Deutsche Bank, Danske, and HSBC, to name but a few, starting with branches in the Baltics and Moldova. Such operations need corrupt judges and inefficient (or absent) bank regulators. They seem to unfold in parallel with, and unembarrassed by, anti-corruption institutional deployment. More important still, these networks are regional and use regional connections and vulnerabilities. But there has never been any *regional* strategy to prevent raiding or criminal behavior of this kind. National strategies endorsed by the EU include some money laundering regulation in general (which frequently is not transposed into national legislation or does not get implemented), but control over private banks varies wildly from one country to another.

Among democracies aspiring to join the union, a stark contrast is provided by Georgia, which, well ahead of any Eastern European partnership or any EU offer, had a good governance revolution of its own making, driven by domestic agency. Between 2004 and 2008, Georgia achieved one of the most spectacular governance advances in the world and one of few known transitions from a neopatrimonial governance regime based on particularism to ethical universalism. While Georgia's transformation remains imperfect and has even shown some recent signs of backsliding, the leadership of Mikhail Saakashvili and his team of Western-educated reformers undoubtedly succeeded in freeing a state captured by private interests and imposing a system where the norms of impersonality and equal treatment became prevalent, even if exceptions remain (Mungiu-Pippidi, 2015b, Chapter 6). The transition is especially remarkable as Georgia was notorious for graft, corruption, and bribery in Soviet times – and in 2003 still ranked 124 out of 133 countries surveyed for Transparency International's CPI, lumped with Tajikistan, Azerbaijan, and Angola (Clark, 1993; Kupatadze, 2016). By 2013, though, the World Bank–EBRD business survey BEEPS captured the fundamental difference between Georgia, on one side, and Ukraine and Moldova, on the other: in the former, 2 percent reported extortion bribes, while in the latter the figures ranged between 30 and 50 percent.[4]

The abrupt "big bang" transition in Georgia started immediately after the Rose Revolution, which brought to power a team of young politicians led by US-educated lawyer Mikhail Saakashvili. They engaged in a vast program of administrative simplification and deregulation, and they vetted and dismissed huge numbers of staff from public institutions. Then they employed new recruits on the basis of merit. They also reinstated merit-based competitions for university enrollment (Kupatadze, 2016). The implementation of a "one-stop" administrative revolution against red tape (where citizens submit just one request and government offices intercommunicate until all necessary hurdles are passed and return *the* answer) is synthesized in the brilliant glass administrative building in Tbilisi, completely transparent both in construction and in operating rules. The funding of this administrative revolution (with the replacement of many policemen after vetting, in fewer numbers and with increased salaries) was obtained in a rather unconventional way: bargaining with the corrupt and the privileged for the return of assets (privatized or presumed

---

[4] Data from the World Bank's Enterprise Surveys: www.enterprisesurveys.org/

Table 7.1 *Georgia's public integrity framework compared*

Components	Component score	World rank out of 109	Regional rank out of 14	Income group rank out of 27
RESOURCES				
Administrative burden	9.54	15	3	1
Trade openness	8.40	45	9	4
Budget transparency	8.85	18	2	1
CONSTRAINTS				
Judicial independence	5.66	45	3	8
E-citizenship	5.84	53	6	1
Freedom of the press	5.50	57	3	6

Source: Index for Public Integrity

withheld through tax evasion) in exchange for not being prosecuted. According to the prosecutor's office, from 2004 to 2012, approximately 9,500 private properties were handed over to the state "free of charges"; although the "voluntary" nature of such returns remains controversial (Hammarberg, 2013). Western (EU) funds came later, after the Russian invasion of 2008. During the reform years when Georgia registered massive progress, the country merely received infrequent technical assistance funding from the EU (Kleenman, 2010). The result of the Georgian reforms was a dramatic reduction in bribery, especially in the sectors where state and citizenry interact, such as the policing of the streets, licensing laws, and public services, as well as a simultaneous reduction in the informal economy (Kupatadze, 2016). With a score of 7.3 out of 10, Georgia moved up to rank 37 out of 109 countries in the Index of Public Integrity 2018 (see Table 7.1), becoming the leader in its income group and region.

The elements of Georgia's success are close to those of Estonia, which had been a source of inspiration (Mungiu-Pippidi, 2015b, Chapter 6). Georgia added the plea bargaining with profiteers of the old regime, an innovation explained by the very different transition periods during which these reforms took place. Estonians had battled the former Soviet establishment before a new corrupt post-communist class could appear, whereas Georgians had to dismantle their already formed post-communist establishment. Not all the rents were destroyed, and the new regime was later accused of inheriting some of them through concessions and privatization.

Some top anti-corruption prosecutions remained, during and after Saakashvili's term, apparently politically motivated (indeed, even the reformers were indicted in the end), and judicial independence has remained the area with the least progress. But this remains nevertheless the most impressive reform scorecard in the region over the past fifteen years, as Estonia's had been in the earlier period. A look at the European public accountability scorecard Europam.eu shows that Georgia scores the best (well above the average) on freedom of information (with a sanction mechanism worthy of adoption by other countries), financial disclosures, and party financing (overregulated), and has an average score on conflict of interest and procurement regulation. In the massive reform years, however, its leadership was reluctant to embark on the well-trodden path of adopting the UNCAC and the international standard approach (Tsitsishvili and Warner, 2010). For instance, while Moldova and Ukraine had ethical codes (part of the international approach) adopted from very early on for civil servants (with zero impact), the Georgians did the reforms first – and only afterwards did they start to address what Mark Warren calls the "appearances of corruption" (2006).

Moldova, Georgia, and Ukraine signed their respective association agreements with the European Union on June 27, 2014. These entered into force on July 1, 2016, for Moldova and Georgia and on September 1, 2017, for of Ukraine. By that time, Saakashvili had failed to be reelected and had conceded defeat to an oligarch. Furthermore, he had to flee, facing the threat of being arrested (*Politico*, 2018). Armenia, which had also been negotiating, got cold feet at the last minute due to Russian pressure. In Ukraine, the Euromaidan revolution was needed to steer the country back toward Europe after former president Viktor Yanukovych's change of heart. He then became the first oligarch charged with corruption, and the population raided his luxurious residence. His closest oligarch cronies also lost some of their influence and assets.

Ukraine's corruption is typical for a post-Soviet society and very similar to Romania's: its independence (and in Romania EU integration) was made possible by a deal between those who wanted emancipation from the east (being too weak to take power on their own, unlike the Baltics) and those with established power from communist times (Wilson, 2015). The effect was to leave untouched the spoils of the first generation of post-communist business-politicians, those who had had the amplest opportunity to become oligarchs navigating between two economic systems. If Yanukovych had resisted Russian pressure and himself gone on with the association agreement with EU, this historical deal would have been practically reconfirmed; his downfall, however, created some hope for good governance independently of EU accession, although it was dearly paid for with the loss of Crimea and war in the east. Moldova and Georgia had already had secession wars with the Russian-speaking population in the early 1990s, and their evolution therefore stalled for many years. They embarked on their Europeanization with only partial control of their territory, and the EU played a weak role in the negotiations about their own borders, Russia remaining *de facto* the most important actor (*Foreign Policy*, 2015).

Resources for corruption had traditionally been very high in Ukraine. On top of the communist legacy and the occasional shortage of cash during the economic crisis in the 1990s, which led to policemen directly extorting from commuters, for instance, Ukraine had subsidized energy prices (as had Russia for many years). It went on to develop a regulatory framework meant to exploit businesses by enhancing red tape and therefore administrative discretion. In 1999 it took the average business owner fifty-five days to register a business, and twenty-six agencies were authorized to inspect businesses and impose fines for infractions of (nontransparent) rules (Lyle, 1999). Equally troubling was the use of the judiciary and the secret services to control political opponents by initially encouraging impunity in order to collect evidence for later use in blackmail, a general practice under President Kuchma and one that was not entirely eliminated (Darden, 2001). Property has always been a shallow institution, allowing state control and manipulation – not individual autonomy. For instance, the Kryvorizhstal steel mill was sold to two oligarchs for USD 800 million to ensure their support in the 2004 election, only to be subsequently nationalized after the election and resold for USD 4.8 billion (Wilson, 2015). The Tartars, previously deported to Central Asia by Stalin, sought restitution of their lands. This proved impossible as most of their Crimean lands had ended up with former publicly owned companies *de facto* controlled by oligarchs and mobsters from Ukraine and Russia. When President Yushchenko introduced a bill to restore land to the Tartars it was blocked in the parliament. A clear majority on good governance issues in the Ukrainian parliament, even a nominal one, has never emerged from the vast archipelago of vested interest-based ad hoc majorities; this is why the integrity of MPs had been and remains a key issue. And finally, Ukraine has no land market, with the land reforms requested by the international donor community still hanging in the balance because vested owners have always managed to control whichever nominal majority existed in the parliament. The problem has only consolidated itself in the nearly thirty years since Estonia already solved the issue. This affects the economic autonomy of many voters to a large extent and is thus a direct subversion of good governance.

Particularism in the broader Ukrainian society (nepotism, extensive use of connections, etc.) blends with Ukrainian officials' directly exploiting public assets and capturing the state through undue connections with business and organized crime, well institutionalized under all regimes (Miller et al., 2011; Varese, 2000; Karklins, 2002). Corruption continued to flourish after the Orange Revolution despite President Yushchenko's promises to fight it (instead, he ended up being charged with corruption himself). It reached its peak during President Yanukovych's mandate. The latter managed to concentrate power in the hands of a narrow circle of oligarchs – his so-called "Family" – with whom he had been acquainted since the days of the Donbas gang wars. This group's undue spoils via state capture are estimated at USD 8–10 billion a year (Åslund, 2013), totaling USD 100 billion according to Ukrainian prosecutors (Bratu, 2016). State procurement levels exploded after open tendering was abolished in July 2012, to UAH 250 billion or USD 21.1 billion over the following twelve months (ibid.). Yanukovitch's "Family" did lose considerable influence after his fall, but a major property redistribution (from profiteers to the state budget) stopped short of the Georgian model. Saakashvili had enjoyed a majority in his parliament and enormous trust due to the Rose Revolution. He deliberately pushed for major reforms early on. For the second time, the Ukrainians did not exploit the initial trust capital that comes with popular change, and they never had a similar majority. On the contrary, after each "revolution," Ukrainian oligarchs nevertheless "owned" many members of parliament, whole political parties, and media stations, and they were successful in limiting reform aimed at reducing their rents. The economic contraction was their biggest enemy so far, not anti-corruption, with the top oligarchs losing nearly half their fortunes as accounted by Forbes (Wilson, 2015).

The underdevelopment of Ukrainian armed forces and law enforcement, and their penetration by organized crime, which varies according to region (Shelley, 1998), considerably weakens official constraints on corruption. Civil society activists face major risks, especially provincial Ukrainians fighting local predators directly. Judicial independence has only regressed over the last decade of unprecedented Western assistance to the judiciary, as shown in both Freedom House and Global Competitiveness Report evaluations, after stagnating through the previous decade as well (as the World Bank's rule of law score shows[5]). Table 7.2, which captures all the essential elements of control of corruption in

---

[5] Ukraine's stagnation across World Bank WGIs is documented in the Country Data Report for Ukraine, 1996–2014 (World Bank, 2015).

Table 7.2 *Ukraine's public integrity framework compared*

Components	Component score	World rank out of 109	Regional rank out of 14	Income group rank out of 27
RESOURCES				
Administrative burden	9.22	25	7	4
Trade openness	8.92	38	7	3
Budget transparency	7.21	63	10	12
CONSTRAINTS				
Judicial independence	2.84	101	13	24
E-citizenship	3.98	74	12	9
Freedom of the press	5.05	66	6	11

Source: Index for Public Integrity

the Index for Public Integrity, shows that the evaluation of the Ukrainian judiciary in 2018 is still at 2.88 out of 10, with a rank of 13 among 14 regional states, 24 out of 27 in the same income group, and a staggering 101 of the 109 countries surveyed globally. Not enough has been done to reverse Yanukovych's highly damaging legal "reform" of 2010, which effectively snuffed out all vestiges of judicial independence, establishing executive control over judicial appointments and salaries (Wilson, 2015), and deepening the notorious system of "telephone justice" (secret executive instructions to judges). A judiciary reform council was set up in the autumn of 2014. The December 2014 Law on the Status of Judges and the February 2015 Law on the Right to a Just Court have brought about some marginal improvements, but were not the big bang reform needed. The chief prosecutor is appointed by the president and accountable solely to him.

A brave step was the 2015 appointment of genuine reformers including Vitalii Kasko and Davit Sakvarelidze, who had held the same posts in Georgia under Saakashvili from 2009 to 2012, as deputy chief prosecutors. They promptly began investigations of corruption in the procuracy itself, resulting in efforts to discredit them by their corrupt colleagues with media connections (ibid.). The interventions of the secret service in 2018 (when they staged the death of a journalist) seemed to come out of cheap movies, showing another essential area where nationalism and anti-Russian sentiment became substitutes for real accountability and modernization (*Le Monde*, 2018).

The only assets in Ukraine's control of corruption seem to be an active civil society and a growing middle class (armed with smartphones), able to assemble quickly on Facebook and in the streets to support good governance causes. Ukraine's scores on civil society and the electoral process have remained more or less constant over the last ten years, according to Freedom House Nations in Transit and these areas received diverse and consistent EU support (even growing over time). Ukraine has always been an outlier when it comes to civil society, whose good ratings do not match the country's poor quality of governance. A deeper look, however, shows that while Ukraine is well rated by Freedom House for its civil society's activism, the e-citizen component of the IPI shows insufficient civil society (too few household internet connections, too few people connected through Facebook; compared to the regional average, Ukraine ranks 12 out of 14, and compared with the world average 74 out of 109). Ultimately, this reveals that although civil society in Kiev and L'viv may impress those giving the ratings, it cannot compensate for the situation in the rest of the country. Additionally, freedom of the press decreased due to media capture by various private or wildly partisan interests, and threats against the few independent journalists remain serious. Ukraine barely scores 6.20 and ranks 68 out of the 109 countries in the Index for Public Integrity, and this only due to recent reforms. The ascending trend seems to be exhausted, however; there was no progress from 2017 to 2018.

The European Court of Auditors divides the EU intervention into before the Euromaidan (a consensus exists that nothing much was achieved by then, budget support being just a resource for corruption, conditionality not being implemented, and so forth) and after, when more substantial reforms were finally initiated (ECA, 2016a).[6] The major reform of gas pricing eliminated the discretionary arbitrage practice that had previously enriched gas traders and intermediaries, and this led to a measurable reduction in the concentration of market winners in the sector. A transparent open-data-based public procurement system, ProZorro, was introduced in 2016 and has increased coverage since. The government started to rid the banking sector of "zombie" banks, for instance by taking over Pryvat, Ukraine's largest bank, which had been plagued by bad loans and accused of serving as a cover for money laundering. A reform of VAT taxation brought transparency and

---

[6] The 41 sector budget support programs were generally designed to disburse a large share of the allocated amount at the very beginning of the program. Budget support frontloading, i.e. the initial fixed tranche paid in full and generally without delay, was carried out despite a relatively poor track record in structural reforms, ranging from 31 to 49 percentup until 2012.

simplification. Through coordinated action by the prosecutor general's office, USD 1.5 billion in assets belonging to the "Family" was confiscated and returned to the state treasury (Karatnycky and Motyl, 2018). Although it only confirmed the public's worst suspicions, the introduction of mandatory and transparent financial disclosures for public officials is a positive step, enabling a future check on their undue profit from office. In exchange for these reductions of resources for corruption, the country was flooded with new opportunities in the form of external funds following the existential threat from Russia after 2014 (Dabrowski, 2017). It is debatable whether the abundance of EU funds for Ukraine has played a rationalizing role in selecting priorities and incentivizing reforms after the Euromaidan (European Court of Auditors found in 2016 that funds were more often than not frontloaded and the progress indicators both poor and not implemented). There is consensus that earlier EU aid in the form of poorly conditioned budget support did more harm than good. In July 2017, Ukrane's finance minister Oleksandr Danylyuk told an IMF meeting in Dubrovnik that the opportunity window for an Estonian-style reform package advocated by this author, among others, "has passed."[7] Unlike Georgia, Ukraine did not manage to pass enough reforms in its window of opportunity in the wake of regime change and popular mobilization against Russian aggression in 2014–2015 (Dabrowski, 2017). Mr. Danylyuk resigned shortly afterwards in the face of huge political pressure to support a spending program for socioeconomic development in Ukraine's regions, which he described as "buckwheat," the practice of bribing voters with food or by similar means during an election campaign (Reuters, 2018). He was not the only reformer who had to go due to vested interests protecting the status quo, even after the "revolution of dignity."

As the European Union did not have real methods for diagnoses of corruption in a country and had no theory of change, its efforts in the ENP area had embraced a one-size-fits-all approach (Börzel et al., 2008). The EU thus followed the recommendations of the Council of Europe's GRECO, the Venice Committee, or the UNCAC. In other words, the EU's approach was grounded 100 percent in the "lawyer approach." This basically involves the checking of a country's integrity legislation against ideal benchmarks, without any pretense of offering strategies on how countries might get from the point where they are to where they should be. Compliance with adopting legislation is simply supposed to deliver change. Implementation is equated with some top "big fish" being arrested, as in Romania. In Ukraine, this mean that by 2018 the

---

[7] Answer to a query from the author.

prosecution of some individuals seemed to be valued more highly by the EU and its international allies than deeper policy reform (Karatnycky and Motyl, 2018). After investing in rule of law for more than a decade with nothing to show for it, the EU and its partners suddenly seemed to abandon the reform of the judiciary and stake everything on the usual anti-corruption agencies. However, Ukraine had a past history of using prosecution for political goals in the post-Soviet environment, and was a systemically corrupt country – hardly a Hong Kong to be cleaned up by one single agency on the basis of common law. The invested champion is the National Anti-Corruption Bureau of Ukraine (NABU), inspired by the Romanian NAD, which immediately entered into conflict with other agencies created in previous rounds of "anti-corruption"; thus, its cases soon stalled in the courts. The EU and the IMF then started to promote a "special" anti-corruption court to pass sentences (as part of the Ukrainian Supreme Court, as once again "autonomous" bodies staffed by magistrates could hardly be constitutional under a legal system based on the Napoleonic code). The international community would even vet the judges of this special court to prosecute NABU cases. By 2017–2018, this had become the EU's main anti-corruption proposal for Ukraine, a kind of mixture of the Romanian and Guatemalan models – at a time when both these models had already been proven unsustainable.[8] For how can sustainable control of corruption in a country be delivered by such anti-corruption "excellence islands" surrounded by a judiciary and a law enforcement community presumably and hopelessly corrupt (otherwise, no special court would be needed to pass sentences on NABU's prosecutions)? However, this seemed to be the main theory of change in both Ukraine and nearby Moldova: that curbing impunity culture by arresting a few top individuals (despite knowledge that such individuals are part of broader networks that can easily supplant individual losses) would result in control of corruption.

Both Ukraine and Moldova were encouraged by donors down the path of relentless buildup of agencies and regulation towards an ever more comprehensive "integrity framework" (as donors also demand implementing agencies for every law or directive). This development has continued despite the evidence that the only regional success cases, Georgia and Estonia, had quite a different strategy (Emerson et al., 2017). The European Bank for Reconstruction and Development remained rather singular in promoting primarily the "market" approach to anti-corruption, including de-monopolization and a reduction of rents in the

---

[8] For Romania, see Mungiu-Pippidi, 2018b. For Guatemala, see the Brookings Institution Blog piece by Charles T. Call (2017).

public sector (*Euromaidan Press*, 2017). By summer 2018, when Ukraine's President Poroshenko finally signed the High Anti-Corruption court into being, the international think tank community had realized that without a reduction in corruption opportunities Ukraine would not change – indeed, that it might run the risk of political destabilization before getting cleaner (Karatnycky and Motyl, 2018; Lough, 2018). However, the court's existence was one of the key conditions for the release of the next tranche of the IMF's USD 17.5 billion support program to Ukraine. The EU and IMF thus answered the demand from local, donor-sponsored civil society, which had spent considerable energy in defending NABU and asking for an anti-corruption circuit parallel to the judicial system and reporting to the donors (Kaleniuk, 2018). There is insufficient attention and protection for civil society anti-corruption fighters in the provincial cities and outlying regions, and they face significant risks, being few and isolated. The bulk of anti-corruption actors in Ukrainian civil society seem engaged in top level political advocacy against grand corruption rather than in aggregating interests by profession and fighting to establish some standards of normalcy.[9] But it is down here at the granular level that change in practice becomes indispensable for the sustainable control of corruption. In the Western history of building control of corruption, divergent group interests helped change the rules of the game, for instance through strategic litigations or strikes. There are very few such attempts in Ukraine, where EU-planned and more generally donor-funded anti-corruption work, including for the use of civil society, often seems the only anti-corruption activity in town.

Even more than Ukraine, Moldova – Europe's poorest country – shows symptoms of the "Samaritan Dilemma." By 2016, Moldova had received the highest amount of EU aid per inhabitant of all of the EU's eastern neighbors. The country, a former Romanian province before the Second World War that splintered out of the USSR in 1991, had its ups and downs, presenting the opposite of stagnation in the charts, and qualified for budget support for some years as it has always had a strong pro-European parliamentary faction. Its urban, Romanian-speaking population valiantly fought election after election against the former communist party, which relied on Russian speakers and state-dependent populations such as pensioners (Mungiu-Pippidi and Munteanu, 2009). Through victories and defeats, they managed to keep the country's democracy

---

[9] In a focus group in Kiev with anti-corruption activists in April 2018 we had a hard time identifying any associations representing corruption "losers" in health and education, for instance, despite many corruption complaints targeting these areas. The level of associativity remains extremely low.

ratings good, but rent opportunities also remained rife and only changed hands between the two sides.

In spring 2009, Moldova preceded Ukraine's Maidan with its own "Twitter Revolution." A public revolt in the capital motivated by fears of being shut out of Europe led to the Communist party losing its absolute majority in parliament. An ad hoc alliance of pro-European parties took over the government in July 2009. Moldova joined the EU's Eastern Partnership in 2009 and on July 1, 2016, the EU–Moldova Association Agreement came into force, which included the introduction of a Deep and Comprehensive Free Trade Area (DCFTA). Moldova's pro-European stance endured through yet another wave of Russian embargos (for instance on wine, which is a major Moldovan export commodity), but Europe rewarded Moldova and its pro-European leaders with visa-free travel, which bought popular support. Moldova committed itself to substantial market and good governance reforms as part of its European agreement, as the European Neighborhood Policy states that in order for countries to reap the benefits of free trade with more advanced European economies, they must adopt many European competition standards. As the EEAS succinctly puts it, "By signing the agreement, Moldova committed to reforming its domestic policies on the basis of EU laws and practice. To do so, the country benefits from substantial EU support."[10]

Corruption has become a major topic in Moldova's politics during the 2001–2009 presidency of Vladimir Voronin, who also has the distinction of being the first freely-elected Communist leader in Europe. The media alleged that Oleg Voronin, his son, enjoyed the largest fortune in Moldova (Anghel, 2009), due largely to rents. The younger Mr. Voronin replied bitterly that Moldova's 2009 EU moment had in fact been a coup d'état, which brought to power a criminal network of "raiders" led by a fast-rising oligarch, Vladimir Plahotniuc, supported by foreign secret services. Comparing his own self-declared "medium-size" businesses to the assets amassed by Mr. Plahotniuc, Mr. Voronin argued that others' success in the current Moldovan economy was based entirely on "raiding" and "smuggling," while he himself, at the most, benefited from exemption from the usual post-Soviet type of discretionary control by tax authorities from the time of his father's presidency. "Raiding" is a term used by criminologists and investigative journalists to designate a specific form of crime involving the violent takeover of a business. Such violence in a post-Soviet environment is rarely entirely private, as few if any businesses

---

[10] The original statement can be seen at https://eeas.europa.eu/headquarters/headquarters-homepage_en/4011/EU-Moldova%20relations,%20Factsheet.

can exist in such an environment without semi-official protection. Mr. Voronin's claims are therefore very much worth discussing because they introduce the fundamental distinction between corruption and organized crime. Unlike "private" organized crime, which always uses corruption to bribe policemen or politicians, organized crime in post-Soviet Europe has frequently embraced the character of *state capture*, with the complete fusion of private and public interests and abuse of law enforcement capability (Varese, 2000; Frye, 2010). While it is difficult to make a distinction between systemic corruption and organized crime because they nearly always go hand in hand, there is one important distinguishing feature, namely the use of coercion over solely material inducements. Furthermore, there is an important conceptual difference between an organized crime group that corrupts politicians and officials, as in the film *The Godfather*, and a corrupt ruling elite with such discretionary power that it *creates* its own organized crime network by "privatizing" (in fact, *patrimonializing*) law enforcement agencies, as portrayed in the Russian film *Leviathan*. Yet Moldova seem to have turned into a state captured by organized crime precisely during its years of EU-sponsored anti-corruption, which makes it an interesting case.

A former anti-corruption official gives this picture of how Moldova works:

Since they politicized every public official appointment by the parties, since [Mr. Plahotniuc's] party has remained practically by itself in what used to be a coalition arrangement they just take over public agencies by appointing their heads or making them switch allegiance to him. And once they have control, they send in a group of their "experts," who take over a council room, ask civil servants for all kinds of documents and regulations in that office and by the end of day they have concocted some corrupt scheme using the loopholes they've found on how to drain public money out of that particular place.[11]

The capture of the state by the second pro-European government alliance was done almost publicly. An appendix of the 2011 cooperation agreement was published by the media, showing how astutely Mr. Plahotniuc managed to gain control of the general prosecutor's office and the Centre for Curbing Economic Crime and Corruption. This meant that Mr. Plahotniuc himself appointed the heads of those organizations and so took control of anti-corruption in exactly the years of the misguided EU and US anti-corruption interventions in the area.[12] Another party of the

[11] Private interview in Chisinau, September 2018.
[12] Agreement of creation of Alliance for European Integration, published January 18, 2011, https://unimedia.info/stiri/doc-acordul-de-constituire-al-aie-a-fost-facut-public–vezi-do cumentul-28687.html; details of the secret agreement, November 16, 2011, https://uni media.info/stiri/detalii-din-acordul-secret-al-aie-41233.html

same coalition gained control of other nominally autonomous agencies, such as the secret service and the national bank. Even the legislation was changed, according to Transparency International Moldova, on the pretext of "decommunization," and a serious amount of politicization followed, most dangerously of the law enforcement agencies. While his colleagues and rivals alike thought they had the most lucrative of rents in their control of, for instance, the customs agency, they had overlooked the fact that whoever controlled anti-corruption controlled everything. By the end of 2018, Mr. Plahotniuc's coalition partners and rivals had been indicted for corruption or landed in jail. His own minority party managed to participate in all ruling coalitions from 2009 onward, and despite ranking only fourth originally by number of seats, he adroitly engineered floor-crossing from all other parties, mostly from communists, thus gaining a functional majority of MPs acquired one by one. In summer 2018, the DPM-controlled majority passed the fiscal amnesty law that allowed people to register assets without providing documents as to how they were acquired, as long as they paid a tax of 3 percent of their value (raised to 6 after many protests).

And so precisely during the years of "Europeanization" Moldova's diverse and contentious kleptocracy, which had traditionally cut across the main political dividing line between supporters of the West and supporters of Russia, was turned into a political monopoly. This meant that a significant step had been taken towards authoritarianism, despite elections having been formally held. A focus group of local investigative journalists depicted this mix of capture methods as follows:

The method these people employ is threefold. First, they have invested in people's personal files through both public and private means of spying. They control the state security agency as well – they know everything about politicians, judges and public officials, of which many are vulnerable. Even those who want to do the right thing are afraid their wives might receive an embarrassing video of them in the mail. So, threats/blackmail are the first tool, and with serious consequences, as they control prosecutors. The second is use of calculated defamation (*kompromat*) until the target complies. Since they own important media, they can frame someone as corrupt or worse even when that particular individual is not. And finally, they buy people off, through simple bribes or others favors – an irresistible offer can be made even to the constitutional judges appointed by others. Few people can resist all three approaches.[13]

Additionally, during the decade when it was ruled by its nominal pro-European coalition the country suffered the worst raiding attacks. First, 2010 saw a complex money laundering operation by cross-border post-

[13] Focus group interview in Chisinau, September 2018.

Soviet crime syndicates. They took advantage of the country's vulnerable judiciary and used tens of corrupt Moldovan judges and bailiffs to enforce money orders for fictitious debts out of Russian banks and then to launder the money further (estimated at least USD 20 billion) (*The Guardian*, 2017a). Second, though a series of fraudulent loans, a group of criminals made the Moldovan National Bank cover a billion in losses belonging to three banks earlier privatized into their hands – the equivalent of 10–12 percent of Moldova's GDP (*CNN Money*, 2015). Then Prime Minister Vlad Filat was recorded talking on the phone to the most visible perpetrator, Ilan Shor, a Russian-speaking businessman. His subsequent fall was celebrated as the end of impunity culture (Carnegie Europe, 2017). With the benefit of hindsight, it appears as just one step in the elimination of rival gangs and the establishment of a power monopoly for Mr. Plahotniuc, as Mr. Filat was judged behind closed doors and Mr. Shor was still free by 2019. Despite the national and international outcry provoked by these moves, there was no attempt or serious conditionality imposed to ensure that anti-corruption agencies were and would remain autonomous. Likewise, bank reform was taken seriously only after the banks had been cleared out. The warnings signs had been plentiful, though. In Chisinau, prosecutors can be easily spotted driving private luxury vehicles, despite their meager salaries. The list of Plahotniuc's critics to be indicted got longer and longer (for instance, mayors who refused to switch to his party).[14]

The trend towards state capture has been clear at least since 2016, when Open Democracy and Carnegie both published papers on Moldova's captured state, each identifying Mr. Plahotniuc as a monopolist and usurper of the pro-EU camp leadership (Levcenko 2016; Chayes 2016). Of course, Mr. Plahotniuc was by then immensely rich and powerful, but not above sanction, as he had been the subject of monitoring by Interpol and had connections with the Romanian intelligence community (he could even boast a second Romanian identity in addition to three passports, Russian, Romanian, and Moldovan).[15] However, no serious attempt has ever been made for the individual sanctioning of Mr. Plahotniuc, even when he was accused of tampering with election results. The US and EU embassies in Moldova did react publicly, but also naively, imagining that such trends could be reversed by a few critical comments. Three European Parliament members even sent messages of

---

[14] September 2018 focus group in Chisinau, IRIS interviews by the author with all parties concerned.

[15] See comments of Armand Gosu, former adviser to Romanian Ministry of Foreign Affairs, on partisan Romanian mishandling: www.contributors.ro/administratie/prizonerii-lui-p lahotniuc-relațiile-dintre-romania-și-republica-moldova/

support to Mr. Shor's party for the February 2019 elections (*Politico*, 2019).

So, what did EU and the bulk of donors do while Moldova was sliding back? They were largely backing "five-year" anti-corruption plans of the likes of the "National Anti-Corruption Strategy 2011–2015," which was intended to reduce corruption in the Moldovan public and private sectors. The strategy included a theory of change "transforming corruption from a low-risk activity with benefits into an inconvenient and high-risk activity" but listed as its goal the completely unrealistic donor objective of "contributing to the creation of a zero-tolerance environment towards corruption in Moldova." Combined with the acquis communautaire, which implies the presence of "autonomous" agencies with the task of implementing EU directives, Moldova embarked on the long road toward building institutions. Agencies created included the National Anticorruption Center (NAC, cna.md), a monitoring group for the implementation of the National Anti-Corruption Strategy, a National Integrity Authority modeled on the Romanian National Integrity Agency, an audit court, a money laundering office, and so forth. Each of the above institutions received a great deal of donor support from the EU, Sweden, the UNDP (generally European donor money), and the US, through various agencies.

Additionally, five-year plans were drawn up, reminiscent of the Communist era. As an assessment of the past UNDP strategy, funded by the Swedish government, noted:[16]

Over the past five years, the approval of the Action Plans for the Anti-Corruption Strategy in Parliament took considerable time (delays were due to elections or the ongoing political negotiations). As a result, only 3.5 years of the five-year implementation period were covered by Action Plans.

And futher:

The Parliament of Moldova receives annual, semi-annual and quarterly progress reports on the Strategy implementation from the Secretariat of the Monitoring Group. It is also informed on the work of the NAC [Anti-Corruption Agency] as one of the MPs who is member of the same Parliamentary Commission for National Security, Defense and Public Order is also the member of the National Anti-Corruption Centre's Board. So, at its quarterly meetings every member receives the Report on the NAC's activity from the previous time period (quarter, semester, year).

---

[16] See www.md.undp.org/content/dam/moldova/docs/3_Anticorruption_inside_print%20 ISBN%2022DE.pdf, page 18.

In addition to its main laws and strategies, Moldova has also issued numerous special documents concerning the prevention and fighting of corruption. These have covered conflict of interest; codes of conduct; prevention and combating of corruption; approval of regulations on the operation of an anti-corruption hotline system; the application of lie detector (polygraph) tests; verification of holders of and candidates for public offices; testing of professional integrity; estimation of corruptibility of draft legislation; approval of the methodology of evaluation of corruption risks in public authorities and institutions; and the establishment of permissible values of gifts and approval of regulations on evidence, evaluation, storage, use, and redemption of symbolic gifts and of gifts offered by courtesy or on the occasions of protocol actions. A 2015 PhD thesis monitored the inflation of legislation over more than twenty-five years, but after a thorough study of existing court cases concerning corruption concluded that the end result was anything but justice (Gatcan, 2015, p. 98). In fact, during its "anti-corruption years" Moldova's place in the corruption perception index fell to the level of Mali and Azerbaijan.

In 2018, a Freedom House report aptly noted that

Anticorruption initiatives did not contribute to reducing corruption in 2017, as none aimed at depoliticizing public institutions and regulatory agencies. Open competitions for positions of responsibility were nontransparent in most instances, organized not by merit but instead relying on controversial regulations and political loyalty to, or membership of, the ruling political group. The year saw an excessive politicization of the fight against corruption. Although the number of big corruption cases grew compared to 2016, these concerned current or former senior figures of political parties other than PDM ... While the local public administration (LPA) is one of most trusted institutions in the society, local governments risk losing independence and are increasingly used as political instruments ahead of the parliamentary elections ... LPA representatives, especially those belonging to parties other than PDM, faced intimidation and verbal threats. The threats seemed to take place because they were reluctant to join PDM or promote certain ideas of the party. (Freedom House 2018)

Instead of delivering effective justice, Moldova's many reforms thus created a national integrity framework consisting only of empty shells. As in Italy, current procedures in Moldovan justice would not support even well-meaning anti-corruption, as cases drag on for years in the most inefficient and dispiriting manner possible. As the European acquis communautaire actually includes demands for reform of criminal and civil procedural codes, the opportunity has always existed to address as part of Europeanization the fundamental problem of the courts' effectiveness in EU-associated countries. But this opportunity has seldom been taken up seriously. By the end of 2018, Moldova has not fully implemented a system of random assignment of court cases, for instance, but instead has managed to develop a string of agencies whose activity all ends up in the judicial bottleneck, a situation that only serves to muddy the waters. Worse still, none of them acts directly on the causes of corruption, so all only create ever more ample opportunity not so much to curtail as to enable the manipulation of anti-corruption for political and personal gain. This is further bolstered by poor regulatory quality that makes all mayors, for instance, vulnerable to accusations of breaking the law in one way or another.

Like Ukraine, Moldova is home to an active noncorrupt civil society sponsored by European and American donors, as well as an informal pro-European opposition that has developed against Mr. Plahotniuc. The EU had been a constant sponsor of Moldovan civil society, but it did not, however, act on its timely warnings that pro-European parties were rapidly turning to organized crime, despite a grassroots anti-corruption coalition, Dignity and Truth, being promptly organized. Finally, when the anti-corruption opposition even managed to win elections in the capital city, Chisinau, in spring 2018 against both socialists and the Plahotniuc camp, and a series of courts annulled the mayoral elections, the EU reacted in protest, interrupting budget support and announcing that the money would instead be put into "projects" (Radio Free Europe, 2016). But how persuasive could the EU's threats be – to scrap the association agreement, for instance – when in every election, as in Ukraine, a serious contender exists (the socialists) to run with a program against EU integration and in favor of Russia? The alternative would have been to acknowledge that the institutions created have no potential to reverse and contain the capture by organized crime of the government of Moldova (as acknowledged by a European Parliament resolution[17]) and that the way to deal with organized crime groups is not through collective sanctions targeted at states, but instead through *individual sanctions* targeted at individuals. A recent European model exists in Council Decisions 2014/145/CFSP and its update of December 10, 2018 (CFSP) 2018/1930 "amending Decision 2014/145/CFSP concerning restrictive measures in respect of actions undermining or threatening the territorial integrity, sovereignty and independence of Ukraine." They establish individual sanctions on 164 individuals and 44 entities (as of December 2018) such as freezing of assets and travel restrictions, for actions including "misappropriation of Ukrainian state funds." The list includes politicians, businesspeople, magistrates from electoral

---

[17] See www.europarl.europa.eu/sides/getDoc.do?pubRef=-//EP//TEXT+TA+P8-TA-201
8–0458+0+DOC+XML+V0//EN&language=EN

courts, and so on. Such sanctions could have been used from the first revelations that law enforcement agencies have been politicized and used unlawfully, and maybe the situation could have been averted in which Plahotniuc's and Shor's parties both ran in the 2019 elections.

The EU has been also chronically unable to play much of a role in solving the problem of the substantial corruption opportunities that have arisen due to the breaking away of Moldova's Transnistria region: the EU has always resigned itself to having a very weak role in resolving the conflict, if any. From its early years Transnistria was a smuggler's paradise, although in time, and while "negotiations" involving Russia and the EU dragged on, it has turned into a major source of rents, with considerable collusion from both banks of the Nistru river to keep it going (Soloviev 2017). For instance, as Moldova's main power station is in Transnistria, Transnistria sold electricity to Moldova via various "favored" companies, allegedly connected to leaders in both countries.[18] The EU and member state Romania have done far too little over the years to prompt energy reforms to make Moldova independent from Transnistria's power supply. EBRD stepped forward to acquire shares in Moldovan banks after the bank disaster, and indeed such a policy – supporting the privatization of the Moldovan economy to EU member state companies to remove them from the influence of Russian or local mafias – has far higher anti-corruption potential than any new agency created.

The European Court of Auditors reported of Moldova that "budget support had had a limited effect. The Commission could have responded more quickly when risks materialized, and programs were not sufficiently aligned to Moldovan strategies. The Commission did not make full use of its ability to set conditions for disbursement, and additional incentive-based funds were not fully justified" (ECA, 2016b). As to Ukraine, the latest audit court assessment acknowledges that the aid could hardly have been better organized due to the ad hoc quality of intervention (following Russian aggression) and achievements remain "partial" (ECA, 2016b). Both reports practice understatement, however. The truth is that donor-sponsored anti-corruption activities in Moldova and Ukraine hardly contributed to progress over long periods of time. In certain cases, these activities had negative consequences. Both countries were flooded with "autonomous" agencies before opportunities for corruption were reduced, exactly the opposite of the successful Estonian or Georgian

---

[18] See reports at http://infoprut.ro/44700-energocapital-plahotniuc-sevciuk-raportul-kroll-doi-experti-se-aplica-schema-din-jaful-secolului.html and https://eurasianet.org/moldova-shadowy-power-deal-fueling-protesters-anger

examples. The roadmap of cutting rents, liberalizing the economy, clear-
ing and consolidating property, simplifying and strengthening financial
management, and reducing administrative burden has been pursued
inconsistently. The result is that dangerous law enforcement agencies,
barely beginning to democratize out of Soviet times (e.g. prosecutors and
secret services), find themselves empowered by the new anti-corruption
mandate. They wield that mandate, in typical post-Soviet fashion, to
harass and intimidate opponents and expropriate independent foreign
businesspeople. They operate regionally with quasi-impunity.[19]

To sell the acquis to the neighborhood, despite the lack of an accession
perspective, the EC used the argument that the EU model is superior to
those of other international actors: first, in terms of regulatory quality;
second, because of its comprehensiveness; and third, given the relative
lack of controversy surrounding it (Emerson et al., 2018). Unfortunately,
the acquis adoption process did not hinder the advance of state capture in
any way, and therefore, the premises emerged for a meaningless legal
transition from Soviet to EU regulation in a context where societies have
in any case long learned to cope with laws by not implementing them
(Ledeneva, 2006). In the absence of a strategic theory of change, EU anti-
corruption policies resorted to the standard formal prescription mechanism (Johnson and Taxell, 2015; Szarek-Mason, 2010).

Other EU interventions not directly marked as means to fight "corruption" delivered more significant contributions to anti-corruption, however: public financial management, support for e-government, civil
society support at the local level, support for strategic litigation by civil
society lawyers, exchange programs for students. Most of these initiatives
have taken off in recent years, after practically unconditional aid before
the Euromaidan saw Ukraine regressing, not progressing, on fiscal transparency. But by and large, as successive reports of the ECA showed,
"political dialogue" combined with aid, either in the form of projects or
unconditional budget support, has not prompted good governance in
Ukraine so far (Euractiv.com, 2016). As the country embarked on a
new electoral cycle in 2018–2019, a strong, credible pro-integrity
electoral alternative was still missing. The focus of politicians remains,
understandably, on securing their survival in power. The relentless anti-
corruption campaign by civil society actors managed to discredit
President Poroshenko and his moderate reformers, but, as in Romania,
there was not much of a ready-made pro-integrity alternative to win a
majority. And the geopolitical situation is so much worse.

---

[19] For more information on the "Russian Laundromat," see the Organized Crime and
Corruption Reporting Project (OCCRP, 2014) at www.reportingproject.net.

The point can be raised that the "ownership" that characterized reforms in Estonia and Georgia was lacking in Moldova or Ukraine, where agency was reduced to merely civil society actors and occasional technocrats. But that depiction would not be accurate. Reformers were present in both countries. The Georgian reformers imported to Ukraine after the Maidan revolution are a good example, and the decision to bring them in was certainly commendable. Their time perspectives and periods of stability, however, have always been too short; their control of the situation, unlike in Estonia, has always been limited in the absence of a consistent group supporting reforms in the parliament. Also, they were caught in the bureaucratic machine of the EU (which did not happen in Estonia or Georgia, as they reformed before the EU showed up), with its false targets and prescription mechanisms, so they could not achieve much. Corruption also fights back. In Ukraine, media capture makes the life of every reformer difficult: it would have been more strategic to start reforms by cleaning up the blackmail (*kompromat*) media, which was frequently wrongly defended on the pretext of freedom of the press. One should never forget that European media did not reach integrity by itself, but by a combination of civil lawsuits that ruined the blackmail tabloids through government policy (Mungiu-Pippidi, 2015b, Chapter 5). Due to political fragmentation, frequent elections, and competition with Russian-backed populists, good governance agendas face an uphill battle to get public support. Such agendas unfortunately require people to give up their rents (e.g. gas subsidies) in exchange for some future uncertain ethical universalistic reward.

If mainstream EU anti-corruption has not delivered very much in both countries, a latecomer to the scene, the separately organized European Endowment for Democracy (EED, created in 2011) proved to be a more efficient and strategic intervener. It gave strategic grants to the opposition media (to great effect in 2018 notably in Armenia and in Moldova, where it funded the only anti-oligarchic TV channel) and supported small groups with a pro-integrity agenda and strategic thinking of their own, not part of the great bureaucratic effort. The EED, an initiative of the Polish presidency, was set up as an independent international trust operating on a minimal budget (EUR 18 million in 2017, of which a European Commission grant covers the EUR 4 million necessary for operation).[20] It is accountable only to a pan-EU political board and operates more like an American charity, free of the EU's bureaucratic constraints, on the basis of appraisal missions and flexible allocation calendars. Simultaneously and in parallel with mainstream bureaucratic EU anti-corruption efforts,

---

[20] Interview at EED in Brussels in June 2018.

the EED has done the real work of identifying veritable agents of change and funding them. It also ties financing to the right conditions to ensure the money funds representative action.[21] In a short amount of time, the EED developed the intelligence needed for a domestic agency-based strategy, for which it had neither the authority nor the means. Yet, armed with only what they knew about the people on the ground, they were able to achieve a lot more than the EU – whose money went through classic channels into aid for democracy and good governance – and to contribute to more evidence-based suggestions for other donors.[22]

The spring and summer of 2019 brought new developments in the two countries, forcing the EU to adjust quickly and bring its policies up to date. In Ukraine, a former television actor won by a landslide in the presidential elections, defeating the nominally pro-EU party of the incumbent president Petro Poroshenko. The challenger, Volodymyr Zelensky, had played the TV role of an ordinary man who suddenly became president, in a series tellingly titled *Servant of the People*. In a campaign helped by both traditional and social media (and not without support from certain oligarchs), Zelensky opened a new chapter of uncertainty about Ukraine for Western diplomats.

In Moldova, the EU found itself blackmailed when Mr. Plahotniuc managed in the February 2019 elections to secure again the role of king-maker between the east (the former communist party, which came first with roughly a third of the vote) and the west (anti-corruption pro-Europeans, Plahotniuc's chief rivals). But then something unprecedented happened. After some weeks of stalemate, Moldova's capital city was visited by three overseas officials in one day, June 3: the Russian deputy prime minister and special representative for trade with Moldova, Dmitry Kozak; the EU commissioner for European neighborhood policy, Johannes Hahn; and the director of the US State Department's Office of Eastern European Affairs, Brad Freden. They met all political parties, and statements followed blessing the alliance between the pro-Russia socialists and the pro-EU anti-Plahotniuc camp.[23] Plahotniuc resisted for about a week, supported by his Romanian allies in the secret services and politics, and then he fled. Russia charged him with money landering and other criminal offences. While the new alliance cannot do much more than call for fresh elections, given its heterogeneity, the cooperation between the EU and Russia to combat state capture is an innovation

[21] Their annual reports are available online: www.democracyendowment.eu/annual-repor t-2017

[22] Focus groups with NGO EU grantees, Chisinau and Kiev, 2019.

[23] See the full story covered by Carnegie Russia at https://carnegie.ru/commentary/79333

and opens new possibilities for anti-corruption, at least for the curbing of international money laundering, which could prove beneficial to both sides.

7.2   Arab Delusion to Arab Confusion

In December 2010, protest rallies erupted in Tunisia following the self-immolation of an unlicensed street vendor, who was prevented from exercising his trade by local police. Protests against the regimes that Michael Johnston (2014) had described as "official moguls" then spread to Oman, Yemen, Egypt, Syria, and Morocco. On January 14, 2011, the Tunisian government was overthrown. Ten days later, massive protests started in Tahrir square in Cairo. In February, Egyptian president Hosni Mubarak resigned. In Libya, street demonstrations erupted that would soon turn into the Libyan Civil War. In June 2012, Mr. Mubarak was sentenced to life in prison by an Egyptian court; ten days later, former Tunisian president Zine El Abidine Ben Ali got his turn for a prison sentence, issued by a Tunisian court. Also, that June, the Egyptians elected the Muslim Brotherhood candidate Mohammed Morsi in the second round of a presidential run-off election, only to see him deposed by an army coup following street protests in the summer of the following year – a year that saw the Syrian government use chemical weapons to prevent the spread of further opposition.

A widespread belief reigns that discontent with patrimonialism and a longing for an ethical universalist democracy fueled these Arab Spring fires. This increasingly looks like just a delusion. The MENA region presents a wide variation of backgrounds on goodness of fit for modernity, with considerable variation across countries in education, income, secularization, treatment of women, and the urban–rural divide. This speaks against some theories of unitary causes of the uprisings (Anderson 2011). As the Tunisian street vendor did not belong to the same social class as the Egyptian students, it seems that the broad street movements assembled together various groups with different agendas – which then separated into several streams after the protests died down, each based on narrower perspectives and self-interest. The main commonality is the ingrained particularistic *modus operandi* of the state across these polities, where rulers have shaped regulation across time to produce rents for the connected and to control access for the rest. The result of this long-time trend was that the World Bank's average control-of-corruption ranking for the region was consistently on the lower half of the scale at 46 (out of 100). Using firm-level data from Tunisia, researchers found the typical landscape to contain market concentration of "connected" firms, accounting for a disproportionate share of aggregate employment, output, and profits, especially in sectors subject to authorization and restrictions on FDI (Freund et al., 2014).

While "official moguls" can certainly be identified behind these connections prior to the popular uprisings of 2010–2011, the prevailing systems – limited access created through restrictive regulation, and long-term privileged market advantage – survived the moguls' downfall and the street rebellion. Pessimism rules across the region, with 50–90 percent thinking that "most" officials are still corrupt (the highest in Yemen) and critical of how governments handle corruption. Reports of bribery are more varied, with under 10 percent paying to access public services in Jordan and Tunisia while one in two respondents to the Afrobarometer survey claimed to have paid a bribe in the past year in Egypt or Morocco (Afrobarometer 2016). Privileged access via connections and nepotism is the rule across the region; even in countries where bribes are relatively low, e.g. Tunisia, privileged access is still a source of much discontent for the young, often jobless generation (CISR, 2018). Red tape conducive to restrictive access and its opposite – legal privilege (various forms of monopolies or privileged allocations) – are also the rule (Goldstraw-White and Gill, 2014). This discontent with limited access, rather than just pure material despair, seemed to have driven the protests, making MENA by the late 2000s the only region in the world where subjective wellbeing had drastically declined, with perceptions of the quality of government services and economic opportunities in particular deteriorating across all countries (Ianchovichina, 2015). Thus, the essential question after the revolutions is to what extent has access been opened and ethical universalism promoted? And whose agenda, if anybody's among the local actors, is to eliminate the rent-prone structure altogether rather than inheriting the rents? Here is where the core of any serious anti-corruption strategy should be.

By 2010, the World Bank was recording declines in extreme poverty under the neopatrimonial regimes, along with increased school enrollment, drops in child and maternal mortality, and even moderate economic growth (World Bank, 2010). The European Union was a direct contributor to this moderate increase in prosperity. Speaking on May 10, 2012, Catherine Ashton, Vice-President of the Commission and High Representative of the Union for Foreign Affairs and Security Policy, announced that "The European Neighborhood Policy is a success story." And Štefan Füle, Commissioner for Enlargement and European Neighborhood Policy, added: "Further strengthening the ENP is no less than an investment in the EU's own stability and prosperity – and this must be reflected in our offer to our partners. The ENP is a win-win game" (EC, 2010a). Some serious facts backed their words: between

2004 and 2008, the EU's exports to the ENP region rose by 63 percent and imports by 91 percent. The EU declared itself ready to negotiate deep and comprehensive free trade areas with all its neighbors as soon as they were ready for them. A press release at the time mentioned that "Much remains to be done in terms of judicial and public administration reforms and effectively tackling corruption" (ibid.), but that was a passing footnote.

The eruption of the region's "anti-corruption revolutions" provoked surprise and confusion at EU level. The EU's dominant development theory of change had been incremental modernization, yet Tunisia's wave of discontent resulted from an immediate demand for better quality of government. The actions of local neopatrimonial dictators in turning budget support into subsidies for basic foods (although with added profit for their families) could hardly have been expected to generate riots – and yet they did. The unaccounted-for factor was social media, a completely new phenomenon that turned the disenchanted and underemployed youth into e-citizens, able to associate fast, albeit temporarily, and to shake political regimes to their foundations. The EU had no choice but to reorient its aid, despite its bureaucratic approach. It worked far better in Tunisia than in Egypt.

Both before and after the uprising, Egypt and Tunisia were beneficiaries of assistance from the European Neighborhood and Partnership Instrument (ENPI), which the EU used to support its European Neighborhood Policy (ENP). Egypt got the lion's share. It began negotiations with the EU in 2005, and the EU–Egypt Action Plan entered into force in 2007. The 2007–2013 Country Strategy Paper (CSP) for Egypt details the financial plan and, for the first time, good governance became a priority area rather than just an issue within the political dialog (Louis, 2017). Following the 2005 Paris Declaration on Aid Effectiveness, the EU shifted its aid towards budget support, considered to be an effective mechanism for boosting reforms in partner countries. By 2013 the EU had become the only international donor to provide sector budget support (SBS) to Egypt (ECA, 2013b, p. 22). For the period 2007–2013, Egypt received an allocation of around EUR 1 billion. Approximately 60 percent of these funds were channeled through SBS to the Egyptian government and the rest to projects agreed upon with the Egyptian authorities. Assessments of the EU's impact on governance are rather negative (Del Sarto and Schumacher, 2011; ECA, 2013; Balfour et al., 2016; Louis, 2017). An audit by the ECA covering the period to September 2012 examined 25 projects and the three main SBS programs. It found that overall the European Commission and European External Action Service (EEAS) had not managed support to improve governance in Egypt effectively (ECA, 2013a). The ECA criticized in particular the failure under the Mubarak regime to improve the public financial management framework, and the EC for having continued to fund it through budget support without implementing any conditionality. According to the ECA, neither the political dialogue nor the projects had worked (only one project was relevant for anti-corruption, but it was poorly implemented, said the ECA). Meanwhile civil society had seen barely any funding before the uprising. Egyptian officials interviewed by ANTICORRP also complained that the EU intervention completely ignored the little, but organically developed, anti-corruption activity that already existed. Instead, it imposed its own bureaucratic prescriptions that did not correspond to Egyptian realities, so had no chance of impact or imposed intermediaries, like the UNODC, which were unwelcome in Egypt (Louis, 2017). By the time the EU finally decided to switch its funding support entirely to civil society anti-corruption activities, local political conditions were too averse.[24]

The post-revolution strategy thus tried to increase support to civil society, reacting to ECA criticism; additionally, the budget for the European Instrument for Democracy and Human Rights was increased, and the strengthened EU delegations were empowered to liaise more with civil society actors (Balfour et al., 2016). Perhaps more importantly, this was the birth of the aforementioned European Endowment for Democracy, which provided grants independently of the commission's funding mechanisms. After the uprising, an ENP review tried to refocus the aid, but the ECA found that not much changed in practice thereafter, due in large part to the political deterioration of the situation. In its fierce answer to the criticism of the ECA, the EEAS defended the decision to continue providing financial assistance – despite all the obstacles encountered "of a political nature" (and therefore no business of auditors), which should be viewed "in the regional context and in consideration of the crucial strategic role Egypt is playing. The decision by the Commission/EEAS, in this respect, is in line with the decisions taken by other development partners including EU Member States" (EC, 2013a). In other words, the European Commission accused the European Court of Auditors of imposing overly high normative standards – standards different from the reality on the ground, where each member state had traditionally pursued its national interest.

Indeed, once the Sisi presidency in Egypt had reinstated stability through repression, assistance resumed on a similar level to the pre-2011 period, without the additional funding for good governance (Balfour et al., 2016). With the pre- and post-revolution efforts

---

[24] Interview with former ambassador James Moran, Brussels, February 2018.

combined, Egypt arrived at an IPI score of 4.78 by 2018 (out of 10 possible), and a country rank of 97 out of 109. The MENA region as a whole fell from a 47 out of 100 rank in the World Bank Control of Corruption indicator to an average of 43 – a change at the limit of significance but that shows that the "revolutions" had brought anything but governance improvement. Political stability, however, fell more dramatically, from 45 to 26 out of 100 on the average for the region.

Tunisia seems definitely the success story compared with Egypt, let alone others in the region; but the same issues arise due to inherent interest-driven policies on the side of the EU (as opposed to normative ones) and the bureaucratic approach to anti-corruption, making consolidation and in particular sustainability of democratic achievements a challenge (Tocci, 2011). By 2018, a majority of Tunisians polled claimed that the country was headed in the wrong direction, and corruption was mentioned as merely the fourth most important problem, far below unemployment (ICSR, 2018). A limited amnesty passed by the parliament (the Administrative Reconciliation Law) encountered major disapproval among the country's youth (ibid.). People interviewed in focus groups claimed that they had joined extremist groups due to the inability to find a path in life in Tunisia's system of limited access, which was strictly based on nepotism and connections (Macdonald and Waggoner, 2018). Although the country had made important constitutional strides and had consolidated its democracy, it was unlikely that any survey respondent would say that the problems leading to the immolation of the street vendor in 2010 had by then been solved. Either the Tunisian revolution had not been about corruption, or the anti-corruption revolution as seen by these young people has simply replaced the socialist revolutions of old. In other words, the ethical universalism demanded by Tunisian youth means taking equality of opportunity to the maximum, and the governments' and donors' offer of anti-corruption blended with austerity has not met their expectations (Murphy and Albu, 2018).

The 2011 regime change in Tunisia was a challenge for the EU, which had been engaged in extensive financial and technical cooperation with the previous regime. In the wake of the Lisbon Treaty, the union was also busy redesigning its own external representation. The newly created European External Action Service had only been launched in December 2010, a mere matter of weeks before the removal of President Ben Ali (Warkotsch, 2017). This resulted in competing visions and ambitions on the EU side, but also a sound acknowledgment of past mistakes (Balfour, 2012, p. 11) along with a total retooling of EU instruments. The EU doubled its aid budget to Tunisia for 2011–2013, to reach some EUR 445 million (ECA, 2017). The stress in 2011 was on "reinforcement of conditionality" (deep democracy criteria) and "differentiation" to promote the "democratization wave" of 2010–2011.[25] Tunisia became the main beneficiary of the governance incentive-based SPRING program, receiving a total of EUR 155 million between 2011 and 2013 (Warkotsch, 2017).[26] Good governance conditions have grown along with the programs, including conditions such as implementing legislation in the media sector, greater budget transparency, and improved access to information (ibid.). Funding from the regional South Program (Strengthening Democratic Reform in the Southern Neighborhood) complemented the ENP. The EU thus funded the Council of Europe (CoE) for the South Neighborhood Anti-Corruption (SNAC) project with a budget of EUR 4.8 million for 2012–2014, and an additional EUR 7.37 million (SNAC II) for 2015–2017. The funds enabled the CoE to support the development of Tunisia's integrity framework, consisting in an anti-corruption agency – the Tunisian National Instance for the Fight against Corruption (INLUCC), its successor, the Independent Constitutional Agency for Good Governance and Fight against Corruption, plus a whole legislative and institutional anti-corruption framework. The OECD had already delivered a comprehensive assessment of integrity in 2013, to be used as a strategic basis for a unitary and broad anti-corruption strategy (OECD, 2013). Domestic "ownership" of anti-corruption policies evolved from lack of interest under Ben Ali to his successors' rather limited competence and authority to negotiate adequate reforms, call for donor coordination and conditionalities appropriate to country context, and fulfill administrative capacities (Warkotsch, 2017). Tunisia was weaker than Rwanda in this respect – maybe because its leadership was less authoritarian – and ownership never really materialized, as no one actually was able to make articulate demands to the donors. Experts working on EU projects interviewed by ANTICORRP also considered that the EU should have backed up conditionality with proper incentives for a better response. For instance, concessions granting access to more mobility and trade (especially on agriculture) would have benefited the local population more directly and given some badly needed credit to reform-minded leaders (ibid.). But then again, the integrity framework designed by the Council of Europe and other EU agencies did not have in mind a constituency made of Tunisia's petty entrepreneurs, or of the educated youth seeking employment in the public sector. Theirs was the typical abstract anti-corruption imagined by lawyers meant to punish deviation and not to build new standards. INLUCC

---

[25] European Commission and High representative Joint Communication, *A New Response to a Changing Neighborhood*, Brussels, 25/05/2011, COM (2011), p. 303.

[26] It was replaced by new "umbrella funds" in 2014 under ENI 2014–20.

was under-resourced and understaffed for the thousands of cases on its docket. The few they managed get through the courts did not progress much further (BTI, 2018b). It remains to be seen how effective INLUCC's successor, the constitutional Good Governance and Anti-Corruption Commission, will be. But the very concept that a single agency can solve a generalized particularistic allocation is doubtful. Meanwhile, Tunisia has twice been sanctioned in recent years and has been added to the tax haven and money laundering lists, despite opposition in the European Parliament and the disastrous economic effects going against what EU aid was trying to achieve (EU Council, 2015).

Tracing the IPI components over time, we find that freedom of the press and internet connections are the only ones to have improved substantially (Warkotsch, 2017). Tunisia still lags behind its income group on red tape on trade (21 of 28) and budget transparency (20 of 28).[27] Obviously, democracy and secularism have been top EU priorities for Tunisia, with good governance relegated to secondary status, but unless the country opens access to public resources further, containing the discontent of the young generation will only become more problematic for democratic sustainability. But even the progress on internet connections should be viewed with skepticism. By 2012, three of the top five most followed Arab personalities on Twitter were religious preachers (MRD, 2012). Promoters of nonmodern content thus seem to operate social media more effectively than the promoters of modern government. While development agencies are right to fund universal access to broadband (and there is still insufficient support for that), the investment is lost if content-wise there is no vision for how the smartphone could empower citizens and constrain authority. In the absence of such a vision, donor-supported agencies cannot achieve much.

The main problem of the EU anti-corruption approach in Tunisia is therefore the lack of a comprehensive vision, of a theory of change other than austerity – which cannot go down well with a young population already starved for opportunities and missing a liberal culture. The diplomats and staff in the field also have to struggle with competing interests coming out of member states. During the ENP years, the Tunisian branches of leading French companies such as Orange and Carrefour were led by Ben Ali's family or their cronies; EADS made irregular payments through Saudi Arabia and Société Générale to the Gaddafi regime in Libya, whose survivors also claim to have funded the

---

[27] See the Index of Public Integrity 2017 for Tunisia: www.integrity-index.org.

presidential electoral campaign in France.[28] EADS and Société Générale (which paid its USD 1.3 billion fine to the American authorities) have the status of quasi-official companies with strong ties to European governments in these countries. Most of the European companies investing in the Middle East fund political parties back at home. It is rather difficult to preach anti-corruption to the locals while at the same time having little or no control over implementation of the OECD anti-bribery convention or over European companies, which are instead quite close to their member state embassies. And yet, although some European companies sinned alongside the region's autocrats preventing regional growth, it is really the local rent-seekers who in the absence of other natural resources have the greatest stake in keeping regulatory rents and avoiding meaningful competition, especially in Tunisia and Morocco.

The European Council's conclusions "on the Review of the European Neighborhood Policy," adopted in 2015, stress in quite a Solomonic manner that a "revised ENP should take into account interests and needs of the EU and its neighbors, neighbors' commitment to reforms, the level of ambition of the partnership as well as different challenges and the geopolitical environment."[29] How to solve the trade-offs if the interests of the EU and the interests of the neighbors do not align is left to the EU representatives on the ground, who in any case struggle daily between the various interests of individual EU member states.[30] The new document thus shifts back towards realism, seeking to strengthen economic cooperation through DCFTAs as well as focusing on security and migration issues (Warkotsch, 2017), which had never been very consistent with the earlier conditions on good governance.

The EU anti-corruption interventions in MENA after the Arab Spring could hardly have been more focused than the overall democratization approach. Scholars criticized older action plans for precisely the absence of clear theories of change in democratization (more established than corruption ones) to conclude that, from the first, the ENP had lacked analytical depth in terms of concepts and processes of democratization (Del Sarto and Schumacher, 2011). This shallowness, combined with an arbitrary and largely useless selection of pseudo-benchmarks, resulted in a lack of clarity, undermining the declared objectives of the union's

---

[28] A variety of media and think tank sources exist on the involvement of European companies with corrupt Middle East regimes to which justice cannot be rendered here. For an official account on SG, see the *Financial Times* coverage on Tunisia and EADS in Saudi Arabia.

[29] Council conclusions on the Review of the European Neighborhood Policy, 20/04/2015, Press release 188/15.

[30] Interview with Ambassador Donato Chiarini, Rome, November 15, 2018.

democracy promotion policy and its leverage more generally (ibid.). Both EU project staff and Tunisian officials complained about lack of consistency on the EU side regarding clear operational indicators (Wouters and Duquet, 2013, p. 231; Warkotsch, 2017). In the end, critics remark that instead of "more for more," the positive conditionality paradigm, EU's policy might have delivered rather "more for less" or "less for less" (Lannon, 2015; Bichi, 2014). The EU has not managed to assert itself either as a strategic actor or as a normative power, being perceived as rather a bystander, "trapped in its internal institutional process and passively reacting to crisis events by proposing long-term solutions with little short-term impact" (Noutcheva, 2015).

Of course, what is missing here is the counterfactual. In such trying circumstances, what could have been done differently, if anything? The agenda for governance reform, while needing in-depth grounding country by country, has some similarities across countries in North Africa, requiring primarily a reduction in resources for corruption and the removal of legal rent-seeking opportunities, at least the petty ones if it is politically unfeasible to address the grand ones. In other words, what these countries need is some basic package of administrative simplification and some policies to reduce informality and increase open access. Simply put, one has to return to the grievances of the man who set himself on fire. Simplifying procedures and creating a better administrative environment for business is a key component of the G20 Compact with Africa for these countries, where the lessons from Estonia and Georgia are all the more valuable. The Georgian example could be the one to allow further concrete improvement, with one-stop administrative offices/portals and "public service halls" – single transparent spaces of interaction with the public where all necessary (reduced) administrative steps are united (IGPDE 2018). Additionally, the innovations of the Indian government, such as the recently developed digital commons sponsored by public funds, both reduce informality and enable good governance (Nilekani 2018). These are platforms for the digital identification of citizens, used to distribute social benefits as well as for the facilitation of private secure financial operations, among many other uses.

7.3   The Distant Battlegrounds

On the eve of UK Prime Minister David Cameron's International Anti-Corruption Summit in April 2016 a letter came to him from Abuja, Nigeria, from anti-corruption activists:

Dear Prime Minister,

As you prepare to host global leaders in London for the International Anti-Corruption Summit, civil society in Nigeria is calling on you to take serious action to end the UK's role as a safe haven for our corrupt individuals, who steal our wealth for their own private gain. . . . Now we are embarked on a nationwide anti-corruption campaign. But these efforts are sadly undermined if countries such as your own are welcoming our corrupt to hide their ill-gotten gains in your luxury homes, department stores, car dealerships, private schools and anywhere else that will accept their cash with no questions asked.[31]

Cameron alluded to Nigeria, although not to this particular letter, a few days later when he opened the event and cheerfully introduced to the queen some of the "most fantastically" corrupt countries in the world (*The Guardian*, 2016b) – all the countries where EU (and British) aid was going to help the poor and build "rule of law" – many of them former colonies. The summit was quite an extraordinary event for, as *The Guardian* aptly put it, a city internationally recognized (by the IMF, among others) as a tax haven and a politician who had admitted a month before that he had personally profited from offshore finance (*The Guardian*, 2016c) and even stepped in to shield offshore trusts from EU tax crack-downs in 2013 (*The Guardian*, 2016a). What the Nigerian civil society actors complained of had been Cameron's official policy for quite a while: opening the door to the kleptocrats of other countries, to the effect that a tour run in London and Oxford by an activist group now takes tourists around the lavish estates of oligarchs, complete with university chairs endowed by them at major British universities (Harding, 2016). And yet, it is Nigeria that is "fantastically corrupt" and Britain quite clean – at least as far as British citizens are concerned.

While colonialism and Western hypocrisy cannot take all the blame for today's African kleptocrats, a short survey of Africa's good governance shows a high degree of path dependency. This is why laughing at Nigeria is neither sensitive nor smart. The governance of Africa, perceived with just cause as the land of kleptocrats, is not explained by a few corrupt leaders landed there from outer space. It is a consequence of the whole history of Africa. Systemic corruption and extreme poverty are insepar-able, because poverty implies a dependent population who can be exploited or bought. More systematically, corruption in sub-Saharan Africa (SSA) draws on both high resources and poor constraints.

First, great resources exist for corruption in the form of both adminis-trative and natural resources. The former colonies in SSA inherited a "gatekeeper" state model, primarily designed to extract rents, not to

[31] Published in a Transparency International press release from April 28, 2016 (Transparency International, 2016).

deliver services or enable business. The incentives for change have been far too few for domestic governments to do anything about it (Somerville, 2015, p. 47). As administrative resources for corruption and power inequality are rife throughout SSA, scarce public resources are allocated preferentially by default. The situation nevertheless has evolved quite a bit from the time when the World Bank began conducting public expenditure surveys (PETS) in Uganda over twenty years ago (1996). Back then, most money for education would never even reach the schools. Oversight increased due to such instruments, although fiscal transparency still leaves much to be desired.[32] Furthermore, an autonomous bureaucracy can hardly be said to exist in many SSA countries, a deficiency that is the legacy of unique party states and particularistic pluralism combined. Although the French and in particular the British tried, at the last possible moment, to build some foundation for an autonomous civil service based on the indigenous population (Public Service Commissions), the late effort was subverted by the African governments' need for control (Adu, 1969, p. 29). The national administrations have always been filled with recruits on the basis of family ties and patronage, with a varying degree of competence. Apart from South Africa during apartheid, only two countries' bureaucracies could be called reasonably autonomous from the political factor, both at appointment level and throughout careers: Botswana and Mauritius (Goldsmith, 1999, p. 540). Moreover, civil service has never been considered a service rendered by a "public servant," but rather a source of status and power, a mentality also originating in colonial times (Adu, 1969, p. 17). The lack of proper separation between the political and the bureaucratic has contributed to a regulatory framework oriented towards the extraction of rents, which is the main enemy to any progress of governance (Somerville, 2015). Many decades of modern state structures fitted poorly with the societies they were based in, and in fact, subverted by informal practices, they have developed a legacy of their own; but the return to some traditional–modern synthesis is not possible either (Medard, 2016, p. 183). The "natural resource curse," despite innovative approaches such as the Extractive Industries Transparency Initiative (EITI), has very much remained a curse. Botswana's old good choice – private management of natural resources with 50/50 profit-splitting with the state – has neither been emulated enough nor been supplanted by a better model. Finally, the many ethnic, linguistic, and other particularistic cleavages are a major resource for corruption. Although many can again be traced to recent elite instrumentalization and do not conform to

---

[32] For a history of such surveys, see World Bank, 2004.

the "ancient hatred" stereotypes, they remain among the most difficult issues to tackle in Africa. In divided societies, accountability towards one's own ethnic group does not work – as demonstrated from Nigeria to the African National Congress in South Africa – for the same reasons that it does not work in Bosnia. A country like Nigeria checks the boxes on all these negative factors, besides being the most populous in Africa, which only adds to its other collective action problems. It is difficult to contain corruption when so much is produced.

Secondly, constraints are poor. The British in particular left behind the common law and a court system, but a combination of poorly paid indigenous judiciaries and political intervention in justice makes SSA the worst performer on rule of law in the world, with an average rank of 30/100 (World Bank rule of law indicator) and little evolution over the past twenty years. Early attempts at building anti-corruption agencies had little impact on overall corruption, but taught leaders how to politically instrumentalize them against opponents (Doig et al., 2007). Freedom of the media and civil society are often insufficient and inseparable from two problems. First, demography: due to intense migration flows and overnight "modernization," the urban population grew between 15 percent and 40 percent across the region in the last half century (Courade, 2016, p. 317). Africa has boundless cities, where collective action is difficult as the population is constantly evolving and unaccounted for. Individuals often have no identification, no property, no electricity account, and no social ties. This does not bode well for collective action, as we know that societies, even if unequal, control corruption better if they have a corporative structure, with each individual belonging to some rule-based group or association (Mungiu-Pippidi, 2015b, Chapter 3). Second, poor social control allows frequent outbursts of violence and deters peaceful civil society and independent journalism. Votes are also conveniently bought, when not extorted (Collier, 2011). On the bright side, the multiplication of smartphones, driven by remittances, has led to increased internet penetration and a growing number of e-citizens. There are scattered but encouraging reports of crowdfunding for civil society work also based on remittances, so it is possible that the diaspora will play a large role in increasing constraints for corruption in the future.

In 2007, the EU adopted the EU Strategy for Africa in Lisbon (EC, 2007b). The strategy provided a long-term framework for interaction between Europe and Africa; its stakeholders include the African Union, regional organizations, and national authorities. It focuses on the targets laid out in the Millennium Development Goals (MDGs). Democratic governance is also an important component, with corruption mentioned repeatedly (pp. 8–10). Regular EU–Africa summits have been held since then, and the heads of state and government adopted the Roadmap 2014–2017 at the Fourth EU–Africa Summit in Brussels on April 2–3, 2014 (ibid.). A key new aspect is the recognition of the need to "increase synergies between the political dialogue and cooperation and to promote contributions from the private sector and civil society."[33] In this way, some elements of the integrity framework can be supported by the EU more openly, in particular civil society and freedom of the press.

The good governance trends in sub-Saharan Africa in recent years reflect deep structural and stability problems, but show also some interesting evolutions. The outstanding performer on governance charts is Rwanda, which progressed the most on regulatory quality and control of corruption. Senegal and Ivory Coast show some progress, while earlier champions, such as Botswana, have not changed so much in the last fifteen years. Botswana remains a good governance achiever, reaching rule of law and control of corruption (a version still far from "ethical universalism"). Its progression has relied rather on a traditional, not a modern path (one family and tribe played a dominant role) and has represented the only African success story for many years. On rule of law, it is still on pair with South Africa, at the top of the list. Rwanda became the development agency poster child (if we do not consider the tiny successful island of Cape Verde, also a darling of anti-corruption consultants) as the country to solve the problem of collective action on the issue of corruption through leadership, albeit by now clearly an authoritarian leadership. The Rwandan Patriotic Front (RPF), led by President Paul Kagame, has ruled the country since 1994. While the RPF is credited with restoring ethnic peace and building an ethnically neutral state, it is also suspected of dealing with dissent quite brutally, including by assassinations. The incidence of bribery in Rwanda has fallen far below that of its regional neighbors, and the country is a champion in red tape reduction and donor funds absorption. Bribery, mismanagement, and embezzlement – particularly at lower levels – were firmly reined in. Research published by ANTICORRP shows, however, that Rwanda's success amounts to anything but democratic governance. Government favoritism remains high and public participation very low; the anti-corruption measures are top-down; civil society is either co-opted or sidelined (Bozzini, 2014). While the authorities are keen and determined to curb administrative corruption, there is simply a monopoly on political corruption. The big winners in public tenders prominently feature companies associated with the ruling party (ibid.). Rwanda is currently

---

[33] From Roadmap Introduction, point 5, p. 2 (Joint Africa–EU Strategy, 2014).

covered by the Eleventh European Development Fund for the period 2014–2020, after receiving nearly EUR 300 million in the previous Tenth EDF. The Country Strategy Paper for Rwanda (2008–2013) and a multi-annual National Indicative Programme for Rwanda outline the main focal sectors of EU cooperation, which include national reconciliation and justice along with accountable governance, rather than anti-corruption *per se* (EC, 2013c; EC, 2007a; EC, 2014a). There has been no word from the EU on "big fish" in this case, of course – such demands are apparently reserved for democracies. General budget support is the preferred form of funding.

Rwanda's success was achieved by a top-down regulatory and communication approach, endorsed by the highest levels of government, including from the Rwandan president himself. For instance, management performance contracts are signed by every public official whereby they commit to achieving a set of performance goals associated with government development programs, to which they are later on held accountable (Imihigo). As these contracts are in practice entered into with the head of state himself, the fear of harsh punishment rather than cultural or behavioral change explains compliance (Bozzini, 2014). Abuse of power, generally a part of the definition of corruption, can thus coexist with anti-corruption as well, but in view of Rwanda's violent past, the donors, including the EU, prefer to see the glass half full. The case highlights the importance of domestic agency, on one side, and the poor correlation between success in controlling bribery and broader good governance based on ethical universalism, on the other. President Kagame meanwhile had the constitution changed so that he can stay in office until 2034. He ran for a third term and won with 99 percent (*The Guardian*, 2017b). Freedom House ranks Rwanda as not free.

If Rwanda has been nearly a success case, but another one clearly driven by domestic agency, Uganda is a showcase of the shortcomings of donor-driven anti-corruption activity. There seems to be some curse at work with Uganda and its donors. This starts from the linking of the clause of aid suspension for human rights infringements (the "Uganda" clause) to the suspension of EU budget support due to its landing in the private account of an individual in the cabinet of the Ugandan PM.[34] Both EU member states, through DFID or SIDA, and the EU itself have invested in Uganda's anti-corruption efforts, very much like in Moldova, enabling repressive agencies in a context that is anything but rule of law and where impunity for the leadership reigns. While indicators, with all their faults, continue to reflect a lack of evolution (CPI among them),

---

[34] Interview with Ambassador Rodolfo Ridolfi, FAO, Rome, October 1, 2018.

Uganda made new headlines in 2018 when the head of Transparency International presented an award to the president for great anti-corruption merits. The corresponding outrage on social media received a response from TI Secretariat acknowledging that "recognising the President in this way has sent an unintentional message to the public and the international community," and stating that in no way was this gesture meant to "condone the anti-corruption track record of the Ugandan Government or the President."[35] TI further presented regrets for "any insult this may have caused to anti-corruption activists in both Uganda and the wider international community," as admittedly there were "serious questions" indeed about "the government's political will to address corruption, despite reforms, laws and new institutions," all assisted by donors and which might threaten rule of law before threatening corruption. Uganda scores 4.6 of 10 in the press freedom component of IPI but has a whistleblower protection law as part of the consultant-assisted anti-corruption system. Instead of reflecting that perhaps press freedom should have come first (or a little bit more of it) the discussion, including in the cited TI document, has moved to deploring the "lack of implementation" of anti-corruption tools such as the whistlebower protection act.[36]

Ghana is the case that for many years seemed to redeem the donors. As a lower-middle-income country, Ghana is not a major focus of European Union development assistance in terms of the volume of aid disbursed, but it had long been the model of successful development in West Africa that donors invested in, despite its recent macroeconomic and public finance management challenges (Champagne, 2016). The EU–Africa Partnership also resulted in the Ghana–EU Partnership, intended to promote peace, democracy, and prosperity. The EU committed EUR 604.64 million to support Ghana between 2007 and 2014 and disbursed a total of EUR 541 million, with 90 percent of the funds committed. On average, the EU disbursed EUR 67.63 million per year during that period. Since 2008, EU official development assistance to Ghana has on the whole been dominated by budget support. General budget support is provided directly to the treasury of the government of Ghana to supplement the national budget and support the second Ghana Poverty Reduction Strategy, 2006–2009, and the first Shared Growth and Development Agenda, 2010–2013. The EU General Budget Support Program (GBS) of EUR 209 million for 2009–2014 was implemented

---

[35] A full press statement can be seen at www.transparency.org/news/pressrelease/statement_on_recognition_of_president_h.e._yoweri_museveni
[36] See www.transparency.org/news/pressrelease/statement_on_recognition_of_president_h.e._yoweri_museveni.

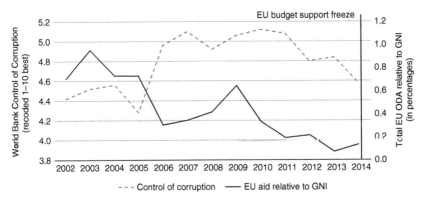

Figure 7.2 Evolution of EU funds and control of corruption in Ghana, 2002–2014

through the Millennium Development Goals Contract (MDG contract), a new generation of contracts designed to help Ghana with a longer-term aid modality in order to achieve the United Nations MDGs adopted in September 2000.[37] In 2013 and 2014, the EU decided to suspend budget support disbursements in order to oblige the government to comply with the public financial management compliance reforms agreed upon in the MDG Contract (Champagne, 2016). Budget support resumed in June 2015, after the two-year suspension, following the Ghanaian government's adoption of an IMF program and a new action plan to improve its public financial management. Ghana scores 6.55 in the IPI, and leads West Africa on judicial independence and freedom of the press. As usual, the quality of regulation is what is dragging down performance on integrity and it has been a hard fight to improve it by external funding. Figure 7.2 sums up the story of Ghana's EU funds and integrity, showing control of corruption increasing at about the same time as a reduction in funds occurs, and then the effort of the EU ten years later to respond again to the decline in quality of government.

In order to support sound public finance management, the EU complemented its GBS with additional capacity-building support to help the Ghanaian government improve country systems and relevant institutions (Champagne, 2016). This support included EUR 1.9 million for the Ghana Audit Service and EUR 9 million to finance the implementation of the Ghana Integrated Financial and Management Information System (GIFMIS) project with the goal of modernizing the management of

[37] See the Millennium Development Goals contract (EC, 2013d).

Ghana's revenue and of increasing internally generated funds of the nontax revenue unit (ibid.). The tenth EDF also grants EUR 45 million to support decentralization in Ghana. As for the financial period 2014–2020, the EU has decided to dedicate EUR 75 million to public sector management and accountability, with an additional cross-cutting EUR 9 million for civil society.

A new dedicated anti-corruption program, the Ghana Anti-Corruption, Rule of Law and Accountability Programme (Ghana-ARAP), has been earmarked with EUR 20 million. It will be commissioned to Spanish and British agencies, the Ibero–American Foundation for Administration and Public Policies (FIIAPP), and DFID through the joint fund Strengthening Transparency, Accountability, and Responsiveness in Ghana (STAR-Ghana).[38] The promotion of civil society engagement in national dialogue and decisions is included as an objective under the tenth EDF (objective 5b, issue 1). In line with Article 8 of the revised Cotonou Agreement, the EU ambassador to Ghana, William Hanna, organized the first official political dialogue with a dozen civil-society organizations on May 28, 2015, ahead of the EU's political dialogue with the government of Ghana on June 12, 2015 (Champagne, 2016). This activity was based on the EU Country Roadmap for Engagement with Civil Society, 2014–17 (EC, 2015c), which was adopted by the EU heads of mission, who represent the EU delegation and EU member states in Ghana. These are significant steps towards a coordinated EU–member state approach, treating country "ownership" more broadly and inclusively: their results remain to be seen, as a clear theory of change and a design inspired from the Georgian administrative revolution does not seem to be on the cards. To start with, Ghana's procurement is not transparent. There are no serious administrative or legal obstacles to tenders being public and awards published (if not digitally, then on the door of every local government office), which would help a lot to deter Ghana's extremely high particularism: yet this particular condition is not tied to EU aid.

The Cotonou–EU conditionality framework actually lists performance criteria. Since the latest revision of the ACP–EU agreement these also include progress on good governance and the Millennium Development Goals (see Articles 1 and 19 of the Cotonou Agreement). The tenth EDF program's indicators, jointly agreed between the EU and the Ghanaian government, are based on the previous policy commitments made by the government (Champagne, 2016). Corruption indicators are the least developed in the framework, as usual. Instead of, for example, transparency of procurement per municipality (since the EU also funds

---

[38] For more information about STAR-Ghana, consult the website: www.star-ghana.org

decentralization), the agreement stresses monitoring of previous commitments: e.g., successful convictions for high-level corruption and uncovered fraud cases for government-funded projects, public information provisions on the successes of the anti-corruption fight, and close consultation with civil-society organizations.

Ghana is a plural particularistic country, where the norm of particularism is still dominant despite the comprehensive public integrity framework. High resources for corruption result in broad clientelism and limit capacity for collective action on behalf of ethical universalism. It has a vibrant civil society, although at sub-national level client–patron ties rule. Its media is pluralistic, although partly captured. Finally, it has one of the most comprehensive anti-corruption frameworks on the African continent (BTI Stiftung, 2018a). The voters, despite belonging to different ethnic groups and client networks, do not agree with predatory corruption and have the capacity to vote out administrations perceived as corrupt if offered better alternatives. However, corruption remains endemic across all levels of government, the economy, and the judiciary. Here, too, the usual vicious circle is at play: high political discretion, administrative politicization, and preferential regulation protect gatekeepers and rentiers. Party politics naturally fuels particularistic allocation, and, combined with an economic decline, it has resulted in control of corruption lagging behind.

The EU has sufficient leverage, funds, and implementing agencies to ask for an evolution on at least the transparency of procurement and government spending. Because the EU also funds decentralization, those same procurement indicators could be used as proxies for local government performance and accountability (examples of indicators were shown in the previous chapter, with single bidding in procurement and publishing of national annual spending reports, as in Romania). And yet routine rules when anti-corruption is concerned, and the only progress seems to be brought about by increased conditionality of including civil society in exchange for budget support. The money could also be better used to reverse the decline of the judiciary, where sector budget support aid could bring in missing resources to improve court logistics and motivate staff. These two strategic moves – investing in a gradual, measurable increase of transparent spending and accountability at sub-national level along with supporting the judiciary to become more effective – might have an impact. Ghana was almost on the borderline between governance norms, but sliding slightly backwards, so wise strategizing by donors could have an impact here, especially taking advantage of the improved donor cooperation framework.

Controlling corruption in poor democracies is a challenge in itself, even when rule of law is present. The proof is the South African anti-corruption front, in a country that used to be the absolute integrity leader (it is still Africa's number one in the Integrity for Public Index or any rule of law chart, with Namibia, Botswana, and Ghana following; Rwanda trails behind, due to zero freedom of the press). The South African case shows that democracy is not sufficient when political elites feel unconstrained by the ethical culture of their voters and where poor constituencies especially rank social and economic justice far higher than they do integrity (though they do make demands for integrity when the others are not met). The indictment of President Jacob Zuma in 2018 was good news for the rule of law, but the system of poor constraints that had allowed his corruption to flourish remained. South Africa is the European Union's only strategic partner on the continent, as the EU is South Africa's primary trading and investment partner, accounting for 25 percent of its trade and 75 percent of foreign direct investments. It is essential that South Africa does not backslide more than it already has on corruption in the past twenty years, as this might provide realists with the example they need to show that control of corruption is just not feasible in democratic Africa and structural constraints will always drag a country down regardless of its human agency.

8 Europe's Choices

8.1 Understanding the Present

"Hey, EU, where are you?" a banner read at the protests in Bucharest, Romania, in December 2017 (Euractiv.com, 2017). Protesters voiced their concern that the majority in parliament were going ahead with changing the criminal code to make prosecution for corruption more difficult. Like other civil society groups in the European sphere of influence, they were calling for the EU to intervene against the majority in the Romanian parliament and in favor of the EU-endorsed anti-corruption agency. Some had really believed the EU could deliver a better quality of governance for Romania, but it did not happen. Others could not understand why Brussels seemed to side with those who had lost elections and against people the electorate had repeatedly voted for. One of the most pro-European constituencies in Europe – according to twenty years of Eurobarometer surveys – wasn't blaming the EU but rather its own political class. But the Romanians' faith in the transformative power of Europe was gone.

And with good reason, because European transformative power over the quality of governance has been proven largely a myth. The EU is many things: a civilizational ideal to emulate, an anchor of geopolitical stabilization, a generous donor, and a historical lesson on cooperation across nations. A fixer of national governance problems, however, it is not. But by trying to be that over the past twenty years, it has created constituencies like the one in Bucharest, which demands that the EU delivers good governance by strong intervention. The size of such constituencies varies (Ukraine, Romania, and Moldova seem to be the leaders), but they are everywhere a minority, or EU intervention would be unnecessary and a popularly elected government would simply undertake the needed reforms. Neither is the pro-EU party in any country reduced to the anti-corruption party, nor is the corruption party entirely anti-European, making the politics of Brussels-driven anti-corruption complex and fraught with risk. In Greece, Brussels and the populists competed over the anti-corruption agenda and the populists won. The risk is that similar European attempts will fail to improve governance and that the backlash will increase Euroskepticism. The stakes for Europe are thus high, especially in the EU periphery and its neighborhood. Moreover, the EU is far from being the single international donor; the ascent of China, in particular in Africa, is unlikely to give a boost to governance reforms now that aid recipients are offered an alternative to conditional development aid. Pro-good-governance constituencies are both smaller and less expectant of the EU in ACP countries, where the lessons well learned by the EU development industry unhappily coincide with an ongoing reduction in the windows of opportunity.

People might dispute the bulk of evidence in this book by claiming that Europe has in fact managed to improve control of corruption and that most evidence to the contrary relies on perceptions. That would be wrong. The evidence in this book might resort to classical expert "perception" scores for the purpose of comparison across countries or broader continental pictures, but all the case studies draw on fact-based indicators. These range from the number of plutocrats owing their fortunes to political connections, to the market share of favored companies winning government contracts and the politicization of public employment. There are a variety of objective indicators, other than perceptions, for assessing the practice of particularism and corruption, with objective and subjective indicators generally consistent with one another. The time when corruption was "hidden" and "unmeasurable" is largely gone. The portal Opentender.eu alone, alongside EC direct sources, makes 17 million contracts in 35 European jurisdictions available with apps to calculate corruption risks per tender. Following the adoption in 2014 of new EU-wide procurement regulations,[1] the European Commission has finally developed (for member states only) a scorecard on procurement, which allows the tracing in real time of indicators on how competitive and transparent national procurement is.[2] A check of the level of 2017 shows that Italy, Greece, Romania, Bulgaria, Cyprus, Portugal, Spain, Slovenia, and the Czech Republic were in the red: their procurement was not transparent enough or competitive enough by EU standards, and it has not improved since. Estonia was the only

---

[1] Directive 2014/24/EU of the European Parliament and of the Council of 26 February 2014 on public procurement OJ L 094 (2014).

[2] An aggregated version as well as one detailed by indicator can be found at http://ec.europa. eu/internal_market/scoreboard/performance_per_policy_area/public_procurement/inde x_en.htm. More data on accession countries such as Serbia can also be found at Opente nder.eu with more corruption risk indicators.

new member country that met the full standards in 2017, while Croatia has 44 percent noncompetitive tenders (single bidding) and Greece shows the most substantial regression. That is a concern, because Croatia is the closest to the equivalent to the successful intervention in Switzerland that I have been able to identify in writing this book. Monitoring began in 2015, and up to 2017 has shown almost wholly negative evolutions, not positive. These are direct indicators of particularism in public allocation, and their use by the EC from now on will allow far more effective and transparent monitoring of control of corruption in Europe. At least in Europe and its neighborhood, open data tools now exist to monitor corruption in ways undreamed of twenty years ago.

Even if they rarely resort to numerical indicators, the selected evaluators of various EU programs also provide data that is consistent with the evidence presented in this book. The *Thematic Evaluation for Justice and Security System Reform* (ADE, 2011), for instance, has as its main recommendations to produce a theory of change in cooperation with EEAS and to provide adequate guidelines on how to link programming and field implementation with it (recommendations 1, 2, 4), to adjust strategies to local contexts so as to avoid standardization (3), and to develop an evidence basis and adequate human resources for anti-corruption projects (6–8).

Table 8.1 offers a simplified synthesis of the EU interventions on governance researched in this book, along with their results. EU tools (negative or positive conditionalities, direct intervention) vary greatly across our categories; the indirect effect on both opportunities and constraints for corruption varies somewhat, but the resulting overall impact on control of corruption in the form of a change of practices (institutional change) varies very little, if at all. For the old member states, where no deliberate promotion of good governance existed (except in Greece after the crisis), but other constraints did, and for the new member states, which joined in 2004 and did have some good governance packages included during accession, I found no impact. OLAF in particular has never triggered significant good governance reforms anywhere, from Greece to Hungary, where a high-profile OLAF disclosure in 2018 came only years after revelations of corruption in the Orban regime by NGOs and open criticism from other EU institutions. Italy and Romania had many OLAF investigations, each leading the OLAF casebook for many years, but that changed little in the way of favoritism as the main distribution practice, regardless of the constant attempts to improve the rules. No significant change came from reforms of OLAF over time, and the adding of a European Public Prosecutor (approved in late 2017) to prosecute fraud against EU financial interests

Table 8.1 *Summary of cases by EU governance intervention tools and impact*

Countries	Effect on resources (funds, red tape)	Effects on legal and normative constraints	EU tools (conditions, direct interventions)	Length of intervention	Impact on control of corruption
Early member states Greece and Italy, but also Portugal and Spain	First increased resources for corruption (EU funds), then decreased dramatically (euro, fiscal constraints)	Some constraints increased in Greece, in particular on procurement	Market participation ECJ, OLAF After 2015 procurement directives (PPD); money laundering and banking pan-EU rules	Decades	Negligible
New member states, 2004 wave	Increased resources for corruption (EU funds plus some red tape)	Insignificant	Accession, then market participation ECJ, PPD, OLAF	>15 years	Some backsliding on corruption and rule of law except Baltics
New member states, 2007: Romania and Bulgaria	Increased resources for corruption (EU funds plus significant red tape)	Romania: creation of a strong anti-corruption agency Bulgaria: insignificant	Major: MCV, suspension of EU funds, besides ECJ, PPD, OLAF	>15 years	Despite top convictions in Romania and none in Bulgaria, no institutional change
Western Balkans, Croatia, Bosnia, Kosovo	Increased resources for corruption (EU funds plus significant red tape)	Significant, due to direct enforcement by internationals	Strong incentives: visa liberalization, status, accession International law enforcement and justice present	>15 years	Progress in Croatia, no institutional change for the rest
Accession country Turkey	Not much despite substantial EU aid, given Turkey's GDP	None (no aid suspension even on rule of law programs before the last coup)	Tukey already part of customs union, no visa liberalization offered	>10–12 years	No institutional change

ENP Ukraine and Moldova	Budget support without *ex ante* conditions, emergency funds, plus significant red tape	Creation of anti-corruption agencies	Governance facility Visa liberalization, DFTA	<10 years	No institutional change
ENP Tunisia and Egypt	Budget support without *ex ante* conditions prior to Arab Spring	Tunisia: creation of anti-corruption and other agencies Egypt: none	Governance facility Black-listing DFTA, no visa liberalization	<15 years	No institutional change
ACP countries	Budget support, effect varying by percentage of contribution to GNI and *ex ante* conditions	Creation of anti-corruption and other agencies	Black-listing, funds withheld, sanctions mechanism	>20 years	No institutional change, some positive signs after reform of budget support

(without closing OLAF) received criticism from the ECA as yet another layer needing coordination with insufficient grounds for superior effectiveness (ECA, 2018b).

Where an EU effect on good governance is present, it is in the pre-accession phase (of course, for accession countries alone): countries either reform in order to be invited to join (and then reforms seldom turn out to have been sustainable) or they are invited by the EU because they are already successful reformers (or both). Such instances can hardly be called EU "interventions." Institutional change remains rare. Croatia's apparent performance is explained by the longer accession period – nearly ten years to try to persuade Europe to let them in. Estonia remains the only solid case of new rules of the game being developed. There is in fact no successful case in the European neighborhood that can be attributed to Europeanization. The sustainability of Georgia's anti-corruption work, despite its EU association agreement, is becoming a problem; Rwanda shines among ACP countries but is an example of effective domestic leadership rather than a success of EU-driven "democratic governance" – for democratic it definitely is not. Ukraine, Ghana, and Tunisia are places where the EU has learned some lessons but an institutional change has not yet occurred. The strong negative conditionality in Romania and Bulgaria has not led to more progress in those countries compared to places with weak conditionality, like Slovakia or Latvia.

Conditionality instruments dedicated to governance such as the "Governance Facility (GF)" or "Initiative" have quietly disappeared after more or less experience with them in the ENP or the ACP area, with the commission blaming their underuse or lack of ownership by countries.[3] Ukraine managed to access about EUR 28.6 million during its first ENPI, which amounted to only 5 percent of Ukraine's 2007–2010 funding from the EU. Egypt was eligible but never seriously considered it. For Tunisia, again, it did not work: funds were too small to be an incentive and the consequences of reform stagnation under GF were practically nonexistent. The "positive conditionality" theory – the more a country reforms, the more support it may obtain from the EU – might have sounded right. But that would have required that good governance become the overriding policy priority; that consistent monitoring would take place, for which the EU was not in fact prepared; and that the weight of the aid linked to good governance, relative to total aid, would be

---

[3] European Commission (2013b), "Report from the Commission to the European Parliament, the Council, the European Economic and Social Committee and the Committee of the Regions on the EU support for democratic governance, with a focus on the Governance Initiative," COM (2013), p. 403.

different. So, after the Arab Spring the funding was canceled and money redirected to the ENP.

There was no reason why conditionality would have worked better in the politically loaded field of corruption, when the scholarly consensus was that conditionality in development had in fact failed in general (Collier, 1997; Dollar and Svensson, 2000; Dreher, 2009). The reasons I found are similar to the ones reported in the literature on World Bank and IMF conditionality: inconsistent application with lack of any credible threat on the part of donors, and strong resistance with lack of ownership on the part of recipient countries. Meanwhile, the EU's budget support has evolved to become increasingly associated with the global trend of selectivity, although many avenues still lie unexplored (Buiter, 2005).

But it was not only conditionality that failed. The differences across instruments recede when the uniformity of results is considered. Ten years ago, the EU's enlargement was still perceived as one of its most successful policies, and the hope was that neighborhood policies could emulate it further. By 2018, the EU was increasingly looking not to take in other countries in but to find ways to penalize the countries it had fought so hard to embrace – Hungary, Poland, Romania. Furthermore, the whole post-Brexit European debate led by Emmanuel Macron has moved to a Europe of different speeds, with a core center-driven perspective by a small group of relatively well governed and more prosperous countries, relegating the others to the margins. Governance convergence ideals have few followers left.

The unwilling contribution of the EU to increasing opportunities for corruption might need some further explanation, as it seems so counter-intuitive. EU funds have better rules and oversight than funds from national budgets. But they do not rule against favoritism, and if favoritism is already the rule of the game, then EU funds will not be excepted, they will become a resource. Furthermore, the methodology of disbursement of EU funds has always relied on a previous history of winning them, which therefore limits access for new entrants and helps in the selection of "specialized" EU-fund-winning companies. That design might actually facilitate favoritism in the allocation of EU funds. That said, in EU member states, as well as in the rest of the world, size matters, so the impact of EU funds on governance is greater where their contribution to the budget is also greater, in places such as Greece or Bulgaria in Europe, or the countries listed in Table 4.3 on development assistance, such as Somalia, the West Bank and Gaza, Djibouti, Afghanistan, or Kosovo, where EU aid is a significant fraction of GNI. In such places, EU funds need special design and supervision if they are not to actually feed corruption. On the other hand, places such as Turkey and Italy, despite attracting significant funds, are just too big for the funds to influence practices in any major way.

As our evidence shows, the funds for good governance in the form of anti-corruption projects have not had much impact so far, good or bad. On the one hand, allocations for anti-corruption have so far been too small for so extraordinarily ambitious a task, and the way EU funds operate is too inflexible for the interventions needed to affect governance. On the other hand, the absence of a sound theory of change consistently followed across years meant that not much could be delivered. The most telling example of such problems is perhaps the politicization of administration, which has actually increased during "Europeanization," despite the EU's insistence on merit-based civil services. That too is an area where significant funds (other than anti-corruption funds) are spent to promote the adoption of ethical codes and to train civil servants in public integrity, although they were originally selected and gained promotion due to political connections. After this review I can suggest no country as a success story of how EU funds and conditionalities created a merit-based administration. Regrettably, from Greece to Kosovo the narrative is exactly the opposite.

Instead of seeing funds having a positive effect on governance, the neighboring and accession countries had to bear significant costs of Europeanization red tape. While the logic of the EU seems sound – countries must adopt EU legislation (for instance, in food standards) if they are to take advantage of trading with the EU – in practice what ensues is not a positive evolution of the regulatory quality of those countries. On the contrary, the regulatory quality of the cases engaged in heavy legal "Europeanization" has only deteriorated, as the process was not used as an occasion for the simplification and streamlining of the legislative framework, ending instead in a confused accommodation of old practices and new rules that qualified as "lack of implementation." In fact, Europeanization unwillingly contributes to the resources of corruption by increasing the distance between formal institutions and real-world practice. Perhaps considerations of stability prevent the EU from throwing its political weight behind deeper transformative processes, leaving only the IMF to deal with them – with the blunt instruments it has at its disposal. However, in the absence of any evolution of public funds allocation towards universalism, the addition of ever more anti-corruption legislation that *presumes* universalism and seeks to punish deviations from particularism only creates the "lack of implementation" we read of in countless EC and ECA reports. Why does the EU not consider strategically sequencing its approach to a country's transformation? Even when the formal process is engaged, a degree of prioritization would greatly help to create the breakthrough that is currently missing.

If the contribution of the EU to resources for corruption is thus ambiguous, its investment in constraints to corruption has only grown over the years. Association agreements with the EU and renewed treaties have never before contained so many mentions of the rule of law and of corruption. Deploring the lack of sanctions and enforcement of negative conditionality seems less justified when one surveys the areas where the EU had maximum power: Bosnia, Kosovo, Romania, and Bulgaria. In the absence of a clear theory of change, such strong interventions by the EU in the Western or Eastern Balkans or the former Soviet Union have not made things better, but have made the EU appear politically partisan, more inconsistent, and generally weaker. Of course, no such interventions existed for Greece and Italy. Georgia, a top reformer, has seen its name on the tax haven blacklist, alongside Tunisia. Moldova was not on the list despite its "laundromats." As to Georgia, the commission candidly stated that its presence on the list was "an error," after news of its inclusion spread.[4] In fact, the evidence points to a far more important contribution to money laundering by certain actual EU member states than by small peripheric countries, and the criteria that the EU lists are not consistently applied.[5] A country's blacklisting is often the result of a bargaining power game between member states.[6]

In conclusion, changing institutions in another country is an uphill battle of enormous difficulty, and its disappointing impact at country level in the first two decades of international good governance promotion is over-explained. Among causes on the side of the assisted countries, it is enough to note that corrupt governments are generally controlled by corrupt elites who are not interested in killing their own rents, although they may find it convenient to ratify international treaties or play the Europeanization game. Europeanization is good business, or it used to be, so leaders paid lip service to the cause of good governance. Countries where informal institutions have long been substituted for formal ones have a long tradition, however, of surviving untouched by any formal

---

[4] The Questions and Answers on the EU list of uncooperative tax jurisdictions on the Commission website specifies "Updated on 6 December to remove Georgia from the jurisdictions who need to improve transparency standards. Georgia was included under this category in error," http://europa.eu/rapid/press-release_MEMO-17-5122_en.htm

[5] See the policy paper of the Tax Justice Network "Financial Secrecy Affecting the European Union" (Janský et al., 2018).

[6] A description of the EU's methodology, as well as a shadow list using the same criteria and arriving at different results, was performed by Oxfam; both report and methodology can be seen at www.oxfam.org/en/research/blacklist-or-whitewash-what-real-eu-blacklist-tax-havens-should-look

changes that may be forced upon them. They have even developed quite ingenious strategies for it. Describing the Hellenization attempts by the ancient Greeks – and their rather poor impact – historian Arnaldo Momigliano wrote: "the Greeks were seldom in a position to check what natives told them: they did not know the languages. The natives, on the other hand, being bilingual, had a shrewd idea of what the Greeks wanted to hear and spoke accordingly. This reciprocal position did not make for sincerity and real understanding" (Momigliano, 1975, p. 8) Successful institutional transformations, therefore, are seen only in countries that know what to ask for from the EU, because they have their own transformation agenda. From Estonia to Rwanda, with all the differences across cases, change is domestically driven; at any rate, no external instruments seem able to drive it.

However, factors internal to the EU also make a contribution, and these could and should be addressed. On top of the usual collective action problems of decision making in an organization of 28 (soon to be 27) member states, each with its own interests, the EU has conflicting priorities: its own and those of the member states. The latter are concerned with their own domestic companies that invest abroad and are interested in their business opportunities. They hope both to reduce immigration from poor countries and to generate jobs for their development industries. The EEAS and the other European agents of good governance are well aware of such conflicting priorities and must navigate – sometimes in rough seas – the narrow channels between completely different objectives. Also, a trade-off exists between human rights and anti-corruption in countries where rule of law does not exist, and this is not fully acknowledged or solved by attempting to impose similar standards to those of "old" Europe. Europe should not encourage selective anti-corruption.

Another cause of poor impact comes with the absence of a competent tailor-made and contextual approach to anti-corruption. The current Europeanization process consists to a large degree of standardization, which enhances the already existing formality of UNCAC and GRECO reviews, upon which the EU relies. However, aligning legal standards and building rule of law or control of corruption are separate endeavors. Institutional transformation does not work if standard approaches are used, and standardization can be introduced only after transformation is achieved. The EU has extended the enlargement methodology from the Eastern to the Western Balkans and to the ENP countries, although in the field of good governance this had not delivered even in accession countries. However, important differences exist across countries on account of their own overall regulatory quality and the extent to which the rule of law is present. The strength of pro-change groups makes a great difference, if indeed there are any present, as does the extent of rents and their concentration. EU intervention (trade treaty, aid, agreement, or a combination) should reflect those differences. For instance, any EU strategy could start with a check to see if a country is below or above average according to the World Bank indicators for the rule of law, voice, and accountability. The figures for regulatory quality, judicial independence, and freedom of the press, too, are highly revealing for the choice of instruments. Impunity problems cannot be solved using instruments that require the rule of law already to be in place, and unintended consequences, as in Moldova, can be quite dramatic. In a similar vein, there seems to be little point in asking New Zealand, at the top of good governance charts, to join the UNCAC when signing a trade treaty with the EU just for the sake of ensuring a uniform approach. New Zealand is the world leader on good governance, so it has better institutions already and needs no institutional change. In practice, EU diplomats or technocrats do adjust to contexts, but as they cannot influence the routine-based approach and instruments they simply choose to apply standards differently, even contradictorily, across countries or even time.

Despite having excellent human resources and access to the best research possible (Eurostat or the procurement scoreboard cited), in the field of rule of law promotion and anti-corruption the EU often displays inconsistent standards and arbitrary methodologies (ADE, 2011). The lawyers in DG Home seem particularly isolated from economic DGs, and in the remote intervention countries the rationality of intervention seems frequently decoupled from the reality on the ground. As the EU insists on the creation of agencies in intervention countries, it seems also keen to create more of its own instead of rationalizing the existing ones or anti-corruption activities in general. Not only have the Balkans and Moldova been filled with agencies, but the list grows in the EU proper as well. Although the ECA remarked that it was the length (measured in years) of OLAF investigations that was mainly responsible to poor follow-up of court cases by national prosecutors, the European Parliament initiated an enhanced cooperation procedure to address precisely the prosecution problem (ECA, 2018c). A European Public Prosecutor (EPPO) was thus created by twenty-two EU member states in 2018 to function alongside already existing agencies, OLAF and Eurojust, and to prosecute in each of the twenty-two jurisdictions those cases of EU financial interest frauds that national authorities deemed fit to decline, despite high transaction costs and predictable turf wars. The ECA also criticized the DG Home "Hercules" anti-corruption program precisely for being insufficiently based on evidence and strategic thinking (ECA, 2018c). In general, the European Audit Court reports, from specific interventions in

developing or accession countries to the evaluation of OLAF or the pro-
posed European Prosecutor, show a clear vision and could serve to teach
lessons or to ground a more strategic approach. The emulation of Europe's
top-performing audit courts in intervention countries is low to nonexistent,
although this is a sound European experience to be promoted abroad.
Instead, the EU-sponsored approach of going after the "big fish" creates
incentives for local political actors to engage in gaming and attract the EU
to their side to eliminate rivals – while leaving rents intact.

Achieving stronger constraints on corruption requires a comprehensive
understanding of its mechanism. That would in turn require more than
the bureaucratic approach that limited the influence of EU anti-
corruption intervention in peripheric Europe. The "prescription model"
(rewarding countries by the number of EU recommendations they take
in) is highly path dependent and has poor potential to break vicious circles
of governance. As EU monitoring is based largely on inputs (adoption of
standard conventions, laws, and regulations) a first phase unfolds when
corrupt countries reach a record number of integrity-related laws
(Montenegro and Moldova shine at it). Even a check of the European
Justice Scoreboard for EU member states sponsored by DG Justice would
show that *de jure* legal equipment and *de facto* judicial independence differ
significantly.[7] The difference is often attributed not to the obvious
cause – that good governance is not the result of formal institutions, but
of a more comprehensive power equilibrium (as the cases of old and new
European achievers show)[8] – but to "implementation deficit." The next
phase of EU anti-corruption interventions and related conditionality then
asks for "autonomous" agencies to be created to step up implementation
of the conventions and laws, although successful countries have never had
them. The "autonomous" agencies are created, with the resulting problems of increased transaction and coordination costs, let alone their
insulation from the rest of the administration; and all of this is reported
back as "progress." Then, if the new agencies do not deliver, additional
ones are created (Kosovo, Ukraine, and Moldova have reached the peak;
Tunisia might well be next in line). That in turn becomes an excuse for
not undertaking substantial reforms that might cut somebody's influential rents.

The main advantage of having the EU in the game, namely the political
weight the EU can add to help reformers in government or civil societies,

---

[7] The European Justice scoreboard is accessible at https://ec.europa.eu/info/sites/info/files/
justice_scoreboard_2018_en.pdf
[8] An evidence review of the European Justice scoreboard, along with an argument trying to
explain why judicial reforms that should be conducive to an independent judiciary may
seem to have adverse consequences, can be found in Gutmann and Voigt (2018).

is therefore largely lost if reform targets are so poorly focused. Furthermore, the EU becomes captured by its own bureaucratic path dependency and the agencies it sponsored, funded, and provided with technical assistance; it has to defend them even when it becomes clear that they cannot deliver much. Hence the avalanche of pages of self-referential progress reports having little correspondence with reality, such as the ones on Turkey and the Balkans cited in this book.

The highest impact of EU intervention is in raising the corruption problem on the public agenda. As the EU has offered little direct support for the media, the improvement of media freedom in countries with an EU anti-corruption intervention (for which we found statistical evidence) means that other EU actions, especially its political actions (its public stands, for instance), have a good effect and manage to offer some protection to the freedom of a critical media. It is therefore rather the machinery of EU anti-corruption that is too bureaucratic and therefore a poor fit to help change. The positive exception is the European Endowment for Democracy (EED), whose projects have impact, flexibility, and timeliness. The EED has the great merit of showing that innovation is possible in the realm of European democracy and good governance promotion. However, the endowment's total budget is well below the level needed for effective intervention to save even one endangered newspaper.

Still, here lies the solution: in the confining to and splitting of intervention between the two institutions that seem to work, EED and budget support (leaving evaluation to the audit court). Labor could thus be divided, with the EED overtaking the anti-corruption projects (with a considerably expanded budget and staff) and the commission dealing with sector budget support only, with *ex ante* conditions covering the good governance agenda in detail (for instance including detailed conditions on the performance of the judiciary or procurement) and with the necessary technical assistance. The progress indicators should be fact based; real judicial statistics, for instance, from the ECHR or random allocation of cases and consistency of judgments across different tiers, and not "more corruption arrests than last year." That is not to exclude civil society from aid, but as already stated, help for civil society development needs radical reform and is better done through the EED. The EU should also press for state–society designs, with mandatory civil society audits, consumer surveys, and participation in policy formulation as *ex ante* conditions for sector budget support. As to support for watchdogs, those are better selected and supported through an organization like the EED. Getting rid of anti-corruption projects by outsourcing them to some member state is also hardly a solution: evidence exists that bilateral aid agencies are an even more inefficient way of going about anti-corruption.

8.2   The Future of EU Good Governance Promotion

If the EU has not succeeded so far in prompting nations ranging from member states to distant ACP countries to ensure a superior control of corruption, the preliminary question becomes not how to improve delivery, but rather whether the EU should engage in this operation at all. In general, audits of rule of law and anti-corruption policies have been negative, in accession areas as well as in neighborhood areas, and there are obvious reasons for that. Auditors assess results in relation to *declared* objectives. The concept that objectives might be rather nominal is simply not taken into consideration by them. Furthermore, the ECA takes the next step of assessing objectives against the means and the results. In other words, for the first time it is providing evaluations based not only on inputs and outputs, as the European Commission traditionally encourages for its EU funds, but on impact, relevance, and opportunity. That is, of course, devastating if those evaluated do not put their money or their strength where their mouths are. It also makes the absence of a theory of change very visible, even if it is called by a term such as "strategy" or "vision." The EC's responses to the auditors' reports, for example on Egypt (EC 2013a), abandon the normative ambition and return to the paradigm of realism. The commission simply points out that its policies are not so different from the pragmatic approach of some member states and are the only ones possible in such difficult circumstances.

In the end, inflated language and objectives are problems in themselves, as they create false expectations. Apart from the matter of the public in the targeted countries hoping for the impossible and potentially being attracted by the offers of populist politicians, rifts will also appear between commitments and disbursements (Balfour et al., 2016). The cost to local regimes of complying with EU requests must also be calculated, for nobody would comply if the cost of compliance were higher than that of refusing to do so. As one retired diplomat remarked to me, "If the president of this East African country stopped replacing ministers every six months in order to allow the various groups to have their fill, a civil war would have erupted, and when he could no longer do so it did." He went on to say, "Our definition of corruption does not allow for such complexities. Every six months I had to introduce myself, explain to another new minister who I was and what the EU stood for. Of course, not much [development] work gets done this way, but his tactics and our money, which was not much anyway, was helping to maintain stability."[9]

The problem with that coherent and perfectly defensible view, shared by many working in development and cooperation, is that an auditor would expect money to do what it was earmarked to do. If budget support is used to pay armies that might otherwise rebel, that's fine. A case can even be made for paying, say, a ransom demanded by terrorists to free a group of schoolgirls; but money earmarked specifically for anti-corruption is expected to have some effect on corruption, or it might as well not have been spent. If anti-corruption is not feasible in a given context, why program it? In other words, the introduction of good governance as a priority and of projects dedicated to anti-corruption exposes the conflict between normative goals and realistic goals even more than the usual development business. The gulf between declared aims and real delivery capacity at the basis of EU foreign policy becomes even more clearly visible than in other policies.

Because of the other policy objectives mentioned here and despite the new trend for supporting private sector investment rather than funding countries directly, the EU will in the foreseeable future continue to assist corrupt countries. And as long as the EU does that, the opportunity question is implicitly answered. Whenever it is deemed as worthwhile to grant assistance to a particular country, preventing European money from feeding predatory elites in the recipient country becomes an obligation to domestic taxpayers, as well as to citizens of the recipient country. Businesses, for their part, even if their risks are partially covered by EU, might still be forced to play by rules of the local game that they cannot influence. It remains to be seen what answer will come from businesses to the commission's call to invest in certain countries, but the concept that this approach would eliminate corruption risks because it is not based on the public sector is mistaken, as the European businesses will still have to face that country's regulations and practices. So, the embedding of an anti-corruption approach in development policy remains indispensable and it should better be fully rationalized through the learning of these lessons.

The business of integrity promotion cannot dispense with some minimal ethical considerations, for the sake of effectiveness if not of ethics. The choice is not between realist and normative objectives, for we are, or should be, constrained by evidence to reconcile both. In fact, the choice is between being "smart" and having some effect, albeit modest; or overstating objectives and making no progress even

---

[9] Interview with retired EU ambassador, Rome, November 2018.

after spending considerable sums of money. Only after agreeing to some principles, albeit not currently enforced or even widespread, are certain decisive choices even worth discussing. The basics are as follows.

1. *Act knowingly.* The first principle must be to acknowledge that a science of institutional transformation has developed that defines corruption comprehensively as equilibrium and is able to measure it, both across countries and in particular across time, in order to measure change. Any anti-corruption intervention, therefore, can now be chosen on a sounder basis than before. We need to answer first some fundamental questions to decide whether there is the opportunity for an intervention and how to shape its nature.

> Is particularistic distribution of public resources (on the basis of some kind of link, whether monetary or personal) the norm or the exception, and does the answer vary across sectors, or is it more or less uniform?

> Does merit (training, hard work, innovation) determine success in the public or private sectors as a rule, or are connections to ruling elites, government, or local gatekeepers more significant? Can institutional status quo winners be changed at elections, or are they permanent? Do elections basically amount to contests over rents, or do rents remain unaffected regardless of who wins?

> Does the rule of law operate, in other words is anybody above the law? Can we be certain that new laws would be applied equally and without discrimination? In simpler terms, is the country above or below average for existing rule of law indicators (World Bank, World Justice Project, GCR, Physical Rights Index)?

> Are there any groups for whom it is in their best interest for the current governance equilibrium to change? What is their state of association and organization and what circumstances would bring them to "critical mass"? They are the group who should have ownership, if not now, then after winning elections. In the absence of such ownership, externally driven anti-corruption efforts will not work and should not be attempted.

If the answers to these questions are not obvious, some research money should be spent before an intervention to answer them and also to define fact-based change indicators (other than legal inputs) and map who is in favor of change and how they can be empowered. We could not find such in-depth diagnoses even in the countries where considerable amounts had been spent, and it is my belief that at least in Ukraine, Turkey, and Afghanistan such early diagnostic studies (NB: not accounts of legislation, as in GRECO) would have shaped the anti-corruption agenda in a better and more meaningful way. There is no good study of this kind even on Bosnia or Kosovo, even after so many years, and the good ones on MENA done by the World Bank and OECD do not seem to have been followed up. EED at least operates a fact finding mission to collect information on countries to which they give grants, and that is the closest to sound research that exists. The EC, instead, replaces research with its own monitoring, which asks only one imperial question, "Has this country done what we asked them to?" There is never any questioning of the justification of the original demands nor of the impact of those actions, even if the country concerned did comply. Such questions are left for the later attention of auditors. That is how Tunisia became a leading money launderer while Moldova did not; it was how Georgia ended up on a list of tax havens "by mistake," but Luxembourg did not. The EU's own rule of law and anti-corruption system suffers from the absence of an evidence-based and organized approach such as can be observed in other areas of EU intervention (markets or trade, for instance). A strategic and evidence-based approach is also the main recommendation emerging from several audit court reports.

2. *Do not add to resources for corruption.* As many examples in this book have shown, it is difficult to make a corrupt situation better, but very easy to make it worse. Scandals, even in the EU proper – in Greece, Spain, Hungary, Slovakia, or Malta – are related to EU funds that opened new opportunities for corruption for local elites. While the EU's financial interests are defended by the fact that funds are – as a rule – advanced by the recipient country, so the EU can always refuse to reimburse them when corruption suspicions exist, no such protection exists for the recipient country's budget. It is essential to prevent EU funds from ever becoming a resource for corruption, rather than simply punishing countries afterwards. That means a shift of philosophy concerning how funds are managed to rely more on social accountability approaches. EU funds simply must be kept away from the hands of gatekeepers and made transparent and democratic, from the very beginning (on the model of citizens' budgets for establishing priorities) to the final evaluations and audits. That would be better public relations for the EU, too, at a time when it sorely needs it. In recent years there has been a degree of evolution, for instance in cohesion funds, which now use *ex ante* indicators. However, the steps taken so far are insufficient to deliver the goals the EC should

be pursuing, which is funding that is free of corruption, meaningfully spent, and fully absorbed.

3. *Do not add to the pile of dead letters.* An inflation of regulations, good and bad but both equally ineffective, is present in countries with poor governance. There is currently a significant association between high corruption and the inflation of public accountability mechanisms. This comes at a cost: the loss of credibility and hope. Rules that are not enforced for decades cannot be resuscitated. A narrower but deeper intervention might be better than extravagant gestures of integrity that can be neither monitored nor enforced.

4. *Ask others to follow only where you are prepared to go.* If development is to be "privatized," rather than sticking to the classical but inefficient government support, we also need to step up implementation of the OECD convention. The present uneven implementation of the OECD anti-bribery convention even across EU members, let alone the rest of the world, raises the question of whether emphasis on laws against bribery that cannot be enforced equally across parties actually brings more equal treatment and market access, or less. The uneven enforcement of laws prohibiting foreign bribery puts at a serious disadvantage those companies that play by the rules while competing in a global marketplace. The mushrooming of "integrity pacts" on which the Siemens judicial fine has been spent begins to look like window-dressing when one notices that even Siemens has been in trouble again since. The same can be said about blacklists of money launderer countries based on double standards. If the EU does not start effectively promoting integrity within itself, it will not be able to do so in the rest of the world.

5. *Identify and support owners of the change process; do not take them for granted.* Successful anti-corruption policies need leadership and comprehensive reforms with broad social support. If that path is not feasible, it is better to avoid interventions in this area altogether. The evidence shows that anti-corruption tools in the wrong hands prove formidable instruments for the repression of dissent and in fact end up subverting the rule of law. EU-designed roadmaps and national anti-corruption strategies are poor substitutes for national governance reform programs driven by broad societal alliances that promote them because those societies genuinely want a change in governance. We must stimulate and support genuine initiative, and not substitute for it a yearly anti-corruption plan rubber-stamped by various prime ministers.

With such preliminaries agreed, and realizing that path dependency remains the thing that shapes the EU's approach to normative EU policy, we have three important options in the specific area of anti-corruption.

1. *Anti-corruption **by market means**. This is the approach long advocated by economists, who believe that competion brings about less
corruption. One focus is on trade facilitation, meaning reduction of
non-tariff barriers and less red tape associated with customs, import–
export, registering a business, payment of tax, and so on. In recent
years we have seen more access asked for and sometimes granted to
what should be transparent markets for public procurement.
A market-based approach should include procurement packages modeled on the GPA or CETA with strong monitoring and prevention
mechanisms based on transparency. Eventually every WTO member
might be asked to join the GPA. Disbarment of corrupt firms or of
firms from countries that break the rules should be considered when
countries have no anti-bribery laws of their own or do not implement
them. Other, more demanding tools requiring enforcement in domestic courts depend on the proper working of the rule of law, so should be
considered only if the country in question already has reasonably
stable rule of law and a good degree of judicial independence.
Everything included should have clear and practical procedures for
monitoring and redress.

   While effective opening of markets is of paramount importance,
there are many ways in which countries, even within the Common
Market or the Customs Union (for instance Cyprus, or Turkey), can
sign up and still manage to sabotage implementation. Italy and Greece
have not seen their governance changed by being in the Common
Market. While on paper there is a lot of evolution in the Doing
Business indicators of the World Bank (and a great deal of gaming)
around the world, in practice few of the changes announced have run
deep. In a market-based approach, the focus must be on equality of
treatment, reduction of transaction costs, and expansion in as many
areas as possible. Simply put, a trade treaty that opens nearly all public
procurement areas to external competition and makes them entirely
transparent makes a far greater contribution than a treaty that invokes
criminal penalties that it cannot enforce. But nothing in international
trade is really self-enforceable, and quite a large role must be played by
commercial attachés, business associations, and other NGOs, all of
whom should use monitoring, naming and shaming, and litigation in
arbitrage or civil courts to force countries to keep their commitments.
The increasing digitization of government is certainly a promising
development in the fight against this kind of corruption "by stealth."
Even when a country is too poor to digitize fast, administrative simplification of the kind Georgia did (one-stop administrative kiosks,
a public service hall, budgets of schools and hospitals regularly posted

on the outside doors) can deter corruption very effectively. The most effective anti-corruption approach by market means, therefore, would stress the systematic reduction of corruption opportunities, on the sides of both donor and recipient countries, and would include as an *ex ante* condition the stimulation of constraints by developing incentives rather than through enforcement. The closest to this design in the European sphere of influence comes the European Bank for Reconstruction and Development, EBRD, whose plans at least for Moldova and Ukraine seem more realistic than those of other donors. Here also belong civil society integrity campaigns tied to elections or performance of government, which have scored some temporary successes in Romania, Ukraine, the Czech Republic, and the Balkans, but proved in the long run unsustainable due to the presence of more *permanent* incentives for politicians to compete on integrity. Such campaigns have occasionally been supported by European donors such as SIDA or by USAID, although their most constant supporter has remained the Open Society Institute.

2. *Anti-corruption by legal means.* The development of a normative framework for international anti-corruption efforts has led to an explosion in the promotion of anti-corruption by legal means, which is now also propelled by the needs of a large consultancy market. The EU has adopted such a framework via GRECO in the accession countries and UNCAC in the rest of the world. It implies the promotion of standard packages, with considerable institutional creation on top of just criminalizing active and passive bribery, and introducing criminal responsibility. This ranges from anti-corruption agencies to legislation to protect whistleblowers, regardless of the country context and so functioning even in the absence of enabling institutions (such as freedom of the press). Other conventions for different geographical areas have additional demands. The theory is that institutional change will be triggered by the strength of the policy messages sent, for instance due to the monitoring of the treaties' implementation. In any case, though, fighting corruption by recourse to the law is bound to remain the biggest game in town because of path dependency. Legal consultants make up a large, well-qualified workforce in need of work, and the legal approach has a routine that is easy to follow for any development promoter who needs to spend a budget and check a box. The problem is when evaluations start coming in showing that impact on reducing corruption is missing even when compliance took place. The GRECO reports cited in this book, for instance on Greece or Italy, draw sound conclusions. Such reports have become less adequate or useful as they expanded in scope and geographical area and encountered contexts

where rule of law did not exist, as the GRECO lawyers were not equipped to deal with the Caucasus, Central Asia, or the informal Mediternnean societies. And GRECO has never claimed to offer more than an assessment of legislation. The problems started when "Europeanization," for want of a better strategy, makes such formal approaches the core of its transformation efforts and equates legal compliance with impact on practices.

3. *Comprehensive donor-induced anti-corruption,* or good governance by means that some would call "imperial." The essence of this last option is in the consistent integration of all external EU policies on trade, development, and any policy that might refer to one country or another. Cotonou has made the first step towards such a comprehensive approach, bringing together political dialogue, trade, and development (Cameron, 2012, p. 194). This option has the potential of controlling the flux of potentially unaccountable money as a resource for corruption, as well as disposing of certain constraints, so establishing better control and coordination over positive and negative incentives. The current EU policy on certain associated areas with distant EU-accession perspectives, such as the Balkans or Ukraine, comes – on paper at least – close to this approach.

Along the same lines, when an agreement is due for renegotiation – for instance Cotonou or other future trade agreements – aid and sanctions could also be tied together in a stronger but more astute package. Lowering of non-tariff barriers, financial transparency, even freedom of the press and judicial independence could all be made preconditions for aid. Additionally, a renegotiated agreement could include monitoring of corruption, in particular to make sure there is competitive procurement in order to work against government favoritism both before and after allocation of contracts. Countries could draw roadmaps to improve their indices for public integrity, alongside their main Millennium Goals development plans. However, the disadvantage had already become apparent in the controversies over Cotonou. Under the guise of anti-corruption efforts, former colonial powers might actually be pushing their own commercial interests or be perceived to be doing so. So far, the EU has had only very limited success in addressing corruption in weak countries such as Kosovo, Bosnia, Macedonia, and Moldova. The reasons for internal EU failures, as described here, need solutions if the EU is to continue trying to promote good governance. A five-year anti-corruption plan invested in by the EU may actually act as a disincentive for local agency, with the result that we see now: very poor ownership, if any. Without a sounder basis in both strategic goals and evidence, andr without more internal coherence among objectives and across EU institutions, such ambitious goals might continue not to be met. This is why this author cannot unreservedly recommend that the EU engage in a general anti-corruption approach using all means at its disposal in countries where it gives aid. In the event that it does engage in anti-corruption efforts, for political reasons of its own, there are seven indispensable steps for a more successful endeavor. I outlined these in a concept paper, "Seven Steps to Evidence-Based Anti-Corruption," commissioned by the Swedish government (Mungiu-Pippidi 2017).

1. Conceptualize corruption as a social context, not as individual cases.
2. Diagnose whether corruption is the exception or the norm, as the strategies for the two contexts differ.
3. Measure the level of the problem by sector of intervention so that you can trace whether you have reduced it or not.
4. Identify the stakeholders with an *interest* in changing the situation.
5. Develop an agency-based theory of change (who would do something to change the status quo and why, and what is missing to empower such agents of change).
6. Get together (with all other international donors, or at least European donors) around one plan where roles are divided, so that all areas of the equilibrium are covered and the effects are synergetic, eliminating redundancies and overlaps.
7. Set an example with your own aid on how social allocation is supposed to work (publish what you pay), and condition your aid on the quarterly publishing of indicators of competitive procurement by the recipient country.

While the three general approaches (market, legal, and imperial) can be seen as general alternatives, they are perhaps better understood as *choices* between different governance contexts. The market option could be applied as the default option in virtually every case, and it is obviously the only thing to do with a country that is below average on the rule of law and where corruption is the norm. Principal agent tools would not work in such contexts and exporting them would be useless, and therefore the aim should be to open markets and level the playing field by way of administrative simplification and transparency. In time, this could create a critical mass of competitive businesses who would be able to articulate demand for better governance in a broader sense. The legal option, currently promoted everywhere, can in fact work only in developed countries with strong rule of law. Some of it is more universal – every country should acquire decent conflict of interest legislation, and basic corrupt offences should be criminalized. But it will only work anti-corruption transformation under the restricted conditions described here: the precedence of robust rule of law. Finally, it remains to be seen if the situation in the Balkans, where the EU has thrown all its weight behind the imperial option, will evolve better than other, more autonomous national anti-corruption efforts that we witness in Brazil, South Africa, and Indonesia. The imperial option should be applied to corrupt countries that are heavily dependent on aid from the EU or that have opted to join the EU. Such ambitious engagement should be weighted by the capability of the country to enforce unitary standards, the ability of the EU to deliver on both promises and threats, and its determination to hold course for a considerable time – as long, in fact, as it might take to change governance for the better. This is because building control of corruption takes more time, not only more skill, than the EU has devoted so far. No good governance promotion should proceed without the implementation of the recommendations in the evaluations cited (ADE, 2013, for instance, or the ECA's) and fixing the serious problems of the EU approach as shown in this book. Otherwise more harm than good might result, and less thanks than deserved, given Europe's good intentions.

Indicators Frequently Used in This Book

Control of Corruption (CoC)	World Bank Worldwide Governance Indicators (WGI) Control of Corruption, recoded 1–10 with 10 best governance. See http://info.worldbank.org/governance/wgi/index.aspx #home
Index for Public Integrity (IPI)	Composite index consisting of six components: judicial independence, administrative burden, trade openness, budget transparency, e-citizenship, and freedom of the press. See full methodology at https://integrity-index.org /methodology/
Government Favoritism	World Economic Forum Global Competitiveness Report (GCR) for Government Favoritism, coded 1–7 with 7 least corrupt. See www.weforum.org/reports/the-global-competitiveness-report-2017–2018
IPI Administrative Burden	Index for Public Integrity (IPI) for Administrative Burden (red tape in opening and closing a businesss and paying business-associated taxes), coded 1–10 with 10 least red tape. See www.integrity-index.org
IPI Trade	Index for Public Integrity (IPI) for Trade Openness (time required for border compliance for export and import procedures, cost required for border compliance for export and import procedures), with 10 most open of non-tariff barriers. See www.integrity-index.org
Physical Integrity Index (measures power discretion)	Additive index constructed from the Torture (ciri_tort), Extrajudicial Killing (ciri_kill), Political Imprisonment (ciri_polpris), and Disappearance indicators (ciri_disap). Details on its construction and use can be found in Cingranelli and Richards (1999). Scaled from 0 (no government respect for physical integrity) to 8 (full government respect for physical integrity. See Cingranelli, D., and Richards, D.L. (2014). The Cingranelli-Richards (CIRI) Human Rights Dataset, http://www.humanrightsdata.com/p/data-documentation.html

(cont.)

Freedom of the Press Index	Freedom House index computed by adding three component ratings: Laws and Regulations, Political Pressures and Controls, and Economic Influences and Repressive Actions. Scaled from 0 (most free) to 100 (least free). See Freedom House *Freedom in the World Reports.*
KOF Index on Economic Openness	Economic dimension of the KOF Globalisation Index, consisting of two sub-dimensions: trade globalization and financial globalization, scaled from 1 (least globalized) to 100 (most globalized). See Gygli et al. (2018).
KOF Index on Social Openness	Social globalization is expressed as the spread of ideas, information, images, and people, scaled from 1 (least globalized) to 100 (most globalized). See Gygli et al. (2018).
Income Group	World Bank Country and Lending Groups. For the current 2018 fiscal year, low-income economies are defined as those with a GNI per capita, calculated using the World Bank Atlas method, of $1,005 or less in 2016; lower-middle-income economies are those with a GNI per capita between $1,006 and $3,955; upper-middle-income economies are those with a GNI per capita between $3,956 and $12,235; high-income economies are those with a GNI per capita of $12,236 or more. See https://datahelpdesk.worldbank.org/knowledgebase/arti cles/906519-world-bank-country-and-lending-groups
Rule of Law (RoL) and Freedom	Compiled by Freedom House. Non-RoL or RoL: countries with WGI "rule of law" scores below or above the sample median; not free, partly free, or free – corresponding freedom status.
Judicial Independence	Global Competitiveness Report Judicial Independence, recoded 1–10 with 10 best. See https://www.weforum.org/reports/the-global-competitiveness-report-2017–2018

Bibliography

Abbott, K. W., & Snidal, D. (2002). Values and Interests: International Legalization in the Fight against Corruption. *Journal of Legal Studies*, **31**(S1), S141–S177.

Acemoglu, D. (1995). Reward Structures and the Allocation of Talent. *European Economic Review*, **39**(1), 17–33.

Acemoglu, D., & Robinson, J. A. (2012). *Why Nations Fail: The Origins of Power, Prosperity and Poverty*, first edition, New York: Crown Publishers.

Adaman, F., Carkoglu, A., & Senatalar, B. (2001). *Corruption in Turkey, Results of Diagnostic Household Survey*, TESEV (Economic and Social Studies Foundation of Turkey).

ADE (Analysis for Economic Decisions) (2011). *Thematic Evaluation of European Commission Support to Justice and Security System Reform*, https://ec.europa.eu/europeaid/sites/devco/files/evaluation-cooperation-ec-justice-1295-main-report-201111_en_0.pdf

ADE (2013). *Public Expenditure and Financial Accountability (PEFA) Assessment Mainland Tanzania (Central Government) (Final Report)*, www.tzdpg.or.tz/fileadmin/documents/external/Aid_Effectiveness/PEFA/2013313736-_Final_Report_PEFA.PDF

Ades, A., & Di Tella, R. (1997). The New Economics of Corruption: A Survey and some New Results. *Political Studies*, **45**(3), 496–515.

Ades, A., & Di Tella, R. (1999). Rents, Competition, and Corruption. *American Economic Review*, **89**(4), 982–993.

Adevarul.ro (2000). EXCLUSIV Interviu cu Oleg Voronin, fiul liderului PCRM: "Sunt un boschetar în comparație cu clica de la guvernare" [Exclusive interview with Oleg Voronin, son of Communist Labor Party leader: I am homeless compared to the governing gang], https://adevarul.ro/moldova/politica/exclusiv-interviu-oleg-voronin-fiul-liderului-pcrm-sunt-boschetar-comparatie-clica-guvernare-1_50d801c5596d7200912f494a/index.html

Adu, A. L. (1969). *The Civil Service in Commonwealth Africa: Development and Transition*, London: Allen & Unwin.

African Union (2018). *African Peer Review Mechanism (APRM)*, https://au.int/en/organs/aprm

Afrobarometer (2016). *People and Corruption: Middle East and North Africa Survey 2016*, http://afrobarometer.org/publications/people-and-corruption-middle-east-and-north-africa-survey-2016

Alesina, A., & Weder, B. (2002). Do Corrupt Governments Receive Less Foreign Aid? *American Economic Review*, **92**(4), 1126–1137.

Ali, A. M., & Isse, H. S. (2003). Determinants of Economic Corruption: A Cross-Country Comparison. *Cato Journal*, **22**(3), 449–466.

Amani, A. (2013, October 22). How Europe Failed Azerbaijan. *OpenDemocracy*, www.opendemocracy.net/can-europe-make-it/aslan-amani/how-europe-failed -azerbaijan

Anand, S., & Sen, A. (1994). *Human Development Index: Methodology and Measurement*, Human Development Report Office (HDRO), United Nations Development Programme (UNDP), https://ideas.repec.org/p/hdr/hdocpa/hdo cpa-1994-02.html

Anderson, C. J. (1998). When in Doubt, Use Proxies: Attitudes toward Domestic Politics and Support for European Integration. *Comparative Political Studies*, **31**(5), 569–601.

Anderson, J. H., & Gray, S. W. (2007). Transforming Judicial Systems in Europe and Central Asia. In F. Bourguignon and B. Pleskovic, eds., *Beyond Transition*, Washington, DC: World Bank, 329–356.

Anderson, L. (2011). Demystifying the Arab Spring: Parsing the Differences Between Tunisia, Egypt, and Libya. *Foreign Affairs*, **90**(3), 2–7.

Anderson, R. D., & Müller, A. C. (2017). *The Revised WTO Agreement on Government Procurement (GPA): Key Design Features and Significance for Global Trade and Development*, World Trade Organization (WTO), Economic Research and Statistics Division.

Andreou, G. (2010). The Domestic Effects of EU Cohesion Policy in Greece: Islands of Europeanization in a Sea of Traditional Practices. *Southeast European and Black Sea Studies*, **10**(1), 13–27.

Anghel, D. (2009, April 16). Oleg Voronin ar avea o avere de 2 miliarde de euro, aproape jumatate din PIB-ul Moldovei [Oleg Voronin Might Own Assets Worth Half Moldova's PIB], *Ziarul Financiar*, www.zf.ro/politica/politica-externa/oleg-voronin-ar-avea-o-avere-de-2-miliarde-de-euro-aproape-jumatate -din-pib-ul-moldovei-4217435/

ANSA.it (2016, June 16). Corruption 40% of Italy Large-Scale Public Works Contracts, www.ansa.it/english/news/2016/06/16/corruption-40-of-italy-large-scale-public-works-contracts_2f515370-dfd4-4e88-bfa5-aae9522c8ff1 .html

Aristotle (2013). *Aristotle's Politics* (C. Lord, ed.), second edition, Chicago: University of Chicago Press.

Åslund, A. (2013). *Ukraine's Choice: European Association Agreement or Eurasian Union? Policy Brief 13-22*, Peterson Institute for International Economics, https://piie.com/publications/policy-briefs/ukraines-choice-european-association -agreement-or-eurasian-union

Autorità Nazionale Anticorruzione (2014). *Appendice dati sulla corruzione fonte amministrativa*, Rome: Autorità Nazionale Anticorruzione.

Ayed, M. K. (2018). *Italy Corruption Report*, www.business-anti-corruption.com /country-profiles/italy/

Balducci, G. (2010). The Limits of Normative Power Europe in Asia: The Case of Human Rights in China. *East Asia*, **27**(1), 35–55.

Balfour, R. (2012). *EU Conditionality after the Arab Spring*, European Institute of the Mediterranean, www.epc.eu/documents/uploads/pub_2728_papersbal four_for_euromesco16.pdf

Balfour, R., Carta, C., & Raik, K. (2015). *The European External Action Service and National Foreign Ministries: Convergence or Divergence?* Farnham, Surrey: Ashgate.

Balfour, R., Fabbri, F., & Youngs, R. (2016). *Report on Democracy Assistance from the European Union to the Middle East and North Africa* (EUSPRING Report).

Banfield, E. C. (1958). *The Moral Basis of a Backward Society*, New York: Free Press.

Baracani, E. (2008). EU Democratic Rule of Law Promotion. In A. Magen & L. Morlino, eds., *International Actors, Democratization and the Rule of Law Anchoring Democracy?* Oxford and New York: Routledge.

Baran, Z. (2000). Corruption: The Turkish Challenge. *Journal of International Affairs*, **54**(1), 127–146.

Barbé, E., & Johansson-Nogués, E. (2008). The EU as a Modest "Force for Good": the European Neighbourhood Policy. *International Affairs*, **84**(1), 81–96.

Barcelona Declaration (1995). Euro-Mediterranean Conference, November 27 and 28, https://ec.europa.eu/research/iscp/pdf/policy/barcelona_declaration.pdf

Barrón, Í. de, & Pérez, F. J. (2016, September 26). Ex-IMF Chief in the Spotlight as Bankia Credit Card Trial gets Underway. *El País*, https://elpais.com/elpais/2016/09/26/inenglish/1474902184_160485.html

Bartels, L. (2007a). The Trade and Development Policy of the European Union. *European Journal of International Law*, 18(4), 715–756.

Bartels, L. (2007b). The WTO Legality of the EU's GSP+ Arrangement. *Journal of International Economic Law*, 10(4), 869–886.

Bass, G. J. (2009). *Freedom's Battle: The Origins of Humanitarian Intervention*, New York: Vintage.

BBC News (2012). How "Magic" made Greek Debt Disappear Before it Joined the Euro, www.bbc.com/news/world-europe-16834815

BBC News (2014). Hundreds of Turkish Police Officers Dismissed, www.bbc.com/news/world-europe-25634542

BBC News (2016). The City Getting Rich from Fake News, www.bbc.com/news/magazine-38168281

Bechev, D. (2018). Meet the EU's Next Member State: Montenegro, Al Jazeera, www.aljazeera.com/indepth/opinion/meet-eu-member-state-montenegro-180418115545134.html

Becker, G. S. (1968). Crime and Punishment: An Economic Approach. *Journal of Political Economy*, **76**(2), 169–217.

Becker, S. O., Egger, P. H., & von Ehrlich, M. (2013). Absorptive Capacity and the Growth and Investment Effects of Regional Transfers: A Regression Discontinuity Design with Heterogeneous Treatment Effects. *American Economic Journal: Economic Policy*, 5(4), 29–77.

Belloni, R., & Strazzari, F. (2014). Corruption in Post-Conflict Bosnia-Herzegovina and Kosovo: A Deal Among Friends. *Third World Quarterly*, **35**(5), 855–871.

Bénassy-Quéré, A., Coupet, M., & Mayer, T. (2007). Institutional Determinants of Foreign Direct Investment. *World Economy*, 30(5), 764–782.

Bentham, J. (1996). *The Collected Works of Jeremy Bentham: An Introduction to the Principles of Morals and Legislation*, Oxford: Clarendon Press.

Berenschot and Imagos (2012). *Thematic Evaluation of Rule of Law, Judicial Reform and Fight against Corruption and Organised Crime in the Western Balkans – Lot 3* (Final Main Report), Brussels, https://ec.europa.eu/neighbour hood-enlargement/sites/near/files/pdf/financial_assistance/phare/evaluation/20 13_final_main_report_lot_3.pdf

Bergel, J.-L., Cherot, J. Y., Cimamonti, S., & Mercadier, M.-F. (2015). *L'Émergence d'une culture judiciaire européenne. Avancées et difficultés d'une culture judiciaire europeene dans l'espace judiciare européen* [The Emergence of a European Judicial Culture. Progress and Difficulties of a European Judicial Culture in the European Judicial Space], Université Paul Cézanne, Aix-Marseille III.

Bertelsmann Stiftung (2016). *Turkey Country Report*, Gütersloh: BTI 2016, www .bti-project.org/fileadmin/files/BTI/Downloads/Reports/2016/pdf/BTI_2016_ Turkey.pdf

Bertelsmann Stiftung (2018a). *Country Report – Ghana*, Gütersloh: BTI 2018.

Bertelsmann Stiftung (2018b). *Country Report – Tunisia*, Gütersloh: BTI 2018, www.bti-project.org/de/berichte/laenderberichte/detail/itc/TUN/

Beugelsdijk, M., & Eijffinger, S. C. W. (2005). The Effectiveness of Structural Policy in the European Union: An Empirical Analysis for the EU-15 in 1995–2001. *JCMS: Journal of Common Market Studies*, 43(1), 37–51.

Bevan, A. A., Estrin, S., & Grabbe, H. (2001). *The Impact of EU Accession Prospects on FDI Inflows to Central and Eastern Europe*, ESRC Research Programme on One Europe or Several.

Bicchi, F. (2014). The Politics of Foreign Aid and the European Neighbourhood Policy Post–Arab Spring: "More for More" or Less of the Same? *Mediterranean Politics*, 19(3), 318–332.

Bilal, S., & Große-Puppendahl, S. (2016). *Blending 2.0: Towards New (European External) Investment Plans*, http://rgdoi.net/10.13140/RG.2.2 .22528.43523

Bilefsky, D. (2012a, November 21). Former Premier of Croatia, Ivo Sanader, is Sentenced for Graft. *New York Times*, www.nytimes.com/2012/11/21/world/ europe/former-premier-of-croatia-ivo-sanader-is-sentenced-for-graft.html

Bilefsky, D. (2012b, October 26). The Curse of Corruption in Europe's East. *New York Times*, www.nytimes.com/2012/10/26/world/europe/26iht-romania 26.html

Birdsall, N., Savedoff, W. D., Mahgoub, A., & Vyborny, K. (2010). *Cash on Delivery: A New Approach to Foreign Aid: With an Application to Primary Schooling*, Washington, DC: Center For Global Development.

BIRN (Balkan Investigative Reporting Network) Kosovo (2016). *Published Annual Public Procurement Monitoring Report*, BIRN, http://birn.eu.com/uncategorized/b irn-kosovo-published-annual-public-procurement-monitoring-report/

Biucchi, B. M. (1973). *The Industrial Revolution in Switzerland, 1700–1914* (C. M. Cipolla, ed.), London: Fontana Collins.

Black, C. E. (1966). *The Dynamics of Modernization: A Study in Comparative History.*, New York: Harper Torchbooks.

Bogmans, E., & de Yong, C. (2011). Does Corruption Discourage International Trade? *European Journal of Political Economy*, 27(2), 385–398.

Bonifazi, C., & Heins, F. (2000). Long-Term Trends of Internal Migration in Italy. *International Journal of Population Geography*, 6(2), 111–131.

Booth, D. (2012). *Synthesis Report – Development as a Collective Action Problem: Addressing the Real Challenges of African Governance*, Africa Power and Politics Programme.

Börzel, T. A. (1999). Towards Convergence in Europe? Institutional Adaptation to Europeanization in Germany and Spain, 37, 573–596.

Börzel, T. A., & Risse, T. (2004). One Size Fits All! EU Policies for the Promotion of Human Rights, Democracy and the Rule of Law. Paper presented at Workshop on Democracy Promotion, October 4–5, 2004, Stanford University Center for Development, Democracy and the Rule of Law.

Börzel, T. A., & van Hüllen, V. (2014). One Voice, One Message, but Conflicting Goals: Cohesiveness and Consistency in the European Neighbourhood Policy. *Journal of European Public Policy*, 21(7), 1033–1049.

Börzel, T. A., Hofmann, T., & Panke, D. (2012). Caving In or Sitting It Out? Longitudinal Patterns of Non-Compliance in the European Union. *Journal of European Public Policy*, 19(4), 454–471.

Börzel, T. A., Stahn, A., & Pamuk, Y. (2008). *Good Governance in the European Union*, https://refubium.fu-berlin.de/bitstream/handle/fub188/19026/2008-7_Boerzel_Pamuk_Stahn.pdf?sequence=1

Bossuyt, J., Lehtinen, T., Simon, A., Laporte, G., & Corre, G. (2000). *Assessing Trends in EC Development Policy: An Independent Review of the European Commission's External Aid Reform Process*, https://ecdpm.org/wp-content/uploads/2013/10/DP-16-Assessing-Trends-in-EC-Development-Policy-2000.pdf

Bozzini, A. (2014). *Background Paper on Rwanda*, ANTICORRP, http://anticorrp.eu/publications/background-paper-on-rwanda/

Bratu, R. (2016). *Case Study Report on Control of Corruption and EU Funds in Ukraine*, ANTICORRP, http://anticorrp.eu/publications/case-study-report-on-control-of-corruption-and-eu-funds-in-ukraine/

Breuilly, J. (2003). Napoleonic Germany and State-Formation. In M. Rowe, ed., *Collaboration and Resistance in Napoleonic Europe: State Formation in an Age of Upheaval, c. 1800–1815*, Basingstoke and New York: Palgrave Macmillan.

Buchanan, J. M. (1975). *The Limits of Liberty: Between Anarchy and Leviathan*, Chicago: University of Chicago Press.

Buchanan, J. M., Tollison, R. D., & Tullock, G. (1980). *Toward a Theory of the Rent-Seeking Society*, College Station: Texas A & M University.

Buğra, A. (1994). *State and Business in Modern Turkey: A Comparative Study*, Albany, NY: State University of New York Press.

Buğra, A., & Savaşkan, O. (2012). Politics and Class: The Turkish Business Environment in the Neoliberal Age. *New Perspectives on Turkey*, 46, 27–63.

Buiter, W. H. (2005). Country Ownership: A Term whose Time has Gone. In S. Koeberle, H. Bedoya, P. Silarky, & G. Verheyen, eds., *Conditionality*

Revisited: Concepts, Experiences, and Lessons, Washington, DC: World Bank, pp. 27–32.

Bull, M., & Pasquino, G. (2007). A Long Quest in Vain: Institutional Reforms in Italy. *West European Politics*, 30(4), 670–691.

Burke, E. (1783). *Speech on Mr. Fox's East India Bill, by Edmund Burke (1/12/ 1783)*, www.ourcivilisation.com/smartboard/shop/burkee/extracts/chap10 .htm

Burlyuk, O. (2015). Variation in EU External Policies as a Virtue: EU Rule of Law Promotion in the Neighbourhood. *JCMS: Journal of Common Market Studies*, 53(3), 509–523.

Burnside, C., & Dollar, D. (2000). Aid, Policies, and Growth. *American Economic Review*, 90(4), 847–868.

Calderoni, F. (2011). Where Is the Mafia in Italy? Measuring the Presence of the Mafia across Italian Provinces. *Global Crime*, 12(1), 41–69.

Call, C. T. (2017). What Guatemala's Political Crisis Means for Anti-Corruption Efforts Everywhere, Brookings, www.brookings.edu/blog/order-from-chaos/ 2017/09/07/what-guatemalas-political-crisis-means-for-anti-corruption-efforts-everywhere/

Cameron, F. (2012). *An Introduction to European Foreign Policy*, second edition, Oxford and New York: Routledge.

Canter, E. J. (2015). Business as Usual: Analyzing Recidivism under the Foreign Corrupt Practices Act. *Journal of Law, Business & Ethics*, 21 (Winter), 77–103.

Capussela, A. (2015a, April 16). Eulex Report Exposes EU Failure in Kosovo. *EU Observer*, https://euobserver.com/opinion/128343

Capussela, A. L. (2015b). *Eulex's Performance of Its Executive Judicial Functions* (SSRN Scholarly Paper), Rochester, NY: Social Science Research Network, www.academia.edu/8980254/Eulex_s_Performance_of_its_Executive_Judicial _Functions

Carbone, M. (2010). The European Union, Good Governance and Aid Co-ordination. *Third World Quarterly*, 31(1), 13–29.

Carnegie Europe (2018). *Explaining Oligarchic Moldova*, https://carnegieeurope .eu/strategiceurope/69856

Carothers, T. (1998). Rule of Law Revival. *Foreign Affairs*, 77(2), https://carne gieendowment.org/1998/03/01/rule-of-law-revival-pub-165

Ceccarini, L., & Bordignon, F. (2017). Referendum on Renzi: The 2016 Vote on the Italian Constitutional Revision. *South European Society and Politics*, 22(3), 281–302.

Champagne, H. (2016). *The EU Good Governance Approach in Ghana: the Growing Focus on Anti-Corruption Measures*, ANTICORRP, http://anticorrp.eu/publica tions/report-on-kosovo/

Chandler, D. (2000). *Bosnia: Faking Democracy after Dayton*, second edition, London: Pluto Press.

Charron, N. (2011). Exploring the Impact of Foreign Aid on Corruption: Has the "Anti-Corruption Movement" Been Effective? *Developing Economies*, 49(1), 66–88.

Chayes, S. (2016). *The Structure of Corruption: A Systemic Analysis Using Eurasian Cases*, Washington, DC: Carnegie Endowment for International Peace.

Chirot, D. (ed.) (1991). *The Origins of Backwardness in Eastern Europe: Economics and Politics from the Middle Ages until the Early Twentieth Century*, Berkeley, CA: University of California Press.

Chirot, D., & Hall, T. D. (1982). World-System Theory. *Annual Review of Sociology*, **8**(1), 81–106.

Chrysolora, E. (2018). EU Officials Slam Gov't over Public Sector Posts, Judiciary, Ekathimerini.com, www.ekathimerini.com/226973/article/ekathi merini/news/eu-officials-slam-govt-over-public-sector-posts-judiciary

Cicero, M. T. (2006). *De Officiis* (W. Miller, trans.), ReadHowYouWant.com, Limited.

Cingolani, L., & Fazekas., M. (2017). Breaking the Cycle? How (Not) to Use Political Finance Regulations to Counter Public Procurement Corruption. *Slavonic and East European Review*, **95**(1), 76–116.

Cingranelli, D. L., & Richards, D. L. (1999). Measuring the Level, Pattern, and Sequence of Government Respect for Physical Integrity Rights. *International Studies Quarterly*, **43**(2), 407–417.

Clark, W. A. (1993). *Crime and Punishment in Soviet Officialdom: Combating Corruption in the Political Elite, 1965–1990*, Armonk, NY: M.E. Sharp.

Clogg, R. (2013). *A Concise History of Greece*, third edition, Cambridge: Cambridge University Press.

CNN Business (2015). How to Steal $1 Billion in Three Days. CNNMoney, ht tps://money.cnn.com/2015/05/07/news/economy/moldova-stolen-billion/inde x.html

Cole, W. M. (2015). Institutionalizing a Global Anti-Corruption Regime: Perverse Effects on Country Outcomes, 1984–2012. *International Journal of Comparative Sociology*, **56**(1), 53–80.

Collier, P. (1997). The Failure of Conditionality. In C. Gwin, J. M. Nelson, & E. Berg, eds., *Perspectives on Aid and Development*, Washington, DC, and Baltimore, MD: Overseas Development Council and Johns Hopkins University Press.

Collier, P. (2011). *Wars, Guns, and Votes: Democracy in Dangerous Places*, New York: Random House.

Collier, P., & Venables, A. (eds.) (2011). *Plundered nations? Successes and Failures in Natural Resource Extraction*, Basingstoke and New York: Palgrave Macmillan.

Collier, P., & Vicente, P. C. (2014). Votes and Violence: Evidence from a Field Experiment in Nigeria. *Economic Journal*, **124**(574), 327–355.

Courade, G. (2016). *L'Afrique des idées reçues*, Paris: Belin.

Dabrowski, M. (2017). *Ukraine's Unfinished Reform Agenda*, Breugel.org, http:// bruegel.org/2017/09/ukraines-unfinished-reform-agenda/

Dadašov, R. (2016). EU Aid and Quality of Governance (ERCAS Working Paper No. 47), www.againstcorruption.eu/wp-content/uploads/2016/01/WP-47-EUAid_QualityofGovernance.pdf

Dadašov, R. (2017). European Aid and Governance: Does the Source Matter? *European Journal of Development Research*, **29**(2), 269–288.

Damania, R., Fredriksson, P. G., & Mani, M. (2004). The Persistence of Corruption and Regulatory Compliance Failures: Theory and Evidence. *Public Choice*, **121**(3–4), 363–390.

Darden, K. A. (2001). Blackmail as a Tool of State Domination: Ukraine under Kuchma. *East European Constitutional Review*, **10**(2/3), 67–71.

Davis, J. A. (2006). *Naples and Napoleon: Southern Italy and the European Revolutions (1780–1860)*, Oxford and New York: Oxford University Press.

Della Porta, D. (2004). Political Parties and Corruption: Ten Hypotheses on Five Vicious Circles. *Crime, Law and Social Change*, **42**(1), 35–60.

Della Porta, D., & Mény, Y. (eds.) (1997). *Democracy and Corruption in Europe*, London and Washington: Pinter.

Della Porta, D., & Vannucci, A. (2005). The Governance Mechanisms of Corrupt Transactions. Introduction: A Neo-Institutional Approach to Corruption. In J. Lambsdorff, M. Taube, & M. Schramm, eds., *The New Institutional Economics of Corruption*, London and New York: Routledge, pp. 152–159.

Della Porta, D., & Vannucci, A. (2007). Corruption and Anti-Corruption: The Political Defeat of "Clean Hands" in Italy. *West European Politics*, **30**(4), 830–853.

Del Monte, A., & Papagni, E. (2007). The Determinants of Corruption in Italy: Regional Panel Data Analysis. *European Journal of Political Economy*, **23**(2), 379–396.

Del Sarto, R. A., & Schumacher, T. (2011). From Brussels with Love: Leverage, Benchmarking, and the Action Plans with Jordan and Tunisia in the EU's Democratization Policy. *Democratization*, **18**(4), 932–955.

Der Spiegel (2010). Complicit in Corruption: How German Companies Bribed Their Way to Greek Deals, www.spiegel.de/international/europe/complicit-in-corruption-how-german-companies-bribed-their-way-to-greek-deals-a-69397 3.html

Diac, M. (2016). *Raport. România – sub ascultare. SRI a cerut și a obținut de 16 ori mai multe mandate de interceptare decât FBI, de-a lungul unui an* [Romania under surveillance: the RSI asked for and was granted 16 more wiretap warrants than the FBI in a single year], https://romanialibera.ro/politica/institutii/raport–ro mania—sub-ascultare–sri-a-cerut-si-a-obtinut-de-16-ori–mai-multe-mandate-de-interceptare-decat-fbi–de-a-lungul-unui-an–431994

Diamond, L. (2008). The Democratic Rollback: The Resurgence of the Predatory State. *Foreign Affairs*, **87**(2), 36–48.

Dietrich, S. (2017). EU Democracy Promotion, Conditionality, and Judicial Autonomy. In A. Mungiu-Pippidi & J. Warkotsch, eds., *Beyond the Panama Papers: The Performance of EU Good Governance Promotion*, The ANTICORRP Project, Anticorruption Report Volume 4, Opladen, Berlin, and Toronto: Barbara Budrich Publishers, pp. 34–45.

Diez, T. (2005). Constructing the Self and Changing Others: Reconsidering "Normative Power Europe." *Millennium: Journal of International Studies*, **33**(3), 613–636.

Di Federico, G. (2004). Independence and Accountability of the Judiciary in Italy. The Experience of a Transitional Country in a Comparative Perspective. In A. Sajó, ed., *Judicial Integrity*, Leiden and Boston: M. Nijhoff Publishers, http://siteresources.worldbank.org/INTECA/Resources/DiFedericopaper.pdf

Dijkstra, A. G. (2002). The Effectiveness of Policy Conditionality: Eight Country Experiences. *Development and Change*, **33**(2), 307–334.

Dimulescu, V., Pop, R., & Doroftei, I. M. (2013). Risks of Corruption and the Management of EU Funds in Romania. *Romanian Journal of Political Science*, **13**(1), 101.

Directive 2014/23/EU of the European Parliament and of the Council of 26 February 2014 on the Award of Concession Contracts (Text with EEA Relevance) (2014). Vol. OJ L, http://data.europa.eu/eli/dir/2014/23/oj/eng

Directive 2014/24/EU of the European Parliament and of the Council of 26 February 2014 on Public Procurement and Repealing Directive 2004/18/EC (Text with EEA relevance) (2014). Vol. OJ L, http://data.europa.eu/eli/dir/2014/24/oj/eng

Directive 2014/42/EU of the European Parliament and of the Council of 3 April 2014 on the Freezing and Confiscation of Instrumentalities and Proceeds of Crime in the European Union (2014). Vol. OJ L, http://data.europa.eu/eli/dir/2014/42/oj/eng

Directorate General for Internal Policies of the Union (2018). *Assessment of the 10 Years' Cooperation and Verification Mechanism for Bulgaria and Romania*, Policy Department for Budgetary Affairs, www.europarl.europa.eu/RegData/etudes/STUD/2018/603813/IPOL_STU(2018)603813_EN.pdf

Directorate General for International Cooperation and Development (2018). *Budget Support and Dialogue with Partner Countries*, https://ec.europa.eu/europeaid/eubudgetsupport_en

Djankov, S., Glaeser, E., Porta, R. L., Lopez-de-Silane, F., & Shleifer, A. (2003). *The New Comparative Economics*, Cambridge, MA: National Bureau of Economic Research.

Dodbiba, A., & Duli, F. (2016). *Improving Governance in Kosovo: Evaluating the Impact of EU Conditionality through Policy and Financial Assistance*, http://anticorrp.eu/publications/improving-governance-in-kosovo-evaluating-the-impact-of-eu-conditionality-through-policy-and-financial-assistance/

Doig, A., Watt, D., & Williams, R. (2007). Why Do Developing Country Anti-Corruption Commissions Fail to Deal with Corruption? Understanding the Three Dilemmas of Organisational Development, Performance Expectation, and Donor and Government Cycles. *Public Administration and Development*, **27**(3), 251–259.

Dollar, D., & Svensson, J. (2000). What Explains the Success or Failure of Structural Adjustment Programmes? *Economic Journal*, **110**(466), 894–917.

Doroftei, I. M. (2016). Measuring Government Favouritism Objectively: The Case of Romanian Public Construction Sector. *European Journal on Criminal Policy and Research*, **22**(3), 399–413.

Drápalová, E. (2016). *Good Apples on Bad Trees : Explaining Variation in Levels of Corruption in South-European Local Government* (PhD thesis, European University Institute, Florence), http://cadmus.eui.eu/handle/1814/39058

Drápalová, E. (2017). Spain: Roads to Good Government? How EU structural Funds Impact Governance across Regions. In A. Mungiu-Pippidi & J. Warkotsch, eds., *Beyond the Panama Papers: The Performance of EU Good Governance Promotion*, The ANTICORRP Project, Anticorruption Report Volume 4, Opladen, Berlin, and Toronto: Barbara Budrich Publishers, 46–58.

Dreher, A. (2006). Does Globalization Affect Growth? Evidence from a New Index of Globalization. *Applied Economics*, **38**(10), 1091–1110.

Dreher, A. (2009). IMF Conditionality: Theory and Evidence. *Public Choice*, **141**(1–2), 233–267.

Duli-Sefaj, F. (2014). *Ethnography of Corruption: The Case of Kosovo* (survey report), http://anticorrp.eu/publications/report-on-kosovo/

Easterly, W. (2007). Was Development Assistance a Mistake? *American Economic Review*, **97**(2), 328–332.

EC (European Commission) (1993). Conclusions of the Presidency (Bulletin of the European Communities), Copenhagen, www.consilium.europa.eu/media/21225/72921.pdf

EC (2001). European Governance – A White Paper (Communication from the Commission), https://eur-lex.europa.eu/legal-content/EN/TXT/HTML/?uri=LEGISSUM:l10109&from=EN

EC (2003a). Governance and Development (Communication from the Commission to the Council, the European Parliament and the European Economic and Social Committee), Brussels, https://eur-lex.europa.eu/legal-content/EN/TXT/PDF/?uri=CELEX:52003DC0615&from=EN

EC (2003b). On a Comprehensive EU Policy Against Corruption (Communication from the Commission to the Council, the European Parliament and the European Economic and Social Committee), https://eur-lex.europa.eu/LexUriServ/LexUriServ.do?uri=COM:2003:0317:FIN:EN:PDF

EC (2003c). Turkey 2003 Regular Report, Brussels.

EC (2003d). Wider Europe – Neighbourhood: A New Framework for Relations with our Eastern and Southern Neighbours (Communication from the Commission), Brussels, http://eeas.europa.eu/archives/docs/enp/pdf/pdf/com03_104_en.pdf

EC (2007a). Country Strategy Paper and National Indicative Programme for the Period 2008–2013 – Rwanda, Lisbon, https://ec.europa.eu/europeaid/sites/devco/files/csp-nip-rwanda-2008-2013_en.pdf

EC (2007b). Joint Africa–EU Strategy, https://ec.europa.eu/europeaid/regions/africa/continental-cooperation/joint-africa-eu-strategy_en

EC (2009a). Attitudes of Europeans towards Corruption: Full Report (Fieldwork September–October 2009), http://ec.europa.eu/commfrontoffice/publicopinion/archives/ebs/ebs_325_en.pdf

EC (2009b). On Progress in Bulgaria under the Co-operation and Verification Mechanism, Brussels, https://ec.europa.eu/transparency/regdoc/rep/1/2009/EN/1-2009-402-EN-F1-1.Pdf

EC (2009c). On Progress in Romania under the Co-operation and Verification Mechanism, Brussels, https://ec.europa.eu/transparency/regdoc/rep/1/2009/EN/1-2009-401-EN-F1-1.Pdf

EC (2010a). Five years of European Neighbourhood Policy: More Trade, More Aid, More People-to-People Contacts, Brussels, http://europa.eu/rapid/press-release_IP-10-566_en.htm

EC (2010b). Strategic / Interim Evaluation of EU IPA Pre-Accession Assistance to Kosovo (under UNSCR 1244/99) (evaluation report), https://ec.europa.eu/

neighbourhood-enlargement/sites/near/files/pdf/financial_assistance/phare/eva
luation/2013/evaluation_report_kosovo_ares_836741.pdf

EC (2010c). The Economic Adjustment Programme for Greece (Occasional Papers 61), https://publications.europa.eu/en/publication-detail/-/publication/ 64c89a77-ddc4-46f4-9bb0-18d7e80f6f0c/language-en

EC (2011a). A New Response to a Changing Neighbourhood: A Review of European Neighborhood Policy (Joint Communication by the High Representative of the Union For Foreign Affairs And Security Policy and the European Commission), Brussels, www.ab.gov.tr/files/ardb/evt/1_avrupa_bir ligi/1_9_komsuluk_politikalari/A_review_of_European_Neighbourhood_Polic y.pdf

EC (2011b). Increasing the Impact of EU Development Policy: An Agenda for Change (Communication from the Commission), Brussels, https://ec.europa .eu/europeaid/sites/devco/files/agenda_for_change_-_com2011_637_final.pdf

EC (2012). Treaty on Stability, Coordination and Governance in the Economic and Monetary Union, http://europa.eu/rapid/press-release_DOC-12-2_en.htm

EC (2013a). Eu Cooperation with Egypt in the Field of Governance (Replies of the Commission and the EEAS to the Special Report of the European Court of Auditors), Brussels, https://eur-lex.europa.eu/legal-content/EN/TXT/HTML/ ?uri=LEGISSUM:l10109&from=EN

EC (2013b). European Development Fund (EDF) – International Cooperation and Development, https://ec.europa.eu/europeaid/funding/funding-instruments -programming/funding-instruments/european-development-fund_en

EC (2013c). Millennium Development Goals Contract, https://ec.europa.eu/eur opeaid/policies/european-development-policy/millennium-development-goals -contract_en

EC (2013d). Report from the Commission to the European Parliament, the Council, the European Economic and Social Committee and the Committee of the Regions on the EU Support for Democratic Governance, with a Focus on the Governance Initiative, https://eur-lex.europa.eu/legal-content/EN/ALL/?u ri=CELEX%3A52013DC0403

EC (2013e). Flash Eurobarometer 374 (Fieldwork: February – March 2013), http://ec.europa.eu/commfrontoffice/publicopinion/flash/fl_374_en.pdf

EC (2014a). European Union – Republic of Rwanda National Indicative Programme for the period 2014–2020, Brussels, https://ec.europa.eu/eur opeaid/sites/devco/files/pin-rwanda-fed11-2014_en.pdf

EC (2014b). Report from the Commission to the Council and the European Parliament EU Anti-Corruption Report, Brussels, https://ec.europa.eu/home-affairs/sites/homeaffairs/files/e-library/documents/policies/organized-crime-and-human-trafficking/corruption/docs/acr_2014_en.pdf

EC (2014c). The Cotonou Agreement and Multiannual Financial Framework 2014–20; Signed in Cotonou on 23 June 2000, Revised in Luxembourg on 25 June 2005, Revised in Ouagadougou 22 June 2010, Luxembourg: Publishing Office of the European Union.

EC (2014d). Eurobarometer 76.1 (2011), Brussels: GESIS Data Archive.

EC (2015a). eGovernment in Italy, https://joinup.ec.europa.eu/sites/default/files/inline-files/eGovernment%20in%20Italy%20-%20February%202016%20-%2018_00%20-%20v1_00.pdf

EC (2015b). Flash Eurobarometer 428: Businesses' Attitudes towards Corruption in the EU, https://data.europa.eu/euodp/data/dataset/S2084_428_ENG

EC (2015c). Third Report on Progress by Kosovo in Fulfilling the Requirements of the Visa Liberalisation Roadmap (Report from the Commission to the European Parliament and the Council), Brussels, https://ec.europa.eu/home-affairs/sites/homeaffairs/files/e library/documents/policies/international-affairs/general/docs/third_report_progress_kosovo_fulfilling_requirements_visa_liberalisation_roadmap_en.pdf

EC (2016a). About the EU Delegation to the African Union, https://eeas.europa.eu/delegations/african-union-au_pt/865/About_the_EU_Delegation_to_the_African_Union

EC (2016b). Eurobarometer 79.1 (2013), Brussels: GESIS Data Archive.

EC (2016c). Evaluation of the Cotonou Partnership Agreement (Joint Staff Working Document), Brussels, https://ec.europa.eu/europeaid/sites/devco/files/evaluation-post-cotonou_en.pdf

EC (2017a). Competitiveness in Low-Income and Low-Growth Regions: The Lagging Regions Report (Commission Staff Working Document), Brussels, https://ec.europa.eu/regional_policy/sources/docgener/studies/pdf/lagging_regions%20report_en.pdf

EC (2017b). EU Official Development Assistance Reaches Highest Level Ever, https://ec.europa.eu/europeaid/news-and-events/eu-official-development-assistance-reaches-highest-level-ever_en

EC (2017c). EU–Western Balkans Media Days: Strengthening media in the Western Balkans – European Neighbourhood Policy And Enlargement Negotiations, https://ec.europa.eu/neighbourhood-enlargement/news_corner/news/eu-western-balkans-media-days-strengthening-media-western-balkans_en

EC (2017d). On Progress in Bulgaria under the Co-operation and Verification Mechanism, Brussels, https://ec.europa.eu/info/sites/info/files/comm-2017–750_en_0.pdf

EC (2017e). On Progress in Romania under the Co-operation and Verification Mechanism, Brussels, https://ec.europa.eu/transparency/regdoc/rep/1/2017/EN/COM-2017–751-F1-EN-MAIN-PART-1.PDF

EC (2017f). Report on the Implementation of the European Neighbourhood Policy Review (Joint Report), https://eur-lex.europa.eu/legal-content/EN/TXT/PDF/?uri=CELEX:52017JC0018&from=EN

EC (2017g). Special Eurobarometer 470 (Fieldwork October 2017), http://ec.europa.eu/commfrontoffice/publicopinion/index.cfm/ResultDoc/download/DocumentKy/81007

EC (2017h). Standard Eurobarometer 88: Public Opinion in the European Union (Fieldwork November 2017), https://ec.europa.eu/commfrontoffice/publicopinion/index.cfm/ResultDoc/download/DocumentKy/82873.

EC (2018a). Montenegro 2018 Report (Commission Staff Working Document), Strasbourg, https://ec.europa.eu/neighbourhood-enlargement/sites/near/files/20180417-montenegro-report.pdf

EC (2018b). Single Market Scoreboard Performance per Governance Tool: Infringements (Reporting Period: 12/2016 – 12/2017), http://ec.europa.eu/internal_market/scoreboard/_docs/2018/infringements/2018-scoreboard-infringements_en.pdf

EC (2018f). Whistleblower Protection: Commission Sets New, EU-Wide Rules (press release), Brussels, http://europa.eu/rapid/press-release_IP-18–3441_en.htm

ECA (European Court of Auditors) (2012). *European Union Assistance to Kosovo Related to the Rule of Law* (Special Report No. 18), www.eca.europa.eu/Lists/ECADocuments/SR12_18/SR12_18_EN.PDF

ECA (2013a). *EU Cooperation with Egypt in the Field of Governance* (Special Report No. 04), www.eca.europa.eu/Lists/ECADocuments/SR13_04/SR13_04_EN.PDF

ECA (2013b). EU Support for Governance in Egypt – "Well-Intentioned but Ineffective", say EU Auditors, http://europa.eu/rapid/press-release_ECA-13–18_en.htm

ECA (2016a). *EU Assistance for Strengthening the Public Administration in Moldova* (Special Report), www.eca.europa.eu/en/Pages/DocItem.aspx?did=37235

ECA (2016b). *EU Assistance to Ukraine* (Special Report), www.eca.europa.eu/en/Pages/DocItem.aspx?did=40134

ECA. (2017). *EU Assistance to Tunisia* (Special Report No. 3), www.eca.europa.eu/Lists/ECADocuments/SR17_3/SR_TUNISIA_EN.pdf

ECA (2018a). *EU Pre-Accession Assistance to Turkey: Only Limited Results So Far* (Special Report No. 07), www.eca.europa.eu/Lists/ECADocuments/SR18_07/SR_TURKEY_EN.pdf

ECA (2018b). Opinion No 8/2018 on the Commission's Proposal of 23 May 2018 on Amending OLAF Regulation 883/2013 as regards Cooperation with the European Public Prosecutor's Office and the Effectiveness of OLAF Investigations, www.eca.europa.eu/en/Pages/DocItem.aspx?did=48309

ECA (2018c). Opinion No 9/2018 Concerning the Proposal for a Regulation of the European Parliament and of the Council Establishing the EU Anti-Fraud Programme, www.eca.europa.eu/en/Pages/DocItem.aspx?did=48336

ECOTEC Research and Consulting (2006). *Support to Public Administrative and Judicial Capacity in Bulgaria and Romania: Thematic Evaluation Report of the European Union Phare Programme*, https://ec.europa.eu/neighbourhood-enlargement/sites/near/files/pdf/financial_assistance/phare/evaluation/zz_pajc_0536_final_version_revised_e4_en.pdf

Ederveen, S., Groot, H. L. F., & Nahuis, R. (2006). Fertile Soil for Structural Funds? A Panel Data Analysis of the Conditional Effectiveness of European Cohesion Policy. *Kyklos*, **59**(1), 17–42.

Efstathiou, K., & Wolf, G. B. (2018). Is the European Semester effective and useful? *Bruegel* (Policy Contribution Issue No. 9), http://bruegel.org/2018/06/is-the-european-semester-effective-and-useful/

Egger, P., & Winner, H. (2006). How Corruption Influences Foreign Direct Investment: A Panel Data Study. *Economic Development and Cultural Change*, 54(2), 459–486.

Eisenstadt, S. N. (1956). Political Struggle in Bureaucratic Societies. *World Politics*, **9**(01), 15–36.

Eisenstadt, S. N. (1966). *Modernization: Protest and Change*, Englewood Cliffs, NJ: Prentice-Hall.

Eleftheriadis, P. (2014). Misrule of the Few: How the Oligarchs Ruined Greece. *Foreign Affairs*, **93**(6), S 139, https://ora.ox.ac.uk/objects/uuid:ed1ecad8-9399-4cf3-a70b-bc71b8d98c5a

ELIAMEP (2013). *Hellenic Foundation for European and Foreign Policy: Evaluation of the Impact EU Budget Policies Had on the Greek Economy* (in Greek), Athens: ELIAMEP.

Emek, U., & Acar, M. (2015). Public Procurement in Infrastructure: The Case of Turkey. In A. Mungiu-Pippidi, ed., *Government Favouritism in Europe*, The ANTICORRP Project, Anticorruption Report Volume 3, Opladen: Budrich, pp. 84–96.

Emerson, M., Cenuşa, D., Kovziridze, T., & Movchan, V. (eds.) (2018). *The struggle for good governance in Eastern Europe*, Brussels: Centre for European Policy Studies, http://search.ebscohost.com/login.aspx?direct=true&scope=site&db=nlebk&db=nlabk&AN=1894537

Emerson, M., Hriptievschi, N., Kalitenko, O., Kovziridze, T., & Prohnitchi, E. (2017). *Anti-Corruption Policies in Georgia, Moldova and Ukraine*, Centrul de Resurse Juridice din Moldova (CRJM), https://crjm.org/wp-content/uploads/2017/10/Anti-corruption-policies-Georgia-Moldova-Ukraine-02.10.07.pdf

Erickson, J. L. (2013). Market Imperative meets Normative Power: Human Rights and European Arms Transfer Policy. *European Journal of International Relations*, **19**(2), 209–234.

EU Council (2004). Council Decision of 21 April 2004 Concerning the Conclusion of a Euro-Mediterranean Agreement Establishing an Association between the European Communities and their Member States, of the One Part, and the Arab Republic of Egypt, of the Other Part, http://data.europa.eu/eli/dec/2004/635/oj/eng

EU Council (2008). Council Decision of 18 February 2008 on the Principles, Priorities and Conditions Contained in the European Partnership with Bosnia and Herzegovina and Repealing Decision 2006/55/EC, https://eur-lex.europa.eu/legal-content/EN/TXT/?uri=CELEX%3A32008D0211

EU Council (2015). Council Conclusions on the Review of the European Neighbourhood Policy (press release), www.consilium.europa.eu/en/press/press-releases/2015/04/20/council-conclusions-review-european-neighbourhood-policy/#

EU Council (2016). Corruption Prevention in Respect of Members of Parliament, Judges and Prosecutors (Public), Strasbourg, www.acts-project.eu/download/117.html

EULEX (2014). Allegations of Corruption Against EULEX Are Being Pursued Vigorously, www.eulex-kosovo.eu/en/news/000528.php

Euractiv.com (2016). Court of Auditors Unable to Say how EU Money Was Spent in Ukraine, www.euractiv.com/section/europe-s-east/news/court-of-auditors-unable-to-say-how-eu-money-was-spent-in-ukraine/

Euractiv.com (2017). Romanians Stage Fresh Anti-Corruption Protests, www.euractiv.com/section/elections/news/romanians-stage-fresh-anti-corruption-protests/

Euromaidan Press (2017). EBRD: Privatisation in Ukraine Has Failed, But There Is Room for Optimism, http://euromaidanpress.com/2017/11/24/ebrd-privatisation-in-ukraine-has-failed-but-there-is-room-for-optimism/

European Anti-fraud Office (2018). *Report of the European Anti-Fraud Office* (activity report for the period June 1, 2000 – May 31, 2001), https://ec.europa.eu/anti-fraud/sites/antifraud/files/docs/body/rep_olaf_2001_en.pdf

European Commission, Directorate-General for International Cooperation and Development & Directorate-General for Neighbourhood and Enlargement Negotiations (2017). *Budget Support: Trends and Results 2017*, http://publications.europa.eu/publication/manifestation_identifier/PUB_MNAP17001ENN

European Commission for Democracy Through Law (Venice Commission) (2017). Turkey: Opinion on the Amendments to the Constitution Adopted by the Grand National Assembly on 21 January 2018 and to be Submitted to a National Referendum on 16 April 2017 [Opinion No. 875/ 2017] (opinion), Strasbourg, www.venice.coe.int/webforms/documents/default.aspx?pdffile=cdl-ad(2017)005-e

European Commission for the Efficiency of Justice (CEPEJ) (2012). Scheme for Evaluating Judical Systems 2011, https://rm.coe.int/european-commission-for-the-efficiency-of-justice-cepej-scheme-for-eva/168078bbbb

European Court of Human Rights (2018). Pending Applications Allocated to Judicial Formation, www.echr.coe.int/Documents/Stats_pending_2018_BIL.pdf

European Endowment For Democracy (2018). *Annual Report 2017*, www.democracyendowment.eu/annual-report-2017/

European Ombudsman (O'Reilly, E.) (2018). Recommendations of the European Ombudsman in the Joint Inquiry into Complaints 194/2017/EA, 334/2017/EA, and 543/2017/EA on the European Commission's Handling of Post-Mandate Employment of Former Commissioners, a Former Commission President and the Role of its "Ethics Committee", Strasbourg, www.ombudsman.europa.eu/en/recommendation/en/90956

European Parliament (2017). Committees Again Reject Blacklist of States at Risk of Money Laundering, www.europarl.europa.eu/news/en/press-room/20170503IPR73255/committees-again-reject-blacklist-of-states-at-risk-of-money-laundering

European Public Accountability Index (EuroPAM) (2018), www.europam.org/

Eurostat (2004). Report by Eurostat on the Revision of the Greek Government Deficit and Debt Figures, https://ec.europa.eu/eurostat/documents/4187653/5765001/GREECE-EN.PDF/2da4e4f6-f9f2-4848-b1a9-cb229fcabae3?version=1.0

Evans, P., & Rauch, J. E. (1999). Bureaucracy and Growth: A Cross-National Analysis of the Effects of "Weberian" State Structures on Economic Growth. *American Sociological Review*, **64**(5), 748.

Exit (2017). Instead of Europeanizing Kosovo, We Have Balkanized EULEX, https://exit.al/en/2017/11/17/instead-of-europeanizing-kosovo-we-have-balka nized-eulex/

Farmer, B. (2017). Russia Plotted to Overthrow Montenegro's Government by Assassinating Prime Minister Milo Djukanovic Last Year, According to Senior Whitehall Sources. *The Telegraph*, www.telegraph.co.uk/news/2017/02/18/rus sias-deadly-plot-overthrow-montenegros-government-assassinating/

Farrell, M. (2005). A Triumph of Realism over Idealism? Cooperation Between the European Union and Africa. *Journal of European Integration*, **27**(3), 263–283.

Fazekas, M. (2017). Red Tape, Bribery and Government Favouritism: Evidence from Europe. *Crime, Law and Social Change*, **68**(4), 403–429.

Fazekas, M., & King, L. P. (2018). Perils of Development Funding? The Tale of EU Funds and Grand Corruption in Central and Eastern Europe. *Regulation & Governance*, January 4, https://doi.org/10.1111/rego.12184

Fazekas, M., & Tóth, J. (2014). *New Ways to Measure Institutionalised Grand Corruption in Public Procurement* (technical report), Bergen.

Fazekas, M., & Tóth, J. (2017). Corruption in EU Funds? Europe-Wide Evidence on the Corruption Effect of EU Funded Public Contracting. In J. Bachtler, P. Berkowitz, S. Hardy, & T. Muravska, eds., *EU Cohesion Policy (Open Access)*, London: Routledge.

Fazekas, M., Chvalkovska, J., Skuhrovec, J., Tóth, I. J., & King, P. L. (2014). Are EU Funds a Corruption Risk? The Impact of EU Funds on Grand Corruption in Central and Eastern Europe. In A. Mungiu-Pippidi, ed., *Controlling Corruption in Europe*, [revised version in R&R in Regulation & Governance], Berlin: Barbara Budrich Publishers, https://docplayer.net/3409461-Controlling-corruption-in-europe.html

Featherstone, K., & Papadimitriou, D. (2008). *The Limits of Europeanization: Reform Capacity and Policy Conflict in Greece*, New York: Palgrave Macmillan, http://public.eblib.com/choice/publicfullrecord.aspx?p=455195

Ferguson, A. (1995). *An Essay on the History of Civil Society* (F. Oz-Salzberger, ed.), Cambridge and New York: Cambridge University Press.

Ferguson, N. (2012). *Civilization: The West and the Rest*, New York, NY: Penguin Books.

Ferguson, N. (2014). *The Great Degeneration: How Institutions Decay and Economies Die*, London: Penguin Books, reprint.

Financial Times (2016, October 18). Former PM Monti Urges Italians to Reject Renzi's Referendum, www.ft.com/content/c2911a0e-9524-11e6-a1dc-bdf 38d484582

Fischer, E. (1946). *Histoire de la Suisse: Des Origines à nos jours*, Paris: Payot.

Fischer, J. (2000). From Confederacy to Federation: Thoughts on the Finality of European Integration – Speech at the Humboldt University in Berlin, 12 May 2000. In C. Joerges, Y. Meny, & J. H. H. Weiler, eds., *What Kind of Constitution for What Kind of Polity? Responses to Joschka Fischer*, Florence: Robert Schuman Centre for Advanced Studies at the European University Institute;and Cambridge, MA:Harvard Law School, pp. 19–30.

Foreign Policy (2015). Putin's Frozen Conflicts, https://foreignpolicy.com/2015/02/13/putins-frozen-conflicts/

Freedom House (2012, April 24). Greece, https://freedomhouse.org/report/free dom-press/2012/greece

Freedom House (2017a). Freedom in the World 2018 : Montenegro, https://fre edomhouse.org/report/freedom-world/2018/montenegro

Freedom House (2017b). Freedom in the World 2018 : Turkey, https://freedom house.org/report/freedom-world/2018/turkey

Freedom House (2017c). Nations in Transit 2017: Romania, https://freedom house.org/report/nations-transit/2017/romania

Freedom House (2017d, April 27). Greece, https://freedomhouse.org/report/free dom-press/2017/greece

Freedom House (2018, April 11). Nations in Transit 2018: Moldova, https://fre edomhouse.org/report/nations-transit/2018/moldova

Freud, S. (2005). *Civilization and its Discontents* (J. Strachey, ed.), New York: W. W. Norton & Company.

Freund, C., Nucifora, A., & Rijkers, B. (2014). All in the Family: State Capture in Tunisia, World Bank, http://documents.worldbank.org/curated/en/44046146 8173649062/All-in-the-family-state-capture-in-Tunisia

Freund, D. (2017). Access all areas: When EU politicians become lobbyists. Transparency International. Available at https://transparency.eu/access-all-ar eas/, last accessed July 15, 2019.

Freyburg, T., Lavenex, S., Schimmelfennig, F., Skripka, T., & Wetzel, A. (2009). EU Promotion of Democratic Governance in the Neighbourhood. *Journal of European Public Policy*, **16**(6), 916–934.

Frye, T. (2010). Corruption and Rule of Law. In A. Åslund, S. Guriev, & A. Kuchins, eds., *Russia After the Global Economic Crisis*, Washington, DC: Peterson Institute for International Economics, pp. 79–94.

Fukuyama, F. (2006). *The End of History and the Last Man*, New York: Free Press.

Fukuyama, F. (2014). *Political Order and Political Decay: From the Industrial Revolution to the Globalization of Democracy*, reprint, New York: Macmillan USA.

Füle, Š. (European Commissioner for Enlargement and Neighbourhood Policy) (2011). Speech on the Recent Events in North Africa, Vol. SPEECH/11/130, Brussels, http://europa.eu/rapid/press-release_SPEECH-11-130_en.pdf

Gambetta, D. (1996). *The Sicilian Mafia: The Business of Private Protection*, Cambridge, MA: Harvard University Press.

Gaṭcan, I. (2015). *Corupția ca fenomen social și mecanisme anticorupție* (unpublished PhD thesis, Universitatea de Stat Din Moldova/Moldova State University), www.cnaa.md/files/theses/2016/24368/iurie_gatcan_thesis.pdf

General Framework Agreement for Peace in Bosnia and Herzegovina. Initialled in Dayton on 21 November 1995 and Signed in Paris on 14 December 1995 (2018), www.osce.org/bih/126173?download=true

Gibson, C. C., Andersson, K., Ostrom, E., & Shivakumar, S. (2005). *The Samaritan's Dilemma*, Oxford: Oxford University Press.

Gilmour, D. (2011). *The Pursuit of Italy: A History of a Land, Its Regions, and Their Peoples*, New York: Farrar, Straus and Giroux.

Ginsborg, P. (2003). *A History of Contemporary Italy: Society and Politics, 1943–1988*, New York: Palgrave Macmillan.

Girardet, R. (1978). *L'Idée coloniale en France de 1871 à 1962*, Paris: La Table Ronde.

Glaeser, E. L., La Porta, R., Lopez-de-Silanes, F., & Shleifer, A. (2004). Do Institutions Cause Growth? *Journal of Economic Growth*, 9(3), 271–303.

Gligorov, V., Holzner, M., & Landesmann, M. A. (2004). Prospects for Further (South-) Eastern EU Enlargement: From Divergence to Convergence? In M. A. Landesmann & D. K. Rosati, eds., *Shaping the New Europe: Economic Policy Challenges of European Union Enlargement*, London: Palgrave Macmillan UK, pp. 315–345.

Golden, M. A. (2000). *Political Patronage, Bureaucracy and Corruption in Postwar Italy*, (versión 1.2), Washington, DC: Ponencia presentada en la reunión anual de APSA.

Golden, M. A., & Chang, E. C. (2001). Competitive Corruption: Factional Conflict and Political Malfeasance in Postwar Italian Christian Democracy. *World Politics*, 53(4), 588–622.

Goldsmith, A. A. (1999). Africa's Overgrown State Reconsidered: Bureaucracy and Economic Growth. *World Politics*, 51(04), 520–546.

Goldstraw-White, J., & Gill, M. (2014). *Bribery, Corruption and Fraud in the Middle East* (First Middle East Bribery, Corruption and Fraud Survey), EY, www.ey.com/Publication/vwLUAssets/EY-bribery-corruption-and-fraud-in-the -me/%24FILE/EY-bribery-corruption-and-fraud-in-the-me.pdf

Gosu, A. (2018). Prizonerii lui Plahotniuc. Relațiile dintre România și Republica Moldova. *Contributors.ro*, www.contributors.ro/administratie/pri zonerii-lui-plahotniuc-rela%C8%9Biile-dintre-romania-%C8%99i-republica- moldova/

Green Cowles, M., Caporaso, J. A., & Risse, T. (2001). Europeanization and Domestic Change: Introduction. In J. A. Caporaso, M. Green Cowles, & T. Risse, eds., *Transforming Europe: Europeanization and Domestic Change*, Ithaca, NY: Cornell University Press, pp. 1–20.

Group of States Against Corruption (GRECO) (2010). *Troisième Cycle d'évaluation. rapport d'évaluation sur la Grèce: Transparence du financement des partis politiques (Thème II) (Public Greco Eval III Rep [2009] 9F Thème II)*, https://rm.coe.int/ 16806c647e

Group of States Against Corruption (2018). *Council of Europe Warns Against Reversal of Progress in Fight Against Corruption*, www.coe.int/en/web/portal/full- news/-/asset_publisher/Dgh51iCGvfbg/content/council-of-europe-warns-against -reversal-of-progress-in-fight-against-corruption

Grzymala-Busse, A. (2007). *Rebuilding Leviathan: Party Competition and State Exploitation in Post-Communist Democracies*, Cambridge: Cambridge University Press.

Güneş-Ayata, A. (1994). Roots and Trends of Clientelism in Turkey. In L. Roniger & A. Güneş-Ayata, eds., *Democracy, Clientelism, and Civil Society*, Boulder, CO: L. Rienner Publishers, pp. 51–64.

Güneş-Ayata, A. (2002). The Republican People's Party. *Turkish Studies*, 3(1), 102–121.

Gutmann, J., & Voigt, S. (2018). Judicial Independence in the EU: A Puzzle. *European Journal of Law and Economics* (ILE Working Paper Series No. 4), https://ssrn.com/abstract=2963028

Gygli, S., Haelg, F., & Sturm, J.-E. (2018). *The KOF Globalisation Index – Revisited* (KOF Working Paper No. 439).

Habib, M., & Zurawicki, L. (2002). Corruption and Foreign Direct Investment. *Journal of International Business Studies*, **33**(2), 291–307.

Hahn, J. (2015). *European Neighbourhood Policy Reloaded*, https://ec.europa.eu/c ommission/commissioners/2014–2019/hahn/blog/european-neighbourhood-policy-reloaded_en

Hammarberg, T. (2013). *Georgia in Transition: Report on the Human Rights Dimension: Background, Steps Taken and Remaining Challenges*, http://eeas .europa.eu/archives/delegations/georgia/documents/human_rights_2012/2013 0920_report_en.pdf

Hancock, G. (1992). *Lords of Poverty: The Power, Prestige, and Corruption of the International Aid Business*, New York: Atlantic Monthly Press.

Harding, L. (2016). *A Very Expensive Poison: The Definitive Story of the Murder of Litvinenko and Russia's War with the West*, London: Guardian Books and Faber and Faber.

Harnischfeger, J. (2004). Sharia and Control over Territory: Conflicts between "Settlers" and "Indigenes" in Nigeria. *African Affairs*, **103**(412), 431–452.

Haughton, T. (2007). When does the EU Make a Difference? Conditionality and the Accession Process in Central and Eastern Europe. *Political Studies Review*, **5**(2), 233–246.

Hayman, R. (2011). Budget Support and Democracy: A Twist in the Conditionality Tale. *Third World Quarterly*, **32**(4), 673–688.

Hayo, B., & Voigt, S. (2007). Explaining De Facto Judicial Independence. *International Review of Law and Economics*, **27**(3), 269–290.

Headley, J. M. (2016). *Europeanization of the World – On The Origins of Human Rights and Democracy*. Princeton: Princeton University Press.

Helble, M., Shepherd, B., & Wilson, J. S. (2009). Transparency and Regional Integration in the Asia Pacific. *World Economy*, **32**(3), 479–508.

Hermes, N., & Lensink, R. (eds.) (2001). Changing the Conditions for Development Aid: A New Paradigm? *Journal of Development Studies*, **37**(6), 1–16.

Herzfeld, T., & Weiss, C. (2003). Corruption and Legal (In)Effectiveness: An Empirical Investigation. *European Journal of Political Economy*, **19**(3), 621–632.

Heywood, A. (2014). *Global Politics*, second edition, London and New York: Palgrave Macmillan.

Holmes, S. (2002). Introduction. *East European Constitutional Review*, **11**(1–2), 90–92.

Hooper, J. (2015). *The Italians*, New York: Viking.

Horowitz, J. (2018). Italy's Populist Parties Win Approval to Form Government. *New York Times*, www.nytimes.com/2018/05/31/world/europe/italy-government -populists.html

Hout, W. (2007). Globalization: A Critical Introduction by Jan Aart Scholte (review). *Development and Change*, **38**(4), 763–764.

Howard, L. M. (2012). The Ethnocracy Trap. *Journal of Democracy*, **23**(4), 155–169.

Hulsey, J., & Stjepanović, D. (2017). Bosnia and Herzegovina: An Archetypical Example of an Ethnocracy. In A. H. Schakel, ed., *Regional and National Elections in Eastern Europe: Territoriality of the Vote in Ten Countries*, London: Palgrave Macmillan UK, pp. 35–58.

Human Development Index (HDI) / Human Development Reports (2018), http://hdr.undp.org/en/content/human-development-index-hdi

Huntington, S. P. (1968). *Political Order in Changing Societies*, New Haven, CT: Yale University Press.

Huntington, S. P. (1981). *The Soldier and the State: The Theory and Politics of Civil–Military Relations*, Cambridge, MA: Belknap Press, revised edition.

Huntington, S. P. (1993). The Clash of Civilizations? *Foreign Affairs*, **72**(3), 22.

Huther, J., & Shah, A. (2000). *Anti-Corruption Policies and Programs: A Framework for Evaluation*, World Bank.

Ianchovichina, E., Mottaghi, L., & Devarajan, S. (2015). *Inequality, Uprisings, and Conflict in the Arab World*, World Bank, http://documents.worldbank.org/curated/en/303441467992017147/Inequality-uprisings-and-conflict-in-the-Arab-World

Innes, A. (2014). The Political Economy of State Capture in Central Europe. *JCMS: Journal of Common Market Studies*, **52**(1), 88–104.

International Monetary Fund (2010). Greece: Request for Stand-By Arrangement, www.imf.org/external/pubs/ft/scr/2010/cr10111.pdf

Jackman, R. W., & Montinola, G. R. (2002). Sources of Corruption: A Cross-Country Study. *British Journal of Political Science*, **32**(01), 147–170.

Jacoby, W. (2006). *The Enlargement of the European Union and NATO: Ordering from the Menu in Central Europe*, Cambridge: Cambridge University Press.

Jacqué, J.-P. (2015). *Review of the EULEX Kosovo Mission's Implementation with a Particular Focus on the Handling of the Recent Allegations*, http://eeas.europa.eu/archives/docs/statements-eeas/docs/150331_jacque-report-annexes_en.pdf

Janský, P., Knobel, A., Meinzer, M., & Palanský, M. (2018). *Financial Secrecy Affecting the European Union: Patterns Across Member States, and What to Do About It*, Tax Justice Network, www.taxjustice.net/wp-content/uploads/2018/09/Financial-Secrecy-affecting-the-European-Union-Policy-Paper-Tax-Justice-Network.pdf

Jenkins, M. (2017). *Anti-Corruption and Transparency Provisions in Trade Agreements*, Transparency International, www.transparency.org/whatwedo/answer/anti_corruption_and_transparency_provisions_in_trade_agreements

Jensen, M. (2014). *Getting to Denmark – The Process of State Building, Establishing Rule of Law and Fighting Corruption in Denmark 1660–1900*, Vol. 2014:04, QoG Working Paper Series.

Jensen, N. M., & Malesky, E. J. (2018). Nonstate Actors and Compliance with International Agreements: An Empirical Analysis of the OECD Anti-Bribery Convention. *International Organization*, **72**(01), 33–69.

Johnsøn, J., Taxell, N., European Parliament, & Directorate-General for External Policies of the Union (2015). *Cost of Corruption in Developing Countries: How*

Effectively Is Aid being Spent? Brussels: European Parliament, http://bookshop
.europa.eu/uri?target=EUB:NOTICE:QA0215389:EN:HTML

Johnston, M. (2014). *Corruption, Contention, and Reform: The Power of Deep Democratization*, Cambridge: Cambridge University Press.

Joint Africa–EU Strategy: Roadmap 2014–2017 (2014), www.africa-eu-partnership.org/sites/default/files/documents/2014_04_01_4th_eu-africa_summit_roadmap_en.pdf

Joly, E., & Beccaria, L. (2003). *Est-ce dans ce monde-là que nous voulons vivre?* Paris: Arènes.

Jun, K. W., & Singh, H. (1999). *Some New Evidence on Determinants of Foreign Direct Investment in Developing Countries*, Washington, DC: World Bank.

Kaleniuk, D. (2018). Actually, the West's Anticorruption Policy Is Spot On. Atlantic Council, www.atlanticcouncil.org/blogs/ukrainealert/actually-the-west-s-anticorruption-policy-is-spot-on

Kalniņš, V. (2017). The World's Smallest Virtuous Circle: Estonia. In A. Mungiu-Pippidi & M. Johnston, eds., *Transitions to Good Governance: Creating Virtuous Circles of Anti-Corruption*, Cheltenham UK: Edward Elgar Publishing.

Kant, I. (1983). To Perpetual Peace: A Philosophical Sketch (1795). In T. Humphrey, trans., *Perpetual Peace, and Other Essays on Politics, History, and Morals*, Indianapolis: Hackett, pp. 109–115.

Kantorowicz, E. H. (1957). *Frederick the Second, 1194–1250*, New York: F. Ungar.

Karadag, R. (2010). Neoliberal Restructuring in Turkey: From State to Oligarchic Capitalism (MPIfG Discussion Paper), Max Planck Institute for the Study of Societies, https://econpapers.repec.org/paper/zbwmpifgd/107.htm

Karadag, R. (2013). Where Does Turkey's New Capitalism Come From? *European Journal of Sociology*, **54**(01), 147–152.

Karatnycky, A., & Motyl, A. J. (2018). How Western Anticorruption Policy Is Failing Ukraine. *Foreign Affairs*, www.foreignaffairs.com/articles/ukraine/2018-05-29/how-western-anticorruption-policy-failing-ukraine

Karklins, R. (2002). Typology of Post-Communist Corruption. *Problems of Post-Communism*, **49**(4), 22–32.

Karp, J. A., Banducci, S. A., & Bowler, S. (2003). To Know It Is to Love It? Satisfaction with Democracy in the European Union. *Comparative Political Studies*, **36**(3), 271–292.

Kartner, J., & Warner, C. M. (2015). Multi-Nationals and Corruption Systems: The Case of Siemens (ERCAS Working Paper No. 45), www.againstcorruption.eu/reports/multi-nationals-corruption-systems-siemens/

Kasekende, E., Abuka, C., & Sarr, M. (2016). Extractive Industries and Corruption: Investigating the Effectiveness of EITI as a Scrutiny Mechanism. *Resources Policy*, **48**, 117–128.

Katsios, S. (2006). The Shadow Economy and Corruption in Greece. *South-Eastern Europe Journal of Economics*, **4**(1), 61–80.

Kaufmann, D. (2004). Governance Redux: The Empirical Challenge. In M. E. Porter, K. Schwab, X. Sala-i-Martin, & A. Lopez-Carlos, eds., *The*

Global Competitiveness Report 2003–2004, Oxford: Oxford University Press [for the] World Economic Forum.

Kaufmann, D., & Kraay, A. (2002). *Growth Without Governance* (SSRN Scholarly Paper), Rochester, NY: Social Science Research Network, https://papers.ssrn.com/abstract=316861

Kaufmann, D., & Vicente, P. C. (2011). Legal Corruption. *Economics & Politics*, 23(2), 195–219.

Kaufmann, D., Kraay, A., & Mastruzzi, M. (2006). *Governance Matters V: Aggregate and Individual Governance Indicators for 1996–2005*, Washington, DC: World Bank, http://documents.worldbank.org/curated/en/265051468322155295/Governance-matters-V-aggregate-and-individual-governance-indicators-for-1996-2005

Kaufmann, D., Kraay, A., & Mastruzzi, M. (2011). The Worldwide Governance Indicators: Methodology and Analytical Issues. *Hague Journal on the Rule of Law*, 3(02), 220–246.

Kearns, I. (2018). *Collapse: Europe after the European Union*, London: Biteback Publishing.

Killick, T. (2004). Politics, Evidence and the New Aid Agenda. *Development Policy Review*, 22(1), 5–29.

Kipling, R. (1998). The White Man's Burden (1899). *Peace Review*, 10(3), 311–312.

Kirişci, K. (2011). Reforming Turkey's Asylum Policy: Is It Europeanization, UNHCR-ization or ECHR-ization? Paper presented at KFG Conference "Faraway, So Close? Reaching beyond the Pro/Contra Controversy on Turkey's EU Accession," June 2–4, Istanbul.

Kleemann, K. (2010). The European Neighbourhood Policy – A Reality Check (ERCAS Working Paper No. 16), www.againstcorruption.eu/reports/multi-nationals-corruption-systems-siemens/

Knack, S. (1999). *Aid Dependence and the Quality of Governance: A Cross-Country Empirical Analysis* (SSRN Scholarly Paper), Rochester, NY: Social Science Research Network.

Knack, S. (2001). Aid Dependence and the Quality of Governance: Cross-Country Empirical Tests. *Southern Economic Journal*, 68(2), 310–329.

Knaus, G. (2005). *Islamic Calvinists: Change and Conservatism in Central Anatolia*, Berlin, Brussels and Istanbul: European Stability Initiative, www.esiweb.org/pdf/esi_document_id_69.pdf

Knaus, G., & Martin, F. (2003). Travails of the European Raj: Lessons from Bosnia and Herzegovina. *Journal of Democracy*, 14(3), 60–74.

Koch, A. (2016). These Spanish Activists have Taken Punishing Bankers into Their Own Hands, *The Nation*, www.thenation.com/article/simona-levi/

Koch, S. (2015). A Typology of Political Conditionality Beyond Aid: Conceptual Horizons Based on Lessons from the European Union. *World Development*, 75, 97–108.

Kochenov, D., & Pech, L. (2015). Monitoring and Enforcement of the Rule of Law in the EU: Rhetoric and Reality. *European Constitutional Law Review*, 11(3), 512–540.

Kochenov, D., & Pech, L. (2016). Better Late than Never? On the European Commission's Rule of Law Framework and its First Activation. *JCMS: Journal of Common Market Studies*, **54**(5), 1062–1074.

Konończuk, W. (2015). Oligarchs after the Maidan: The Old System in a "New" Ukraine. OSW (Ośrodek Studiów Wschodnich / Centre for Eastern Studies), www.osw.waw.pl/en/publikacje/osw-commentary/2015-02-16/oligarchs-after -maidan-old-system-a-new-ukraine

Kosovo Law Institute (2017). KLI: No High Profile Individuals were Sentenced with Effective Imprisonment for Corruption, Solution – Vetting, http://kli-ks.org /en/kli-no-high-profile-individuals-were-sentenced-with-effective-imprisonment -for-corruption-solution-vetting/

Kossow, N., & Kukutschka, R. M. B. (2017). Civil Society and Online Connectivity: Controlling Corruption on the Net? *Crime, Law and Social Change*, September, 1–18.

Kristeva, J. (2000). Europe Divided: Politics, Ethics, Religion. In *Crisis of the European Subject*, New York: Other Press, pp. 114–115.

Krueger, A. O. (1974). The Political Economy of the Rent-Seeking Society. *American Economic Review*, **64**(3), 291–303.

Kubicek, P. J. (2003). International Norms, the European Union, and Democratization: Tentative Theory and Evidence. In P. Kubicek, ed., *The European Union and Democratization*, London and New York: Routledge, pp. 13–41.

Kupatadze, A. (2016). Georgia's Break with the Past. *Journal of Democracy*, **27**(1), 110–123.

La Porta, R., Lopez-de-Silanes, F., Shleifer, A., & Vishny, R. W. (1998). Law and Finance. *Journal of Political Economy*, **106**(6), 1113–1155.

Laar, M. (2008). Leading a Successful Transition: The Estonian Miracle. *European View*, **7**(1), 67–74.

Ladrech, R. (1994). Europeanization of Domestic Politics and Institutions: The Case of France. *Journal of Common Market Studies*, **32**(1), 69–88.

Lannon, E. (2015). More for More or Less for Less: From the Rhetoric to the Implementation of European Neighbourhood Instrument in the Context of the 2015 ENP review. In *Mediterranean Yearbook*, Barcelona: IEMed, pp. 220–224.

Lavenex, S., & Schimmelfennig, F. (2011). EU Democracy Promotion in the Neighbourhood: From Leverage to Governance? *Democratization*, **18**(4), 885–909.

Ledeneva, A. V. (2006). *How Russia Really Works: The Informal Practices that Shaped Post-Soviet Politics and Business*, Ithaca, NY: Cornell University Press.

Leff, N. H. (1964). Economic Development Through Bureaucratic Corruption. *American Behavioral Scientist*, **8**(3), 8–14.

Lejárraga, I., & Shepherd, B. (2013). Quantitative Evidence on Transparency in Regional Trade Agreements (OECD Policy Paper No. 153), www.oecd-ilibrary.org/trade/quantitative-evidence-on-transparency-in-regional-trade -agreements_5k450q9v2mg5-en

Le Monde. (2018). La Fausse Mort de Babtchenko, une aubaine pour le pouvoir russe, www.lemonde.fr/international/article/2018/05/31/la-fausse-mort-de-babtchenko-une-aubaine-pour-le-pouvoir-russe_5307607_3210.html

Lerner, D. (1958). *The Passing of Traditional Society : Modernizing the Middle East*, New York: Free Press, https://trove.nla.gov.au/version/45410724

Levcenko, M. (2016, February 25). Vlad Plahotniuc: Moldova's Man in the Shadows, Open Democracy, www.opendemocracy.net/od-russia/maria-levcenco/vlad-plahotniuc-moldova-s-man-in-shadows

Levitz, P., & Pop-Eleches, G. (2010). Why No Backsliding? The European Union's Impact on Democracy and Governance Before and After Accession. *Comparative Political Studies*, 43(4), 457–485.

Leys, C. (1965). What Is the Problem About Corruption? *Journal of Modern African Studies*, 3(02), 215.

Liargovas, P., Petropoulos, S., Tzifakis, N., & Huliaras, A. (2016). *Beyond "Absorption": The Impact of EU Structural Funds in Greece*, Berlin: Konrad Adenauer Stiftung, www.kas.de/c/document_library/get_file?uuid=03cc85bb-4f7a-36f3-84ee-f12897eebd6e&groupId=252038

Linz, J. J., & Stepan, A. C. (1996). *Problems of Democratic Transition and Consolidation: Southern Europe, South America, and Post-Communist Europe*, Baltimore, MD: Johns Hopkins University Press.

Lipset, S. M. (1960). *Political Man: The Social Bases of Politics*, Garden City, NY: Doubleday, http://archive.org/details/politicalmansoci00inlips

Lofranco, Z. T. (2014). Report on Bosnia and Herzegovina (ANTICORRP [Anticorruption Policies Revisited: Global Trends and European Responses to the Challenge of Corruption] policy paper), http://anticorrp.eu/publications/d4-1-report-on-bosnia-and-herzegovina/

Lopez, A., Rodriguez, M., & Valentini, M. (2017). How Does Political Finance Regulation Influence Control of Corruption? Improving Good Governance in Latin America (ERCAS Working Paper No. 50), www.againstcorruption.eu/publications/how-does-political-finance-regulation-influence-control-of-corruption-improving-governance-in-latin-america/

Lough, J. (2018). Ukraine Must Focus More on Reducing Opportunities for Corruption (expert comment), Chatham House, www.chathamhouse.org//no de/37306

Loughlin, J. (2001). *Subnational Democracy in the European Union: Challenges and Opportunities*, Oxford and New York: Oxford University Press.

Loughlin, J. (2004). The "Transformation" of Governance: New Directions in Policy and Politics. *Australian Journal of Politics and History*, 50 (1), 8–22.

Louis, J. (2017). Egypt: The Failed Transition. In A. Mungiu-Pippidi & J. Warkotsch, eds., *Beyond the Panama Papers: The Performance of EU Good Governance Promotion*, The ANTICORRP Project, Anticorruption Report Volume 4, Opladen, Berlin, and Toronto: Barbara Budrich Publishers, 89–104.

Lyle, R. (1999). Ukraine Under Corruption Spotlight. *Ukrainian Weekly*, 67(10), www.ukrweekly.com/old/archive/1999/109905.shtml

Macdonald, G., & Waggoner, L. (2018). Dashed Hopes and Extremism in Tunisia. *Journal of Democracy*, 29(1), 126–140.

MacFarlane, A. (1978). The Origins of English Individualism: Some Surprises. *Theory and Society*, 6(2), 255–277.

Madar Research & Development (MRD) (2012). Arab ICT Use and Social Networks Adoption: Report, www.unapcict.org/ecohub/arab-ict-use-and-social-networks-adoption-report/at_download/attachment1

Magalhães, P. C. (1999). The Politics of Judicial Reform in Eastern Europe. *Comparative Politics*, 32(1), 43–62.

Mancini, P. (2009). *Elogio della lottizzazione: La via italiana al pluralismo*, Rome: GLF editori Laterza.

Manners, I. (2002). Normative Power Europe: A Contradiction in Terms? *JCMS: Journal of Common Market Studies*, 40(2), 235–258.

Manners, I. (2008). The Normative Ethics of the European Union. *International Affairs*, 84(1), 45–60.

Marzouk, L. (2009). Protesters Overturn 25 EULEX Cars. *Balkan Insight*, www.balkaninsight.com/en/article/protesters-overturn-25-eulex-cars

Mauro, P. (1995). Corruption and Growth. *Quarterly Journal of Economics*, 110(3), 681–712.

Mbaku, J. M. (1996). Bureaucratic Corruption in Africa: The Futility of Cleanups. *Cato Journal*, 16(1), 17.

Mbaye, H. A. D. (2001). Why National States Comply with Supranational Law. *European Union Politics*, 2(3), 259–281.

McLean, N. M. (2012). Cross-National Patterns in FCPA Enforcement. *Yale Law Journal*, www.yalelawjournal.org/note/cross-national-patterns-in-fcpa-enforcement

McMullan, M. (1961). A Theory of Corruption. *Sociological Review*, 9(2), 181–201.

Médard, J.-F. (2016). L'État en Afrique ne fonctionne pas . . . . In G. Courade, ed., *L'Afrique des idées reçues*, Paris: Belin.

Medina, L., & Schneider, F. (2017). *Shadow Economies Around the World: New Results for 158 Countries Over 1991–2015* (SSRN Scholarly Paper), Rochester, NY: Social Science Research Network, https://papers.ssrn.com/abstract=2965972

Mendelski, M. (2012). EU-Driven Judicial Reforms in Romania: A Success Story? *East European Politics*, 28(1), 23–42.

Mény, Y. (1996). "Fin de Siècle" Corruption: Change, Crisis and Shifting Values. *International Social Science Journal*, 48(149), 309–320.

Meyer-Sahling, J.-H. (2011). The Durability of EU Civil Service Policy in Central and Eastern Europe After Accession. *Governance*, 24(2), 231–260.

Meyer-Sahling, J.-H., & Veen, T. (2012). Governing the Post-Communist State: Government Alternation and Senior Civil Service Politicisation in Central and Eastern Europe. *East European Politics*, 28(1), 4–22.

Michel, L. (2006). *The European Consensus on Development*, Luxembourg: Office for Official Publications of the European Communities.

Migdal, J. S. (1988). *Strong Societies and Weak States: State–Society Relations and State Capabilities in the Third World*, Princeton, NJ: Princeton University Press.

Milio, S. (2007). Can Administrative Capacity Explain Differences in Regional Performances? Evidence from Structural Funds Implementation in Southern Italy. *Regional Studies*, 41(4), 429–442.

Mill, J. S. (1984). A Few Words on Non-Intervention (1859). *Foreign Policy Perspectives*, 8, www.libertarian.co.uk/lapubs/forep/forep008.pdf

Millard, F. (1999). *Polish Politics and Society*, London and New York: Routledge.
Miller, W. L., Koshechkina, T. Y., & Grödeland, A. B. (2001). *A Culture of Corruption? Coping with Government in Post-Communist Europe*, Budapest: CEU Press.
Mitsopoulos, M., & Pelagidis, T. (2007). Rent-Seeking and Ex Post Acceptance of Reforms in Higher Education. *Journal of Economic Policy Reform*, **10**(3), 177–192.
Mitsopoulos, M., & Pelagidis, T. (2009). Vikings in Greece: Kleptocratic Interest Groups in a Closed, Rent-Seeking Economy. *Cato Journal*, **29**(3), 399–416.
Mitsopoulos, M., & Pelagidis, T. K. (2011). *Understanding the Crisis in Greece: From Boom to Bust*, Basingstoke and New York: Palgrave Macmillan.
Momigliano, A. (1975). *Alien Wisdom: The Limits of Hellenization*, Cambridge: Cambridge University Press.
Monnier, V. (2002). *Bonaparte et la Suisse*. Geneva: University of Geneva.
Moore, B., Jr. (1966). *Social Origins of Dictatorship and Democracy: Lord and Peasant in the Making of the Modern World*, Boston: Beacon Press.
Moore, Jr., B. (1978). *Injustice: The Social Bases of Obedience and Revolt*, White Plains, NY: M. E. Sharpe.
Moravcsik, A. (2009). Europe: The Quiet Superpower. *French Politics*, **7**(3), 403–422.
Morlino, L., & Tarchi, M. (1996). The Dissatisfied Society: The Roots of Political Change in Italy. *European Journal of Political Research*, **30**(1), 41–63.
Mouzelis, N. P. (1986). *Politics in the Semi-Periphery: Early Parliamentarism and Late Industrialisation in the Balkans and South America*, Basingstoke: Macmillan.
Mulgan, R. (2012). Aristotle on Legality and Corruption. In M. Barcham, B. Hindess, & P. Larmour, eds., *Corruption: Expanding the Focus*, Canberra: Australian National University Press, www.jstor.org/stable/j.ctt24hbwc.6
Mungiu-Pippidi, A. (2006a). Corruption: Diagnosis and Treatment. *Journal of Democracy*, **17**(3), 86–99.
Mungiu-Pippidi, A. (2006b). Democratization Without Decommunization in the Balkans. *Orbis*, **50**(4), 641–655.
Mungiu-Pippidi, A. (2007). Is East-Central Europe Backsliding? EU Accession is No "End of History." *Journal of Democracy*, **18**(4), 8–16.
Mungiu-Pippidi, A. (2011). A House of Cards? Building the Rule of Law in the Balkans. In M. Abramowitz & J. Rupnik, eds., *The Western Balkans and the EU: "The Hour of Europe"*, Paris: Institute for Security Studies, pp. 145–163.
Mungiu-Pippidi, A. (2012). Corruption: Diagnosis and Treatment. *Journal of Democracy*, **17**(3), 86–99.
Mungiu-Pippidi, A. (2013). Controlling Corruption through Collective Action. *Journal of Democracy*, **24**(1), 101–115.
Mungiu-Pippidi, A. (ed.) (2015a). *Government Favouritism in Europe*, The ANTICORRP Project, Anticorruption Report Volume 3, Opladen: Budrich.
Mungiu-Pippidi, A. (2015b). *The Quest for Good Governance: How Societies Develop Control of Corruption*, Cambridge and New York: Cambridge University Press.
Mungiu-Pippidi, A. (2017). *Seven Steps to Evidence-Based Anti-Corruption: A Roadmap*, Stockholm: EBA.
Mungiu-Pippidi, A. (2018a). *Anti-Corruption Provisions in EU Free Trade and Investment Agreements Delivering on Clean Trade* (workshop report), www

.europarl.europa.eu/RegData/etudes/STUD/2018/603867/EXPO_STU(2018)603867_EN.pdf

Mungiu-Pippidi, A. (2018b). Explaining Eastern Europe: Romania's Italian-Style Anticorruption Populism. *Journal of Democracy*, **29**(3), 104–116.

Mungiu-Pippidi, A., & Dadašov, R. (2016). Measuring Control of Corruption by a New Index of Public Integrity. *European Journal on Criminal Policy and Research*, **22**(3), 415–438.

Mungiu-Pippidi, A., & Dadašov, R. (2017). When Do Anticorruption Laws Matter? The Evidence on Public Integrity Enabling Contexts. *Crime, Law and Social Change*, **68**(4), 387–402.

Mungiu-Pippidi, A., & Hartmann, T. (n.d.). Corruption and Development. *Oxford Research Encyclopedia of Economics and Finance*.

Mungiu-Pippidi, A., & Johnston, M. (eds.) (2017). *Transitions to Good Governance: Creating Virtuous Circles of Anti-Corruption*, Cheltenham, UK: Edward Elgar Publishing.

Mungiu-Pippidi, A., & Krastev, I. (eds.) (2004). *Nationalism after Communism: Lessons Learned*, English edition, Budapest and New York: Central European University Press.

Mungiu-Pippidi, A., & Munteanu, I. (2009). Moldova's "Twitter Revolution." *Journal of Democracy*, **20**(3), 136–142.

Mungiu-Pippidi, A., & Warkotsch, J. (eds.) (2017). *Beyond the Panama Papers: The Performance of EU Good Governance Promotion*, The ANTICORRP Project, Anticorruption Report Volume 4, Opladen, Berlin, and Toronto: Barbara Budrich Publishers.

Mungiu-Pippidi, A., Dadašov, R., Fazekas, M., et al. (2016). *Public Integrity and Trust in Europe*, European Research Centre for Anti-Corruption and State-Building (ERCAS), Hertie School of Governance (commissioned by the Dutch Ministry of the Interior and Kingdom Relations [BZK]), https://doc player.net/29157008-Public-integrity-and-trust-in-europe.html

Mungiu-Pippidi, A., Dadašov, R., Alvaro Pachon, S. N., & Norman, C. (2017). For a More Effective Link between EU Funds and Good Governance (ANTICORRP [Anticorruption Policies Revisited: Global Trends and European Responses to the Challenge of Corruption] policy paper drawing on previous studies with recommendations on governance conditionality), http:// anticorrp.eu/publications/for-a-more-effective-link-between-eu-funds-and-goo d-governance/

Mungiu-Pippidi, A., & Kukutschka, R. M. B. (2018). Can a Civilization Know its Own Institutional Decline? A Tale of Indicators. In H. Anheier, M. Haber, & M. Kayser, eds., *Governance Indicators: Approaches, Progress, Promise*, Oxford: Oxford University Press.

Murphy, C. (2007). *Are We Rome? The Fall of an Empire and the Fate of America*, Boston: Houghton Mifflin Co.

Murphy, J., & Albu, O. B. (2018). The Politics of Transnational Accountability Policies and the (Re)Construction of Corruption: The Case of Tunisia, Transparency International and the World Bank. *Accounting Forum*, **42**(1), 32–46.

Nilekani, N. (2018). Data to the People. *Foreign Affairs*, September/October, www.foreignaffairs.com/articles/asia/2018–08-13/data-people

Nisbet, R. A. (1992). *Social Change and History: Aspects of the Western Theory of Development*, New York: Oxford University Press.

NORAD (2011). *Contextual Choices in Fighting Corruption: Lessons Learned*, Norwegian Agency for Development Cooperation.

North, D. (1993). *The New Institutional Economics and Development*, St. Louis: EconWPA, http://econwpa.repec.org/eps/eh/papers/9309/9309002.pdf

North, D. C. (1991). Institutions. *Journal of Economic Perspectives*, 5(1), 97–112.

North, D. C., Wallis, J. J., Webb, S. B., & Weingast, B. R. (eds.) (2013), *In the Shadow of Violence: Politics, Economics, and the Problem of Development*, Cambridge: Cambridge University Press.

North, D. C., Wallis, J. J., & Weingast, B. R. (2009). *Violence and Social Orders: A Conceptual Framework for Interpreting Recorded Human History*, Cambridge and New York: Cambridge University Press.

Noutcheva, G. (2015). Institutional Governance of European Neighbourhood Policy in the Wake of the Arab Spring. *Journal of European Integration*, 37(1), 19–36.

Nye, J. S. (1967). Corruption and Political Development: A Cost-Benefit Analysis. *American Political Science Review*, 61(2), 417–427.

OCCRP (2014). *The Russian Laundromat*, www.reportingproject.net/therussian laundromat/russian-laundromat.php

O'Dwyer, C. (2006). *Runaway State-Building: Patronage Politics and Democratic Development*, Baltimore, MD: Johns Hopkins University Press.

OECD (2013). *Integrity Scan of Tunisia*, OECD CleanGovBiz, www.oecd.org/cl eangovbiz/Tunisia-Integrity-ScanEN.pdf

OECD (2016). *The Principles of Public Administration: Kosovo* (monitoring report), www.sigmaweb.org/publications/Monitoring-Report-2016-Kosovo.pdf

OECD (2017). *Data on Enforcement of the Anti-Bribery Convention*, www.oecd.org /corruption/data-on-enforcement-of-the-anti-bribery-convention.htm

OECD (2018a). *OECD Convention on Combating Bribery of Foreign Public Officials in International Business Transactions*, www.oecd.org/daf/anti-bribery/oecdanti briberyconvention.htm

OECD. (2018b). *QWIDS – Query Wizard for International Development Statistics*, https://stats.oecd.org/qwids/

Offe, C. (2015). *Europe entrapped*, Cambridge ; Malden, MA: Polity.

Office of the High Representative for Implementation of the Peace Agreement on Bosnia and Herzegovina to the Secretary-General of the United Nations (2010). *37th Report*, www.ohr.int/?p=34492

Osborne, S. (2017). Turkey's Erdogan Warns Europeans "Will Not Walk Safely on the Streets" if Diplomatic Row Continues. *The Independent*, www .independent.co.uk/news/world/europe/turkey-erdogan-germany-netherlands -warning-europeans-not-walk-safely-a7642941.html

Osterhammel, J. (2014). *The Transformation of the World: A Global History of the Nineteenth Century* (P. Camiller, trans.), Princeton, NJ: Princeton University Press.

Ostrom, E. (2013). Overcoming the Samaritan's Dilemma in Development Aid. In J. Y. Lin & C. P. Sepulveda, eds., *Annual World Bank Conference on*

Development Economics 2011: Development Challenges in a Post-Crisis World, World Bank Publications.

Paris, R. (1997). Peacebuilding and the Limits of Liberal Internationalism. *International Security*, 22(2), 54–89.

Paris Declaration on Aid Effectiveness (2005) and Accra Agenda for Action (2008) (2009), www.oecd.org/dac/effectiveness/34428351.pdf

Parsons, T. (1997) *Introduction to Max Weber: The Theory of Social and Economic Organization*, New York: Free Press.

Parsons, T. (1951). *The Social System*, Glencoe, IL: Free Press, http://archive.org /details/socialsystem00pars

Pasquino, G. (2006). Studying the Never Ending Italian Transition. *European Political Science*, 5(4), 423–433.

Passas, N. (2010). Anti-Corruption Agencies and the Need for Strategic Approaches: A Preface to this Special Issue. *Crime, Law and Social Change*, 53(1), 1–3.

Pech, L. (2012). *Promoting the Rule of Law Abroad: On the EU's Limited Contribution to the Shaping of an International Understanding of the Rule of Law* (SSRN Scholarly Paper), Rochester, NY: Social Science Research Network, https://papers.ssrn.com/abstract=2598953

Persson, A., & Rothstein, B. (2015). It's My Money: Why Big Government May Be Good Government. *Comparative Politics*, 47(2), 231–249.

Persson, T., & Tabellini, G. E. (2003). *The Economic Effects of Constitutions*, Cambridge, MA: MIT Press.

Phinnemore, D. (ed.) (2006). *The EU and Romania: Accession and Beyond*, London: Federal Trust.

Piattoni, S. (ed.) (2001). *Clientelism, Interests, and Democratic Representation: The European Experience in Historical and Comparative Perspective*, Cambridge: Cambridge University Press.

Piccio, D. (2014). Tackling Corruption, Finally? How Domestic and Supranational Factors Have Led to Incremental Policy Change in Italy. In J. Mendilow & I. Peleg, eds., *Corruption in the Contemporary World: Theory, Practice, and Hotspots*, Lanham, MD: Lexington Books.

Pieth, M. (1997). International Cooperation to Combat Corruption. In K. A. Elliot, ed., *Corruption and the Global Economy*, Washington, DC, pp. 119–131.

Piga, G. (2001). *Derivatives and Public Debt Management*, Zurich: International Securities Market Association (ISMA), www.icmagroup.org/ assets/documents/Derivatives%20and%20Public%20Debt %20Manageme nt.pdf

Plato (2018). *The Republic* (B. Jowett, trans.), New York: Clydesdale Press.

Podumljak, M. (2016). *The Impact of EU Conditionality on Corruption Control and Governance in Bosnia and Herzegovina*, http://anticorrp.eu/publications/the-impact-of-eu-conditionality-on-corruption-control-and-governance-in-bosnia -and-herzegovina/

Podumljak, M., & David-Barrett, E. (2015). *The Public Procurement of Construction Works: The Case of Croatia*, http://anticorrp.eu/publications/report-on-croatia/

Politico (2017, May 18). Spain's Never-Ending Corruption Problem, www
.politico.eu/article/spain-corruption-pp-rajoy-never-ending-problem-graft-
ignacio-gonzalez/

Politico (2018, February 12). The Rise and Fall of Mikheil Saakashvili, www
.politico.eu/article/the-rise-and-fall-of-mikheil-saakashvili/

Politico (2019, February 22). MEPs Help Campaign of Moldovan Convicted in
$1B Fraud, www.politico.eu/article/ilan-shor-fulvio-martusciello-barbara-
kappel-richard-milsom-meps-help-campaign-of-moldovan-convicted-in-1-bil
lion-fraud/

Portela, C., & Orbie, J. (2014). Sanctions Under the EU Generalised System of
Preferences and Foreign Policy: Coherence by Accident? *Contemporary Politics*,
20(1), 63–76.

Power Distance Index – Clearly Cultural (2018), http://clearlycultural.com/geert-
hofstede-cultural-dimensions/power-distance-index/

Pridham, G. (2003). *EU Enlargement and Consolidating Democracy in Post-Communist
States – Formality and Reality* (SSRN Scholarly Paper), Rochester, NY: Social
Science Research Network, https://papers.ssrn.com/abstract=369691

Prodi, R. (2000). "2000–2005: Shaping the New Europe": Speech to the
European Parliament. Speech/00/41, Strasbourg, http://europa.eu/rapid/press-
release_SPEECH-00–41_en.htm

Pronk, J. P. (2001). Aid as a Catalyst. *Development and Change*, **32**(4), 611–629.

Proposal for a Thematic Evaluation on IPA Support to Fight Against Corruption
Evaluation Mandate (2018), https://ec.europa.eu/neighbourhood-enlargement
/sites/near/files/pdf/financial_assistance/phare/evaluation/2014/20140822-final
-evaluation-mandate-corruption.pdf.pdf

Putnam, R. D., Leonardi, R., & Nanetti, R. (1994). *Making Democracy
Work: Civic Traditions in Modern Italy*, Princeton, NJ: Princeton University
Press.

Radaelli, C. M. (2003). The Europeanization of Public Policy. In C. M. Radaelli
& K. Featherstone, eds., *The Politics of Europeanization*, Oxford: Oxford
University Press, www.oxfordscholarship.com/view/10.1093/0199252092
.001.0001/acprof-9780199252091

Radaelli, C. M. (2006). Europeanization: Solution or Problem? In M. Cini &
A. K. Bourne, eds., *Palgrave Advances in European Union Studies*, London:
Palgrave Macmillan UK, pp. 56–76.

Radio Free Europe (2016). Vlad Plahotniuc, om de afaceri, politician – o schiță de
portret [Vlad Plahotniuc, Businessman, Ex-Politician. A Portrait Sketch],
https://moldova.europalibera.org/a/27329569.html

Rajan, R. G., & Zingales, L. (2003). *Saving Capitalism from the Capitalists:
Unleashing the Power of Financial Markets to Create Wealth and Spread
Opportunity*, London: Random House Business Books.

Rand, A. (1957). *Atlas Shrugged*, New York: Random House.

Rehn, O. (EU Commissioner for Enlargement) (2008). Europe's Smart Power in
its Region and the World (speech at the European Studies Centre, St Antony's
College, University of Oxford), http://europa.eu/rapid/press-release_SPEEC
H-08–222_en.htm

Reporters Without Borders (2018). Montenegro, https://rsf.org/en/montenegro

Reuters (2009). FACTBOX – Seven Scandals from Bulgaria, www.reuters.com /article/bulgaria-scandals-idUSLH84274420090630

Reuters (2017). Ukraine Prosecutors Open Case as Inter-Agency Conflict Escalates, www.reuters.com/article/us-ukraine-corruption/ukraine-prosecutors-open-case-as-inter-agency-conflict-escalates-idUSKBN1DH1NE

Reuters (2018). Ukraine Finance Minister Says was Told to Back Corruption or Quit, www.reuters.com/article/us-ukraine-finmin-dismissal-idUSKCN1J213I

Rodrik, D. (2006). Goodbye Washington Consensus, Hello Washington Confusion? A Review of the World Bank's "Economic Growth in the 1990s: Learning from a Decade of Reform." *Journal of Economic Literature*, **44**(4), 973–987.

Rodrik, D. (2010). Who Lost Europe? *International Economy*, Summer, www .international-economy.com/TIE_Su10_Rodrik.pdf

Rodrik, D. (2011). Ergenekon and Sledgehammer: Building or Undermining the Rule of Law? *Turkish Political Quarterly*, 10(1), 99–109.

Rodrik, D., & Subramanian, A. (2003). The Primacy of Institutions. *Finance and Development*, **40**, 31–34.

Rodrik, D., Subramanian, A., & Trebbi, F. (2004). Institutions Rule: The Primacy of Institutions Over Geography and Integration in Economic Development. *Journal of Economic Growth*, 9(2), 131–165.

Romanian Academic Society (2018). Harta corupției județene [Map of County Corruption], www.romaniacurata.ro/harta-coruptiei/

Rose-Ackerman, S. (1998). Corruption and Development. In *Annual World Bank Conference on Development Economics 1997*, Washington, DC: World Bank, pp. 35–57.

Rosecrance, R. (1998). The European Union: A New Type of International Actor. In J. Zielonka, ed., *Paradoxes of European Foreign Policy*, The Hague: Kluwer, pp. 15–25.

Rostow, W. W. (1959). The Stages of Economic Growth. *The Economic History Review*, **12**(1), 1–16.

Rothstein, B. (2011). Anti-Corruption: The Indirect "Big Bang" Approach. *ResearchGate*, 18(2), 228–250.

Rothstein, B., & Tannenberg, M. (2015). Making Development Work – The Quality of Government Approach. *SSRN Electronic Journal*, www.ssrn.com /abstract=3023883

Rothstein, B., & Teorell, J. (2012). Defining and Measuring Quality of Government. In S. Holmberg & B. Rothstein, eds., *Good Government: The Relevance of Political Science*, Cheltenham, UK: Edward Elgar.

Ryan, N. J. (1967). *The Making of Modern Malaysia: A History from Earliest Times to 1966*, third edition, Kuala Lumpur : Oxford University Press.

Sampson, S. (2010). The Anti-Corruption Industry: From Movement to Institution. *Global Crime*, 11(2), 261–278.

Sandweiss, M. A., Milner, C. A., & O'Connor, C. A. (1994). *The Oxford History of the American West*, New York and Oxford: Oxford University Press.

Savona, E. U. (1995). Beyond Criminal Law in Devising Anticorruption Policies: Lessons from the Italian Experience. *European Journal on Criminal Policy and Research*, 3(2), 21–37.

Sberna, S., & Vannucci, A. (2013). "It's the Politics, Stupid!" The Politicization of Anti-Corruption in Italy. *Crime, Law and Social Change*, 60(5), 565–593.

Schiltz, C. B. (2009). Rumänische Ministerin: Ex-Glamour-Girl verwaltet jetzt EU-Milliarden, *Die Welt*, www.welt.de/politik/ausland/article5688791/Ex-Glamour-Girl-verwaltet-jetzt-EU-Milliarden.html

Schimmelfennig, F., & Scholtz, H. (2008). EU Democracy Promotion in the European Neighbourhood: Political Conditionality, Economic Development and Transnational Exchange. *European Union Politics*, 9(2), 187–215.

Schimmelfennig, F., & Sedelmeier, U. (2004). Governance by Conditionality: EU Rule Transfer to the Candidate Countries of Central and Eastern Europe. *Journal of European Public Policy*, 11(4), 661–679.

Schmidt, V. A. (2013). Democracy and Legitimacy in the European Union Revisited: Input, Output and "Throughput." *Political Studies*, 61(1), 2–22.

Schneider, F. (2010). *The Influence of the Economic Crisis on the Shadow Economy in Germany, Greece and the Other OECD Countries in 2010: What Can Be Done?* Linz: Johannes Kepler University of Linz, http://citeseerx.ist.psu.edu/viewdoc/download?doi=10.1.1.709.3857&rep=rep1&type=pdf

Scott, J. C. (1969). The Analysis of Corruption in Developing Nations. *Comparative Studies in Society and History*, 11(03), 315.

Segal, D. (2018). Where in the World is Denmark's $2 Billion? *New York Times*, www.nytimes.com/2018/10/05/business/denmark-skat-tax-scandal.html

Sforza, C. (1948). Italy, the Marshall Plan and the "Third Force." *Foreign Affairs* (April), www.foreignaffairs.com/articles/italy/1948-04-01/italy-marshall-plan-and-third-force

Shelley, L. (1998). Organized Crime and Corruption in Ukraine: Impediments to the Development of a Free Market Economy. *Demokratizatsiya*, 6(4), 648–63.

Shleifer, A., & Vishny, R. W. (1993). Corruption. *Quarterly Journal of Economics*, 108(3), 599–617.

Shore, C. (2005). Culture and Corruption in the EU: Reflections on Fraud, Nepotism and Cronyism in the European Commission. In D. Haller & C. Shore, eds., *Corruption: Anthropological Perspectives*, London and Ann Arbor, MI: Pluto.

Siebenhaar, H.-P. (2010). WAZ-Gruppe: Konzernchef Hombach sagt dem Balkan ade. *Handelsblat*, www.handelsblatt.com/unternehmen/it-medien/waz-gruppe-konzernchef-hombach-sagt-dem-balkan-ade/3505254.html

SIGMA (2016). *The Principles of Public Administration: Kosovo* (Monitoring Report), http://sigmaweb.org/publications/Monitoring-Report-2016-Kosovo.pdf

Smith, A. (2007). *An Inquiry into the Nature and Causes of the Wealth of Nations*, Petersfield: Harriman House.

Smith, K. E. (1998). The Use of Political Conditionality in the EU's Relations with Third Countries: How Effective? *European Foreign Affairs Review*, 3, 253–274.

Soloviev, V. (2017, July 21). An Ideal Conflict on the Dniester. *OpenDemocracy*, www.opendemocracy.net/od-russia/vladimir-soloviev/ideal-conflict-on-dniester

Somerville, K. (2017). *Africa's Long Road Since Independence: The Many Histories of a Continent*, London: Penguin.

Sotiropoulos, D. A. (2004). Southern European Public Bureaucracies in Comparative Perspective. *West European Politics*, 27(3), 405–422.

Sotiropoulos, D. A. (2018). *The Backsliding of Democracy in Today's Greece*, Bonn: Friedrich-Ebert-Stiftung, http://library.fes.de/pdf-files/bueros/athen/15078.pdf

Soyaltin, D. (2017). Public Sector Reforms to Fight Corruption in Turkey: A Case of Failed Europeanization? *Turkish Studies*, 18(3), 439–458.

Spanou, C. (1996). Penelope's Suitors: Administrative Modernisation and Party Competition in Greece. *West European Politics*, 19(1), 97–124.

Spanou, C. (2008). State Reform in Greece: Responding to Old and New Challenges. *International Journal of Public Sector Management*, 21(2), 150–173.

Spiegel Online (2013). Wasted EU Funds: Brussels Ignores Tip-Offs from Greek Official. www.spiegel.de/international/europe/report-eu-officials-ignore-tip-offs-of-fraud-at-greek-institution-a-928639.html

Spitzer, A. B. (1962). The Good Napoleon III. *French Historical Studies*, 2(3), 308–329.

Stark, D., & Bruszt, L. (1998). *Postsocialist Pathways: Transforming Politics and Property in East Central Europe*, Cambridge: Cambridge University Press.

Statista (2018). Forbes Ranking of the 10 Richest People in Italy 2018, www.statista.com/statistics/729819/forbes-ranking-of-the-10-richest-people-in-italy/

Stefanov, R., & Karaboev, S. (2015). The Bulgarian Public Procurement Market: Corruption Risks and Dynamics in the Construction Sector. In A. Mungiu-Pippidi, ed., *Government Favouritism in Europe*, The ANTICORRP Project, Anticorruption Report Volume 3, Opladen: Budrich, pp. 35–53.

Stiglitz, J. E. (1999). Keynote Address: More Instruments and Broader Goals: Moving Toward the Post-Washington Consensus, German Foundation for International Development (DSE), https://pdfs.semanticscholar.org/657d/d9ec1d1631b3d46e19e6657bad7a8de5de4f.pdf

Stille, A. (1995). *Excellent Cadavers: The Mafia and the Death of the First Italian Republic*, New York: Vintage.

Stone, N. (2017). *Turkey: A Short History*, London: Thames and Hudson.

Sung, H.-E. (2004). Democracy and Political Corruption: A Cross-National Comparison. *Crime, Law and Social Change*, 41(2), 179–193.

Szarek-Mason, P. (2010). *The European Union's Fight Against Corruption: The Evolving Policy towards Member States and Candidate Countries*, Cambridge and New York: Cambridge University Press.

Tannous, I. (n.d.) The Programming of EU's External Assistance and Development Aid and the Fragile Balance of Power between EEAS and DG DEVCO. *European Foreign Affairs Review*, 18, 329–354.

Tanzi, V., & Davoodi, H. (1998). Corruption, Public Investment, and Growth. In H. Shibata & T. Ihori, eds., *The Welfare State, Public Investment, and Growth*, Tokyo: Springer Japan, pp. 41–60.

The Economist (2014). Small Balkan Scandal, www.economist.com/europe/2014/11/15/small-balkan-scandal

The Economist. (2016). Comparing Crony Capitalism Around the World, www.economist.com/graphic-detail/2016/05/05/comparing-crony-capitalism-around-the-world

The Economist (2018). Time Off for Bad Prose – Romania's Jail Literature, www
.economist.com/europe/2015/10/22/time-off-for-bad-prose

The Guardian (2014). Alleged Connections between Top Kosovo Politicians and
Assassin Investigated, www.theguardian.com/world/2014/nov/07/kosovo-
hitman-inquiry-eulex-hashim-thaci

The Guardian (2016a). Afghanistan and Nigeria "'Possibly Most Corrupt
Countries", Cameron Lets Slip, www.theguardian.com/uk-news/2016/may/1
0/david-cameron-afghanistan-nigeria-possibly-most-corrupt-countries

The Guardian (2016b). Cameron Stepped in to Shield Offshore Trusts from EU
Tax Crackdown in 2013, www.theguardian.com/politics/2016/apr/07/david-
cameron-offshore-trusts-eu-tax-crackdown-2013

The Guardian (2016c). The Guardian View on Corruption: David Cameron
should Look Closer to Home, www.theguardian.com/commentisfree/2016/m
ay/10/the-guardian-view-on-corruption-david-cameron-should-look-closer-to
-home

The Guardian (2018). EU says Greece can "Finally Turn the Page" as Bailout
Ends, www.theguardian.com/world/2018/aug/20/eu-greece-bailout-ends-
pierre-moscovici

The Observer (2017). The Miracle of Matera: From City of Poverty and Squalor to
Hip Hub for Cave-Dwellers, www.theguardian.com/world/2017/jun/17/mater
a-italy-culture-capital-cave-homes-from-squalor-to-airbnb-film-sets

The Observer (2018). Is Matera's Crumbling Beauty Ready for Its Year in
Europe's Cultural Sun? www.theguardian.com/world/2018/sep/22/matera-
italy-capital-of-culture-2019-unbuilt-roads-and-venues

Tilly, C. (2009). Astonishing Switzerland. *Swiss Political Science Review*, 15(2),
321–331.

Tipps, D. C. (1973). Modernization Theory and the Comparative Study of
National Societies: A Critical Perspective. *Comparative Studies in Society and
History*, 15(02), 199.

Tocci, N. (2011). *State (Un)Sustainability in the Southern Mediterranean and
Scenarios to 2030: The EU's Response* (MEDPRO Policy Paper No. 1/
August 2011, updated April 2012), http://aei.pitt.edu/58348/

Tomasi di Lampedusa, G. (1960). *The Leopard*, New York: Pantheon Books.

Transparency International (2016). Nigerian Civil Society Calls on UK to End Role
as a Safe Haven for Corrupt Individuals, www.transparency.org/news/pressrelease/
nigeria_civil_society_letter_ahead_of_international_anti_corruption_summit

Transparency International (2017). State Capture: The Case of the Republic of
Moldova, www.transparency.md/wp-content/uploads/2017/06/TI_Moldova_
State_Capture.pdf

Transparency International Secretariat (2018). Montenegro: Parliament
should Refrain from Voting on Dismissal from Council of Anti-
Corruption Agency until Court Makes Decision, www.transparency.org/ne
ws/pressrelease/montenegro_courts_should_decide_before_parliament_vote
s_on_dismissal_from_a

Treaty of Amsterdam Amending the Treaty on European Union, the Treaties
Establishing the European Communities and Certain Related Acts – Final Act
(1997), www.europarl.europa.eu/topics/treaty/pdf/amst-en.pdf

Treaty of Lisbon Amending the Treaty on European Union and the Treaty Establishing the European Community (OJ C 306, 17.12.2007); Entry into Force on 1 December 2009 (2018), www.europarl.europa.eu/ftu/pdf/en/FTU_1.1.5.pdf

Trebilcock, M. J., & Daniels, R. J. (2008). *Rule of Law Reform and Development: Charting the Fragile Path of Progress*, Northampton, MA: Edward Elgar.

Treisman, D. (2000). The Causes of Corruption: A Cross-National Study. *Journal of Public Economics*, **76**(3), 399–457.

Treisman, D. (2007). What Have We Learned About the Causes of Corruption from Ten Years of Cross-National Empirical Research? *Annual Review of Political Science*, **10**(1), 211–244.

Tsitsishvili, D., & Warner, C. M. (2010). Georgia: Corruption Developments and Anti-Corruption Activities since 1990s (ERCAS Working Paper No. 6), www.againstcorruption.eu/wp-content/uploads/2012/09/WP-6-Corruption-developments-in-Georgia-new.pdf

Tsoukalis, L. (2016). Greek Myths and Reality. In K. Derviş et al., *Greek Myths and Reality*, Hellenic Foundation for European & Foreign Policy (ELIAMEP), pp. 4–5.

Turkish Economic and Social Studies Foundation (TESEV) (2014). *Corruption Assessment Report Turkey*, Istanbul: TESEV Publications.

UNCAC (United Nations Convention Against Corruption) (2005), www.unodc.org/documents/brussels/UN_Convention_Against_Corruption.pdf

U.S. Securities and Exchange Commission (SEC) (2016). *Novartis Charged With FCPA Violations (3–17177)*, www.sec.gov/litigation/admin/2016/34-77431-s.pdf

Uslaner, E. M., & Rothstein, B. (2016). The Historical Roots of Corruption: State Building, Economic Inequality, and Mass Education. *Comparative Politics*, **48**(2), 227–248.

Vachudova, M. A. (2005). *Europe Undivided*, Oxford: Oxford University Press, www.oxfordscholarship.com/view/10.1093/0199241198.001.0001/acprof-9780199241194

Vannucci, A. (2009). The Controversial Legacy of "Mani Pulite": A Critical Analysis of Italian Corruption and Anti-Corruption Policies. *Bulletin of Italian Politics*, **1**(2), 233–64.

Varese, F. (2000). Pervasive Corruption. In A. V. Ledeneva & M. Kurkchiyan, eds., *Economic Crime in Russia*, London and Boston: Kluwer Law International, pp. 99–111.

Vargas, G. A., & Schlutz, D. (2016). Opening Public Officials' Coffers: A Quantitative Analysis of the Impact of Financial Disclosure Regulation on National Corruption Levels. *European Journal on Criminal Policy and Research*, **22**(3), 439–475.

Venanzi, D., & Gamper, C. (2012, December 4–5). *Public Investment across Levels of Government: The Case of Basilicata, Italy* (report of OECD Territorial Development Policy Committee), www.oecd.org/cfe/regional-policy/basilicata_edited.pdf

Verheugen, G. (2003, April 9). Let Us Not Hesitate in Seizing This Opportunity (speech to Plenary Session of the European Parliament, Strasbourg), http://europa.eu/rapid/press-release_SPEECH-03-187_en.htm

Volintiru, C. (2016). *Clientelism and Cartelization in Post-Communist Europe: The Case of Romania* (PhD thesis, London School of Economics and Political Science), http://etheses.lse.ac.uk/3611/

Warkotsch, J. (2016). *EU Governance Promotion in Tunisia: Lessons from the Arab Spring* (report), http://anticorrp.eu/publications/eu-governance-promotion-in-tunisia-lessons-from-the-arab-spring/

Warkotsch, J. (2017). Tunisia: Great Expectations. In A. Mungiu-Pippidi & J. Warkotsch, eds., *Beyond the Panama Papers: The Performance of EU Good Governance Promotion*, The ANTICORRP Project, Anticorruption Report Volume 1, Opladen, Berlin, and Toronto: Barbara Budrich Publishers, 104–116.

Warner, C. M. (2002). *Creating a Common Market for Fraud and Corruption in the European Union: An Institutional Accident, or a Deliberate Strategy?* Florence: European University Institute.

Warner, C. M. (2007). *The Best System Money Can Buy: Corruption in the European Union*, Ithaca, NY: Cornell University Press.

Warren, M. E. (2006). Democracy and Deceit: Regulating Appearances of Corruption. *American Journal of Political Science*, **50**(1), 160–174.

Weber, M. (1947). *The Theory of Social and Economic Organization* (A. M. Henderson & T. Parsons, trans.), New York: Free Press.

Weber, M. (1968). Asceticism, Mysticism and Salvation. In *Economy and Society: An Outline of Interpretive Sociology*, New York: Bedminster Press.

Weber, M. (1978). *Economy and Society: An Outline of Interpretive Sociology*, Volume 1. Oakland: University of California Press.

Weber, M. (1991). *From Max Weber: Essays in Sociology* (H. H. Gerth and C. Wright Mills, eds.), Oxford: Routledge.

Welzel, C., Inglehart, R., & Kligemann, H.-D. (2003). The Theory of Human Development: A Cross-Cultural Analysis. *European Journal of Political Research*, **42**(3), 341–379.

Westad, O. A. (2007). *The Global Cold War: Third World Interventions and the Making of Our Times*, Cambridge and New York: Cambridge University Press.

Wilson, A. (2015). Ukraine's Uncertain Reform Process. In A. Mungiu-Pippidi, ed., *Government Favouritism in Europe*, The ANTICORRP Project, Anticorruption Report Volume 3, Opladen: Budrich, pp. 97–104.

Wilson, J. Q. (1993). The Moral Sense. *American Political Science Review*, **87**(01), 1–11.

Wolff, S. (2009). Constraints on the Promotion of the Rule of Law in Egypt: Insights from the 2005 Judges' Revolt. *Democratization*, **16**(1), 100–118.

World Bank (2004). *Public Expenditure Tracking Surveys – Application in Uganda, Tanzania, Ghana and Honduras*, Washington, DC: World Bank, http://documents.worldbank.org/curated/en/577081468117881604/Public-expenditure-tracking-surveys-application-in-Uganda-Tanzania-Ghana-and-Honduras

World Bank (2010). *MENA Regional Economic Update: Recovering from the Crisis, April 2010*, www.worldbank.org/en/news/feature/2010/05/01/mena-regional-economic-update-recovering-from-the-crisis-april-2010

World Bank (2015). *Country Data Report for Ukraine, 1996–2014*, http://documents.worldbank.org/curated/en/398041468195838838/Country-data-report-for-Ukraine-1996-2014

World Bank (2018a). *Historical Data Sets and Trends Data*, www.doingbusiness.org /en/custom-query

World Bank (2018b). *The Worldwide Governance Indicators (WGI) project*, http:// info.worldbank.org/governance/wgi/#home

World Economic Forum (2017). *The Global Competitiveness Report 2017–2018: Insight Report* (K. Schwab, ed.), Geneva: World Economic Forum.

Wouters, J., & Duquet, S. (2013, June 7). The Arab Uprisings and the European Union: In Search of a Comprehensive Strategy (Leuven Centre for Global Governance Studies Working Paper No. 98). *SSRN Electronic Journal*, https:// papers.ssrn.com/sol3/papers.cfm?abstract_id=2274741

Wright, J., & Winters, M. (2010). The Politics of Effective Foreign Aid. *Annual Review of Political Science*, **13**(1), 61–80.

You, J.-S. (2015). *Democracy, Inequality and Corruption: Korea, Taiwan and the Philippines Compared*, Cambridge: Cambridge University Press.

Young, D. (2016, March 25). Claims Against Petrobras Highlight Prospects for Shareholder Enforcement in US Courts, *Global Anticorruption Blog*, https://glo balanticorruptionblog.com/author/daniellecyoung/

Youngs, R. (2004). Normative Dynamics and Strategic Interests in the EU's External Identity. *JCMS: Journal of Common Market Studies*, **42**(2), 415–435.

Youngs, R. (ed.) (2010). *The European Union and Democracy Promotion: A Critical Global Assessment*, Baltimore, MD: Johns Hopkins University Press.

Zielonka, J. (2008). Europe as a Global Actor: Empire by Example? *International Affairs*, **84**(3), 471–484.

Zielonka, J. (2011). America and Europe: Two Contrasting or Parallel Empires? *Journal of Political Power*, **4**(3), 337–354.

Zucman, G. (2015). *The Hidden Wealth of Nations: The Scourge of Tax Havens* (T. L. Fagan, trans.), Chicago: University of Chicago Press.

Index

Lightning Source UK Ltd.
Milton Keynes UK
UKHW021158130421
381697UK00021B/943

9 781108 459662